Using TRIZ For Anti-Virus Development

Building Better Software Through Continuous Innovation

An innovation guide
For Inventing Anti-Virus Technologies
And Developing Anti-Virus Tools
Engineered through
The powerful techniques of TRIZ

Umakant Mishra

The patent details and patent drawings referenced in this book are sourced from USPTO website (http://www.uspto.gov) within the permissible limits of the site. The author sincerely accredits USPTO site for sharing such valuable information.

First Edition
July 2013

Author and Publisher
Umakant Mishra
208-A, Prime Classic
2nd Main, Chinappa Garden,
Bangalore-560046

ISBN 978-93-5126-882-6

This book is printed by
CreateSpace.com

CONTENTS

Foreword

This book was written by my friend Umakant Mishra who is a genius in the world of computers and software. His skills and achievements in this arena, speak for themselves. This is his second book where he merges the application of TRIZ and computer science. With deep knowledge of both technologies, Umakant is able to show us how TRIZ can be used to develop powerful deterrents to the nagging problem of our computers being attacked by viruses and worms. Corruption of our business and personal computers is an insidious attack on our lives and livelihood. By using the key concepts and tools that TRIZ provides, he explains in great detail how these malicious corruptors can be defeated thus protecting our personal and business information.

For those of you who are not familiar with TRIZ, let me share a little about who developed this technology and how it works. The "Theory of Inventive Problem Solving" or TRIZ was developed by Genrich S. Altshuller, by screening hundreds of thousands of patents to arrive at some common principles of evolution and common methods of problem solving. Altshuller found that the same problems are being solved again and again at different times in different contexts. He analyzed the pattern of these solutions and found that all these inventions have emerged out of only 40 dominant Inventive Principles. In Addition to the 40 Principles, Altshuller research outlined 9 rules for the evolution of systems and 76 Standards techniques for resolving standard problems found in various industries and scientific applications.

TRIZ provides a systematic approach to solve any real problem by using a set of logical steps, starting from defining a problem through finding and solving a contradiction which leads to developing solution concepts. This provides a great advantage over the conventional trial and error approach of innovation which is time consuming and expensive.

Umakant, in this books, shows many interesting applications of Inventive Principles to anti-virus inventions, such as, scheduling a virus scan (Principle-10: Prior action), user sensitive scanning (scan when the user is not working) (Principle-15: Dynamization), partial scanning (Principle-16: Partial or excessive action), store-scan-forward scanning (Principle-19: Periodic Action), stream scanning (Principle-20: Continuous action), fast virus scanning (Principle-21: Skipping), auto-updating of virus database (Principle-25: Self Service), emulation techniques (Principle-26: Copying, Principle-27: Cheap and disposable), and so on.

Umakant shows several examples of contradictions with improving and worsening parameters and solutions. He illustrates dozens of examples on applications of S-Fields and Inventive standards, especially using standards of class-4: for detection of viruses and standards of group-1.2 for removing the harmful effects of the viruses on a the computer system. This book shows application of powerful TRIZ concepts like Ideality, Trends of Evolution, Resources etc. which can help solving some of the strong challenges faced by the anti-virus developers:

- to overcome limitations of current generation anti-virus programs,
- to stay ahead of the virus creators,
- to assist anti-virus developers and
- to find all new possibilities of virus/ malware solutions.

This book is packed with valuable information for the casual computer user to the expert computer guru's who develop great programs for our use.

Richard Langevin

July 2013

Executive Director,

Altshuller Institute for TRIZ Studies, Inc. and

CEO of Technical Innovation Center

Worcester, MA 01606, USA

Preface

The battle between viruses and Anti-Viruses

With the increasing number of viruses and the superior techniques employed by the virus creators, the virus attacks remain one of the core security issues everywhere in the world. The virus creation engines available on the Internet enable even a layman to generate powerful metamorphic viruses. The current day viruses have got the capability of exploiting emails and Internet for spreading their code across the globe. There is a threat of viruses, malware attacks and cybercrime looming over any computerization activity whether at home, office or business.

The battle between virus writers and anti-virus researchers started since the viruses first appeared on microcomputers in 1980s. The virus writers constantly adapt new obfuscation techniques, such as, encryption, polymorphism, metamorphism etc., to keep their viruses hidden and undetectable. On the other hand the AV researchers go beyond the conventional method of pattern matching and implement various heuristic techniques and emulation to detect even the most advanced and complicated viruses.

Both virus and anti-virus technologies are improving rapidly. While virus creators want their dirty creations to spread over the whole world, the anti-virus developers intend to catch even the last piece of virus hidden inside any corner of a computer or network. The simple scanning of early age scanners has changed to complex scanning involving a range of multiple detection techniques. The current scanners adopt all possible methods in order to leave no chance for any virus to survive.

While the traditional virus scanners were providing only off-access scanning, i.e., scanning the computer when not in use, the current day virus scanners provide both off-access and on-access scanning. The on-access method scans a file when there is an attempt to access the file thereby leaving no scope for virus proliferation.

Why the Anti-Viruses are still behind

Although the virus detection programs employ all available methods, off-access scanning, on-access scanning, heuristic scanning, code emulation etc. to combat the malware code, the journey is far from being over. As the virus programs are outcome of malefic brains they can cause nuisance to any extent including deleting files and corrupting data. Even a simple virus can be dangerous as to erase the hard disk and bring down the computer system.

The anti-virus developers are in a weaker position, as they have no co-operation or collaboration among themselves. They are all carrying out the same activities in order to compete with each other. As each of them duplicates the same sort of activities, even an addition of ten or hundred more anti-virus companies or products may not necessarily strengthen the anti-virus system. While on the other hand the virus developers have at least some level of collaboration such as to share some of the virus codes. Even if they work individually without collaboration still each of them independently contributes to aggravate the virus problem.

Publication of anti-virus techniques and future threats is another problem. If the anti-virus researchers or organizations publish the details of virus detection mechanism then the virus creators will come to know about the detection techniques and modify their viruses to make them immune to those techniques. Besides if they publish the exact details of the detection techniques then their competitors will come to know about their secrets which may weaken their position. This situation compels the anti-virus organizations to publish only thematic information and maintain confidentiality of the exact specifications.

Detecting malware is a difficult task as a slightest mistake may allow viruses to escape. If a detection method is over tightened then the method can reduce false negatives but may lead to false positives. The objective of the anti-virus developer is to catch every single virus without raising any false positive. While on the other hand the virus creators don't have any strict objective. Even if a virus creator wrongly codes a virus, which hangs and crashes, that still creates a new type of virus and adds to the nuisance. While anti-virus developers are still struggling to protect the personal computers and networks the virus creators are moving to mobile and handheld devices.

While some of the new techniques make scanning stronger and more reliable, to their drawback they typically consume additional scanning time and system resources. While an on-access scanning provides maximum amount of security it causes delay in accessing every file and increases consumption of system resources. Until now there is no good method of stream scanning or scanning data moving on a network or Internet.

Need for Improving Anti-Virus

During recent ages many people and businesses have become significantly dependent on computers and Internet. Unfortunately with the popularity of computers and Internet, the growth of viruses also has seen a great surge. The virus creators no more work just because of their criminal mentality but many of them are also secretly funded by terrorist organizations. The creation of computer viruses has gone from an academic curiosity to a persistent problem engaging thousands of professionals worldwide to find solutions out.

Some of the important problems in anti-virus applications are, (i) problem of detecting stealth viruses, (ii) problem of slowness of virus scanning, (iii) problem of detection of new viruses, (iv) problems in extracting virus signatures from complex/ metamorphic viruses, (v) problems in fast distributing virus signatures to clients, (vi) problem of eliminating false positives and false negatives, (vii) problem of managing the anti-virus program code in a continuously changing environment, (viii) problem of scanning compressed, encrypted and password protected files, (ix) problem of scanning realtime network traffic, (x) protecting secrets of scanning technologies from virus writers and anti-virus competitors etc..

Although the anti-virus developers adopt various advanced techniques to reduce the scanning time and scanning load the result is far behind success. Every anti-virus today significantly slows down the computer and affects the computer worse than an average virus. There is a need to use system resources more efficiently during virus scanning.

With the rapid development of computer technology, the virus developers also equip themselves with advanced tools and techniques. The recent trend is to develop metamorphic viruses which change the viral code in each infection. The virus developers aim at developing viruses with high degree of metamorphism leaving nothing in common between two generations of the same virus which can be extracted as a signature.

While some data mining techniques try to differentiate the pattern of viral code from that of the normal genuine code, the virus creators try to make their viral code look very similar to ordinary computer program so that no scanner can differentiate them from the ordinary programs. Under the scenario the challenge for the anti-virus developers has become extremely difficult, as they have to discern the indiscernible, find the invisible and detect the undetectable.

How can TRIZ help in developing anti-virus

TRIZ provides a systematic approach of solving any kind of problem through a sequence of logical steps, viz., (i) Defining the problem, (ii) Finding Technical Contradictions, (iii) Defining Ideal Final Result and Physical Contradictions, (iv) Solving Contradictions by using various solution tools, (v) Evaluating various solutions and implementing the best solution. After the whole cycle is over, the problem solver goes back to the first step and changes the way the problem is analyzed. This provides higher probability of finding better solutions compared to the conventional trial and error methods of innovation and creativity.

TRIZ can help solving some of the strong challenges faced by the anti-virus developers, such as overcoming limitations of current generation anti-virus programs, staying ahead of the virus creators and other anti-virus developers and finding all new possibilities of solving the malware problem. TRIZ believes that all systems, including computers, operating systems, software and anti-virus, are moving towards an ideal stage that is full of only useful functions and devoid of any weaknesses. The book illustrates application of various TRIZ techniques such as Contradictions, Resources, Trends, Ideality, S-Fields, Inventive Standards and Inventive Principles in the course of explaining various patented and non-patented anti-viral solutions.

Using TRIZ for overcoming current limitations of anti-virus by means of solving contradictions

While developing a virus scanner, the anti-virus researchers do face a lot of constraints. Although some researchers have come up with new methods of virus detection, such as machine learning, data mining etc. they typically need huge computation load and make the system and/or scanning unbearably slow. This situation creates a contradiction. **We want to scan for viruses but don't want to slow down our system.**

With the increasing size of hard disks, increasing number of viruses and increasing number of scanning methods a complete virus scan takes enormous time. A speed scanning leads to partial or insufficient scanning which leads to vulnerability. **While it is necessary to speed up a virus**

scanning it is also important to ensure that no compromise is made on the security aspect.

There is a contradiction in scanning confidential files. For example, some files are encrypted and/or password protected to maintain privacy of the information inside. As the anti-virus has no way to read the content of the encrypted files many viruses inside encrypted files easily escape the security gateways. On the other hand if the password is broken to decrypt the content for virus scanning then there is a breach of the intended privacy. **We want to read the encrypted content for virus scanning but at the same time we don't want to break the privacy of the encrypted content.**

About half a century contradictions are discussed throughout the book while analyzing various limitations of the anti-virus technology. While the traditional solutions provide efficient compromise or tradeoff between the two conflicting situations, TRIZ teaches to eliminate the contradictions and get the complete benefit without doing any compromise. Solving contradictions not only leads to new inventions but also sometimes creates new directions in solving problems.

Using TRIZ for staying ahead of virus developers

The conventional anti-virus technology is reactionary. That means an anti-virus is developed only when a virus is released. This process is guaranteed to fail as it always keeps the viruses (and virus developers) ahead of the anti-virus (and anti-virus developers). What is necessary is to keep the anti-virus ahead of the viruses. In other words the anti-virus has to be created and implemented before a virus is created and distributed.

For example, if the anti-virus has to extract signatures of all the newly found viruses then the detection method will always remain days behind the creation and spreading of new viruses. The conventional methods may attempt to reduce this time lag from weeks to days but that even is enough for the fast moving viruses to spread across the globe and wreck havoc with substantial damages. **Hence the solution is not to detect or vaccinate the known viruses but to implement vaccines for the future age viruses that are not yet born.**

The virus creators can reverse engineer the anti-virus programs to know the algorithms that are used for virus scanning. This method enables them to create viruses that can cheat and escape the current scanning techniques. The anti-virus programmers stay behind because they don't know the future strategy of the virus creators and the possible characteristics of the future viruses. TRIZ can help the anti-virus developers to see the characteristics of the future viruses and forecast the futuristic problems that are not yet seen or known. As the virus developers have access to all the technologies and infrastructure (like compilers, code generators, Internet etc.) that the anti-virus developers have access to, it is only the matured techniques of TRIZ that can help the anti-virus developers to win over their opponents.

Using TRIZ for staying ahead of competitors

It is not enough to stay ahead of virus creators, it is also important to stay ahead of other competitors working on anti-virus technology. Currently there are about fifty large organizations working on anti-virus technology including McAfee, Symantec, Kasperasky, Lenovo, Microsoft, IBM, Trend Micro, AVG, Network Associates etc. In this scenario patenting inventions on anti-virus technology potentially keeps an organization ahead of its competitors. As every organization is as competent as the other there is no guarantee for an organization to invent at a faster pace unless it follows a superior process of invention. The superior technique of TRIZ can help the anti-virus developer to move faster in the process of invention and gain the desired competitive advantage. The philosophy of TRIZ takes the inventor away from the conventional track of racing with the competitors to an innovative track of moving towards the Ideal Final Result or the Ultimate Solution.

For example, almost all the inventions on virus scanning followed a file-based approach until Patent 6021510 (by Nachenberg) first suggested a sector-based approach to store the hash values of each storage sector in a critical sectors file for checking the integrity. This solution opened up a new possibility of sector based approach of virus scanning. Later Patent 7401361 (Freeman et. al.) suggested to maintain a protective archive bit for each sector on the hard disk and scan only the changed sectors instead of scanning the changed files. Similarly Patent 7581250 (invented by Sitze) teaches to scan only the changed sectors of the hard disk in successive scanning instead of scanning all the data in the hard disk.

Often we feel that invention is a difficult job and might take years to accomplish it. While the matter may be true for revolutionary inventions or discoveries, the scenario is different for the current day inventions which are solely intended for patenting. Every minor improvement on the prior art is patented for the sake of competition. For example, Patent 7591001

(Liquidware Labs, Inc., Sep 2009) teaches to ensure the security status of a second computer is up-to-date and acceptable before establishing a network connection to it in order to reduce the risk of infection. While the method prima facie does not seem to be saying anything new which none of us know but the patent is granted.

Similarly, Patent 7591018 (Trend Micro Incorporated, Sep 2009) discloses to use a removable rescue device to disinfect a computer infected with virus. Although the concept of rescue disk, boot disk, anti-virus disk etc. were there in the prior art, nobody had exactly specified the possibility of a removable rescue device containing a scanning engine which is upgradable and which can be used to rescue any infected computer wherever necessary. A very similar invention disclosed in Patent 7930531 (Super Talent Electronics, Inc., Apr, 2011) to use a multi-partition USB flash disk with multiple operating systems and boot the infected system with an alternate operating system which is not sensitive to the viruses of the primary operating system. Although some inventions may not appear to be so impressive it is true that every invention takes our knowledge a step forward towards the ultimate solution.

Using TRIZ for finding all new possibilities of solutions

Some people feel that there is nothing much to research on computer viruses as the anti-virus technologies have gone far ahead to detect/ prevent any kind of virus. But the truth is that even today a large number of viruses escape from virus scanners and remain undetected in all of our computers. We don't face any problem in their presence because either they are actionless or their payload condition/time has not arrived.

Secondly, TRIZ does not perceive the purpose of an anti-virus just to scan and detect viruses. The Ideal anti-virus is a no virus situation where there is no need of any anti-virus (TRIZ IFR). The anti-virus technology may be implemented in such a way that the virus creators may not succeed in creating viruses or may result in self-damage in making such efforts. Thus TRIZ provides a very different angle of looking at the problems.

When the ultimate IFR is not possible TRIZ suggests considering a lower level IFR that has greater achievability. Taking a step back from the above IFR provides us many interesting solutions. For example, the anti-virus measures may be implemented on the Internet to prevent movement of viruses from one place to another. The anti-virus measures may be implemented in gateways and firewalls to prevent the malicious code entering into a LAN or subnet. The security mechanism of OS should not allow viruses to operate. The servers should not allow viruses to reside. And finally the files and data should have their own protection mechanism to prevent virus infection.

It is not enough an achievement to scan the computer for hours and affect the performance of other programs. Even a lower level IFR suggests that the anti-virus should prevent the viruses from entering into the system (TRIZ Principle-9: Prior Counteraction). The running of anti-virus should not demand much system resources (TRIZ Ideality: No negative effects on super system or adjacent systems). The anti-virus should demand no updating of virus definitions. It should be simple for any novice user and should work automatically in a networked computers and servers without demanding any attention of the system administrator (TRIZ Principle-25: Self Service).

TRIZ not only changes our perception of looking at the problem but also provides different techniques of solving the problems. By applying the powerful techniques of resources, contradictions, Ideality, trends of evolution etc. a researcher may come up with revolutionary solutions. According to the concept of "resources" the best solutions are those which solve the problem by using the freely available existing resources. The best solutions are those which convert harmful effects to useful actions. The TRIZ concept of Ideality and trends of evolution helps us to visualize where do we currently stand in the process of development and what should we focus to accelerate the innovation for future improvement.

For example, the current anti-virus programs look each other in suspicious manner. Hence, running multiple anti-virus programs leads to deadlocks or unpredictable results. While Patent 8171552 (Chang, May 2012) shows a possibility of "simultaneous execution of multiple anti-virus programs" there are umpteen number of scopes for collaborating multiple anti-viruses to supplement each other's deficiencies.

Currently the anti-virus developers have to maintain a lot of secrecies in the exact techniques of scanning as otherwise the virus creators would misuse that information in creating detection-proof viruses. But looking at the technology trend we can predict that there will be a time in future when the anti-virus techniques will be openly published but the virus creators cannot utilize that knowledge for improving viruses.

Why this book

While the term "innovation" has become very common and every software organization aspires to have an advanced innovation department with trained professional innovators, the real "invention" still remains a mysterious high-end topic. The book intends to demystify the techniques and simplify the difficulties of invention. The book discusses all the critical aspects of the current day anti-viruses and illustrates the TRIZ way of addressing the issues by solving the contradictions.

Many people say or believe that the concepts and Principles of TRIZ are not applicable to Software Inventions. They have definitely some reasons for saying so. First of all, the theory of TRIZ is based on the observation of technical systems and techniques of TRIZ are derived from the analysis of technical patents (i.e., relating to machines). Secondly, many TRIZ rules use terms like "Gravity Field", "Oxidization", "Thermal Expansion", "Ferromagnetic systems" etc. which do not make any sense in the context of software or Information Technology.

While it is true that the theory of TRIZ was originally designed for technical or mechanical systems, the author finds that the philosophy of TRIZ holds true for any branch of study whether sociology, psychology, management or computers. What is missing a "super-system" above the current technical TRIZ which is "non-disciplinary" TRIZ. This proposed super-system can easily hold other "subsystems" of TRIZ like "technical-TRIZ", "software-TRIZ", "social-TRIZ", "biotech-TRIZ", "management-TRIZ" etc. with minor changes in narrations and interpretations while keeping the rules and concepts unchanged.

TRIZ can be used as a great potential for the software inventions. The author has written a book "TRIZ Principles for Information Technology" illustrating thousands of examples on application of the 40 Principles for software. The author also finds that the concept of contradictions is straight forward applicable to software inventions and is authoring a book "Solving Software Contradictions using TRIZ". Similarly the concepts of "Ideality", "trends of evolution", "S-Fields" and "Inventive Standards" are perfectly applicable in software and illustrated in several places throughout the current book.

As the traditional TRIZ experts don't have enough exposure in software development field, there is no authoritative guideline on how to apply TRIZ for software inventions. Hence there is a need for a series of books which can give clear guidelines to the problem solvers and inventors on how to use TRIZ techniques for various software solutions. This book is intended to be one such book in the series, focusing only on one specific field of software, i.e., anti-malware.

One might ask why a whole book is devoted to a single topic like anti-malware while a general book on "TRIZ for software" could have addressed the issue. The answer to that question is multifaceted. Although many people including me have been talking about TRIZ for software since last 15 years, no body so far has drawn a single S-Field diagram on any software issue demonstrating how to apply the technique in software. Although this book is specifically on anti-malware, the methods of application of TRIZ are generic and exemplary which can be applied on branches of software. So this book may be considered as more a book on "TRIZ for software" than a book on "TRIZ for anti-virus".

Who the book is meant for

The book is meant for people who want to apply TRIZ for software inventions. Many people have learnt TRIZ to some extent but confuse to apply them successfully in software problems. This book intends to solve that problem by providing practical examples to the readers at any level, be an experienced anti-virus developer or an enthusiastic beginner.

As the book deals with all the basic theories of anti-virus techniques, their intrinsic drawbacks and chronological improvements, it will certainly be a valuable companion for anti-virus researchers, anti-malware developers and security specialists. The book intends to be an essential handbook for every anti-virus developer, IT inventor and TRIZ researcher around the world. Besides it is expected to be useful for TRIZ trainers and practitioners, Network/Security Managers, IT students, professionals and solution developers.

How to read this book

The language of the book has been kept simple for any reader to follow the internal substance. But from technical point of view some parts of this book may appear very simple and some other parts may appear difficult depending on individual experience. Unlike some academic research papers this book contains no ornamentation of heavyweight jargons and no statistical formulas, tables or graphs.

The chapters are organized in an order that may be suitable for most readers to follow the sequence. So the easiest way is to read from chapter to chapter. However, if somebody is interested on specific types of viruses (like worms) or specific types of detection technology (such as, emulation) or specific TRIZ technology (like, Ideality) then he can jump to the specific chapter of interest. Readers having knowledge on anti-virus may read the chapters in any sequence. Readers who have no knowledge on TRIZ are suggested to read some basic materials on TRIZ (may be from triz-journal and trizsite journal) before reading this book. This book directly jumps into the application of TRIZ without introducing enough on TRIZ concepts. All patents cited in examples are selected from US patent database (USPTO) unless mentioned otherwise.

Acknowledgement

I would like to thank Mr. Richard Langevin who has been kind enough to write a foreward for this book. Mr. Langevin has been a continuous source of encouragement to me since he published my first TRIZ book in 2007.

I cannot thank and praise enough to Mr. Vladimir Petrov, TRIZ master, who has taken the pain of reading the manuscript of this book and guiding me on avoiding some critical mistakes in presenting TRIZ concepts.

I am extremely grateful to Mr. Yuri Salamatov, TRIZ Master, who happily read the manuscript and spent his valuable time in giving his comments, suggestions and guidelines chapter by chapter for the whole book. His guidance has helped me to improve the book from one revision to another.

However, all the mistakes and misinterpretations whatever is there in the book is the sole responsibility of mine and don't in anyway involve the above dignitaries.

Umakant Mishra

Bangalore, India

June 2013

Chapter 1.

Introduction to Computer Viruses

1.1 What is Computer Virus

Generally speaking a computer virus is a manmade computer program or code that is illegal and destructive. A simple definition of computer virus is *a program that is able to infect other programs by including a copy of it.* But it is difficult to give an accurate definition of computer viruses because some malware like Trojan horses, rootkits etc., although very different from typical viruses, are generally called as computer viruses for convenience.

In common terms computer viruses include certain species of malware including viruses, worms, Trojans, backdoors, rootkits etc. Although each of these malware is different in structure and behavior, they are all called as viruses for convenience. In this book we will also call them all as viruses except in places cases where we will discuss about specific types of viruses like “worms” or “rootkits”.

The viruses generally get into a computer system without the knowledge of a user and cause unauthorized and unwanted changes to the information stored on the computer. It is important to note that every software that causes damage is not a virus. Popular legal software may cause damages because of certain unfixed bugs. But they are different from viruses as those bugs cannot infect other programs. The viruses are intentionally designed to infect other programs for troubling others, which the legal software are not.

Computer viruses are called viruses because they share some of the traits of biological viruses. A computer virus passes from computer to computer like a biological virus passes from person to person. A computer virus increases its population, infects computers and causes damage to the computers like a biological virus does to the human beings.

1.2 History of computer viruses

The initial form of computer viruses came into existence during mid 1980's till mid 1990's, when the use of PCs started to grow for businesses and homes. During that period computer games were very popular and applications like word processors and spreadsheets were very commonly used. The viruses typically attached themselves to games and other bona fide computer programs to travel from one computer to another.

During that period, floppies were predominantly used for booting and for data transfer. The virus creators took advantage of this scenario and created viruses revolving around the usage of floppies exploiting the drawbacks of the media.

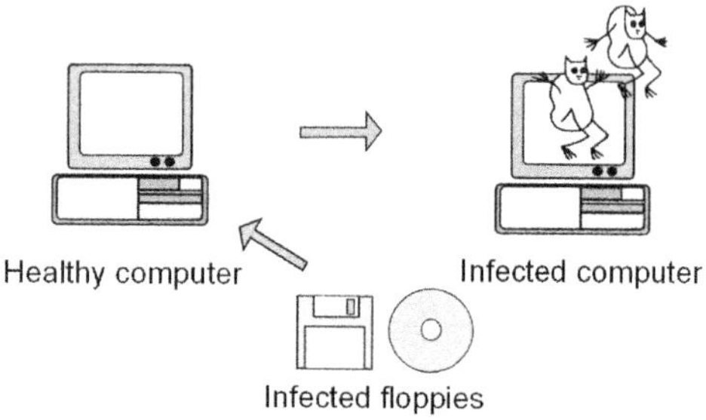

The primitive viruses were infecting executable files by typically appending the viral code and inserting a JUMP instruction at the start of the program to run the viral code. When the infected program was executed, the control was passing to the virus code before executing the host program. The virus scanner had to detect the executable files (e.g., .exe, .com, .bat etc). These types of viruses are known as file viruses or file infectors.

Later in mid nineties a new type of virus was identified which infected Microsoft Office files. These viruses are called macro viruses as they remain in the form of macros. Macros are small executable programs which are included in Microsoft Word, Excel or Access or similar files. Macro viruses are written in high-level macro languages such as VBA (Visual Basic for Applications). The first wide spread macro virus was WM/Concept virus which appeared in 1995.

Gradually the viruses are evolving with new capabilities and infection techniques. While the advanced worms are communicating with their siblings through the network, the metamorphic viruses are changing their bodies in each infection to avoid detection. Some virus have the capabilities to infect various types of files and spread automatically on different operating systems and platforms. The passive files like .jpg pictures and .pdf documents are not even fully secured. There is hardly any computer user who has never faced any virus problems.

Names of some infamous viruses

There are at least dozens of infamous viruses which have created horror throughout the world at different period of times and damaged significant amount of data causing loss of billions of dollars to various business organizations. Although we have no purpose of getting into those details, we will just spot the evolution of some viruses on a time line.

In March 1999, the Melissa virus forced many large companies to turn off their email systems until the virus was brought under control. In May 2000, ILOVEYOU virus wrecked havoc through a piece of code in the email attachment. When a user double clicked the attachment the attachment executed to send copies of itself to every email address stored in the victim's computer.

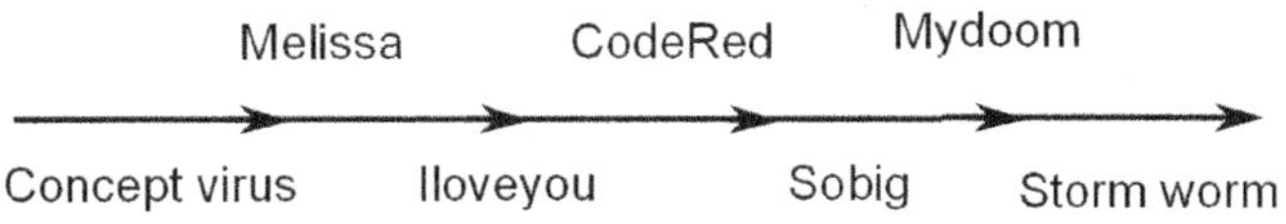

Virus Appreance Timeline

The CodeRed worms made huge damages in July 2001 infecting over 250,000 machines within a couple of days which was targeting Windows machines and IIS servers. In August 2003, the Sobig virus/worm infected millions of MS Windows computers connected through internet. There were varieties of Sobig virus, from Sobig.A through Sobig.F, which were replicating by emails sent through their own SMTP engines.

In January 2004, Mydoom worm infected approximately a quarter-million computers in a couple of days. Mydoom has a payload that allows backdoor on port 3127/tcp to allow remote control of the subverted PC. In late 2006, Storm Worm carried a message through emails having subject like "230 dead as storm batters Europe" or similar important headline. This storm worm is a Trojan horse program that turns computers into zombies or bots.

1.3 Different Types of Viruses

It is important to note that every malware is not a virus. For example, keyloggers, spyware and adware etc. are typically not viruses. But many malware like Trojans and Worms are included in the broad category of viruses for convenience although technically they are different from viruses in their structure and behavior. The following types of malware are generally called as viruses for general purposes.

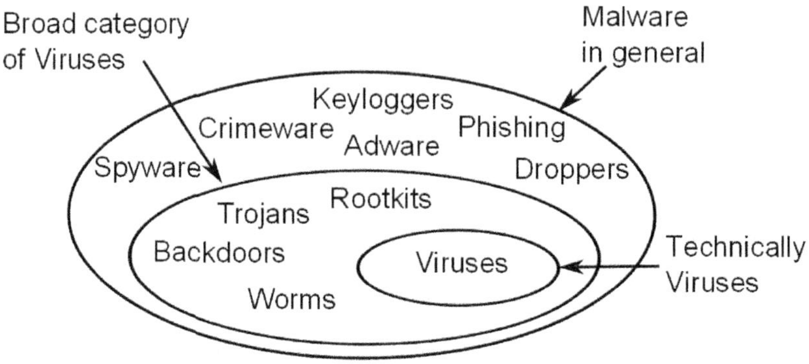

The Subset of Viruses within Malware

Viruses

A virus is a computer program that is capable of infecting other programs by attaching its code in such a manner that the virus code is executed when the infected program is executed. Thus a typical virus is parasitic in nature, as it has to mount on a host program in order to execute and spread. The innermost ellipse in the above diagram represents this category. There are different types of viruses, such as, file viruses, boot sector viruses etc. which we will discuss in later pages.

Worms

Unlike viruses, worms don't depend on other programs to execute or spread. Worms are self-sufficient programs that can execute independently. They typically use computer networks and security holes to replicate themselves. They are capable of spreading functional copies of themselves to other computers via network connections. Hence, they can consume excessive network resources and slow down or choke the network. They have the potential to do any kind of harm to a computer.

There are different types of worms. The host computer worms run entirely on the host computer and use the network connections only to copy themselves to other computers. Network worms consist of multiple parts or "segments" each running on different machines and using network connections for communicating between themselves.

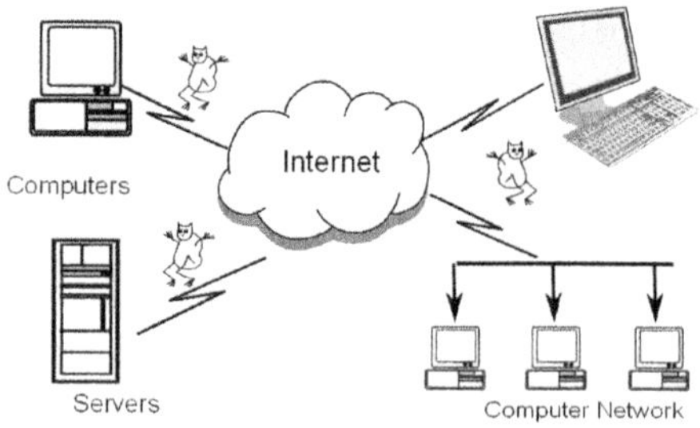

Spreading of Worms

Morris worm was one of the earliest worms which crippled the internet for several days in 1988. It exploited buffer overrun flaws in the common "sendmail" and other programs. It was causing a buffer overrun by inputting a large chunk of garbage data. Mydoom and ILOVEYOU are other examples of infamous worms. The detections and preventions for worms are discussed in a separate chapter.

Trojan horses

A Trojan horse is another type of virus which contains dangerous code inside but appears to be a benign and legitimate from outside. In other words, it is different from what it appears to be. For example, a Trojan horse claims to do something useful, such as a game, and may also do its job as a game. But when its payload comes it does very harmful operations, like erasing the disk.

The term "Trojan horse" comes from a story in Homer's Iliad in which the Greeks presented a giant wooden horse to their enemies, the Trojans, as a peace offering. But actually they deceived Trojans as the Greek soldiers were hidden inside the hollow belly of the wooden horse. When the Trojans brought the horse inside their city walls, the Greek soldiers sneak out of the horse and opened the city gates to allow their Greek compatriots to come enter and capture Troy.

The characteristics of Trojan horses are the following:

- Trojans are complete programs capable of running independently. Unlike viruses they don't depend on other programs.
- Trojans claim to be doing something good like gaming, registry cleaning etc. Hence, they may have legal names and even advertisements on Internet.
- Trojans use a deceiving strategy. They claim to be doing something good but do something harmful during their payload.
- Unlike viruses, Trojans don't replicate themselves automatically. People often download them and install them with consent.

- ⇨ While doing their advertised jobs (like gaming) they do an additional heinous job/s of a dropper, downloader, keylogger, backdoor, spyware, adware, rootkit etc. Some advanced Trojans are quite complex having multiple functionalities.
- ⇨ There are some FTP Trojans which opens your FTP port 21 for attackers to access your computer through FTP.
- ⇨ Some Trojans try to defunct or paralyze the anti-virus products so that the viruses can flourish without fear.

Backdoor programs

Backdoor programs allow a secret access to a computer bypassing the normal authentication procedure. The situation is like your house having a door at the backside which can be opened by outsiders. Such backdoor programs are generally installed by viruses, worms, Trojan horses or spyware. The program opens up a particular IP port for remote access. Although just having a backdoor is not seen as a problem, the backdoors can be exploited to infect your computer, steal your data and do many more things that you have not imagined.

Rootkits

A rootkit is different from viruses and worms. They are the modified versions of system programs or tools for administering the computer. These modified programs try to gain administrative-level control over a computer system and provide protection to other malware. The rootkit is used to prevent detection of backdoors and other malware. When operating system is infected by rootkits the anti-virus can be ineffective.

There are user-mode rootkits (which runs with administrator privileges), kernel-mode rootkits (which runs with operating system privileges) and firmware rootkits (could be anything from microprocessor code to PCI card firmware). The later rootkits are more difficult to remove.

Spyware and other malware

Spyware are not so dangerous to damage your system like viruses. They basically get into your computer without your permission and do their work in the background without your notice. Generally they do unwanted changes to the settings. A spyware may generate pop-up ads, hijack the browser to unwanted sites and display adulterated results to search queries, ultimately leading the web browser to be slow and unusable.

Some spyware collect information from your computer without your knowledge. Some of them (called adware) display popup advertisements. Spyware don't come within the broad category of viruses. They are like other malware such as JavaScript malware, VBScript malware, key loggers, Dialers, Hoaxes, Mallicious mobile code (MMC) etc. which are not viruses but no less harmful than viruses.

1.4 Classification of computer viruses

As we saw above, the viruses are technically different from Worms and Trojans in their structure and behavior. So the actual viruses are only a subset of the group of malware called as viruses. Viruses are parasitic and live in the body of other programs. While infecting a file/program they attach their code to the target file/program.

Viruses are classified into different categories from different angles. From the angle of their infection type, they may be classified as file infectors, boot-record infectors, worms and macro viruses. From their propagation method, they may be classified as viruses and worms. From their infection strategies, they may be classified as "residential" viruses and "non-residential" viruses. However, we will not get into the technicalities of these classifications. We will just mention some predominant types of viruses.

Boot sector virus

The master boot record (MBR) is a small program which is executed every time a computer boots. The boot sector virus or MBR (Master Boot Record) virus infects the boot record of the floppy diskettes or hard disks. The boot sector virus generally transfers through infected floppies. When an infected diskette is placed into a floppy drive during system boot up, the boot sector virus transfers itself to the hard disk by overwriting the disk's original boot sector with its own code.

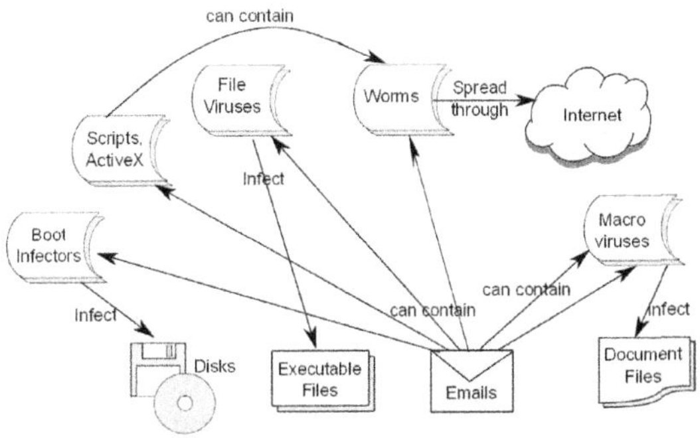

Virus Infection Relationships

File viruses

A file virus is a typical virus, which attaches itself to a program file, driver file or other executable file. This virus infects other programs when the infected program is executed. Generally file viruses attach themselves to executable files with extensions such as .COM, .EXE, .OVL, .DLL, .DRV, .SYS, .BIN, and .BAT etc. Generally they don't infect data files or text files which don't contain executable codes.

A file virus doesn't run automatically. When the host program (the infected genuine program) is executed the virus code gets activated and carries out its mischief. The infected host program generally executes the virus code before executing the host program and tries to infect other programs in the system.

Macro Virus

Macro virus is a recent type of virus written in scripting languages like Visual Basic for Applications (VBA) used to write macros in Office Suite applications. A macro virus can reside in documents like word processing or spreadsheet. The macro viruses run when the host document is accessed or triggered by certain user actions, such as specific keystrokes or menu choices. They can spread through general file transfer and even by e-mail. We will discuss macro viruses later in a separate chapter.

Email viruses

The email virus exploits the strengths and weaknesses of an email messaging system and spreads itself through the emails. An email virus usually replicates itself by automatically mailing virus mails to people in the victim's email address book. As an email can travel fast to distant places an email virus can therefore spread very quickly to distant geographical locations. Email viruses are actually not a separate category as they are either macro viruses or worms or similar. One of the worst destructive email viruses is "ILOVEYOU" virus which many firewalls failed to detect during initial outbreak.

Network viruses

Network viruses are proficient in spreading across a LAN, WAN and even over the Internet. They adopt various method of spreading themselves, such as, by infecting the shared folders and shared resources. They continuously look for potential targets by searching the networks and infect the vulnerable systems when found. Network virus is also just a functional classification like email viruses. They can be either worms, macro viruses or even email viruses.

Multi-partite viruses

Multipartite viruses combine the characteristics of more than one type of viruses. For example, a virus may infect the boot sector and executable files also. It can be memory resident and may travel through emails as well. As a multi-partite virus infects multiple types of files and finds multiple methods of replication it is more difficult to be controlled.

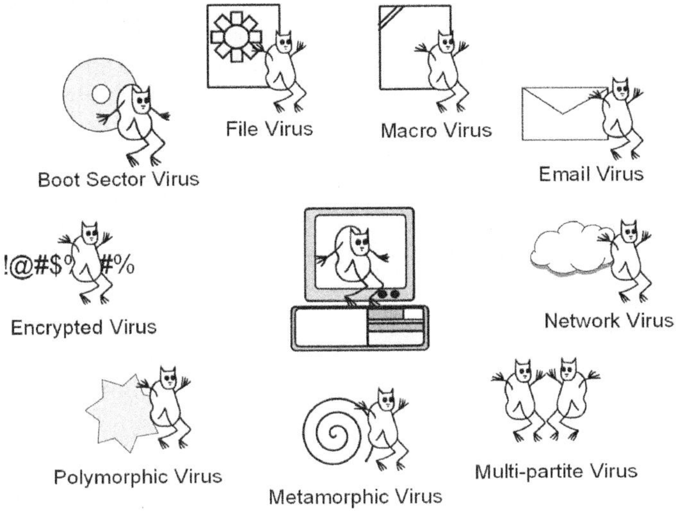

Encrypted viruses

Simple viruses copy themselves to each executable file they infect. They can be detected by searching their signatures extracted from their viral bodies. On the contrary, the encrypted viruses are hidden from view. As they are encrypted with different keys their encrypted bodies don't have any signature. However, those viruses comprise a decryption routine to decrypt their viral body before execution. They are usually detected by searching the signatures of their decryption routine.

Polymorphic and metamorphic viruses

A polymorphic virus is another type of virus, which produces varied copies of itself having the same functionality. The viral body is encrypted with different keys so that they vary in every infection. Besides the decryptor is also mutated in every infection thus leaving nothing common in two different infections. A polymorphic virus is often difficult to detect.

Metamorphic viruses also vary the instructions in the viral body with each infection. As the polymorphic and metamorphic viruses don't have any specific type of signature, they cannot be detected by signature scanning. They are generally detected by emulator-based antivirus technology. We will discuss more about polymorphic and metamorphic viruses in a separate chapter.

1.5 Characteristics of computer viruses

There are thousands of viruses developed by different people at different times. Their operating platforms, modes of operations, levels of nuisances are all different. But **one thing is common to all of them is that they are all unlawfully developed with malefic intentions which make them different from the genuine or benign programs**. The following are some of the common characteristics of different types of viruses.

- ➪ Virus programs are illegitimate and secretly developed. No software company publicly declares to be developing viruses. No Government allows virus development to be legitimate.

- ➪ The most fundamental characteristic of a computer virus is that it is executable, whether it executes directly (like worms) or it attaches its code to another file to get executed (like viruses). Without execution capability it can do no harm and will gain no importance.

- ➪ Another fundamental characteristic of a computer virus is that it replicates. A virus infects other programs generally by attaching its copies to those programs. Without replication the viruses cannot grow or survive. **Exceptions:** some viruses like Trojan horses don't replicate. They are replicated by human users. Some non-viral malware like droppers, transporters and generators also may not replicate.

- ➪ Viruses are capable of transmitting from one computer to another. They may transmit through an infected file or an infected disk. Some viruses or worms are capable of transmitting themselves across networks even bypassing security systems.

- ➪ Although the viruses can transmit from one computer to another, they cannot move from one Operating System to another. This is because the low level language that is understood by one OS will not be understood by another as they have different internal instructions or command sets. **Exceptions**: Macro viruses can move from one OS to another. But macros accessing OS commands cannot work in a different OS.

- ⇨ Different types of viruses have different capabilities and limitations. For example, a boot sector virus infects the boot sector and not the data files; a macro virus infects the documents and not executable files.
- ⇨ The viruses are harmful whether intentionally or unintentionally. The so-called harmless viruses may appear to be harmless but they at least replicate themselves and utilize some memory in the computer system, which by itself is a harmful behavior.
- ⇨ Every virus does not act immediately. Some viruses, like Trojan horses, wait patiently as benign programs until their events are triggered to become active. Some viruses may live just to help their successors or other viruses.
- ⇨ Virus writers don't want their viruses to be detected. So they adopt various stealth techniques. Some viruses use encryption techniques to hide their code. Some even use polymorphism and metamorphism to change their viral body as they travel from one host to another.
- ⇨ One of the weaknesses of viruses is that they are generally small in size and they generally don't do too much calculation that would draw attention towards them. For example, although a virus may be aware of the original checksum of a file it would be uncommon for the virus to add itself to the file without changing the checksum of the file.

These are only some of the general characteristics of viruses. But all viruses are not the same. Different types of viruses have different features. We have already discussed about the features of Trojan horses earlier. The special features of file viruses, boot sector viruses, macro viruses, worms, email viruses etc. are described later in respective chapters.

1.6 Virus infection strategies and results

Viruses may cause various kinds of damages to a computer system. Some viruses may cause simpler problems like displaying notorious messages on the screen, whereas some others may cause serious dangers like formatting the hard disk, causing permanent destruction of data and making the system completely unusable and irreparable.

Some people consider the term "VIRUS" as an acronym for "Vital Information Resources Under Siege".

Virus Infection Strategies

- Some viruses remain residential in memory (e.g., boot sector viruses) and do their job continuously.
- Some viruses do their action when their payload comes. Some others are activated only when triggered by an event.
- Some viruses get activated only once and destroy themselves after doing their job.
- Some viruses don't do anything except replicating themselves (the so called harmless viruses).
- Some viruses wait patiently to help their successors in future.
- Some viruses, like rootkits, take over some actions of the operating system, such as opening a file, in order to hide the infection of that file, before other programs can read that file.
- Generally viruses try to exploit the loopholes of the operating system. Some viruses are carefully written to exploit the loopholes of anti-virus programs. As the users blindly believe on the anti-virus programs, the intelligent viruses can attack the anti-virus program to rule over the computer.

The infection strategy of worms, Trojans, rootkits etc. are all different. We will discuss some of them in specific context as necessary.

1.7 The danger of Virus Payloads

The payload is the execution of the disastrous code that a virus ultimately intends to do. The payloads of different viruses vary greatly. Some viruses don't do anything other than consuming some memory and/or network bandwidth. But many others carry a more malicious payload.

- Some viruses wait until a specific time comes or some specific conditions are met. "Friday the 13th" was a popular time bomb virus which executed when the 13th of a month was falling on a Friday.
- Some viruses wait for a period and then become active for a period. The waiting period may be long or short or random. Similarly the active period may be long short or random.

- Every virus does not infect every file or at every time. Some viruses attack only specific system files or application files while some others attack the document files.
- Some viruses infect an email program to create new mails and send them to other recipients whose address is available in the address book.
- Some viruses consume a large amount of memory to slow down and ultimately hang the computer. Some viruses consume more and more network bandwidth to slow down and ultimately choke/paralyze the network.
- Some viruses attack every time the host file is run, some others attack in specific intervals and some may attack only once in life.
- Some viruses may target specific IP addresses or websites of specific organizations and not others,
- Some viruses attack specific operating systems, such as, specific versions of Windows or specific language editions of Windows etc.

1.7.1 Damages caused by virus infection

The types of damages caused by viruses can be categorized as direct and indirect. The direct damages include corruption or damages of electronic data, damages causes by crashes etc. Mishandling of a virus infection can also cause great losses. For example, a person may format the hard disk when the computer shows "non system disk or disk error", while the problem could have been solved by just removing the boot sector virus. The level of direct damages may be ranked from minor problems to fatal problems.

Direct Damage

Indirect Damage

While the indirect damages include wastages of administrative and computing resources, lost productivity because of downtime, expenditures on anti-virus products, expenditures on system administrators and implementing security measure. Let's mention some of the common problems caused by the viruses in the order of their severity.

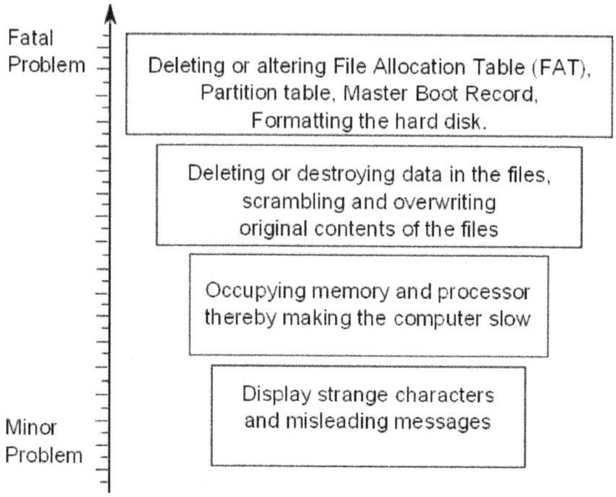

Different levels of harms made by computer viruses

- The so-called benign viruses don't do anything. But they typically take up some computer memory which slows down the speed of genuine programs.
- Some viruses interfere into the display system by scrambling characters on the video display screens, displaying misleading text, video or audio messages to users. Some viruses display poetry on the screen. However these viruses are less dangerous.
- Some viruses consume excessive amount of computer resources thereby preventing users from performing the desired tasks or possibly bringing the computer down.
- Many viruses like Trojan horses, have very malicious payload. The payload may be triggered on a certain date or by a certain action done by the user.
- Some viruses intend to alter or destroy data stored on the disks. They damage the computer by corrupting programs, erasing files, scrambling data on the hard disk, attacking FAT (File Allocation Table), altering partition table and even by formatting the hard disk thereby causing the system to be completely inoperable.

- Some viruses open a port as a backdoor. A hacking program can access the computer to steal data or do other harmful activities. The virus writers can make money out of phishing credit card information, passwords etc.
- If an infected computer system is part of a network then viruses can be transmitted to other systems in the network causing widespread damage.
- Some viruses may attack network servers, network traffic or even the whole network. They may use excessive amount of network resources and choke the network traffic to cause a denial of service (DoS) attack.

Chapter 2.

Evolution of Virus Technology

2.1 The functions and components of a Virus

The early age viruses came to the world with two minimum objectives, one is to replicate and another is to execute something uncommon. Many virus creators wanted to show their technical skills out of academic curiosity. But slowly with the growth of anti-virus programs, the survival of early age viruses became difficult. Like any other branch of computer science, the virus creation technology also evolved. The recent viruses have gone far beyond the capability of early viruses.

Considering the above basic functionalities of a virus it has to have two important components. One is to manage its replication or spreading mechanism and another is to manage its payload or side effects. The payload can be relatively harmless like consuming some amount of memory to highly destructive such as deleting or destroying files or even formatting a hard disk.

Gradually the viruses adopted another objective, i.e., concealing. So they had to have another component, a concealer, to hide itself from detection. Thus most viruses have the following three components. But special viruses also contain other special components.

- Replicator: When the host program is activated, the virus code is executed and the first priority of the viral malcode is to propagate.
- Concealer: Some advanced computer viruses employ various methods to hide its presence from anti-malware.
- Payload: The malcode payload of a virus can be purposed to do just about anything, from disabling computer functions to destroying data.

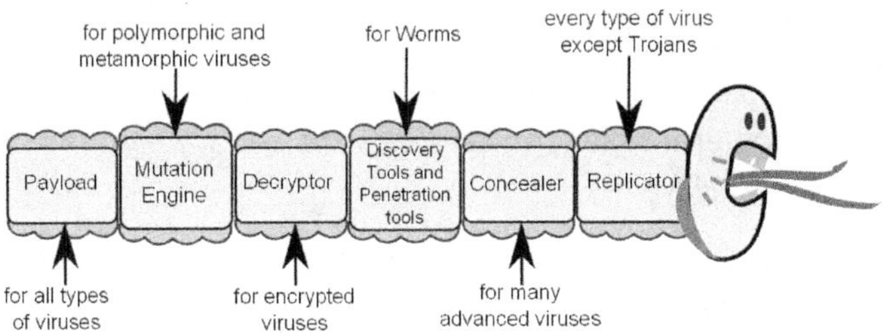

Components of Virus

Different types of viruses like Worms, Trojans, Rootkits, Backdoors etc. have different additional functions and different structures accordingly. For example, worms have two additional components apart from the above, a discovery tool to discover other computers on a network and a penetration tool to leverage the vulnerabilities on the victim computer. As Trojan horses don't replicate themselves, they don't have a replication mechanism. The components of backdoors are different. They use methods to exploit vulnerabilities of the target computer and install the infected files in order to provide remote access. Let's take a journey with the viruses from their early stage of minimal functionality to their current stage of advanced features and intelligence.

2.2 The minimum function- the virus must execute

Any virus should have this minimal capability of execution. Without execution the virus will remain as a dead file and it will not be recognized. The virus can be famous only if it can do something mischievous and draw attention of others.

Limitations:

- Doing more tasks requires more code that increases the size of the virus. But bigger size viruses are easier to be caught. **Contradiction**: The virus writers want to do as much task as possible but with minimum amount of code.

- Most viruses are written in assembly language which don't work on dissimilar platforms. For example, a virus written form IBM PC is generally unable to infect an Apple computer and vice versa.

- In some other cases viruses created on English version of Windows may not work on Chinese or Russian version of windows.

Options for virus writers:

- ✓ One option for the virus writers is to convert the virus code for each different platform and release separately (TRIZ Principle-3: Local Quality).
- ✓ Another option is to create cross platform viruses which will include the codes for different architectures in the same virus body and the virus will execute the relevant code depending on the detected architecture (TRIZ Principle-6: Universality).
- ✓ Another option is to make the virus capable of translating itself to different machine language depending on the architecture detected by the virus (TRIZ Principle-15: Dynamize, Principle-36: Conversion).

2.3 Better if it does some mischief to be infamous

One of the objectives of many virus writers is to draw people's attention in order to make their creation popular. Hence, a virus generally carries a payload to do something in consequence.

Some viruses carry nasty and disastrous payloads to gain quick popularity. Some others don't intend to draw attention immediately. Some viruses intend to hide from detection and live longer. Some are intended to create specific damage and vanish. Some are interested to silently survive in order to help their future generations aiming to cause bigger mischief in future.

Limitations:

- The more a virus draws attention the more the chances of its being caught and eliminated.

- I would like to quote from VLAD (Virus Labs and Distribution) site: *"If you have a virus killing hard drives everywhere, isn't it slightly obvious that your machine is infected? ... Without the extra code those few* crucial *extra bytes can be saved to make the overall virus more compact and much more likely to spread. ...*

  So the virus creators have a contradiction before them. **"Their viruses should do harm to all the computers other than their own".** As far as my knowledge goes, they have not been able to solve this contradiction successfully yet.

2.4 Most essential function- the virus must spread

Spreading the population of virus is very important for virus creators. Every virus creator wants to see his creation getting into every computer and spreading across the whole world. Early age viruses were mostly carried in floppies by human beings. Gradually when the floppies became obsolete, the later age viruses focused around the capability and weakness of Internet and email technology. Some important issues regarding spreading of viruses are:

- ⇨ Launching of the virus- (i) sometimes the virus creators launch their virus from a different machine/ location than their own in order to avoid detection. (ii) Secondly, they launch it from several different sources simultaneously, so that even if one source were blocked, the other sources would still work.
- ⇨ Propagation through self replication- replication is very important for the virus as otherwise it has to extinguish from the world soon. The viruses adopt various strategies to explore, exploit and infect the victim computers. The infection strategies and infection methods are illustrated in the next pages.

Limitations:

- If the virus is distributed through wrong channels it may get detected at early stage and cannot spread further.
- Most viruses are Operating System dependent. A 32-bit Windows virus can only infect PE (portable executable) files and will not execute on MS DOS. Similarly most Windows viruses will not work on Linux or Macintosh.
- Worms are protocol dependent. Worms written for one protocol will not work for another protocol.

Options for virus writers:

- ✓ Making the virus small and intelligent. If the virus is small in size then it can spread much faster.
- ✓ The virus creators strategically launch new viruses simultaneously from different locations, so that if one route is detected other routes can still flourish.

- ✓ Another option is to embed virus codes inside a good-looking program and deceive users as in case of a Trojan horse. The creator may release a good version through its official channel and Trojanized versions through other channels.
- ✓ Taking the help of email and Internet to spread. A popular method is to use the victim's email address book and spread virus code through emails. Another method is to scan IP addresses on the Internet and exploit vulnerable computers (as done by worms).
- ✓ Some recent viruses facilitate the entry of their next generation viruses. Conceptually a virus may give birth to another virus. There may be male and female viruses in future and when they meet together may give birth to new viruses.

2.4.1 How does a virus enter into the computer

As the function of a computer system is very complex, there are many possible ways for a virus to get into a computer system. A virus may come through an infected file, an infected email or an infected media. It may come through an infected computer, LAN, WAN or Internet.

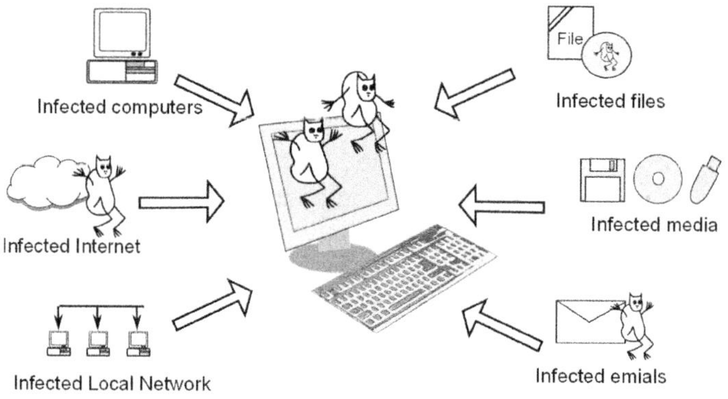

How a Virus gets into a Computer

A boot sector virus enters through infected floppies. When a user transports an infected floppy disk to a second computer the virus infects the second computer and so on. The boot sector virus changes the master boot record of the hard disk and permanently resides in the computer system.

A file virus spreads by copying itself to (or infecting) different executable programs. When the infected executable program executes, the virus gains control of the computer and attempts to infect other files. Some viruses attach themselves to the outgoing emails and get transferred to the destination computer.

Since a virus is a piece of software code it can be transmitted along with any software (even legitimate software) that enters the computer. For example, a virus can spread from a file server to the client systems attached to the server. The same can happen in the other direction. If an infected system is connected to a LAN the other computers may get infected by way of sharing files and infected resources.

In most cases the users spread the virus without their knowledge. For example, a person might download an infected program and run it. In this case the virus loads itself into memory and infects other programs on the disk. Although the virus goes on infecting one file after other the user has no way to know even that a virus had ever ran. The phases of virus infection are as follows.

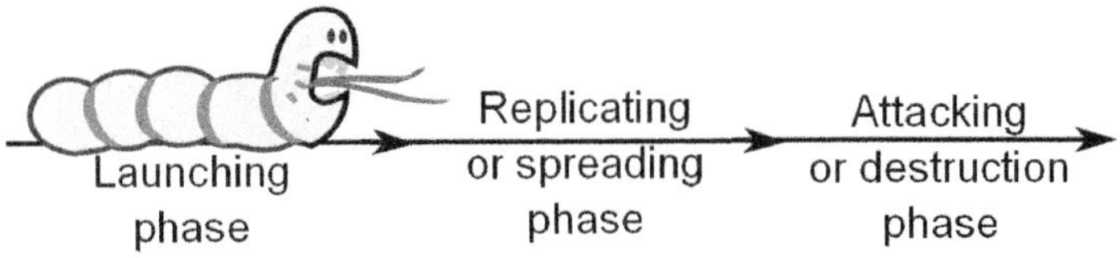

Phases of Virus Infection

2.4.2 Virus replication strategies

The virus creators follow various strategies to attack a victim computer. Some of the popular strategies are as follows.

- One strategy is to convince the user that the virus is a genuine program such as a game or a word processor. The user installs it with confidence and may even reliably use it for a period of time. But the virus shows its color when its payload comes. This strategy is followed by Trojan horses.
- Another strategy is to persuade the user to click on a link or open an email or unzip an attachment for viewing bank statement, or parcel delivery or win a lottery or read confidential mail etc. When the user clicks on the link the virus code is downloaded. This strategy is called social engineering strategy followed by Trojans and spyware.

- Drive-by is another most recently used method of propagating malware through website where the malware code is downloaded without the user's knowledge while the user is visiting a website or viewing a streaming video etc.
- Another strategy is to attach the malicious code to an executable or other active file type. The malicious code travels with the infected host file through floppy, CD, pen drive, email, internet or similar. When the user executes the host program, the virus code is executed causing further infection. Often the original program also works in its expected way so that the user does not suspect that the virus has ever run. This strategy is followed by file viruses.
- A similar strategy is followed by macro viruses to get embedded in a document file as active scripts and get executed when the document is opened.
- Another strategy is to infect the boot sector and get loaded to the system memory every time when the computer boots. This method is followed by boot sector viruses.
- Another strategy is to get attached to the emails. When a user opens the attachment the attachment executes to send copies of itself to every email address stored in the victim's address book. This method is followed by email viruses like ILOVEYOU virus.
- Another strategy is to get loaded into the main memory and stay resident. This method gives a virus greater control over the machine. The memory resident viruses will not go out of the memory unless rebooted.
- Another strategy is called drive-by infection where the viruses exploit ActiveX, Java and similar technologies and get into a system when the user views a streaming media or clicks on a link.
- Another strategy is to replace critical system files with infected files. The infected file does its additional jobs along with the job of the original system file. This strategy is followed by rootkits.
- Another strategy is to scan for security holes in the network and OS to replicate itself to other computers. The copy again looks for

other machines to make further copies. This strategy is followed by worms.

- Last but not the least, many viruses follow a combination of multiple strategies out of the above. For example, a Trojan horse may be attached to an email to travel from one machine to other.

2.4.3 Virus infection method

A typical virus (not worms or Trojans) generally wants to get executed first before the host program is executed. Hence the virus typically adds its executable codes to the beginning of the program. Alternatively it may insert its code in the middle or at the end of the host program and then add a JUMP instruction in the beginning causing the program to execute the virus instructions first before executing the host program.

A typical virus may infect a file through the following steps.

1. Check the availability of any EXE or COM or other suitable file
2. If the file is suitable then open the host file
3. Append, prepend or insert the virus code somewhere in the host file
4. Change the starting point of the host file to point to the starting location of the virus code.
5. Add a return command at the end of the viral code so that original program will execute after the virus is executed.
6. Save the changes to the host file
7. Close the infected host file

The worms spread very differently. Unlike viruses they are independent executable programs. They scan the network for another machine that has a specific security hole. When it finds the desired security hole it copies itself to the new machine by using the security hole. When the new machine becomes its den it starts replicating from there as well.

Many Trojans and spyware spread through websites. Some attackers host malicious software on their websites and attract visitors to download their program. Once the visitors install the malicious programs or ActiveX controls on their computer, the security of their computers is compromised.

Many recent viruses follow drive-by infection methods where the infection takes place without users knowledge when he is browsing a website or viewing a streaming media.

2.5 Better if it spreads to all types of files

The first age viruses were infecting only boot sectors and executable files. The boot viruses were staying memory resident and spreading to all removable media used in the infected system. The file viruses were spreading when their host programs were run. But this led to a very limited scope of proliferation.

Gradually macro viruses came into existence which infected document and spreadsheet files and executed when the host files are opened. Some viruses (particularly VbScript and JavaScript malware) are embedded in HTML files to get executed at the time of browsing the HTML. Some new viruses are infecting pdf files and shockwave movies and get activated when they are opened. The objective of virus writers is to enable their virus to infect all types of files to facilitate fast spreading.

Limitations:

- DOS cannot load .com files beyond a size limit. Hence the file viruses cannot infect very large .com files whose size grows larger than the acceptable size after infection.

- Infecting text files, Jpeg files etc. are meaningless as they are not executable.

Options for virus writers:

- ✓ Many viruses check the size of the file and don't infect files which are larger than the acceptable size limit.
- ✓ Some virus writers create multipartite viruses which can infect different types of file formats (or boot sectors) and capable of jumping one environment to another.
- ✓ When the computers improve with new operating systems and networking environment, the viruses and worms also exploit those features.
- ✓ Some viruses append themselves to the Jpeg files. These infected jpegs cannot do anything on a clean system. But if the computer is

already infected by their counterpart viruses then the virus codes in the jpeg files are executed.

2.6 The virus must escape signature scanning

With the growing usage of anti-virus programs most viruses were caught by their signatures and contained. As their proliferation was greatly restricted, the virus writers were urged to adopt stealth techniques to make their creation escape from signature detection.

Options for virus writers:

- ✓ One method followed by viruses is to infect known types of files and zip them with a password. The zip files can escape from anti-virus gateways as the anti-virus program cannot break the password to decrypt the content.
- ✓ The virus can be launched along with a rootkit which will protect the virus from being detected (TRIZ Principle-8: Counterweight).
- ✓ The virus creators use three powerful techniques, (i) Encryption (ii) Polymorphism and (iii) Metamorphism, to make viruses stealth and undetectable.
- ✓ Another method is to reduce the virus size. **Ideal Final Result:** Ideally if the size of the virus can be made too small (say zero bytes) then it will have no signature.
- ✓ **Using TRIZ Resources:** Another possibility is to create a virus out of the existing code available inside a program. The virus will contain only jumps from location to location within a legitimate program to produce a viral behavior.

2.6.1 Hiding viral body by encryption

One of the easiest methods to hide virus code is through encryption. The virus uses different keys to generate different viral bodies in each infection. There was no way for a scanner to understand what is there inside the encrypted viral body.

Limitation:

- However, there is a drawback in this method. The virus code cannot execute in its encrypted state. The virus must decrypt itself in order to execute. This requires the encrypted virus to include a decryption module. This creates a problem for the virus as this decryption module remains constant in each infection and gets detected by its signature.

Options for virus writers:

- ✓ Change the decryption routine in every infection as in case of encrypted polymorphism.
- ✓ Change the code/ structure of the complete virus in each infection as in case of metamorphism.

2.6.2 Polymorphism– changing decryptors in each infection.

Polymorphism creates different decryptors in each infection thus without leaving any specific signature of the decryptor which could be detected by a scanner.

Limitation:

- However, there is still a weakness. Although the viral body is different when encrypted with different keys, they are all the same when decrypted. The anti-virus programs use emulation techniques to execute the virus in a virtual machine. Once the virus decrypts its body it is caught by signature scanning.

Options for virus writers:

- ✓ The virus may decrypt its body part by part in such a way that only a small window of the decrypted code will be visible at a time. In such case the scanner will fail to match the signature (TRIZ Principle-1: Segmentation).

2.6.3 Metamorphism– changing viral body in each infection

Metamorphism is a step beyond polymorphism. Metamorphic viruses completely change themselves in each infection. As there is nothing common between one infection and another there is no scope for extracting any signature. These viruses became really difficult to detect.

Limitation:

- But at the same time it is also very difficult to develop such viruses. Only persons with immense technical knowledge can develop such a virus. But why such genius people would develop viruses for no benefit?

Options for virus writers:

- ✓ The virus creators solved this problem by providing virus construction kits. The expert virus creators create virus construction kits and make available on the Internet. This method enables even amateur virus writers to create strong metamorphic viruses by using simple copy paste actions.

2.6.4 Hiding viral codes through steganography

Steganography is an art of concealing a message, image or file within another message, image or file. Using this technology a malware can remain hidden inside genuine files, pictures, movies, music etc. This is done by making minor changes to the original files which are not noticeable by human perception.

2.7 The virus must escape from integrity checking

Integrity checking is a simple but foolproof method of detecting virus infection. No virus can infect a file without changing the original code of the file. Even though a virus can escape from signature scanning, it cannot escape integrity checking so easily.

Options for virus writers:

- ✓ One option is to infect the backup file (or hash value) along with the original file. In that case the integrity checker will not find any difference. **Limitation**: a virus will have to be large in size in order to do so much calculation.

- ✓ **Rootkits**- Another method is to fool the integrity checkers with the help of rootkits. When the scanner tries to access a file for integrity checking, the rootkit may intercept to return a “file missing” error or return a copy of the original file stored in a different location.

- ✓ **Companion Viruses**- Another method is to write companion viruses by creating a .com file having the same name as the original .exe file. When the user types the program name (without extension) the.com file gets priority and gets executed.

- ✓ **Directory infection**- another method to escape from detection is by infecting directories instead of infecting files. A virus can change the cluster pointer in the directory entry of the file to point to the virus instead of the actual program so that the virus code executes before executing the target program. This method infects the computer without modifying the code of the host program.

2.8 The virus must escape all types of detection methods

When the viruses apply different stealth techniques to escape from signature scanning, the anti-virus manufacturers created many more techniques to detect and eliminate them. Hence, the virus must target to escape all types of scanning and detection methods in order to survive.

2.8.1 The worms must escape from network anomaly detection

Worms self-replicate by sending network packets to other elements in the network. But this communication of the worms raises network traffic and is detected by traffic anomaly detection methods.

Contradiction before worm/ virus writer:

The worm should communicate through the network for identification of vulnerable computers and self-replication. But this behavior of the worms should not raise network traffic to be detected by network anomaly detection methods.

Options for worm/ virus writers:

- ✓ Some worms send very less number of packets. As the signal-to-noise ratio (SNR) remains very low, the worm is not detected by traffic anomaly methods (TRIZ Principle-30: Thin and Flexible).
- ✓ Another method followed by the worm writer is to adjust the worm transmission rate based on actual network traffic (TRIZ Principle-15: Dynamize). If the SNR remains less than 0.01% then it is virtually impossible to detect any traffic anomaly.

2.8.2 The virus must escape from baits and traps

Some virus detection techniques employ baits and traps to catch the viruses. The bait files (or goat files) are files that are specially created by anti-virus software to be infected by a virus in order to catch the infector. Hence, the virus creators must feed necessary anti-bait intelligence inside their viruses.

2.8.3 The virus must avoid infecting emulated hosts

Some anti-virus programs employ emulation techniques to allow the virus to execute and decrypt its viral body. The virus is recognized after decrypting its viral body. In order to escape emulation the virus must be intelligent to avoid infecting emulated hosts. Hence, the virus creators must feed the necessary anti-emulation intelligence within the virus to avoid and/or fool emulated hosts.

2.8.4 The virus must escape from heuristics detection

Advanced anti-viruses use behavior monitoring techniques and various heuristic techniques to analyze the nature of the viral code and behavior of viruses. How to escape from behavior monitoring and from heuristic detections?

Contradiction before the virus writer:

- The virus should behave like a virus (so that it can do its desired mischief), but at the same time, the virus should not behave like a virus (so that the anti-virus cannot detect it by its behavior).

- The virus must contain viral codes (in order to infect and do its mischief) but the viral code should look like normal code (so that the anti-virus cannot differentiate the virus from other benign programs).

Options for virus writers:

✓ **The virus should be cleverly written to show only a normal behavior-** If the virus does not show any abnormality, then the behavior monitoring method cannot raise any suspicion. However, recent anti-virus researchers have developed many other heuristic techniques which differentiate the pattern of benign programs and malicious programs.

- ✓ **It should be disassembly protected**- As the virus detection techniques disassemble the virus code for analysis in order to get the signature and other characteristics, the virus writers use different techniques to prevent disassembling of the virus code.

And finally,

2.9 Offence can be a defense for the mischievous viruses

It is often too difficult for the virus to escape from the modern detection techniques. Some virus creators take an offensive stand to attack and defunct the anti-virus system or paralyze its crucial functions. The virus explores and exploits the loopholes not only of the operating system but also of the anti-virus program and penetrates into the loopholes to take offensive steps. There are enough incidences of malware attacks in the past on almost all the popular anti-virus products.

In this chapter we discussed how the viruses evolved from their basic features and functions to their current stage of intelligence and capability. We also discussed how the new generation viruses use various anti-detection techniques to escape from different virus scanning methods employed by the anti-virus programs. As the evolution of virus technology is making the viruses intelligent, powerful and virtually undetectable, the situation is posing a great challenge before the anti-virus researchers. The anti-virus developer has to discern the indiscernible, find the invisible and detect the undetectable.

Chapter 3.

What is the Exact Problem to be Solved- Analysis of the Virus Problem

3.1 The TRIZ Approach

The "Theory of Inventive Problem Solving" or TRIZ was originally developed by Genrich S. Altshuller, the famous Russian patent scientist and inventor. Altshuller screened hundreds of thousands of patents and found that the SAME TYPES OF PROBLEMS are being solved again and again by different people at different times in different contexts. The problem solver spends enormous amount of time and energy to solve the problem because he is unaware of the similar problem or problems solved by other people (may be) at other places and (may be) in other contexts. Had he known about those solutions he could have solved the problem with utter easiness.

Altshuller analyzed the patterns of all these solutions in order to find the key solution strategies. He discovered that all these inventions had emerged out of the application of only 40 Principles, 76 Standards and 9 trends. He also found that every system is moving towards its ideality and the technology trends are predictable. He invented a set of tools and techniques, and a new approach to solving the inventive problems, known as *Teoriya Resheniya Izobretattelskikh Zadach* (TRIZ) in Russian or "Theory of Inventive Problem Solving" in English.

The philosophy of TRIZ or the "Theory of Inventive Problem Solving" is different from all other problem solving methods. While large majority of creativity and problem solving tools follow an "internal approach" propagating their own methods to be the best, TRIZ follows an external approach looking for solutions from outside. According to TRIZ philosophy,

the problem that we are facing now has been faced by many people in the past and most likely has been solved by many people in many different ways. Hence, it is not always necessary to build a solution from the scratch. In most cases it's easy and wise to look at other people's solutions and see if any of those solutions is suitable in our situation after due customization.

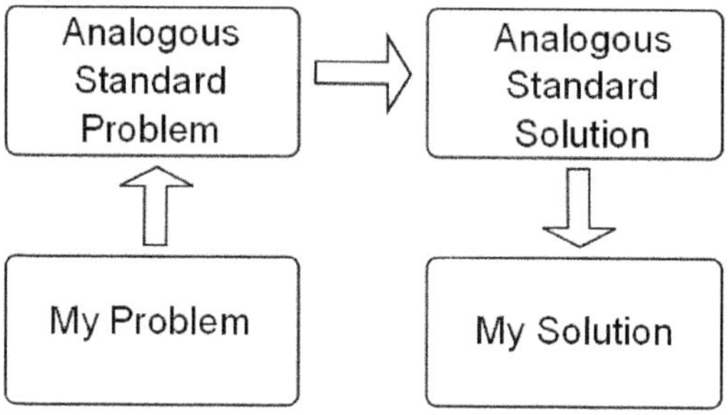

The TRIZ Approach

In the above diagram, "my problem" is a specific individual problem that any of us may be facing or trying to solve. According to TRIZ the individual problems can be generalized and solved by a set of generic solutions. TRIZ provides a set of generic solutions, such as, Inventive Principles, Inventive Standards, Trends of Evolution etc. for solving any kind of inventive problems. A problem solver has to find which generic solutions are suitable for his generic problem and arrive at the specific solutions for his specific problem.

TRIZ is a repetitive process of moving from specific to generic and generic to specific. Moving from specific to generic is called an "inductive" process in the study of Logic. This process is tricky and difficult as any mistake in the process can lead to wrong generalizations. Luckily Altshuller and his team of TRIZ developers have already done this part of the job and provided us with different sets of ready-made generic solutions. We just need to apply some of these generic solutions to solve our specific problems. For example we may be facing a problem to dry our clothes in a specific situation. But if we know all the drying methods, it becomes easy for us to find the best drying method that may be suitable in our situation.

	Individual Problems	**More general Problem**	**More General Problem**
1	Drying my pant	Drying clothes	Drying methods
2	Disinfecting my file	Removing viruses	Removing malware

Interestingly when we generalize the methods of solutions at a very high level they get detached from the domain of their origin (such as dress materials, transportation or computers) and remain as just pure rules applicable to any domain. The rules originating from one problem or problem domain sometimes yield miraculous results when applied to a different problem or problem domain.

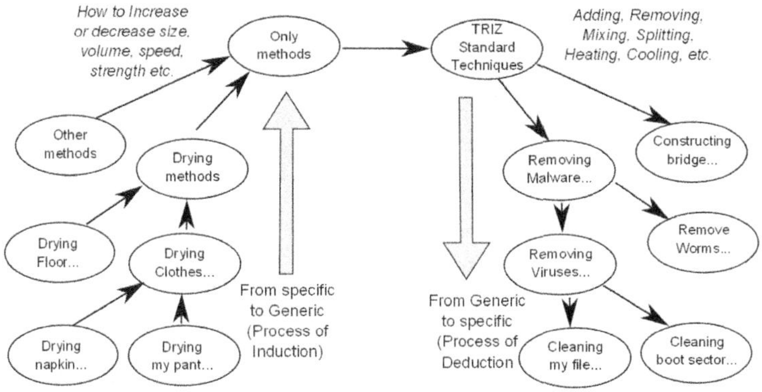

Travelling from specific -> generic -> specific in TRIZ process

How is TRIZ approach different from other approaches

While every problem solving method has restrictive views, TRIZ accepts and embraces all other methods without any hostility. The objective of TRIZ methods is to look for solutions from the past inventions, solutions from other branches of studies and solutions even from dissimilar systems. Thus TRIZ allows us to combine both "internal" and "external" approaches in order to get the strengths of both the approaches.

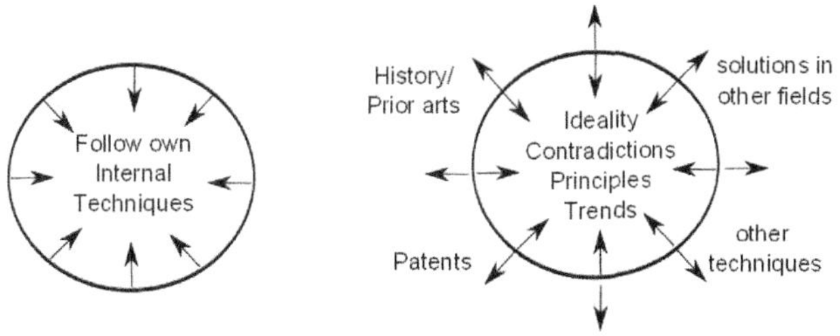

Other Approaches TRIZ Approach

As the methods of TRIZ are derived from a large number of past inventions or patents, they are most suitable for similar purposes, i.e., for making new inventions. Besides TRIZ is driven by powerful concepts like Ideality and Resources both of which conceptually intend to achieve all the desirable functions without much of investment and complicacy.

3.2 The TRIZ method of problem solving

The theory of TRIZ provides a systematic approach to solve any problem starting from defining the problem through applying a solution. The method of problem solving is clearly elaborated in ARIZ (Algorithm of Inventive Problem Solving), a technique of TRIZ. The TRIZ approach of problem solving broadly involves the following steps, viz., analysis of the problem, finding and solving technical contradictions, finding IFR, formulating and eliminating physical contradictions, evaluating alternative solutions and selecting the best solution.

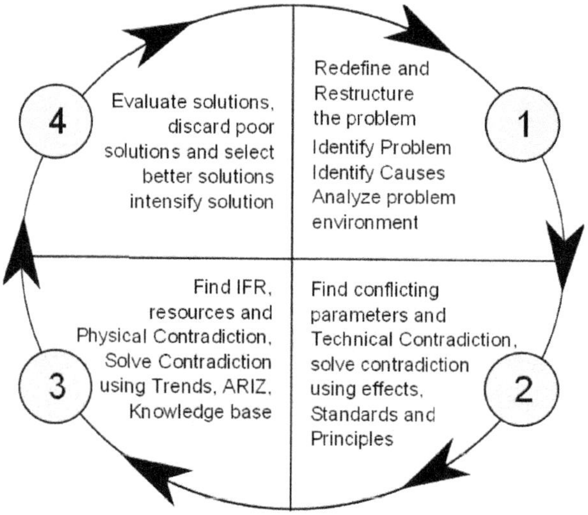

TRIZ Process of Solving a Problem

After the whole cycle is over, the problem solver again goes back to the first step of analyzing the problem situation and redefining or reformulating the problem and change the way the problem is analyzed. **According to TRIZ the best way of solving a problem is to move to a more general problem thus avoiding the need for solving that problem.**

3.2.1 Analyzing and defining the problem

According to TRIZ, analyzing and defining a problem is the first and most important step of problem solving. During this stage the system is analyzed in the context of its functions, resources and conflicts. The analysis of functions involves Useful Functions (UF), Harmful Functions (HF) and the Main Useful Function (MUF) of the given system. The analysis of conflicts indicates which functions of the system lead to conflicting situations or contradictions.

Analysis is important because the same event (or action or situation) may be causing different problems (or benefits) to different people (or co-systems or subsystems) under different conditions. Some solutions may appear to solve a problem but may give rise to other problems, or may solve the problem in the short term but may escalate the problem in long term. Similarly, some solutions may solve the problem in the main context (or system), but may cause problems in other contexts (such as, co-systems or super-system or sub-system). A good solution should be holistic in approach and should not cause any harm to the other parts of the system or the environment.

Analyzing Problem Environment

For example, the computer virus is not a problem to everybody, at least not to the people who don't use computers. Besides, *the same virus infection may be a problem to one person at one time but may not be a problem to another person (different co-systems) or to the same person at a different time (different time segments).* For example, creation of virus is an undesirable phenomenon for a computer-user but is a desirable phenomenon for an anti-virus manufacturer.

To explain further *the same virus may be a problem to one operating system but may not have any impact on another operating system (different super-systems).* The problem analysis is usually done with the help of System Operator, S-Curves etc.

3.2.2 Finding and Solving Technical Contradictions

While the initial description of the problem remains vague (called as administrative contradiction) the next step is to pinpoint the problem by finding out the conflicts or contradictions in the system that inhibit in achieving the intended result (called Technical Contradictions). For example, we found a problem that **"connecting our computer to Internet makes it vulnerable to virus infections".** We found a solution **"don't connect to Internet"**. But that leads to another problem that "**we cannot check our emails or browse websites unless we connect to Internet"**. This situation creates a contradiction - "**we want to connect our computer to Internet but we don't want any virus to come to our computer through Internet".**

Finding the right Contradiction is a key step in the process of problem solving. Once the contradiction parameters are identified a solution is sought. For example, in case of the above contradiction, one may think of various solutions like, can there be an Internet connection which will allow only good data and not viruses? Can there be a subsystem within the "computer system" or within the "internet connection system" which will inhibit infiltration of viruses? TRIZ provides tools like Inventive Principles, Inventive Standards, IFR and trends etc. to solve such contradictions.

3.2.3 Finding IFR and solving Physical Contradictions

The next part of problem solving is to pinpoint the problem by finding the Ideal Final Result (IFR) or Ideal Final Goal (IFG). Ideal Final Result is obtained by answering a question "what do we want in an ideal situation?"

For example, when we are trying to solve virus problems, we may ask a question like "what would we like to see as an ultimate solution?" The answer we get may be like "there should be no virus in our computer" or "the virus should have no power to do any harm to our computer". In many cases an IFR is just a fantasy or imagination; they are not achievable. But formulation of an IFR helps the inventor to think the solutions in the right direction. For example, the above IFRs may help us to think radical solutions like "what if our computer is immune to viruses" or "what if our programs are immune to viruses"! We may also think more generic solutions like "What if the virus creators stop creating viruses"! We will discuss more on Ideality later in this chapter and also in a separate chapter.

After finding the IFR, in many cases a Physical Contradiction is formulated to strengthen the problem further. A Physical Contradiction creates a conflict with the same parameter of the system. For example, "the anti-virus researchers should publish their virus detection techniques so that all the anti-virus developers can benefit from that knowledge, but at the same time they should not do so because the virus creators will misuse that knowledge to make their viruses immune to those methods".

After the contradictions are formulated they are next supposed to be solved. The contradictions are generally solved by applying Inventive Principles, Inventive Standards, Pointers to Effects, Trends of Evolution, ARIZ and Knowledge sources like patent databases. TRIZ does not prohibit using any existing knowledge or method, rather recommends and advises to apply the techniques from the existing knowledge and past inventions. It is recommended to bring solutions that are closer to the IFR.

It is recommended to solve problems by using the resources that are freely available in the system and avoid using external or expensive resources. We will discuss more about contradictions in a separate chapter.

3.2.4 Analyzing and weighing the solutions

While solving a problem we may come up with a multitude of alternative solutions. The final step of solving the problem is to weigh each of these solutions, discard the weaker solutions and select the stronger ones. The strength of a solution is considered in the context of its space, time and environment. As a thumb rule,

- The stronger solutions are those, which solve the contradictions by themselves and turn the harmful elements to useful resources.
- The stronger solutions are those, which solve the problem with the resources already available to the system without requiring additional expensive resources.
- The stronger solutions are those, which not only solve the problem of the system concerned but also solve problems of its super-systems and subsystems.
- The stronger solutions are those, which should not lead to any other problem, either in short term or in long term, whether to the system or to its environment.
- In short, the stronger solutions are those, which are closer to the Ideal Final Result.

3.2.5 Restructuring the Original Problem

After the whole process is over, the problem solver comes back to the first step again to restructure the original problem by changing the context of the problem. This way the problem solver may select a more general problem thereby avoiding the need for solving the original problem. Restructuring and redefining the problem is an important step in problem solving as about 90% of the problems are found to be solved during this step itself without needing to go further.

For example, our initial problem "how to remove viruses from my computer" may be changed to "how to remove viruses from any computer" or "how to remove viruses from Windows operating system" or "how to make my computer immune to viruses" or "how to make an operating system immune to computer viruses" or "how to stop virus creators stop creating viruses" and so on. **According to TRIZ, The best solution of a problem is that which avoids the need for solving that problem.**

3.3 What is the Exact Problem to be solved- the First Step of Solving Virus Problem with TRIZ

If we analyze a virus environment we find several actors and elements, such as users, computers, operating systems, networks, servers, network administrators, viruses, anti-viruses etc. Prima facie a virus is a harmful and unwanted element in the system which needs to be eliminated. But the current form of anti-virus is not an ideal solution. The user has to pay for an anti-virus year after year continually as long as he uses his computer. If he is not paying money for renewal of the anti-virus then his computer is at risk. He has to download signatures on every alternative day otherwise his computer is at risk. The user has to accept the slow performance of his computer for hours during a virus scan. The user tries to escape from the trap of viruses but effectively falls into the trap of anti-viruses. The anti-viruses are no less harmful than an average virus in terms of consuming system and network resources. There is no common general user who willfully wishes to install an anti-virus. The anti-virus has become a compulsion and a necessary evil.

Let's first analyze who are the people facing the problem of computer viruses. For example, a person not using computer does not face this problem. Only a computer user faces this problem. However, there are different types of computer users as we see in the following diagram.

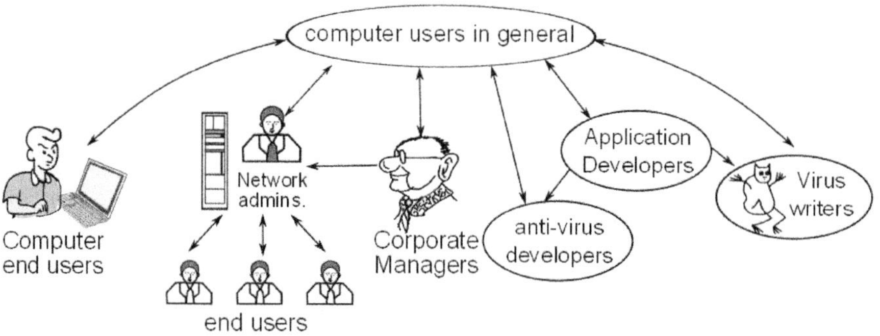

Different types of computer users around virus problem

Almost all types of computer users face this problem whether he is a common type of end user or a special type of user (with higher skills) like system administrator or an application developer. Interestingly a virus creator also faces the problem of computer viruses but that is not our concern at the moment. Our main concern is the larger group of end users who are the main victims of this problem. At the same time we may not ignore a small group of system administrators and corporate managers who take the responsibility of providing computer facilities to the corporate users. The other group of people we are concerned are the anti-virus developers as they hold the key responsibility of solving this problem.

Different problems faced by different level of users

When we analyze a virus problem in detail, we see that the problem is not the same for every level of user. The nature of problem may vary according to the knowledge and experience of the user. For example, the problem faced by a novice user (who does not know how to install an anti-virus) may be different from the problems faced by an advanced user (who might have installed an anti-virus) but is facing the adverse effects of anti-virus or difficulties in updating the virus database or removing a virus undetected by the virus scanner.

As a large number of people use computers, their knowledge and experience on computer technology and computer viruses vary to a great extent. Many computer users may be experts in their own fields like graphic designing, film editing, word processing or web designing etc. but may not be so good in dealing with computer viruses. Thus, the same scenario of virus infection may cause different problems to different users at different levels, such as, a novice computer user, an advanced computer users, an application developer, a systems administrator, a corporate manager and an anti-virus developer because of the differences in their experience, visions, requirements and goals.

Different Solutions for different situations and different people

As the problems are different for different people, the solutions are also different. For example, if a user's computer is infected in office, one of his solutions can be to leave the office and work on his personal computer at home, as his goal is probably to submit the report by a dead line. But in a similar situation the Systems Administrator cannot leave the office and do something similar at home, as his goal is to remove the virus from the infected computers in the office.

While talking about solving virus problems different experts we may suggest different types of solutions. Let's analyze the following figure, which depicts four different types of solutions suggested for eliminating virus problems.

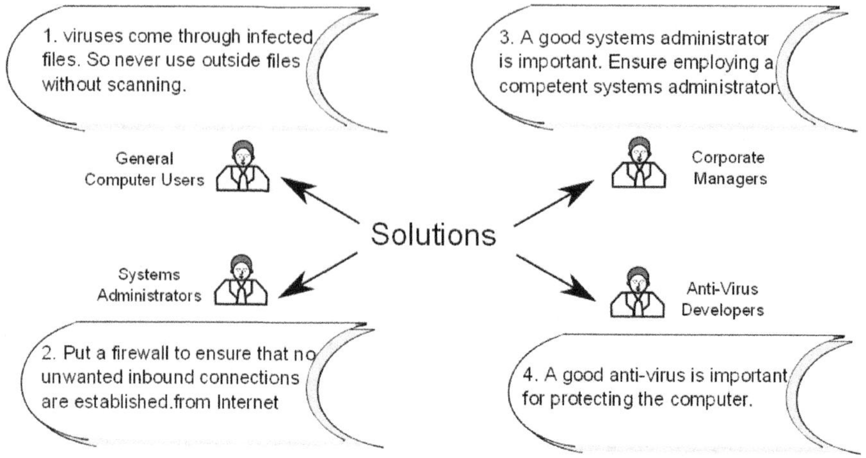

Different solutions for Controlling Viruses

If we analyze the four solutions illustrated above we find that all four are quite valid and very important solutions. But interestingly they are very different from each other and cannot be advised to the same person. This situation often creates confusion and needs to be explained.

Suggestion (1) “to avoid using external files” is meant for the end user, suggestion (2) “to put a firewall in the network” is meant for the systems administrator, suggestion (3) “to employ a good systems administrator” is a suggestion to the corporate manager and suggestion (4) “to develop a good anti-virus” is meant for the anti-virus developer.

Thus we see that the same root cause (in this case, the computer virus) creates different problems to different people. The problems are narrated in different terms and solved in different methods. No single solution is always the best. A good solution may work for some group of people but may not work for every group of people. A better solution works for a larger group of people in a larger environment for a longer period of time.

3.4 Analyzing the Virus Problem of the End Users

Let’s analyze what problems an end user has to face because of computer viruses. An end user uses a computer for specific purposes, say, word processing or gaming or emailing. When the computer is infected, his work is disturbed. His main objective is not to remove the virus but to do his work. If he can continue his word processing or gaming without removing the virus (may be unusual) he wont probably mind sheltering viruses in his computer.

3.4.1 The apparent problems reported by the end users

Often an end user may not recognize a virus problem properly and report it in vague terms. For example the user may say *"The computer is behaving erratically, some program is not running, the system is hanging, the system is not booting"* and so on. The user may say *"Everything was fine till I worked in the morning, but I don't know how suddenly my file became corrupt."* Although the problems are described very differently, an experienced Systems Administrator can link all these complaints to just one problem, i.e., virus infection.

These problems reported by the end user are called "Administrative Contradictions" in TRIZ. The Administrative Contradictions are just the expressions of needs without knowing how to satisfy those needs. It will be interesting to analyze different types of complaints reported by the end users before going for a solution.

- The computer is behaving erratically, some executable is not running, pen drive is not reading, system is hanging, and system is not booting etc.
- The user is facing virus like problems in one particular computer or in one of his friend's computer or in one particular cyber café.
- The user's file is missing or corrupted, so he cannot produce the desired output in the given time.
- The user's boss will be angry; his job will be in stake.
- The virus may come out of his computer and infect his body.

3.4.2 Analysis of the Problems Reported by End Users

Each of the above-described problems appears to be different. Each of them is analyzed individually in the following table.

However the following table illustrates just a few examples and not a complete list of alternative ways a problem is perceived and addressed. The readers of this book might have come across many more interesting manifestations of the same virus problem. What we try to show in all these cases, although the main problem is nothing but the virus, the perceptions of the problem are different and sometimes the objectives are different. When the objectives are different, the approach to solving a problem can be different.

	Problem	Analysis
1	The computer is behaving erratically, some executable is not running, pen drive is not reading, system is hanging, and system is not booting etc.	This is the user's personal problem while interacting with the computer. He may not be doing any significant work, may be just gaming, but he expects his computer to behave in an orderly way. He is worried of the erratic behavior of his computer. If his pen drive is not reading, he may be happy to get a new pen drive, or if his system is hanging he may be happy to see it repaired or get a new system.
2	The user is facing (virus like) problems in one particular cyber café or in one of his friend's computer.	This situation is different from the above. The user doubts or knows about the virus infection in some specific computers. But he will not bother to heal those computers. He will try to avoid that cyber café and prefer to visit a different cyber café in future.
3	The user's file is missing or corrupted. So he cannot produce his output in time.	This situation is more of target related. The user faces problem because his targets are affected. He will not bother about the virus if he can produce his result within the target period. The user will be happy to get a copy of his lost file, or to extend his submission deadline than wasting time on the virus.
4	His boss will be angry, as he has not been able to do his work.	This situation is slightly different from the above. The user although has lost his work or file because of virus, his worry is the boss or the job. He can manage the situation if the boss is satisfied by other means.
5	The virus may come out of his computer and infect his body.	This problem is purely psychological based on a false notion. When the user knows that the computer virus cannot work upon human body, his problem will be solved.

3.4.3 Analysis of alternative solutions

Let's find some possible solutions for the above problems reported by an end user who is affected by computer viruses.

- In the first case the user may be given a new pen drive to replace the old pen drive which was not reading, or given a new joystick to replace the old joystick which was not functioning, or given an additional 1 GB memory as the previous memory was slow. However, all these solutions will work for a short period. Unless the virus is cleaned, the user is likely to face similar problems soon because of virus infection.
- In the third situation, the problem is solved by given a backup of the file. The user continues working on the backup file and his problem is solved. But unless the virus is cleaned from his computer, he may loose his file again or face similar other obstacles in progressing his work.
- The alternative solution in the third instance is to extend the target date. As the target date is extended, the user gets more time to redo his lost work. But again unless the virus is cleaned he might face similar or other obstacles while doing his work.
- The fourth situation is again different. The focus is not on the work rather on the goal of the work, i.e., the job or boss or business. If the boss is happy or job is secured then no care for the virus. However, in such cases, although the user is saved for a short period, the loss will burden on somebody else, such as the boss (co-system) or the business (super-system).

What we see above is that the same problem is seen from different angles by different people and apparently solved by different methods in different situations. But some of these solutions work temporarily in specific conditions without addressing the core issue, i.e., the virus in this case. Now the million-dollar job is to decide which solution is better? Whether should the user finish his document first using a different computer or should he virus-clean his computer first and then continue on his document?

A good solution provides a long-term solution. Besides a good solution not only solves the problem reported (e.g., file corruption) but also solves the problems not reported (e.g., virus infection in this case). A good solution works not only for the person concerned but also works for all other users of the computer. Besides a good solution should not cause any harm or negative results to his peer groups and environment, such as, other users, systems administrators, anti-virus developers etc. And lastly a good solution should be easy and free.

Some good solutions for End Users

Let's now illustrate some good solutions usually advised to the end users. By and large, the end user (of whatever level) has to follow one of the two main strategies, viz., Isolate your computer from other computers, (TRIZ Principle-2: Taking out) or, use an anti-virus program (TRIZ Principle-8: Counterweight). All other do's and don'ts revolve around these two main strategies. The following are some specific methods and their corresponding Inventive Principles.

- Don't use external storage media (like floppies, CDs, DVDs, pen drives etc.) coming from unknown sources. Carrying information from one computer to another can carry viruses with them (TRIZ Principle-9: Prior Counteraction).
- Don't download programs (such as games, screensavers, freeware etc.) from unreliable websites. Programs from unreliable sources can contain viruses (TRIZ Principle-9: Prior Counteraction).
- Don't open emails coming from unknown sources. Don't automatically open email-attachments. If you are not sure about the attachment, better delete it. Never run attachments from unknown sources (TRIZ Principle-9: Prior Counteraction).

These solutions here are exemplary and not exhaustive. A longer list of do's and don'ts are available in my article *"Solving Virus Problems by Computer Users"* in March 2007 issue of TRIZsite Journal.

3.5 Analyzing Virus Problems faced by Systems Administrators

The problems faced by the systems administrators are different from those faced by the end users, because of the difference in their responsibilities and functional goals. When the functional goals are different, the problems are different; the solutions can also be different.

(Note: The term "System Administrator" may be understood in generic sense that is synonymous to Network Administrator, LAN Manager etc. whosoever is responsible for taking anti-viral measures for a group of computers or networks as part of his job responsibility.)

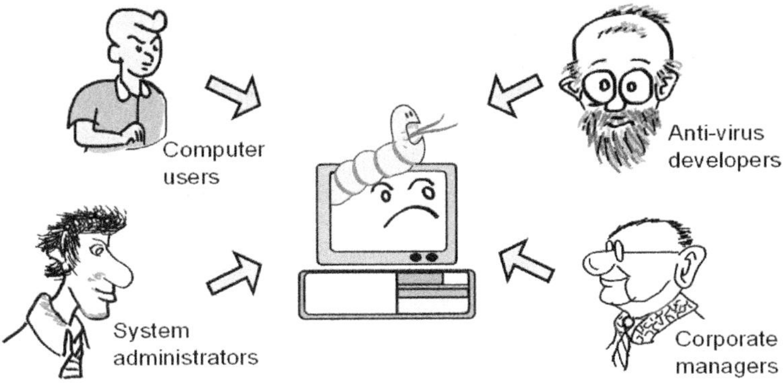

The same virus problems is seen differently by different perspectives

For example, if a user's computer is virus infected he can leave office and work on his personal computer at home, because his goal is to submit a report by a target date. But a systems administrator cannot leave office to work at home, because his goal is to remove virus from the computers in the office.

Later we will see that the problems faced by corporate managers or anti-virus developers are different from the end users and systems administrators, because of the differences in their experiences, visions, requirements and goals.

3.5.1 The problems faced by systems administrators

The job of a Systems Administrator (or Network Administrator or LAN Manager) is to keep the computers and network safe and free from virus attack. When there is a virus infection in a computer system or a virus outbreak in a network environment the systems administrator typically faces the following problems.

- His stress level goes up as because various users start complaining about virus problems.
- His workload goes up, as he has to scan and remove virus in a large number of computers. He may have to apply patches or updates or may have to change the anti-virus software or anti-virus policies.

- His boss gets angry and blames him because he has not been able to tackle the virus problem.

It is interesting to note that unlike the end user he does not want all the computer viruses to vanish completely from the world, as in such a case he will loose part of his job and salary. Unlike the home user he does not mind procuring an anti-virus product, as because he does not have to pay from his pocket, rather his company will pay for the procurement. All he wants is to keep the virus within his control.

3.5.2 Anti-Viral Solutions taken by System Admins

The anti-viral actions taken up by the systems administrators can be broadly categorized as either preventive or curative.

Preventive Actions

- Selection, procurement and deployment of a suitable anti-virus product. The parameters of selection may include price of the product, reliability of the product, product features, OS compatibility etc.
- Implementing anti-virus policy – the network administrator may include an anti-virus policy into the network security policy in order to ensure that the anti-virus measures are properly implemented. The anti-virus policy may include a minimum version of an anti-virus product, minimum update of signature database, a minimum scanning at system startup, specific configurations for automatic scanning of files etc.

The above are only exemplary and not exhaustive. A detailed list may be found in my article *"Solving Virus Problems by System Administrators"* in March 2007 issue of TRIZsite Journal.

Curative Actions

- Downloading the latest anti-virus updates and ensure scanning of each individual computer in the network (TRIZ Principlce-9: Prior Counteraction).
- When there is an outbreak of ferocious virus the Network Administrator may physically unplug the network cables (TRIZ Principle-2: Taking Out).
- And so on...

3.6 Comparing the problems faced by a Corporate Manager

A corporate manager does not face the problems that are faced by the Systems Administrators or LAN Managers. The corporate manager perceives the same virus problem differently as he has a different set of challenges before him, such as,

- Budget allocation and financial provision for virus prevention in the corporate environment.
- Employing right personnel as network administrators and network security managers. Ensuring that the network administrators work according to the conventions followed in the industry.
- Provisioning alternative arrangements to provide working environments in case of virus outbreaks. Ensuring backup of critical data and protection of sensitive data by the security managers in compliance with industry standard.

The role of a systems administrator is crucial in a data center because he has to look after the health of the data center, implement security policies, take data backup, assess requirements etc. On the other hand the high cost on employing a systems administrator (or multiple systems administrators) increases the cost of managing the data center. This situation poses the following contradiction before the corporate manager.

Contradiction	*It is necessary to employ network administrators in order to administer a data center or computer network or web-hosting environment. But employing good network administrators is expensive. The company Manager wants to ensure network administration and system security but he doesn't want to spend money on employing network administrators.*

3.7 What is the Real Problem

As we saw in the above paragraphs, whether it is a *booting problem* for the end user or a *network problem* for the systems administrator or a *recruitment problem* for the corporate manager, the root cause of the problem remains the "virus infection". We can draw a system diagram to depict the position of "viruses" and its impact on other systems around it.

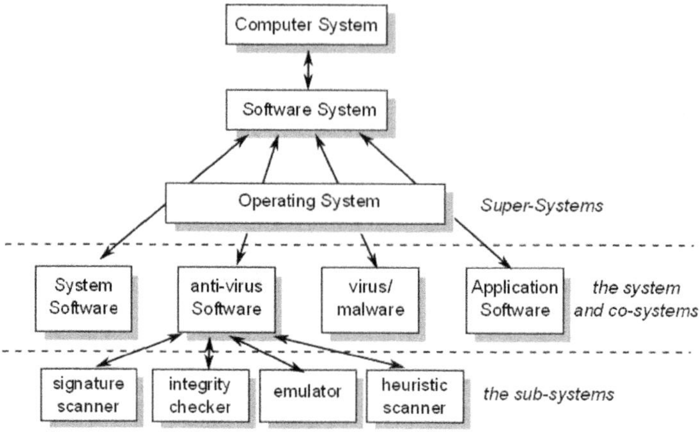

The adjacent-systems of virus and anti-virus systems

In the above system-diagram the virus is a subsystem that affects its super-system (i.e., operating system) and co-systems (i.e., application programs and data). In order to solve this problem we have to either remove this virus system totally or remove the harmful effects of this virus system or add some protections to the other systems or add something that will counter to the harmful effects of the virus system etc.

3.7.1 Creation of viruses- analyzing the broader problem

If viruses are causing harm to other systems around then what is the cause of virus coming into the world? If human beings create the viruses then why do they create such elements? Creating virus is a cyber crime, a form of terrorism and considered as an illegal activity everywhere in the world. No government, no law, no sensible organization supports such criminal activities. Creating viruses is also not an easy job. But yet there are some people who devote their valuable time and effort in such kind of activities. What is the reason? What benefit do they get out of creating viruses? Some answers are:

- Inherent Criminal mentality
- Frustration because of non-recognition of talents
- Hatred towards some group of people
- Encouragement from similar like-minded groups
- Thrill of doing something unusual and watching how things blow up. When the virus gets spread their creators get more fun.
- Experimental mentality or curiosity of the teen-agers

- There are some (relatively) good virus writers who don't like destructive payload routines. They consider their viruses as their creations, like works of art.
- Availability of virus-creating tools and technical support on the Internet/ websites
- Financial sponsorship from criminal organizations- availability of secret funding and sponsorships for such unlawful activities.
- Intellectual curiosity– a person might create viruses out of intellectual curiosity to see how a piece of code copies itself to different machines and applies different tricks to survive under different challenges.

3.7.2 Loopholes in the operating system- analyzing the broader problem

The virus is a computer program like any other program and it has to run on the operating system. No virus can enter unless there are loopholes in the operating system. No virus can run without being supported by the operating system. In fact most viruses are developed for Windows operating system because of its loopholes. Very limited number of viruses exists for Unix/Linux operating system.

3.7.3 Using a system operator

The system operator is a two-dimensional model of the system depicted in both space and time. Using a system operator helps us to visualize and study the components of a system in respect of both space (i.e., super-system, system and subsystems) and time (i.e., past, present and future).

It may be worth mentioning that the terms "super-system" and "subsystem" are relative because every system is a subsystem of its super system and is a super-system of its subsystems. The super-systems of an anti-virus system are "software system", "operating system" and "computer system" etc.. The sub-systems of an anti-virus system include various modules/ methods of virus scanning and detection.

The following is a System Operator model for anti-virus system having 9 windows, three on vertical and three on horizontal. In the model the x-axis represents time and y-axis represents hierarchy of the system.

The 9 Windows of System Operator

Super-systems	People, The jobs to be done by using a computer	Computer Operating System Software Programs Programming environment	An output, a report, a software product
System	Extracting virus signatures. Creating scanning logic	The anti-virus program	Updating virus definition files Scanning and detecting viruses Disinfecting and repairing files
Sub-systems	Installing anti-virus	Offline scanning module On access scanning module Virus signature update module	Periodical scanning and maintenance activities. Vaccination and file repairing
	Past	Present	Future

Studying the adjacent systems are important as sometimes the problem is solved by transferring the main useful function of the system to another system. Sometimes the problem is also solved at a super-system level. Besides studying the adjacent systems gives a clear picture of the system environment. This knowledge helps to propose a solution that is compatible to all the systems in and around the system. If we forget this law, we may bring some benefit to one part of the system at the cost of another part of the system or sub-system or super-system.

3.8 Whose responsibility is it to prevent viruses

All of us agree that the viruses are harmful for the computer and troublesome for the computer users. If "virus" is the real problem, then the question arises who is supposed to solve this problem? Is the end user supposed to solve the problem or the system administrator or the anti-virus developer?

- As the end user is directly suffering from the virus problems it is definitely important for the end user to take necessary precautions to get rid of viruses. They may install anti-virus programs and take necessary preventive measures and follow various hygienic habits in order to prevent virus infections.

- However, in a corporate environment there may be some security policies and the end users may be unaware of those policies or may not be allowed to choose their own anti-virus. In those cases the system administrators take care of anti-virus measures for individual systems and the network.

- Even the OS developers has a critical role to play. Most viruses are platform dependent. If an OS is more transparent and layered like Linux then viruses may infect some external files but cannot attack the operating system. Traditionally virus creators have targeted Microsoft operating systems whether it's MS DOS or MS Windows. Hence people who have used different versions of Microsoft OS have faced higher virus problems. It is important that the OS developer should not leave any vulnerability that would provide scope for proliferation of worms and viruses.

- Similarly the application developers may play a role in virus prevention. If the applications can self check viral infection then viruses cannot flourish.

- Last but not the least, an anti-virus program is found to be crucial for virus protection. Hence, the job of anti-virus developers remains very important, as they must provide a bulletproof anti-virus product to their customers.

Role of different people in solving virus problem

Thus everybody is responsible to play a role for preventing viruses in different contexts. The user has to install an anti-virus program which the anti-virus developer has to develop. Thus, the bigger responsibility lies with the anti-virus developer, as he has to produce an effective tool that is to be used by others. Although everybody needs to be innovative and use TRIZ techniques, the anti-virus developers are bound to be innovative because they have to ensure that their product is capable of fighting with the viruses. Besides they must gain the competitive advantage to survive in the business competition.

3.9 Applying TRIZ for Solving Virus Problem

In the above paragraphs we analyzed the causes of virus creation and the causes of virus infection. We analyzed the technical system illustrating the subsystems and super-systems of the virus and anti-virus systems. Now let's see what are the interesting ways of solving the virus problem.

- The main problem is that the viruses (or other malware) are deliberately created by some human beings. If for some reason they stop creating viruses then there wont be any virus problem or need of any anti-virus solution.
- The virus writers are getting more confident because there is no strong method of tracing the origin of viruses or detecting the virus creator. It is necessary to make virus detection systems competent to find the exact geographical location (or IP address) where a virus has started its first journey. If the virus writers can be traced back and caught by the cyber-police then they will restrain from such activities.
- From a different angle, the viruses are not the real problem. The real problem is their harmful payload routines. If the viruses would have no malicious functions then people can ignore them to settle peacefully as harmless inhabitants. But can we detach the malicious payloads from the viruses?
- Loopholes in the operating system is a real problem. As Microsoft Windows has more loopholes, all viruses are revolving around the Windows operating system. It is necessary to build more robust operating systems having multiple layers of protection so that the viruses cannot enter into the system or don't get an environment to run or make virus writing extremely difficult.

- The problem occurs because there is no built-in defense with the application software. If the application software will have built-in defense mechanism then nobody would bother about the existence of viruses.
- Last but not the least, the problem can be solved by building a powerful anti-virus system which can not only detect and eliminate viruses in the system but also prevent the malware from entering into a computer system.

3.9.1 Can we restrain virus creators from creating viruses?

In an Indian mythological story once there were two benevolent people, one king and another saint, both of them were always helping the poor. The king was always distributing food and money to the poor. The saint was also helping the poor up to his capacity. In the heaven there was confusion with regard to who of them was more benevolent. So lord Vishnu came in disguise to examine them. First he went to the king and offered him a boon. The king said, "Please give me so much of wealth that I can distribute sufficient money to every beggar on everyday". Then lord Vishnu went to the saint and offered him a boon. The saint said, "Please remove poverty from earth so that nobody will ever have to beg".

The meaning of the story is clear. If poverty is eradicated then there will be no poor and no need of giving money to the poor. The desire to give money to the poor is out of one's vanity and a weaker benevolence than the desire to eradicate poverty. If we apply the same wisdom on our virus problem, the best solution would be to stop creating viruses. This solution would not only solve virus problem but also eradicate all the subservient problems under the virus and anti-virus systems. If no virus is created, then no virus problems are faced and no remedies are required. But the question arises is it really possible to do so? How to prevent virus creators from creating viruses? Some thinkers might advise to:

- ✓ Create moral and ethical awareness among people to judge what is good (or right or useful) and what is bad (or wrong or harmful).
- ✓ Improve detection systems to trace and catch cyber criminals- training to investigators, reward to people giving crucial information etc.
- ✓ Create strong cyber laws to punish cyber criminals

- ✓ Change the technology framework in such a manner so that the virus creators will not be successful in their effort
- ✓ Change the technology so that creating viruses should result in damaging the virus creator's system
- ✓ Create coordination between countries to catch cyber criminals from any part of the world and punish the organizations that are financing or patronizing such people.
- ✓ Counterstrike the attackers through similar means like creating viruses to attack the creator's system. (Note: generally an offensive counterstrike in any manner is not allowed by any law).
- ✓ And various other measures which will drag us to social, economic, moral, legal, political and international issues.

Exploring the Virus Problem

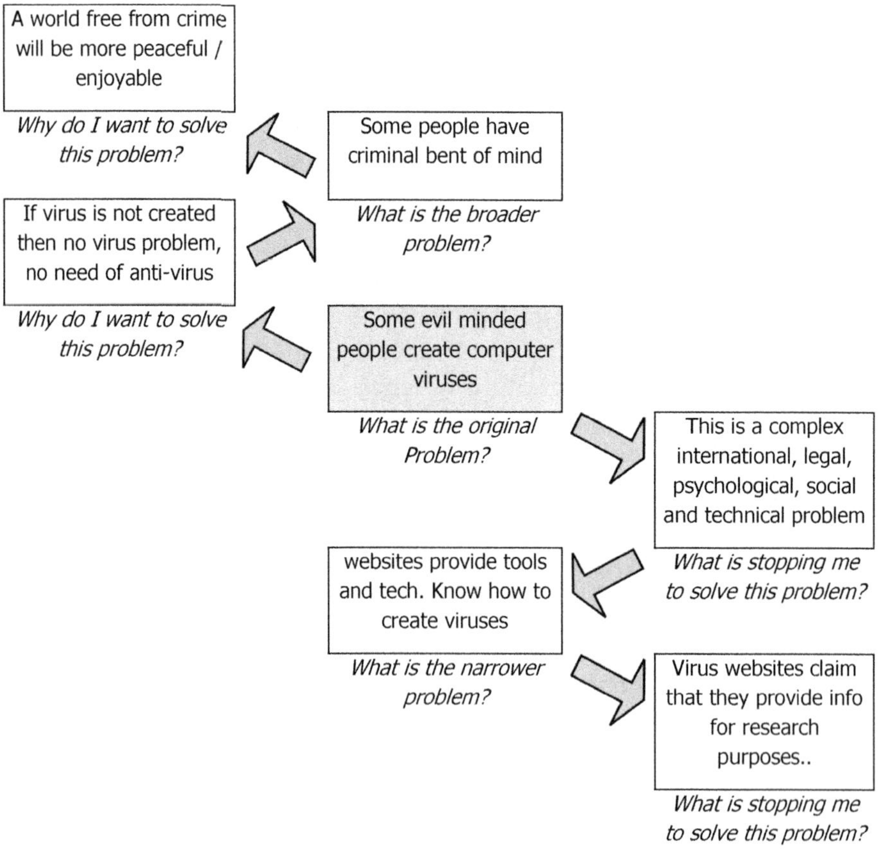

The above diagram explores the problem of virus creation in both directions upward and downward thereby finding the broader and narrower problems. The query begins from the fact that "some evil minded people create viruses". The upward movement continues by asking the question "what is the broader problem?" and "why do I want to solve this problem?". The downward movement continues by asking the question "what is the narrower problem" and "what is stopping me to solve this problem?". (Note: This model is based on a format suggested by Darrell Mann in Hands on Systematic Innovation).

Although preventing virus creators from creating viruses is an ideal method of stopping virus creations and one of the surest methods of solving virus problems at a higher level, there are certain limitations in proceeding longer in that direction.

- If the virus programmers are restricted from creating viruses they may get involved in other criminal activities.

- Demotivating virus developers is rather a socio-psychological issue. There are other systems like education systems, social reformation systems, criminal detection systems and legal systems etc. which should work collaboratively in this direction.

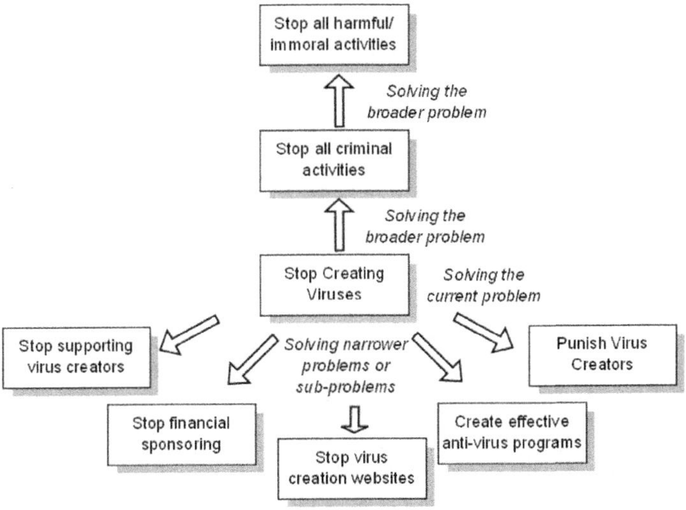

The Hierarchical Structure of Probem Solving

The question arises, whether it will be technically possible to make the virus creation mechanism fail, so that the virus creators will restrain from such activities out of frustration?

INVENTION-1: Using polymorphic protection method to frustrate virus writers

The virus writers always remain one step ahead because they can reverse engineer and know what protection techniques are incorporated in the anti-virus program. This helps them to make their new viruses more intelligent to escape the existing scanning techniques. On the other hand the anti-virus writers are in a weaker position, as they have no clue to know what features the new viruses are going to have.

Patent 5684875 (invented by Hans Ellenberger, Nov 1997) suggests a polymorphic protection method in order to deceive and frustrate the virus writers. The invention although includes a large number of detection algorithm, does not show off all the algorithms in each installation. It installs only a few selected algorithms in each installation of the anti-virus. Hence, even if a virus writer reverse engineers the detection method he can view only limited number of algorithms which are installed on that machine. Even if the new viruses include the counter measures for those algorithms they cannot escape from other algorithms available in other installations. Thus all his effort of escaping the anti-virus will go waste.

The invention uses another method to frustrate the virus writers. The anti-virus will include sufficiently large number of algorithms to detect the viruses. This will require the virus body to include large amount of codes to escape from all these detections. Interestingly the enormous size of the virus will make it easy to be detected (Inventive Standard 4.2.2. Add something in the element to help detection). As the development of new viruses will be less promising the potential virus developers will terminate such activities.

According to TRIZ, if the problem can be solved at a higher (or super-system) level then it can yield a better result as it can automatically solve most of the lower (subsystem) level problems. For example, imagine, if the virus creators can be motivated to stop creating viruses, what will happen to our system chart (in 3.7) above? The current system (virus problem) will disappear along with all its sub-problems (signature extraction, distribution, scanning etc) or sub-systems. The systems chart will completely change its shape. Similarly the problems diagram (in the previous page) will also change its shape. All the narrower problems and sub-problems will vanish out of the diagram.

3.9.2 Can we build a virus resistant Operating System

The other method of solving the problem as we discussed above is to make the operating system virus resistant. For example Linux operating system provides several layers of protection that does not allow viruses to operate at kernel level. A virus can at best operate at a surface level to affect user files but cannot affect the core system files.

The viruses are generally written in assembly language and are completely operating system dependent. That means viruses written for Windows OS cannot work for other OS.

Imagine if the operating system will not allow viruses to operate then the viruses cannot do their malicious activities. This is definitely a thought for the future. But what about the current operating systems!

3.9.3 Using a hardware based operating system and hardware based booting

Imagine if there will be no software! Fifty years ago there was no software and no viruses. Now we are dependent on computers and cannot live without it. But imagine if the functionality of software is achieved by hardware or some other means. For example if the whole operating system and all the applications will be loaded from a ROM! Actually many embedded systems load their OS from ROM and therefore have no fear of viral infection. But there is no easy way of putting the current day huge Windows operating system in ROM. Is there any clue of any possibility? Some inventors have definitely tried in that direction.

- Huntington, et al. suggested to copy the boot sector of the hard disk to a non-volatile memory so that there can be no boot sector infection (Patent 6907524).

- Similarly Zaitsev suggested to use a hardware based anti-virus module in combination with the AV application for better security (Patent 7657941).

- Lawrence Kates (US patent application 20090183253, July 2009) discloses a virus resistant computer which does not make use of a hard disk. The computer boots from a read only media like CD or DVD which once created cannot be infected with virus. Even if a virus finds its way into the computer, the user can easily eliminate it by shutting down the computer and restarting to its default condition. **Limitation**: the method of this invention will not work for the current operating systems like Windows which requires frequent updates and service packs.

3.9.4 Can we remove the loopholes in Windows operating system?

The viruses and worms generally find an entrance to the computer by exploiting the loopholes of the operating systems. In fact, the virus creators first explore a vulnerability in the operating system and develop a malware to exploit that vulnerability. As every version of windows launches with numerous loopholes, the virus creators take advantage of this situation. Therefore Windows operating system has been most vulnerable to virus attacks.

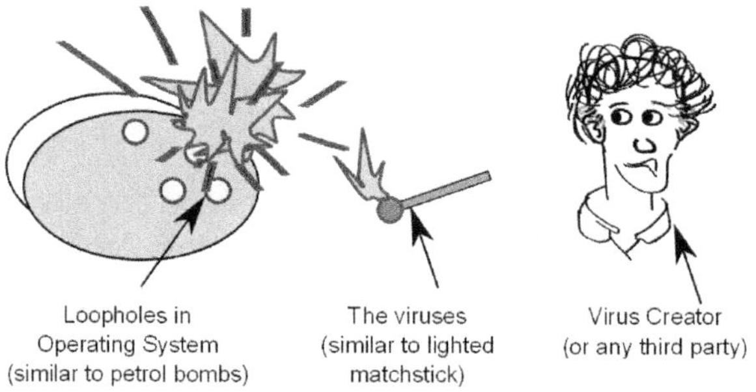

Many viruses are written to exploit specific loopholes of the operating system and critical system services. These viruses become powerless when the specific loopholes are closed by applying security patches. That means if all the computes in the world will apply security patches then all the viruses based on those security holes will automatically die out of the world. The loopholes (in the operating system or critical system files or other executable files) are like bombs which catch fire by the malicious codes to cause explosion. The fire is thrown by the virus creators, hackers or other types of attackers.

Microsoft changed the Windows® architecture drastically in Windows 2000 and later versions. But the new architecture also had many loopholes which were exploited by virus creators. While Microsoft has been continuously trying to fix the loopholes one after the other most of the earlier vulnerabilities are disappearing and most viruses are having limited scope for proliferation only through machines which are not updated with service packs and security patches. The question remains whether Microsoft will be able to fix all the security holes in the future versions of Windows operating system?

3.9.5 Solution by changing the Super-System and/or adjacent systems

TRIZ teaches that many problems in a system can be eliminated by introducing changes in the super system and/or adjacent systems. The above solutions (3.9.2, 3.9.3 and 3.9.4) were based on introducing changes in the super-system (i.e., the operating system). Let's see other possibilities of changing the adjacent systems.

Changing the Macro Interpreting Environment

The macro viruses are all executed by the macro interpreter of the MS Office environment. If something can be changed in the macro interpreting environment so that the macros containing viruses will not be executed then the problem of macro viruses can be resolved.

Introducing changes in the Compilers and Interpreters

The programs are either compiled by a compiler or interpreted by an interpreter. If the compilers and interpreters are changed in such a way that they can recognize the virus codes and will not compile or interpret the virus codes then the problem of compiled or interpreted viruses can be resolved.

3.9.6 Possible Solution - Adding a Super-System above Anti-Virus Development system

There is a big drawback in the current anti-virus system. Although a few anti-virus companies dedicatedly work on developing anti-virus programs there is no coordination between them. They all work independently with hostility and suspicion to each other. This situation has many drawbacks.

- The task of collecting of new virus information becomes repetitive for each of them. The signatures of the same viruses are being extracted in each anti-virus laboratory.

- Every anti-virus company is doing the same type of R&D. The anti-virus researchers of every anti-virus company are developing same type of heuristics. This results in huge wastage of resources.

- Different anti-virus software have incompatibility between themselves. The anti-virus developers become weaker because they have to fight not only with the virus developers but also with their fellow developers.

What is missing is a super-system above the anti-virus development system. A creation of a new super-system, i.e., an anti-virus consortium (or similar) above the anti-virus developers can solve the problem.

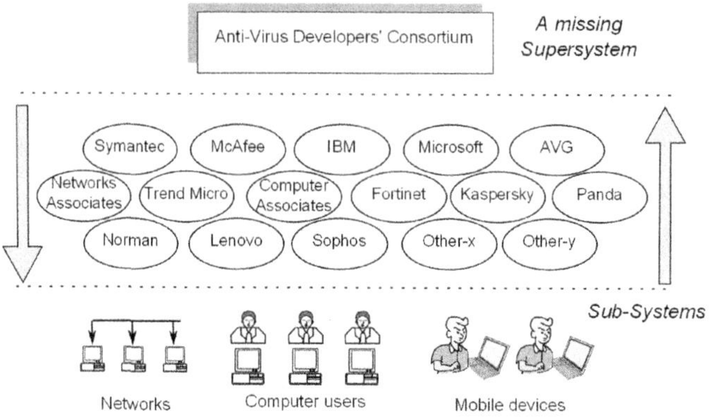

Creation of a Super-System above the Anti-Virus Developers

This super-system can play a vital role by taking the feedback from the end users and share new virus information and other critical information among the anti-virus developers. Actually a body called Anti-Virus Product Developers Consortium (AVPD) was established in nineties to provide an open forum in which the product developers could work towards common goals such as product testing, product certification, surveys, studies and market research. But these functions are only ancillary business functions away from the core functions of virus detection technology.

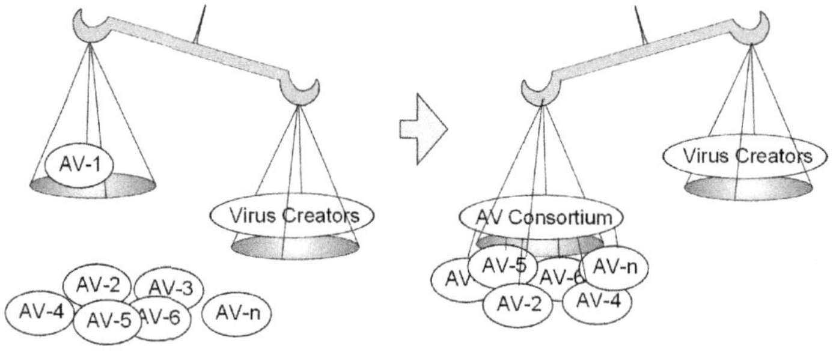

Currently each individual AV developer has to fight with the whole group of virus creators. This situation weakens and defeats the AV developer. If there will be a proper super-system above all the current anti-virus development systems (which can take up the common activities, such as, virus detection, signature extraction and development of core detection technologies) then more than 90% of time and resources that is wasted on the repetitive activities can be saved. Utilization of that saved resources can easily outweigh the strength of anti-virus creators.

Besides there can be a government-private collaboration to strengthen the virus defense mechanism. The government has access to certain critical network data and has got more legal scope of doing experiments on cyberspace than private sectors. On the contrary the private sectors are better equipped with research and technology, which is probably not available with the government. A similar benefit can also be obtained by collaboration between one government and another.

3.9.7 Possible Solution - Transferring the anti-virus functionality to the super-system

Another powerful solution is achieved by "transition to super-system" where the main useful function (MUF) or certain other functions are delegated to the super-system. If the functionality of an anti-virus system (i.e., virus detection and prevention) can be included in its super-system (i.e., the operating system) then there is no need of having a separate anti-virus system. But the question is whether the operating system developer, e.g., Microsoft, will take such an attempt in a foreseeable future?

3.9.8 Possible Solution - Transferring functionality to the co-systems

Another powerful method of achieving IFR is to transfer the main useful function (MUF) or other useful functions of a system (i.e., anti-virus) to its co-systems or adjacent systems. For example, the anti-virus functionality may be taken over by the gateways or firewalls. The anti-virus functionality may be taken over by the interpreters or virtual machines.

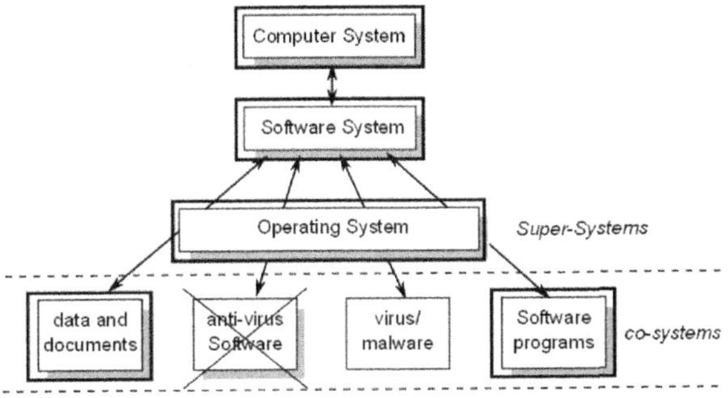

Each adjacent system having protection agains viruses

The functionality may be transferred to one single adjacent system or may be transferred partially to multiple different adjacent systems. For example, the email scanning may be done by the email server and document scanning may be done by the Office Suite environment.

For example, the applications can be built with some kind of virus resistance so that the viruses cannot infect them. Alternatively, the application may self check any infection and inform the user in case infected or take necessary corrective measures. An invention below:

INVENTION-2: Computer program with built-in malware protection

Patent 8195953 (by Yue et. al., Jun 2012) discloses a method of integrating the security functions within the target software itself. The method is based upon the concept that a computer program (or its developer) knows the best about the normal behavior of the program. This knowledge can be used to detect if the behavior of the program is abnormal.

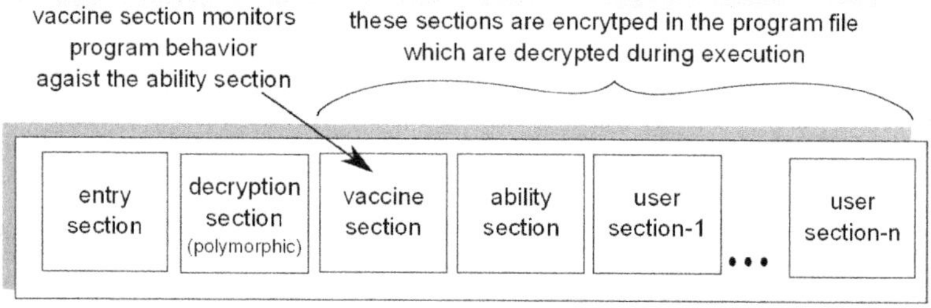

Structure of Executable Program with built-in Vaccine

For example, the developer knows what are the abilities of the program which he enters into the ability section of the program. A vaccine code is entered into the executable program to monitor the behavior of the executable program and compare with the allowed and not-allowed behaviors entered in the ability section. If it detects any non-allowed behaviors then takes necessary corrective measures. This method protects the software both from traditional virus attacks and from modern worms, Trojans and other threats.

3.9.9 Possible solution- strengthening the anti-virus system

Thus we find many possible solutions which are applied to prevent viruses at different points in between the virus creator and the end user computer. The first attempt is to prevent the virus creator from creating viruses by punishing the virus creator or employing technical measures so that the virus creator will not be successful in his attempt. Even if the virus is created, it should not be successful to travel through Internet (honeypots, counter viruses etc.). Even if it travels through Internet it should not be able to enter a local area network (anti-virus at the firewall). Even if it enters a LAN the OS should not allow it to get inside or stay active (Layers of protection like Linux). Even if it remains in a computer it should have no power to infect (programs may be virus resistant or anti-virus may detect and remove viruses etc.).

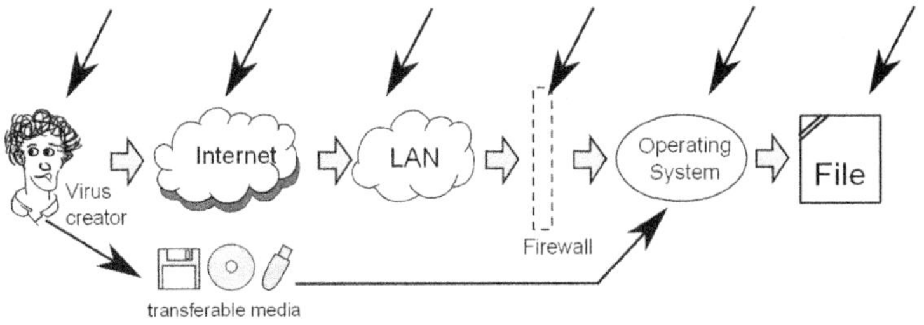

Countersriking Viruses at Different Stages

Using an anti-virus is the most familiar and conceivable solution compared to other solutions described in the previous paragraphs. Besides it is purely a technological solution and does not involve social, political, legal or other domains into the matter. The above picture illustrates that the anti-virus technology has to work at different points in order to prevent or nullify the malware forces. This defensive system has to protect our operating system, programs and scripts, active documents and even passive data. The protection model may be purely passive (such as, a virus scanner) or active (like sandbox, honeypot, on-access scanning etc.)

However, neither every anti-virus system is strong enough to protect our system nor a foolproof anti-virus system is easy to build. The following are some challenges typically faced by the anti-virus developers.

3.10 Analyzing Challenges faced by Anti-Virus Developers

In the previous pages we analyzed the virus problems faced by end users and systems administrators. Let's now see the difficulties faced by the anti-virus developers, who undoubtedly play a much greater role in solving the virus problem. Their goal is not just to sell the product and make profit out of it, but to ensure the quality of the product in order to practically defend the system from viruses. The following are their typical challenges.

- **Growing number of Viruses:** As viruses are created regularly on an ongoing basis, it is difficult to discover and analyze every new virus, and provide remedies for them.

- **Recognizing the virus type:** as there are numerous types of viruses, it is a challenge for the anti-virus developer to say which family a particular variant belongs to.
- **Too many Platforms:** Different operating systems function differently. Even if the developer builds a powerful anti-virus engine for one platform, the same engine **may not** work on other operating systems and operating environments.
- **Boot Sector Viruses:** anti-virus has to work within the framework of an OS. Hence, the anti-virus can be loaded only after the OS is loaded. But the boot sector viruses are loaded before the OS is loaded and infect the system to function maliciously.
- **Memory resident viruses:** There are many memory resident viruses which do not go even after repairing or removing all the infected files because the viruses remain active in the main memory of the computer.
- **Intelligent Viruses:** with the maturity of computing technology, the virus programmers explore newer methods and create viruses with anti-detection intelligence to fool the anti-virus programs.
- **Stealth viruses:** some viruses adopt various stealth techniques in order to escape detection. For example, some viruses don't act immediately. Hence the anti virus cannot detect any negativity in their behavior. But the viruses may act dangerously later when their payload is triggered.
- **Polymorphic and metamorphic viruses:** Some viruses like polymorphic viruses and metamorphic viruses change their signatures on every infection. As they don't have any specific signatures the anti-virus has to apply complicated techniques like emulation, data mining etc. to detect those viruses.
- **Professional Virus Programmers:** The viruses are no more programmed by hobbyists. In some cases they are programmed by software professionals paid by criminal organizations.
- **Virus construction kits:** there are many virus construction kits available on the Internet. Common people without sufficient programming skills can create great metamorphic viruses within no time. While a virus creation kit can create thousands of new viruses, the anti-virus company needs to go through each virus created with the kit in order to prevent them all.

- **Attack on anti-virus products:** Many virus programmers explore the loopholes of the anti-virus products and attack the anti-virus programs to paralyze the protection system.
- **Problem of decompression**: In order to scan the compressed files the anti-virus has to decompress the files using complex calculations. Any mistake in the decompression may lead to vulnerability.
- **Problem of scanning password protected files**: the virus checker cannot see what is there inside a password protected file. A password protected file is generally an encrypted file and has much more chances of bypassing Anti-Virus defenses.
- **Problem of disinfecting and repairing:** When the system is critically damaged by virus infection, it becomes extremely difficult for the anti-virus to repair the infected components and restore the system. Similarly if the content of the file is scrambled or overwritten by the virus the anti-virus remains incapable of repairing them.
- **Problem of email viruses:** Scanning an email file is different from scanning conventional files, as an email is a composition of various types of attachments. Besides it is desirable that the anti-virus must detect and remove the virus before an infected email finally reaches its destination and opened by its recipient.
- **Scanning encrypted emails:** It is difficult to virus scan the emails at the email server because many email servers encrypt the email files using proprietary encryption techniques to maintain the privacy of the emails. In such cases the virus scanners cannot scan the emails as they fail to decrypt the encrypted files.
- **Controlling virus outbreaks:** The conventional techniques of virus scanning cannot handle virus outbreaks. Virus outbreaks can infect a large number of systems very quickly and make the situation out of control. There should be special techniques to prevent and control such outbreaks.
- **Controlling Network Viruses:** The conventional techniques of virus scanning are meant for individual computers and may not work well for network environments. The network viruses may use different strategies to attack, network servers, gateways and even the whole network including the network traffic.

- **Competing with other anti-virus products and difficulty of marketing:** an ordinary user is not capable of comparing various aspects of an antivirus product to choose the right one. Often the sell of the product is not guided by the quality of the product but by advertisements and various other marketing techniques.
- **Problem of renewal of anti-virus:** the earlier convention of one time selling of an anti-virus program was found to be not suitable as because the anti-virus vender had to give the updated virus definitions free for all times in future. This problem was solved by selling the products for an annual fee. But that leads to another problem as the user may either forget to renew or prefer to choose a different product.
- **Anti-virus consumes system resources:** The execution of anti-viruses generally consumes a lot of system resources. If a virus plays intelligently with an anti-virus then the anti-virus can end up consuming a large portion of the system memory and affect the system worse than any average virus.
- **Problem of publishing research findings:** if the findings of anti-virus research are documented and published then that will help the virus creators and competing anti-virus developers and put the publisher into a weaker position in the competition.
- **Stealing of virus signatures**- some anti-virus companies try to steal the virus signatures created by other companies in order to avoid expenses on human experts. The stealing company changes the virus names in order to make them appear as their own research. This results in losses to the other company.
- **Ethical issues on anti-virus research:** the anti-virus researcher has to continuously experiment with dangerous virus codes to the extent as much as or even more than a virus creator. It is possible that some of his experiments may fail and go out to public to harm the innocent users.

The anti-virus developer has to overcome all the aforesaid problems in order to develop a product that is powerful and intelligent to detect and prevent all types of viruses, old and new, known and unknown.

Chapter 4.

Limitations of Anti-Virus Programs and Methods

4.1 Functions of Anti-Virus Programs

While the viruses attempt to get into our systems and destroy our valuable files and data, the anti-virus programs strive to restrain the viruses from being successful. The important functions of an anti-virus software may be summarized as (i) protecting the computer from virus attacks (before the virus could attack), (ii) detecting the presence of viruses (after any virus attack), (iii) removing viruses (after detection of any virus) and restoring the damaged files and system (after removing the virus).

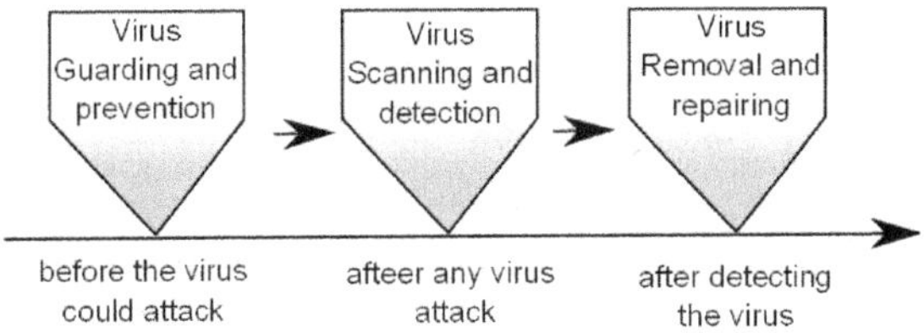

Functions of an anti-virus program

4.1.1 Virus guarding and virus prevention

One of the most important functions of an anti-virus program is to protect the computer from any type of attack by any type of malware, including viruses, worms, Trojan horses, spyware, adware and others. The anti-virus program runs as a service or a memory resident program to detect and remove the viruses when found. Typically every file is scanned before it is accessed by a requestor and after its content is changed by a write operation.

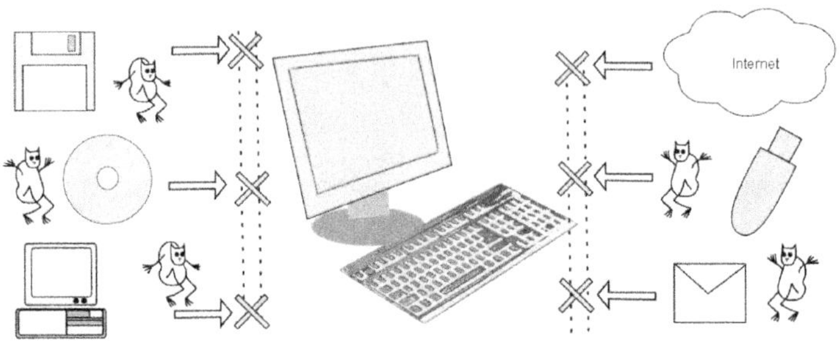

Protection of computer from external attack

- ✓ When an external media, such as, CD, DVD, pen drive etc. is connected to the computer, the anti-virus ensures that no virus from the attached media gets into the computer.
- ✓ When the computer is connected to LAN, WAN or Internet, the anti-virus ensures than no virus comes from other computers through these connections.
- ✓ When the user downloads files from Internet or copies files from other computers or checks his emails, the anti-virus ensures that the incoming files contain no viruses.
- ✓ The anti-virus remains active in the memory to check each and every file for viruses when the file is opened or closed by any application.

4.1.2 Virus scanning and detection

The most commonly known function of an anti-virus is virus scanning. Scanning is the process of detecting the viruses in the main memory and in the secondary memory like hard disk, and removable media like floppy, CD and USB based drives.

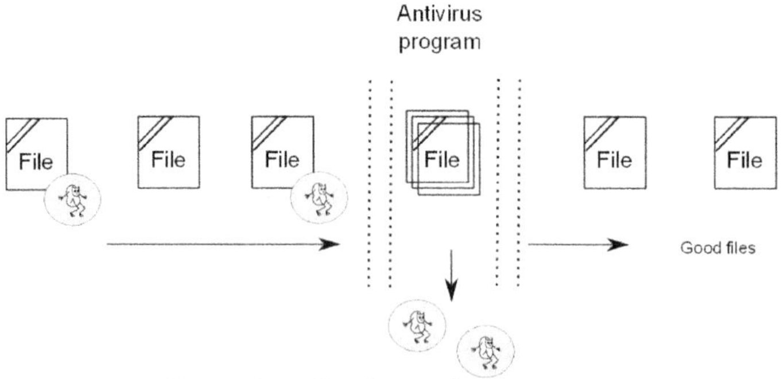

Scanning files by anti-virus programs

A scanner employs various methods, such as, signature scanning, heuristic scanning etc. to scan different parts of a computer. Besides, there are different modes of scanning. For example, scanning can be done in the background without disturbing the regular activities of the user, or can be scheduled to be done during leisure hours. Besides the scanning can be complete or partial depending on user requirement.

4.1.3 Virus removal and file repairing

The last but not the least important function of an anti-virus is virus removal and file repairing. The anti-virus applies various methods to remove the virus code from the infected file and restore the original file.

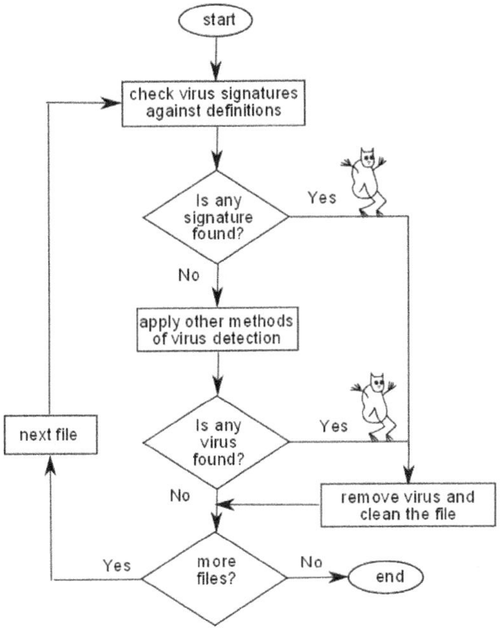

The flowchart shows the cycle of scanning files typically followed by an anti-virus program. When a file or sector is found to be infected, the anti-virus first tries to disinfect and repair the infected file or sector of the disk.

There are situations where the nature of infections is not exactly identified or the method of disinfection is not known to the anti-virus. In such cases the anti-virus isolates the infected file to a quarantine. However, if the virus is too dangerous or the file is too much damaged then the anti-virus is left with no option but to delete the infected file.

4.2 Drawbacks of anti-virus programs

Although an anti-virus is useful for every computer that is exposed to any sort of virus threat, it causes numerous disadvantages to the user. That is why many people think an anti-virus as a necessary evil. Some of the significant disadvantages of the anti-virus programs are as follows.

- An anti-virus product involves a cost. Although there are powerful free anti-virus products like AVG, in many situations there are also reasons to select a paid product to get some extra advantage.

- Some commercial antivirus software are subscribed on an annual basis and the end-user license agreements include a clause that the subscription will be automatically renewed. In that case the purchaser's credit card is automatically billed without his explicit approval.

- As there is a wide range of anti-virus products in the market, it is a difficult job to decide which anti-virus product is better and cost effective.

- Inexperienced users may face problems in understanding various prompts and alerts that the anti-virus software presents before them. An incorrect decision by the user may lead to a security breach.

- No anti-virus product gives a one-time solution. As the viruses are created on a regular basis, the anti-virus products are also updated on a regular basis. This situation involves a lot of maintenance activities.

- Virus scanning is a time consuming job. A full virus scanning on a loaded computer can easily continue for several hours.

- A virus scanner consumes significant amount of system resources. As the scanner has to be more intelligent and work faster than a virus, it puts significant load on the memory and processor and affects a computer's performance.

- Anti-virus software work at the highly trusted kernel level of the operating system. Any loophole in its architecture opens up avenues for serious attack.

- The success of virus scanning depends on achieving a right balance between false positives and false negatives. False positives can be as destructive as false negatives.

- There are many instances where running of certain anti-viruses had disrupted the functioning of other bona-fide programs. That is because although the anti-viruses are tested for a majority of programs, a minority of programs still face some conflicts. Moreover, an anti-virus tested for one version of OS does not accept an upgrade of the OS without getting itself updated.

- Sometimes running of an anti-virus might cause problems in installing some applications. My updated anti-virus falsely detected my handset driver as a virus dropper and did not allow me to install. I had to temporarily disable the anti-virus protection and install the driver.

- Some anti-viruses are supposed to work with the network policies in order to maintain network security. If the anti-virus is not compatible or don't recognize the network access policy then the anti-virus may not provide the expected protection.

- There is not an accepted convention of naming the viruses. Different anti-virus companies call the same virus in different names. With the ever-increasing number of viruses and multiple names for each virus, the situation creates infinite number of virus names leading to an unmanageable situation.

4.3 Popular methods of virus detection

The earliest method of detecting viruses was through their signatures. As the viruses used various stealth techniques to escape from signature scanning, the anti-viruses had to apply various other methods for detecting those viruses. However, different techniques are employed to detect different types of viruses. All types of viruses cannot be detected by any single method. The popular methods used by the anti-virus programs for detecting viruses are as follows:

Signature Scanning

Signature scanning is the most common method of detecting virus. This method is useful for detecting about 80% of viruses. This is implemented by scanning each file for extracted bytes or signatures form the virus. An anti-virus expert first extracts the virus signature from a virus. The anti-virus programs use these signatures to scan each vulnerable area of a computer - including executable files, boot records, document files with macros etc. - to detect the presence of any of those signatures. If any of those signatures is found then the target program is deemed infected, otherwise the target program is deemed uninfected.

Signature scanning may be either **simple signature scanning** or **generic signature scanning**. Simple signature scanning uses exact signatures of specific viruses. This has a limitation, as it cannot detect other variants of a known virus although the differences between their signatures are very minor. A generic signature scanning takes care of this deficiency. A generic signature scanning uses wildcards to detect viruses of specific families. This is a quicker method to detect all the viruses belonging to the same family. This method also works for new and future viruses of the same family. We will discuss more on the limitations of signature scanning and possible improvements in chapter-10.

Integrity checking

Integrity checking is the fastest method of virus detection. The method detects the existence of viruses by comparing the hash values of a file with the hash value of its uninfected version. If no difference is found between the two hash values then the file is deemed to be uninfected. This method works because the viruses must make changes to infect their host programs. We will discuss more on integrity checking in chapter-12.

Behavior monitoring

Behavior monitoring is another method to detect viruses by their type of activity. A behavior blocker is a TSR program which monitors the behavior of computer programs from the time they are loaded on to memory till they finish their execution. If it detects any suspicious or virus like behavior, such as, attempts to format a disk, low level file access, strange modifications to executable files, moving files to operating system folders etc. (which are generally not the activities of a common program) then the behavior blocker immediately flags these programs and issues alerts to the user. Behavior based detection may be of two types, viz., anomaly based malware detection and specification-based malware detection.

Heuristic scanning

Heuristic scanning is another method of virus detection that is different from signature scanning and integrity checking. Heuristic scanning does not scan for specific virus signatures but scans for virus-like codes. While signature scanning is ineffective for polymorphic and metamorphic viruses, heuristic scanning is capable of detecting these viruses.

Heuristic scanning is a powerful generic method and is capable of detecting almost all types of viruses. There are different types of heuristics detection, such as, code anomaly detection, protocol anomaly detection, mixed heuristic detection etc. Often heuristic methods are improved by using simulation, data mining and other complicated mechanism. We will discuss more on heuristic techniques later in chapter-15.

4.4 Comparing virus detection strategies

As the viruses are getting sophisticated the anti-virus programs have to employ a variety of strategies to detect and remove the viruses.

4.4.1 Signature Based Detection vs. Behavior Based Detection

The signature-based detection (or footprint based detection) is based on pattern matching. This method compares the contents of files against a library of known virus signatures. If the signatures are matched then the presence of a specific virus is confirmed.

Advantages: this method is fast and more reliable. The possibility of mistakes or false positives is extremely rare. **Disadvantages**: new viruses cannot be detected whose signatures are not yet known or not yet included in the signature database.

The behavior-based detection (also called heuristic detection) examines the behavior of suspect programs and checks its pattern of code. If the pattern of the code looks to be virus-like then it may flag the program as a possible virus and ask for user intervention.

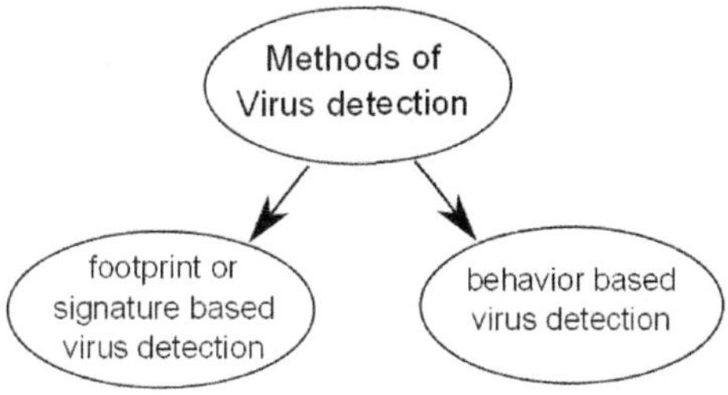

Advantages: as this method does not depend on specific virus signatures it can detect even new viruses whose signatures are not yet known. **Disadvantages**: as there is no exact method of defining a virus-like code or virus-like behavior the method may not identify some real viruses or may identify false positives.

4.4.2 Specific Methods vs. Generic Methods

The specific methods intend to detect only specific known viruses or virus types. Signature scanning is a specific method. Specific methods are more certain in detection and leads to less false positives. However, specific methods cannot detect new and unknown viruses.

On the contrary, generic detection methods are intended to detect all types of viruses whether old or new, whether known or unknown. There is not any particular method called generic method. Integrity checking, behavior monitoring, heuristic scanning etc. are all generic methods. The generic methods are becoming more and more popular in order to detect complex and intelligent viruses.

4.4.3 Static vs. Dynamic detection methods

Static methods detect viruses by scanning and examining the files without running any viral code. Signature scanning, wild card scanning, integrity checking, static heuristics etc. are examples of static methods.

Dynamic detection method observes the behavior of the code during execution. As running a viral code is dangerous, the dynamic methods use a simulated environment or virtual machine.

4.4.4 On-the-fly (or real time scanning or resident scanning) vs. on-demand scanning (or offline scanning)

Scanning can be done either (i) on demand (i.e., when the user clicks a button to start scanning), or (ii) on-the-fly (i.e., automatically when a file is accessed by a program for copying, opening or modifying).

On demand scanning is generally offline scanning. The user clicks on a scan button to initiate a scanning operation (or schedule a scanning later during non-business hours) and carry out his work without waiting for the scanning to finish. On demand scanning can be a full scanning to scan all the files on all the drives or a partial scanning to scan specific files, locations or system components. This method generally scans a long list of files in sequence.

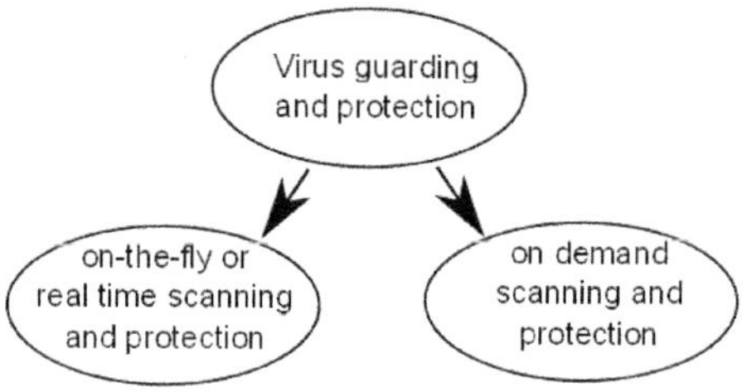

Drawbacks- although it scans the infected files and detects the viruses it does not prevent the files from being infected. A virus may go on infecting other files at the same time while the scanning is carrying out detection.

On the contrary, **on-the-fly or real time scanning** operations are triggered automatically by a memory resident component of the anti-virus whenever there is a file operation, such as, opening or copying a file, receiving an email etc. For example, when an application is going to open a document for modification, the real time scanner scans the document first before the document is opened. If the document is not infected, then the scanner leaves the handle to the application to open the document. On the other hand if the file is found infected, then the scanner first displays a message to the user about the infection and then either disinfects the file or does not allow the file to open.

Advantages: This method provides a real time protection to virus infections. It can detect viruses immediately when they become active. As the virus has to access a file for infection, the on-access scanner detects the infection and prevents the virus from spreading.

Disadvantages: The drawback of this method is that it takes some time to scan the file and delay the process of accessing the file for opening, copying, modifying and other such operations.

4.5 Limitations of conventional scanning methods

Each of the above-described methods has its strengths and weaknesses. Signature scanning is an easy and definite method for detecting known specific viruses, but it does not work for new or unknown viruses. Generic methods may detect new viruses but may not detect with certainty. The following are some drawbacks of the conventional scanning methods.

4.5.1 Time lag between virus creation and detection

One of the worst drawbacks of signature scanning is the time lag between virus creation and virus detection. As the method requires the process of detecting the signature, distributing the signature files to the customers world wide and using the new signature database for scanning, a new virus can easily spread and cause damage during that period without being detected.

Time gap between
Virus Creation and Virus Detection

Because of a potential time gap between virus creation and possible detection, the new viruses, which are not included in the virus definition database, are not detectable by this method. The longer this gap the higher the possibility of creation and spreading of new viruses.

4.5.2 Problem of updating signature database

A signature-scanning engine is of no use without the signature database. The scanning engine has to refer the signature database in order to scan the files. Unfortunately updating the signature database is not a onetime phenomenon, it has to be updated time and again on a regular basis.

As new viruses are created almost on everyday, it requires the anti-virus companies to update their signature database frequently and urges the users to download the same regularly.

4.5.3 Burden of scanning time and resource

The number virus signatures increase according to the increase in the number of viruses. This situation increases the size of the signature database and increases the scanning time as well. With thousands of possible virus types and hundreds of gigabytes of file storage, a scanning operation often demands unacceptably long time. However, on the other hand, if we cut short the scanning process, then we may have to compromise with security. This situation leads to the following contradiction.

Contradiction	*If a scanner includes less number of algorithms then there is possibility of some viruses being escaped. On the other hand if the scanner includes all detection algorithms then the scanning process becomes unbearably slow. We want to include all scanning methods to detect all types of viruses, but we don't want the scanning process to take long time.*

4.5.4 Limitations of integrity checking

Integrity checking is of no use if the computer is already infected at the time when the programs are first fingerprinted. In such situations the computer will be inoculated with virus-infected files and create a safe haven for viruses to infect other programs.

Besides integrity checking works only for the system files that are generally not changed during the normal operation of a computer. But this method does not work for data files which are generally updated by users. Moreover, the checksum method does not work for external drives (such as, CDs or pen drives) whose fingerprints are not available.

4.5.5 Limitations heuristic scanning

A static heuristic detection can recognize only a few of the numerous different ways of virus-like operations. For example, different viruses may open files by using different codes and different methods. In such cases the static heuristic detection mechanism must look for a large number of different ways each virus-like operation may be implemented in order to reliably detect a virus-like behavior. This situation becomes unmanageable with a large number of possible permutations of such operations.

Although a dynamic heuristic technique is superior in detecting virus-like operations, there are many problems in implementing emulation techniques.

4.5.6 Limitations of emulation techniques

Some viruses require extensive emulation before the virus-like operations occur. For example, a virus may idle-loop thousands of times before executing a "file open" operation. In that case, the emulator has to do a lot of processing before the file open operation is reached. Some viruses use anti-emulation techniques. The intelligent viruses can detect an emulated host and avoid execution of viral code or change their behavior. Emulations are discussed later in chapter-14.

4.5.7 Vulnerability of anti-virus programs

Some clever virus makers target the anti-virus programs in various ways. For example, the virus may remain resident in memory and deceive the anti-virus program, paralyze crucial functions of anti-virus program or exploit the loopholes of the anti-virus program to harm the computer.

As the detection gets sophisticated so also the techniques of virus creation. Many polymorphic and metamorphic viruses use anti-anti-virus techniques and become extremely difficult to be detected.

4.5.8 Other problems of anti-virus programs

- Problem in scanning network viruses- the conventional scanners are meant to scan the viruses on the local machine. They are not suitable for network viruses that adopt various special techniques to travel from one machine to another in a network.

- Problem of scanning remote files- a typical virus scanner resides on the local machine and scans the local files. But it cannot scan viruses operating in a different machine. For example, when you are accessing a file on a remote server, the scanner cannot scan the remote file to determine whether it is infected.

- Scanning of a computer is not possible if the machine is extremely infected and is not able to boot from the hard disk.

- If a malware has taken control of the operating system, then it can fool the integrity checker by providing the clean version to the program to calculate the hash codes.
- Problem of false positives- No method of scanning is fool proof. However, generic scanning methods are more susceptible to false positives (i.e., identifying a non-infected file as containing a virus).
- Problem of incompatibility with application software- sometimes the anti-virus developers fail to test of their products with all types of application software and all types of device drivers. Hence sometimes some anti-viruses quarantine or delete various device drivers and thereby make the device dysfunctional.
- Chaos in virus counting- as there is no naming convention, the same virus is named differently by different anti-virus companies. This results in innumerable names without knowing what is what.
- As the anti-virus programs are competitive to each other, they have many incompatibilities. Each has its own method of hiding its procedures and manipulating virus definitions. They look each other suspiciously and if installed on the same machine then end up with deadlocks.
- The original concept of computer virus has expanded to various types of malware with different features and functions. Some of the current day malware include rootkits, mass-mailers, rabbits, logic bombs, backdoors, downloaders, dialers, droppers, virus-generators, keyloggers, hoxes, adware, spyware and many more. Hence the focus is now moving from virus to malware and from anti-malware to computer security in general.

Chapter 5.

Contradictions in Solving Virus Problems

5.1 What is a contradiction

Contradictions are conflicting situations inside a system which cause problems and restrict the performance of a system. For example, *"Increasing speed of a motor generates heat. A high level of heat damages the coil of the motor. We want to increase the speed of the motor but don't want the heat."* In this example, ***speed*** and ***heat*** are two parameters which conflict with each other. Speed is desirable but heat is undesirable.

Let's take an example from virus problem. "*Scanning for all possible viruses requires too much time. We want to scan all viruses but don't want to wait for scanning".* In this example, ***quality of virus scanning*** and ***time required for scanning*** are two parameters which conflict with each other. Here ***quality of virus scanning*** is desirable but ***time required for scanning*** is not desirable. *"The anti-virus involves many scanning techniques and consumes a lot of system resources. We want to run the anti-virus but we don't want to slow down our system*". In this example, ***running of anti-virus*** is desirable but ***sacrificing system performance*** is not desirable. In all these examples achievement of one desired goal affects the achievement of another desired goal.

5.1.1 Types of contradictions

According to TRIZ, the contradictions may be Physical or Technical. ("Physical" and "Technical" are just the names. Otherwise "Physical" contradictions are also equally technical as "Technical" contradictions).

Physical contradictions create a conflict with the same parameter of a system. For example something needs to be hot (for some reason) and cold (for another reason), dynamic and static, big and small etc. Thus the same parameter is desirable and undesirable. For example, *the size of the database should be large enough to contain all the virus definitions and small enough for faster download.*

Technical Contradictions (or Ordinary Contradictions) are situations where improving one part of the system affects another part of the system. Thus it involves two parameters, improving one parameter of the system causes deterioration of the other parameter *"scanning for viruses making the system slow"* in the example above.

5.1.2 Contradictions in Software

Although TRIZ was originally developed for technical systems, the concept of Contradictions is found to be applicable not only in Technical systems but also in every other system including Software systems. According to TRIZ, a contradiction is created when solving one problem leads to creation of another problem or expanding one limitation narrows down another limitation. For example, *"releasing virus signatures with sufficient testing will cause delay while releasing virus signatures with insufficient testing will cause false positives. We want faster release of signatures but no false positives."*

5.1.3 Why to solve contradictions

As contradictions limit the functionality of a system, it is necessary to solve the contradictions in order to extend the functionality of the system. If the contradiction is not solved then we have to do a compromise between the two conflicting parameters which will yield a very limited result. **According to TRIZ, it is necessary to improve the system (or its part) without impairing its adjacent systems (or other parts).**

It is necessary to solve contradictions in order to solve an inventive problem in a Software System.

- ✓ Contradictions restrict the features of software. Solving contradictions expand the benefits of the software.
- ✓ Sometimes contradictions do not allow adding a new feature. Removing that contradiction may lead to successful insertion of that feature.

✓ Solving contradictions may sometimes lead to revolutionary improvements and sometimes a new discovery.

5.1.4 What are Contradiction Parameters

Altshuller found that there are 39 Standard Parameters which might conflict to each other in a system. While some of the 39 Parameters contribute to improve the system the same or other of the 39 Parameters contribute to worsen the system. Thus these 39 parameters can create 1521 (39 x 39) possible conflicts. Each of these conflicts is addressed by different Inventive Principles.

Although the concept of contradiction is fairly applicable in any branch of study, whether social, technical, management or software, the original 39 technical parameters do not hold good for other fields. For example, the parameters like, "Weight of moving object", "Weight of stationary object", "Volume of moving object", "Volume of Stationary object" etc. don't convey their desired meaning in a software system. But they can be modified as below to fit into in a software environment.

Sl.	**Conventional Technical Parameters**	**Corresponding Software Parameters**
#7	Volume of moving object	Volume of data transmission Volume of conversion required
#8	Volume of stationary object	Volume of memory required Volume of storage required
#9	Speed	Speed of Execution Speed of data Transmission

However, all the original technical parameters do not have corresponding Software Parameters. There are many additional/ special parameters for Software problems, which remain out of the scope of this book and are being prepared by the author to be published in a separate book.

5.1.5 How to solve a contradiction

A traditional way of addressing the contradictions is by compromising or balancing between the two opposites. Although a good compromise reduces the intensity of the problem, it doesn't solve the problem effectively. For example "*If the edge of the razor blade is very sharp, then the blade will cut the skin. If not very sharp, then it cannot do a closer shave*". A traditional compromise is to make the blade medium sharp, so that it will shave the beards (although not very well) but not cut the skin (although sometimes may).

TRIZ advises not to compromise but to solve the contradictions. For example, the blade should be sharp for good shaving, but it will have protectors at both sides (as in safety razor) so that it will not cut the skin. All types of contradictions can be solved using TRIZ techniques whether the contradiction is physical or technical.

A physical contradiction is normally solved by Separation in Time, Separation in Space, separation in condition, System Transformation and Phase transition. For example, "*I have to attend the meeting in office and I have to attend the birthday party in hotel*", in which case, I can schedule my meeting first and party afterwards (Separation in Time).

A Technical contradiction is addressed by applying one or more of the 40 Inventive principles as found appropriate. All principles are not appropriate for each contradiction. Generally 1 to 5 principles are found appropriate for solving any specific contradiction. The contradiction matrix shows us which principles are appropriate for solving which contradiction. Solving a contradiction often leads to revolutionary improvements and sometimes to a new invention.

5.1.6 Irrelevance of Conventional Contradiction Matrix

A contradiction matrix is an organization of contradiction parameters in a tabular form, with the corresponding Inventive Principles those are most effective to solve the specific contradictions. In the Technical contradiction matrix, there are 39 improving parameters in horizontal direction and the same 39 worsening parameters in vertical direction, thus creating a total of (39 x 39 =) 1531 possible conflicts. Each cell in the Matrix represents a particular type of conflict which is addressed by specific inventive principles.

It will be appropriate to mention that we will not refer *the contradiction matrix* as a tool to solve virus related problems, because, (i) the use of contradiction matrix has several limitations, (ii) as the conventional contradiction parameters are irrelevant in software context, the conventional matrix remains irrelevant.

5.1.7 Contradictions relating to anti-virus program

When the anti-virus developer is building its anti-virus system it must take various factors into consideration including reliability of the product, user friendliness and system administrators' convenience. As we have discussed earlier, every inventive problem has a contradiction to be solved. Let's illustrate some examples of contradictions that the anti-virus developer faces while improving the anti-virus.

5.2 Contradiction of making an Anti-Virus Program

When the virus scanners and virus definition files are available in the market, they are also available to virus makers. In such cases, the virus makers also test their viruses using the scanner and modify their viruses with various anti-anti-virus techniques until they remain undetected by the anti-virus. The virus writers release the virus to outside only when the anti-virus does not detect the virus as a threat. This way the new viruses can spread easily as the existing anti-viruses fail to detect these viruses.

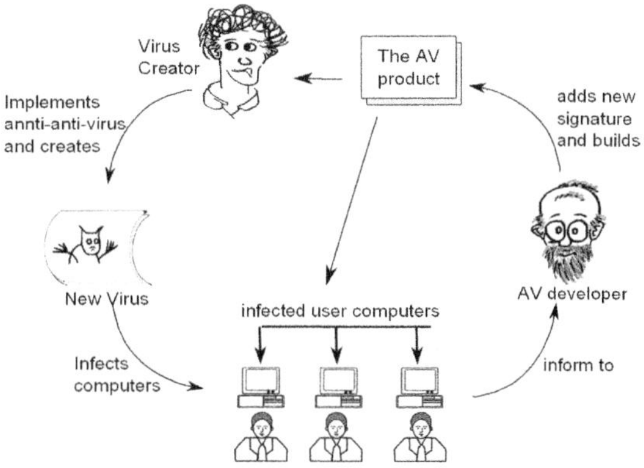

Virus creators using anti-virus to build stronger viruses

Contradiction	*The virus scanners and updated virus definition files are made available to the computer users for scanning of latest viruses. But the same tools are misused by the virus creators to fortify the viruses. We want the scanners and virus definitions to be available only to the general users and not to the virus creators.*

Analysis of Parameters

Improving Parameter: Security

Worsening Parameter: Security

Possible solutions

- The anti-virus should have different virus definition database for general users and different virus definition database for virus makers (TRIZ Principle-35: Change Parameter). **Drawback:** a general user can turn into a virus creator.

- The scanner should capable to detect whether there is a virus creating program on the machine. If it finds a virus creating program then it changes its behavior. **Limitations**- the method will not work if the virus creator tests his virus on a separate machine.

- Using a fuzzy logic that will randomly change the virus definition files for different machines (Patent 7284273 described later).

5.3 Contradiction of Scanning Time

As the population of virus increases, the size of signature database also increases which in turn increases the scanning time. With thousands of possible virus types and hundreds of gigabytes of file storage a complete virus scan can take several hours which is not acceptable to any user.

Contradiction	*If a scanner includes less number of signatures or less number of algorithms then there is possibility of some viruses being escaped. On the other hand if a scanner includes all available signatures and all possible algorithms then the scanning will take very long time. We want to apply more scanning methods to detect all types of viruses, but at the same time we want to apply less scanning methods to finish the scanning fast.*

Analysis of Parameters

Improving Parameter: Volume of execution

Worsening Parameter: Loss of time

Possible solutions

- One of the solutions to the above problem is to spread over the scanning process in several sessions. The scanning should end when we stop it and resumes again in future from the point where it left in the previous session (TRIZ Principle-1: Segmentation). **Drawback:** a full scanning may take several days to finish.

- If the scanning is performed in a distributed network the scanning load may be distributed to multiple computers implementing a distributed scanning. (TRIZ Principle-1: Segmentation).
- Applying Filters in scanning- it is not necessary to scan all types of files for all types of virus signatures. For example, scanning EXE files for macro virus signatures will be meaningless effort. It is better to eliminate irrelevant signature types before scanning a file so that scanning can be faster and efficient (TRIZ Principle-2: Taking out) (Patent 6898712).
- Another solution is to do a partial virus scanning of the core elements like main memory, boot sector, file system etc. A partial virus scanning is done every time the computer boots (TRIZ Principle-16: Partial or Excessive Action). **Limitation**: Partial scanning is useful only in special cases.
- Speed scanning or fast mode virus scanning may be implemented whenever necessary. The fast mode scanning will scan only the memory, system files and critical areas of the disk and will not scan the individual files on the disk (TRIZ Principle-21: Skipping).
- Patent 7644352 suggests copying the data from the source computer to a scan computer for virus scanning. The scan computer creates a log of the suspicious files and sends back to the source computer for scanning. This method reduces the scanning load on the source computer (TRIZ Principle-26: Copying). **Limitation**: This is useful for servers but not convenient for personal computers.

5.4 Contradiction of Virus Scanning and System Performance

Running an anti-virus consumes significant amount of system resources and affects the system performance negatively. An anti-virus loaded system takes more time to boot, more time to shutdown and runs slow while executing other programs. This is one of the reasons why many users don't like running an anti-virus.

Contradiction	*We want to run an anti-virus to keep the computer free from virus. But we don't want the other programs to run slow because of the burden of anti-virus on the computer. In other words, we want the anti-virus to scan the computer, but we don't want it to affect the performance of the computer or other programs.*

Analysis of Parameters

Improving Parameter: Volume of Execution

Worsening Parameter: Load on Machine

In this case the problem solver must look for some solution that helps segregating the volume of execution (TRIZ Principle-1: Segmentation), offloading the volume of execution (TRIZ Principle-2: Taking out), reducing the load on machine or improving the capability of machine.

Possible solutions

- One solution is to put the anti-virus on the gateway. This will protect the system by scanning all incoming and outgoing files but will not affect the system performance (TRIZ Principle-2: Taking out). **Limitation**: this will not protect the computer from infections within the firewall.

- Another solution is to offload the scanning load to a separate scanning server (TRIZ Principle-1: Segmentation, Principle-2: Taking out). **Limitation**: This method is useful for scanning server computers but not suitable for personal computers.

- Use a virus co-processor to improve speed of virus scanning without affecting system performance (TRIZ Principle-8: Counterweight). **Drawback**: requires additional hardware and expenditure thereof.

- The solution is to schedule virus scanning during nights or on holidays when people are not working. The self-running feature of the anti-virus program can run automatically at the pre-scheduled day and/or time (TRIZ Principle-25: Self Service).

- Another solution is to run the anti-virus when the system is running but the user is not working. Some anti virus programs can be scheduled to run when the system is left idle for certain time (TRIZ Principle-25: Self Service).
- Scanning only selected signatures according to file type. For example, a boot sector signature need not be used to scan a macro file. This method reduces the total number of search operations. (TRIZ Principle-21: Skipping)
- Another technique is to scan only the specific areas of a file, which are more likely to be altered by the viruses, instead of scanning the whole file. (TRIZ Principle-21: Skipping)
- Another solution is to take a backup of the data to a different machine and scan the backup data in the second machine. (TRIZ Principle-2: Taking out, Principle-26: Copying). **Drawback**: requires another machine, not suitable for personal computers.
- Use a more powerful processor so that the load on the processor can be neutralized. Similarly, use better scanning techniques so that there will be less load on the processor. (TRIZ Principle-38: Enrich).

5.5 Contradiction of repetitive scanning at every client

In a corporate environment, many files are shared by users just by copying them from one computer to another. Although the files were already scanned in their previous location they are usually scanned again and again in every computer they are copied to. It would be better to avoid repetitive scanning in order to save time and system resource.

Contradiction	*While copying files from one location to another we want to ensure that each copy of the file is free from virus infection. But we don't want to waste time and resources to scan each copy of the file which has been scanned earlier to be virus free.*

Analysis of Parameters

Improving Parameter: Volume of Execution, Security

Worsening Parameter: Loss of Time

Ideal Final Result

IFR Only the infected files should be scanned and others not.

IFR Once a file is scanned as virus-free its future copies should also be deemed virus-free without scanning further.

Possible solutions

- The results of the previous scan may be stored in cache or in a status database which can be referred in subsequent scanning in order to skip the already scanned files (TRIZ Principle-24: Intermediary).
- When a file is copied from one computer to another its virus-scan status should also be copied along with to avoid further scanning (TRIZ Principle-26: Copying).
- Subsequent scanning can be done only when a file has been modified and not just because the file has been opened and closed by a program. (TRIZ Principle-35: Parameter Change).

5.6 Contradiction of putting anti-virus in network gateway

There are two methods of administering anti-virus software in a network. One is to install on each individual computer and the other is to install on the network gateway or firewall. But both the methods have some disadvantages. Having a single point protection in the gateway overburdens the scanning machine. Besides it does not provide protection from inside the LAN. On the other hand installing anti-virus on individual computers increases administrative workload. This situation leads to the following contradiction.

Contradiction	*Implementing anti-virus directly into the firewall prevents viruses from entering from the Internet but fails to provide protection from viruses spreading within the LAN. Implementing anti-virus on every computer within a LAN protects individual computers from virus, but increases administration activities for each computer. We want to protect the computers from both external (Internet) and internal (within the LAN) infections without much of administration load.*

Analysis of Parameters

Contradiction#1

Improving Parameter: Ease of Maintenance and Administration

Worsening Parameter: Reliability

Contradiction#2

Improving Parameter: Reliability

Worsening Parameter: Ease of Maintenance and Administration

Ideal Final Result

IFR Implementing antivirus in large networks should require no maintenance and administration.

IFR Implementing gateway based scanning should also protect infection from internal sources.

Possible Solution

- Patent 6728886 (described later) suggests distributing virus scanning load between central scanning servers and local host computers without managing anti-virus programs at each host computer. This has the advantage of centrally managed scanning while does not have the disadvantage of admin load at each individual computer.

5.7 Contradiction of false positives

There are situations where the anti virus program finds a system file has been modified but is not sure about whether the file has been modified by a virus or by the user. In such a situation, if the program generates a virus alarm it may lead to a false positive.

Contradiction	*If the anti-virus program is not definitive about a suspicious alternation in a system file and raises a virus alarm then it may lead to a false positive. On the other hand if it ignores such a suspicious alteration then it may lead to a false negative. Both the situations are dangerous.*

Analysis of Parameters

Improving Parameter: Ease of manufacturing

Worsening Parameter: Loss of Quality

Possible Solution

- One solution to the above problem may be to ask the user to take a decision (TRIZ Principle-23: Feedback). **Drawback**: the user may not be adequately knowledgeable to take a proper decision.
- Patent 6338141 (RAVEN detection system) suggests to use a combination of multiple signatures and flags (up to about 70 different data items depending on the virus type). Using multiple signatures for each virus allows RAVEN to verify infections with a high degree of certainty and avoiding possibility of false identifications.(TRIZ Principle-40: Composite)

5.8 Contradiction of confirming virus infection

Generally an anti-virus program generates an alarm signal when it detects a virus like activity such as modifying a system program. But in order to be sure about a viral infection the anti-virus has to wait and allow the virus to do its damages.

Contradiction	*The anti-virus program should generate an alarm signal only when it gets sufficient proof about a virus operation. But, by the time it get sufficient proof about a virus operation, the virus would have already made undesirable changes and damages to the program. We want alarms only on confirmed infection but don't want damages caused by virus infection.*

Analysis of Parameters

Improving Parameter: Reliability (of virus detection)

Worsening Parameter: Security

Possible Solution

- The anti-virus may keep a copy of the program before any modification is done to it. If the modification is detected to be virus made then the original file is retrieved from the copy (TRIZ Principle-26: Copying)

- The anti-virus allows the virus to run in an emulated system. The emulated system is destroyed when infected by the virus (TRIZ Principle-27: Cheap and disposable).

5.9 Contradiction of Publishing Virus Research

Sometimes a virus researcher may find some knowledge about a threat by examining the viral codes but he may not publish it because if the knowledge becomes public then the virus writers will take benefit of it and modify their viral code accordingly. On the other hand if the researcher does not publish his findings then the anti-virus developers cannot use that knowledge (Ref. "Future threats" by John Aycock and Alana Maurusat).

Contradiction	*The anti-virus researcher should publish his research findings because that will help the anti-virus developers to put a defense in place. At the same time the anti-virus researcher should not publish his research findings, as that will help the virus creators to refine and improve their virus code.*

Analysis of Parameters

Improving Parameter: Confidentiality (Privacy)

Worsening Parameter: Confidentiality (Privacy)

Possible Solution

- The researcher will publish it within his organization so that at least one anti-virus product can make use of the knowledge (TRIZ Separation in Space). **Limitation**: other anti-virus products cannot make use of that knowledge.

- The researcher will publish the theoretical aspect of it and not the practical aspect. This will help the anti-virus developers to develop their own practical methods but don't help the virus creators much (TRIZ – Separation in Condition). **Limitation**: only the part of his research is utilized not the full.

There is also another contradiction related to the same issue.

Contradiction	If the anti-virus researcher or organization publishes his knowledge then the knowledge becomes public and the organization looses its competitive advantage. If on the other hand the anti-virus researcher or organization does not publish the information then it becomes a moral issue of hiding the knowledge about a malware or a future threat.

- The above contradiction is found not only in malware related knowledge but in any kind of knowledge, which is solved by the concept of patenting. Although the patented knowledge becomes public the rights of the invention remain with the inventors. **Limitations**: Patenting is not an easy task. Besides all types of knowledge cannot be patented.

5.10 Other contradictions

There are many other contradictions in performing an effective virus scanning which are illustrated in other chapters. For example,

Contradiction of detecting boot sector virus

The boot sector viruses are loaded before loading of the operating system and take control of the OS functions. The anti-virus programs can be loaded only after loading of the operating system. Hence, the anti-virus programs cannot work effectively for boot sector viruses.

Contradiction of prolonged scanning

If an anti-virus does not terminate (or time-out) a protracted scanning, then the anti-virus will unnecessarily use system resources and impact system performance. On the other hand if an anti-virus terminates a protracted scanning it may inappropriately terminate a scanning operation in a slow or overloaded computer thereby compromising vulnerabilities.

Contradiction of scanning emails

Most mail servers use proprietary encryption mechanism for email protection. If the mail servers handover their decryption formula to the anti-virus developers then they will fail to maintain the privacy and confidentiality of the mails in their mail server. On the other hand if they maintain the privacy of mails then the anti-virus programs cannot scan the content of the encrypted mail files.

Contradiction of scanning encrypted Viruses

The decrypted viral body can be read only in the runtime when the decryption module of the virus decrypts the viral body. But if we run the infected program then we may well damage our computer system. We want to run the infected program to see its decrypted viral body, but we don't want to run the program as that will infect and damage the computer system.

Contradiction of Freedom of Speech and Publication of Virus Techniques

Freedom of speech and expression is considered as a fundamental right in most of the countries which allows virus writers to publish about virus technologies. Although publishing virus content is not accepted by any law, many publications cannot be categorized whether they are virus technologies or anti-virus technologies, because most anti-virus publications include virus code and vice-versa.

Contradiction of uniform documentation

As the anti-virus companies are competing with each other there is no commonly accepted documentation on virus names, types, signatures etc. Documenting all their research findings by any company will help its competitors to get their valuable research free and affect their competitive advantage.

Contradiction of Legal Implications

Usually the anti-virus researcher has to work with a lot of virus code which is legally risky when investigated by cyber police. However, the anti-virus researcher may take the plea of his research activity and show the support of his organization. But the same also holds true for a virus creator who can prove himself to be an anti-virus researcher.

Chapter 6.

Using Ideality to find the Ideal Anti-Virus Solution

6.1 The concept of Ideality in TRIZ

Ideality is one of the simplest but most powerful concepts of TRIZ. The ideal state of a system is where there is no problem in the system, the system is better, faster, error free, low cost, easy to maintain and so on. In other words, the ideal system consists of all positives and no negatives.

According to TRIZ, the Ideal System is a system that does not materially exist while its functions are achieved. In the absolute sense Ideality is impossible to achieve, it is a fantasy, a dream. But in a relative sense ideality is achievable. (A lift is an ideal staircase so far the climbing functionality of the staircase is concerned, a motorcycle is an ideal bicycle so far its paddling aspect is concerned. But they are not absolutely ideal as they contain other disadvantages.)

According to TRIZ, each product or system or organization automatically moves towards its ideal state. Thus an IFR (Ideal Final Result) is the ultimate state (or function) of a system (or organization) at the end of its evolution. The Ideal Solution (or Ideal Final Solution or Ideal Final Result) is obviously the most powerful solution than all other conceivable solutions.

6.1.1 Ideal Final Result and Ideal Final Goal

The Ideal Results depend upon the Ideal Goal and the Ideal Goal determines the Ideal Results. Thus the Ideal Final Result (IFR) and Ideal Final Goal (IFG) are correlated and interdependent. In a problem-solving environment, the IFR can be derived from IFG and vice versa.

Other applications of the concept of Ideality are found in the concept of "the ideal product" or "the ideal process". "The Ideal product is a product that delivers all the useful functions of the product without its existence". "The ideal process is a process that gives all the desired outcome without involving any time, effort, energy or resources".

6.1.2 Calculation of Ideality

Thus an "Ideal Final Result" or "Ideal Final Solution" is the ultimate solution of any problem. In case of a virus problem, although various people may adopt various solutions, all of them are not ideal or not even close to ideal. The ideal solution must address the root cause of the problem and ensure the main useful function (MUF) i.e., protecting computer from virus infection.

However, protection from virus is neither easy nor free. One may have to spend money (for buying anti-virus program), spend time (for updating virus definitions), upgrade knowledge (to ensure that the virus is removed), spare resources (for running anti-virus) etc. As per TRIZ concepts, the ideality is calculated by the formula:

$$\text{Ideality} = \frac{\sum \text{useful functions and benefits}}{\sum \text{harmful functions} + \sum \text{costs}}$$

To present differently, ideality increases by "increase in benefits", "decrease in costs" and "decrease in harms". Hence, in this case just removing the virus is not a good solution if the user looses his valuable data or wastes his valuable time. Ideally, the computer resources should be protected but without spending too much time, money and effort.

6.1.3 Methods of improving Ideality

Although 100% of Ideality is not achievable, a lower level of ideality or partial ideality is achievable. The solutions closer to IFR are always better solutions. It is possible to improve ideality by increasing the useful functions (in the numerator of the function) and decreasing the harmful functions (in the denominator of the function). The ideality of a system may be increased by:

- ✓ Increasing its main useful function (MUF)
- ✓ Delegating its functions (in part or full) to the super system or to a subsystem or to its adjacent systems.

- ✓ Adding new subsystems or removing unwanted subsystems
- ✓ Introducing a subsystem that counters the harmful functions (HF) of the system.
- ✓ Using freely available resources and making optimal use of resources available to the system.
- ✓ Ensuring that the solution considers not only the interest of the system, but also the interest of the super-system and subsystems etc.

6.2 What is the Ideal Final Solution of a Virus Problem

According to TRIZ the Ideal Final solution (IFS) or the Ideal Final Result (IFR) is the ultimate imaginary solution of a problem irrespective of whether it is achievable or not. In most cases the Ideal final solution is a solution that avoids the need for solving the original problem.

Now what is the Ideal Final Result (IFR) in this scenario of virus problem? Following the concept of Ideality we can derive that **the Ideal Final Result is to achieve a "no virus" environment where there is no need of any anti-virus.** As the Ideal Final Product is no product – but only its functions, **the Ideal anti-virus software is no anti-virus software.**

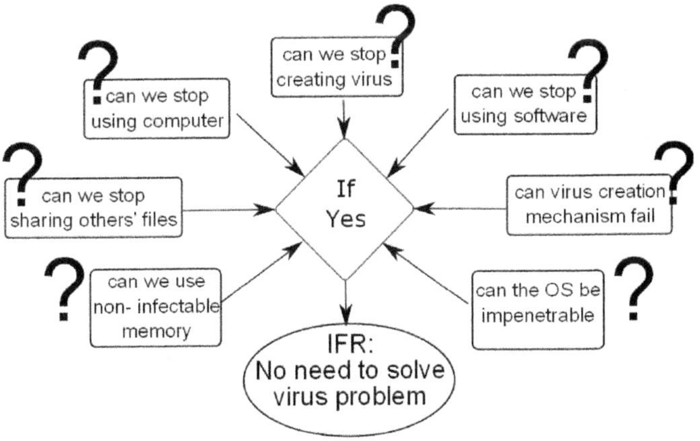

Alternative methods of avoiding virus problem

But is there a situation that eliminates the need for solving the virus problem? Is there a method that leads to a "no virus" environment? How is it possible to achieve the functions of anti-virus program without installing an anti-virus program?

Yes there are alternative ways to avoid virus problems. Some of them may sound absurd, unrealistic or insane but one should still think of alternative ways of achieving that result. For example,

- Can we stop using computer? There was no computer virus before 1980, because there was no computer. If we stop using computers and use a better alternative then there may not be virus problem.
- If we use computer memory that virus cannot infect (such as, ROM) then we are safe from virus. Can we stop using hard disks or other type of infectable memory and use only ROM that cannot be infected by virus? Can we stop using current form of software and use something else that does the function of software?
- Can we make the architecture of the Operating System so robust that viruses cannot penetrate into its environment. Virus infects vulnerable operating systems like Microsoft Windows. Will it be alright to migrate to a non-vulnerable or less vulnerable OS like Linux, then there will be no/less virus problem. If viruses cannot penetrate into the operating system then realizing the futility of viruses the virus-writers may stop creating viruses.
- Virus has to come from a source computer. If we don't use any external file (or network or internet) then there will be no infection.
- The ideality may be achieved by transferring the functionality of an anti-virus to the super-system (such as, operating system) or the grand-super-system (such as, Internet) so that there will be no need for a separate anti-virus on individual machines.

Although the above solutions can lead to a no-virus situation and solve the problem of viruses, it is true that they are extremely difficult to implement and lead to serious contradictions which are extremely difficult to solve. Hence the most practical option at this moment is to put a strong anti-virus that can protect the computers from any type of viruses.

6.3 The hierarchy of IFRs in Virus Problem

As we have discussed earlier, an IFR is a fantasy or dream, which is often not achievable. That is why TRIZ suggests forming multiple levels of IFR in a hierarchy. When the top level IFR is not possible to achieve a lower level IFR is framed with a lesser degree of ideality and a higher degree of achievability.

While the highest-level ideality is called as "global ideality" the lower level ideality is called as "local ideality" where the later is selected based on the local resources. Let's have a look at different levels of IFRs.

As we saw earlier the top level IFR is "a no virus environment".

IFR **Computer viruses should not be created at all or computer viruses should not exist in the world**– if there is no virus then no virus problem and no need of anti-virus.

As the above IFR is difficult to achieve, we have to take a step back to frame a second level IFR which is something as below:

IFR **The computer should never become infected by any computer virus** – the viruses may be created or may exist in the world. But they should not be able to enter into our computer, or they should be destroyed as soon as they enter into our computer".

When the second level IFR is difficult to achieve a third level IFR may be framed which is as below.

IFR **Our files and programs should never be damaged by any computer virus** – the virus may enter into our computer but should have no power to damage anything in our computer.

Now the question arises whether should we frame still lower level IFRs? Sometimes yes and sometimes no. In some cases it is useful to frame lower level IFRs as the lower level IFRs are more achievable. A still lower level IFR is;

IFR Let the virus damage any file or object, but we should have a system (something like an anti-virus) to repair those damages. Even if a file or object is damaged to the extent that it is not repairable there should be a mechanism (may be a backup) to recover the file or object to its most recent condition.

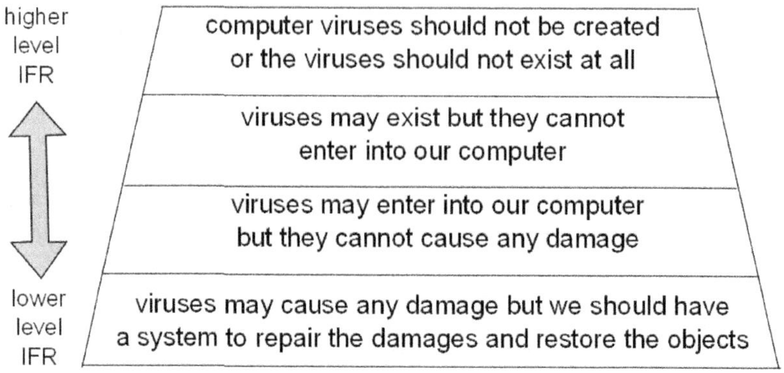

The Hierarchy of IFRs in Solving Virus Problem

In the above hierarchy of IFR, the problem solver should first try to achieve the top level IFR. When that is not possible the problem solver has to take a step back and try to achieve the second level IFR. If that is not possible to achieve then he has to try for an IFR below that level and so on. In principle, a solution closer to a higher level IFR is always a better solution.

According to TRIZ the viruses (and the creators of viruses) and anti-viruses (and the creators of anti-viruses) are two opposite systems, both of which try to achieve their goals. This is like many other competing systems in the world like the policemen and gangsters, the Central bank and counterfeiters, sea artillery and the armored ships, the manual weapon and protective waistcoats, etc. Each of such systems aspires to achieve maximal main useful function (MUF). For example, while one system wishes to make the armored ships, other system wishes to punch the armor. Similar is the case of virus developers and the anti-virus developers.

In this scenario of two antagonistic systems the end users belong to the same side as the anti-virus developers (because the later try to save the former from virus attacks). But the goals and expectations of end users and anti-virus developers are different. For example, **while creation of virus is an undesirable phenomenon for a computer-user, it is a desirable phenomenon for an anti-virus manufacturer.** This situation creates a big contradiction.

Contradiction	*The users neither want creation of viruses, nor want to be panic over virus infection, nor want to pay for the anti-virus software. But the software venders want some new viruses to be created and want the public to be panic over the threat to pay more for the anti-virus product. In such a case, the loss of one party leads to the gain of the other.*

In such situations the best solution is decided based on the calculation of Ideality. According to TRIZ, the Ideality is higher when a system provides more benefits and less harms. Thus the ideality of an anti-virus product is higher when it solves more problems and causes less harm. The formula of calculating ideality of anti-virus is as below.

$$\textbf{Ideality of anti-virus} = \frac{\begin{array}{l}\textit{capability of detecting all types of viruses +}\\ \textit{speed of scanning + platform independence +}\\ \textit{ease of installation, maintenance and admin + ...}\end{array}}{\begin{array}{l}\textit{load on machine + difficulties for the end user +}\\ \textit{burden on network admin + false positives +}\\ \textit{false negatives + price of the produce +}\\ \textit{frequency and difficulty of updating a/v program}\\ \textit{and data + burden on system resources + ...}\end{array}}$$

As per the above formula, the ideality of an anti-virus is higher when it detects more viruses, scans at faster speed, works on all platforms, easy to update, requires no support from system admin, puts less burden on the machine etc.

6.4 Meeting the expectations of different groups

The ideality or perfection of an anti-virus is higher when it meets the expectations of different types of users, such as, ordinary users, system administrators, corporate managers, advanced level users etc. Their expectations from an anti-virus program are different because of their differences in knowledge, experience, responsibilities and goals. The anti-virus developer should keep everybody's expectations in mind while developing the product. The overall ideality of the product may be evaluated based on its suitability for different types of users.

Evaluating an anti-virus program

	Expectations from anti-virus program	Whether expectations are met
Ordinary user		
Corporate Manager		
Systems Admin		
Anti Virus developer		

Expectations of the End Users

A common user does not know much about the "macro viruses" or "trojan horses". He just wants to "run a program", or "edit a file" or "browse a site" or "check an email" or "play a game". He does not bother about cleaning viruses as long as he does not face any problem in doing his job. Apart from the IFR mentioned above his expectations from an anti-virus are:

- Implementing anti-virus should cost no money, no time and no special skill. The anti-virus program should be free and automated. Should be easy to install, update and maintain.

- The anti-virus should not slow down the system performance by consuming valuable system resources. Besides it should not cause other disadvantages to the user.

It may not be possible to satisfy all the expectations of an end user. But like an IFR it is important to keep the expectations of different user groups in mind in order to develop the right product.

Expectations of the Systems Administrator

As we saw in the previous chapter, the problems faced by a systems administrator are different from those faced by the end users, because of the differences in his job responsibilities. When there is a virus outbreak in a corporate network, the systems administrator has to take various course of action, such as, taking data backup, downloading anti-virus updates, scanning computers and servers etc. If the situation goes beyond his control then he may seek help from experts from external sources.

Common users face different problems than System administrator

It is interesting to note that the expectations of a systems administrator are different from that of an end user. Unlike the end user he may not want all the computer viruses to vanish completely from the world, as in that case he will loose his job and salary. Unlike a home user he does not mind procuring an anti-virus product, as his company will pay for the procurement. His expectations are as below:

- The anti-virus software, which he has selected and deployed in the network, should adequately protect the computers and the network from virus infection.

- The anti-virus software should be easy to install, easy to configure, easy to update and easy to maintain so that his workload remains well within limits.

The expectations of the Corporate Manager

A corporate manager or a small business owner is important because he has to take financial decisions and decisions on manpower requirements. His expectations are generally as follows.

- There should be minimal expenditure on procuring the anti-virus products.

- The anti-virus product should require no support or minimal support of system administrators (which will reduce the burden of expenditures on system administrators).

Note that the expectations of a business owner (or corporate manager) and a home user are very similar.

Expectations of Anti-Virus Developers

While the end users don't want the virus to be created at all, the anti-virus companies don't want so because they gain financial incentives for viruses written and spread. Hence they want some new viruses to be created in order for the survival of their business.

- The anti-virus product should be capable of fully protecting a computer from any type of viruses.

- The anti-virus product should be adopted by maximum number of users and sold for a good price.

Although the anti-virus developers do not really want the viruses to vanish totally out of the world, they carry a great vision of their anti-virus product. They wish to develop a powerful anti-virus product that is capable of protecting the user computer from all kinds of viruses.

6.5 The Features of the Ideal Anti-Virus Product

While everybody in the chain (including end user, systems administrator, corporate manager, software vender and anti-virus developer) wants something in common (i.e., to keep the computer free from virus), everybody's goals and expectations are different. While the end user wants a "virus free environment", the systems administrator and anti-virus developer look forward to a "controlled virus environment" by using an anti-virus program. Let's see what are the desired features of an ideal anti-virus product.

IFR The computer should never get infected after using the anti-virus product. The virus should be immediately detected and destroyed as soon as it attempts to enter into the computer.

IFR If the virus has already entered into the computer then the anti-virus product should be able to detect and remove all types of viruses from the users' computer (Note that the goal of anti-virus developer is not to destroy viruses completely out of the world but only from the AV users' computer).

IFR The anti-virus product should include all (or maximum number of) virus signatures to detect all (or maximum) types of viruses. The signature database should include the signatures of new viruses as soon as they are created.

IFR The Ideal Anti-Virus should work without updating the virus database or provide easy and automatic methods of updating virus database.

IFR The product should virus scan the computer in a fast speed and consume minimum amount of system resources.

IFR The product should automatically install, automatically update and automatically function.

IFR The product should protect the user computer, the server, the network and all vulnerable objects from any types of virus infection.

IFR The product should not burden the user or systems administrator for updating virus database. It should work without updating virus database or provide automatic methods of updating.

IFR The anti-virus should detect and prevent viruses with full certainty. The chances of error should be nil and it should not raise any false positives or false negatives.

IFR The product should be able to remove all viruses and repair all infected files and restore the damaged system.

IFR No virus should be able to cripple the Anti-Virus. It may first undergo a self-test to ensure that it has not been infected.

Thus the concept of ideality helps us to visualize the ultimate objective of an anti-virus system (IFR), the main useful function (MUF) and desirable functions and features of an ideal anti-virus product. Although the highest-level IFR is “no virus” (and “no anti-virus”) environment, the most practical IFR is to protect the computer by a powerful anti-virus system. The concept of ideality helps us to visualize the features and functions of an Ideal anti-virus product.

Chapter 7.

Using Inventive Principles for Solving Virus Problems

7.1 What are Inventive Principles

Applying Inventive Principles is one of the simplest but most powerful techniques in TRIZ. According to the findings of TRIZ, there are only forty Inventive Principles, which have been applied in all the inventions so far. Putting differently, the same forty Inventive Principles can be applied to solve any kind of problem in future. Thus the Inventive Principles have tremendous scope to be used as an essential problem solving method.

Each of these 40 Inventive Principles is a unique approach to address a problem. Although some principles appear to overlap each other, it happens only in limited cases and that does not affect their usefulness thereby. It is not necessary that only one Principle can be applied to a situation, rather in most cases, a combination or set of principles are found to be applicable. For example, a method "to detect and isolate an infected machine in a network automatically" uses two principles, viz., Principle-2: Taking out and Principle-25: Self Service.

7.1.1 Some Facts about Inventive Principles

While applying inventive principles we often come up with many doubts and confusions. It will be worth mentioning the following facts about the Inventive Principles.

- The forty Inventive Principles are not mutually exclusive. Some solutions may appear to be (or may actually be) an application of more than one Inventive Principle. In such cases the problem solver should not debate on the definition of Principles in order to distinguish one from the other or focus on determining which principle exactly was applied. The objective is to get the solution and not to brood over definitions.

- Most solutions use more than one Principles. Hence it is not enough to try out only one of the forty principles. We must consider complex solutions which involve multiple Principles. For example, the CPU emulation uses a virtual machine (Principle-26: Copying) in order to decrypt the encrypted viruses (Principle-36: State Change and Conversion) and the virtual machine is destroyed every time after it is infected by the virus code (Principle-34: Discard and Recover).

- In many cases there are alternative names for the same principles, for example, Principle(2):"Extraction" is also known as Principle(2):"Taking Out", Principle(13):"Reversing" is also known as Principle(13):"Other way round" and so on. These differences in the "Proper Names" should only be seen as translation limitations from Russian to English and should not be interpreted otherwise.

- All the principles are not used with equal frequency. There are some principles like Principle(1): "Segmentation", Principle(2): "Taking Out", Principle(5): "Merging", Principle(6): "Universality" , Principle(10): "Prior Action", Principle(15): "Dynamize", Principle(24): "Intermediary", Principle(25): "Self Service", Principle(26): "Copying", Principle(35): "Parameter Change" etc. which are found to be used more often than other principles.

- Inventive Principles can be applied independently or in combination with other TRIZ tools. If somebody is not comfortable with other TRIZ methods he can still go ahead with applying only the forty principles. Applying forty Principles is a powerful tool to arrive at great solutions.

- TRIZ principles are the abstractions of thousands of inventions. Hence, they are not very different from our knowledge and practice. In fact they are derived or abstracted from our (world's) knowledge and practice. The idea behind the TRIZ Principles, like any other TRIZ tool, is not to teach us something new rather to remind us about the existence of various solutions and guide us to apply the existing generic solutions to arrive at some specific solution for any given problem.

7.1.2 Inventive Principles in Software context

Some Principles like “Phase Transition”, “Thermal Expansion”, “Strong Oxidizers” etc. are confusing in software context and are rephrased suitably in Annex-1 as applicable in the field of Software or Information Technology. (For more on Software Principles you may refer the book “TRIZ Principles for Information Technology” by the author).

Although some of the terms used in the original Technical Principles are not suitable in the field of Information Technology, their underlying concepts are very much applicable. For example, the Principle: “Segmentation” reminds us that “a big volume of work can be distributed among several people”, “a large software can be divided into several modules”, and “a long software project can be divided into several phases”. But it is ultimately up to the implementer to decide about how many modules the software should be divided and how many people are to be engaged per module, although the Principles can be applied again to arrive at further details of the solutions.

7.2 How to Apply Inventive Principles

Inventive Principles are generally applied to solve contradictions in complex problems. Most Inventive Problems comprise one or more contradictions and each contradiction can be solved by one or more Principles. However, the Principles can also be applied in situations where there is no contradiction or the contradiction is not yet found.

There are different ways of applying the inventive Principles. The user, after getting acquainted with the principles, can actually find his own way of applying the technique according to his convenience.

- ✓ One method is to apply all the principles sequentially from 1 to 40. This method gives an advantage of checking the possible applicability of each Principle. But this process is time consuming.
- ✓ Referring to the Contradiction Matrix is helpful in case of technical contradictions. But this method is ruled out in case of Software Contradictions.
- ✓ One may also apply the Principles randomly or based on one's personal experience. Although this is not a good practice, this is the often-used method, as because it takes less time to start.

7.3 Examples of Applying Inventive Principles to Improve Anti-Virus Programs

The most important application of Inventive principles is to resolve contradictions. In the previous chapter we discussed a series of contradictions related to improving anti-virus techniques and presented alternative solutions by using Inventive Principles. In this chapter we will just illustrate some examples for each different Inventive Principles. Although some examples may look duplicate as they might have been discussed in other chapters, I think putting them here under this section will help understanding and visualizing the application of Inventive Principles in a better way.

Principle-1: Segmentation

- One of the problems of virus scanning is that it takes very long time. One solution to this problem is to spread over the scanning process in several sessions. The subsequent sessions may start from the same point where the previous sessions left (Principle-1: Segmentation).

- Another solution to the above problem is to divide the scanning load on multiple computers. For example, a distributed virus scanning distributes the scanning load on multiple computers in a distributed network (Principle-1: Segmentation).

Principle-2: Taking out

- If a file or email is virus infected, then remove the virus to disinfect the file or email (Principle-2: Taking out). If the virus cannot be removed from the file then delete the file or email in order to prevent further infection (Principle-2: Taking out).

- When a network device is infected it is important to ensure that the infection does not spread further to other devices. It is advised to first detect the infected device and then disable and thereby isolate from the network. If a user is associated with the detected device the user is also disabled and prevented from accessing the network (Patent 7571483).

- If the hash tables or fingerprints (for integrity checking) are stored on the same machine then there is a possibility of the hash tables getting virus infected. One solution is to store the hash tables or fingerprints on a separate machine or server computer so that they remain safe for integrity checking.

Isolating Fingerprint Database to a separate computer

- The structure of an email is complex to be scanned along with its attachments. Hence the attachments are first detached from the email in order to be scanned by the anti-virus application (Principle-2: Taking out). Once detached the anti-virus does a thorough scanning of the attachments. If found infected the repaired files are reattached to the original email message (Principle-5: Merging).

Principle-3: Local Quality

- Releasing anti-virus programs and updates for each different versions of an operating system.
- Creating a custom cleaner for a computer (Patent 7836500 detailed later).
- Sometimes the virus writers reverse engineer the anti-virus in order to enable their viruses to escape the detection mechanism. Patent 5684875 suggests a polymorphic protection method that installs only a few of a huge set of algorithms in each installation. (Principle-3: Local Quality). Even if a virus writer reverse-engineers the detection method he can view only limited number of algorithms that are installed. So his virus is likely to get caught in other systems that include a different set of algorithms.

Principle-4: Asymmetry

Principle-5: Merging

- Generally different anti-virus programs look suspiciously at each other and lead to unpredictable results if co-exist. But it would be nice to run multiple anti-virus programs on the same system and supplementing each other to provide a stronger protection.

- Spyware and adware etc. cause a lot of problem and need to be scanned. But scanning spyware by a separate scanner will cause performance impact on a computer. Patent 7441273 suggested integrating spyware detection capabilities with the virus scanner so that the same scanner can scan viruses and spyware both. When the virus signatures are updated from the Internet, the spyware signatures will also be updated together at the same time (Principle-5: Merging).

- A network policy ensures that the rules and guidelines are uniformly implemented across the network. US Patent 7010807 suggests to implement an anti-virus policy into the firewall. This way the anti-virus policy is integrated into the network policy (Principle-5: Merging).

Principle-6: Universality

- Signature scanning cannot detect new and unknown viruses. This drawback of signature scanning is overcome by using generic methods of virus detection, such as, heuristic scanning, CPU emulation and integrity checking which can detect any type of viruses, known or unknown.

Principle-7: Nested Doll

- As it is not possible to detect all new macro viruses accurately, Patent 6577920 suggests to suspect all macros and check the macros against three databases, viz., the database containing signatures of known viruses, the database containing signatures of certified commercial macros and the database containing local user created macros. (Principle-16: Partial or Excessive Action). If the signature of the macro is found in first database or not found in the second or third database then the user is given an alert (Principle-7: Nested doll).

Principle-8: Counterweight

- If you are using an unsecured operating system like Windows, install an anti-virus program on your computer (Principle-8: Counterweight).

- ⇨ Use a virus co-processor in order to accelerate scanning of virus signatures (Patent 8079084).

Principle-9: Prior Counteraction

- ⇨ It is not advisable to open emails coming from unknown sources. Never run attachments from unknown sources (Principle-9: Prior Counteraction).
- ⇨ Many current day viruses target to paralyze the virus scanner. Hence the virus scanner should first check itself in order to ensure that its own files are not infected (Principle-9: Prior Counteraction, Principle-25: Self Service).
- ⇨ A malware is generally invited into the machine by web browsing, email downloading and using external storage like pen drive, CD, DVD etc. If we can guard all these incoming routes we can narrow down the chances of virus infection.
- ⇨ If there is a need to turn off anti-virus temporarily in order to restore a computer, the systems administrator may disconnect the computer from the network before disabling the anti-virus program. He may enable the anti-virus program again after the restoration is complete.

Principle-10: Prior Action

- ⇨ Keep a file scanned much before it is required to be opened by a program or user so that the file is not detained for scanning at the time when it is required to be opened by the user (Principle-10: Prior Action).
- ⇨ As the major threat of viral attack remains from outside, it would be useful to screen all the data on the way when transferred from one computer to another through the network. This method avoids the need of scanning at every client machine.
- ⇨ Using a front-end pre-scanner card to do a preliminary scan of network packets (US Patent 7992206). If the pre-scanner card fails to determine whether the packet is infected or not then the packets are passed to the computer for a detailed scanning by a file-based scan engine.

Principle-11: Cushioning

Principle-12: Equipotentiality

Principle-13: Reversing

- The boot sector viruses are loaded before the operating system is loaded. Hence the anti-virus cannot work upon the boot sector virus that is already loaded prior to the anti-virus. One option to solve this problem is to load the anti-virus program before the OS.
- While computer viruses cause problem to the user, a counter-virus agent (Patent 6813712) can detect and control viruses. Like viruses it attaches itself to files for replication but helps detecting all types of viruses, including new and unknown. This method of deploying counter-viruses is opposite to the conventional methods of virus removal.
- The "cheese worm" which was released to counter the infections of LiOn worm for Linux. The cheese worm scans for infected machines and removes the LiOn worm.
- How to disinfect a virus infected file without knowing the infection pattern? Heuristic cleaning tries to follow exactly a reverse method of virus infection to disinfect the infected file (Frans Veldman, http://mirror.sweon.net/madchat/vxdevl/vdat/epheurs1.htm).

Principle-14: Curvature

Principle-15: Dynamize

- Configuring the anti-virus to start scanning when the user stops working and stop scanning when the user starts working. This method utilizes system resources but does not affect the user. Some anti virus programs can be scheduled to run when the system is left idle for certain time (Principle-15: Dynamize, Principle-25: Self Service).
- As there is a possibility of viruses coming from Internet it is advisable for a user to connect the computer to Internet (or external network) only when necessary and disconnect at other times (Principle-15: Dynamize). **Drawback**- this may reduce the chances of infection, but cannot fully avoid infection.

- ⇨ Data may be scanned while being downloaded from a server. If an infection is detected during download, then the anti-virus program can cure the virus or delete the partially downloaded file. This will prevent unnecessary downloading of infected files which need to be deleted later when detected to be infected (Principle-9: Prior Counteraction, Principle-15: Dynamize)

Principle-16: Partial or Excessive action

- ⇨ An exact identification scanning, although more reliable, takes more time to scan. Hence some methods use heuristics to arrive at "almost exact identification" which is much faster and often considered as sufficiently reliable.
- ⇨ As a complete virus scanning takes very long time, one solution to is do a partial virus scanning of the core elements like main memory, boot sector, file system etc. A partial virus scanning may be done every time the computer boots.
- ⇨ Sometimes it is necessary to terminate a protracted scanning in order to escape from endless loops. But a simple timeout may not be justified for large files. Patent 6968461 considers the size of the file as an additional parameter. If the size of a file is large, then it is not early terminated as it may legitimately require a large amount of data to be processed during scanning operation.

Principle-17: Another Dimension

- ⇨ All the conventional scanning methods provide local scanning. But a local scanning may not be useful when there is no scanner or the scanner is infected or the computer is unable to boot from the hard disk. One solution to this problem is online scanning. Patent 6347375 suggests booting from a bootable virus utility and scanning the computer by a remote computer using an online scanning service.

Principle-18: Vibratation

Principle-19: Periodic Action

- ⇨ As new viruses, worms and Trojan horses are born on a daily basis, an outdated virus database cannot be effective to detect such new viruses. Hence, users must update their anti-virus software and download latest virus databases periodically.

- While a fast scanning is done during system boot up or once in a day, a complete virus scanning can be done once in a week or so (Principle-19: Periodic Action).

- Store-scan-forward virus scanning in a network environment- this method stores the packets in a buffer till the whole file is arrived for a file level virus scanning. This type of scanning is more reliable than stream scanning.

Principle-20: Continuity of Useful Action

- Configure your anti-virus program to run automatically on system start-up and run at all times as a resident program (Principle-25: Self service, Principle-20: Continuous action).

- Stream Scanning for computer virus (as opposed to store-scan-forward scanning) is a continuous scanning of packets as and when they arrive. This method gives a faster throughput (although less reliable).

Principle-21: Skipping (Hurry)

- Speed scanning or fast mode virus scanning- which scans the memory, system files and critical areas of the disk. The fast mode does not scan the individual files on the disk.

- One method to reduce the scanning time is to avoid repetitive scanning. Once a file is scanned to be virus free, it should not be scanned again and again in subsequent scanning sessions (Principle-21: Skipping). This method saves scanning time and makes scanning faster.

- The anti-virus may maintain the results of the previous scan so that the files that were scanned earlier to be virus-free need not be scanned again unless found altered.

- Generally an anti-virus scans a file when the file is opened and closed. But this wastes scanning time. Ideally subsequent scanning can be done only when a file has been modified and not just because the file has been opened and closed by a program (Patent 6928555).

- Scanning complete body of files can take long time. To speed up scanning, some advanced scanners don't scan the whole files for virus signatures. They search only the vulnerable area of the files such as the beginning and the end of the file, which makes scanning much faster.

Principle-22: Turn Harms to Benefits

- While the viruses are destructive and problematic, the same technology may be used to spread a (virus like) program that would check the security flaws of a computer and fix the flaws with necessary patches and updates. Once the flaws are fixed it can move to another machine or destroy itself.

- In order to skip the previously scanned files, it is necessary to store the result of the previous scan. But if the previous scan information is stored in a separate file then it takes more time and system resource to access it. Patent 6763466 suggests to store the anti-virus state information in the directory database where the file system stores the file information. This method works fast as it uses an already existing database that is used for storing file information.

- Patent 7512808 suggests modifying the viruses that caused infection in such a way that they would perform a reverse action for cleaning and repairing of the damage done by the virus on the client device.

Principle-23: Feedback

- In some cases an anti-virus program may not be definitive about suspicious alterations in a system file. To solve these situations the anti-virus program may ask the user whether the alteration made is genuine or not and then take a decision based on the user feedback (Principle-23: Feedback).

- Sometimes the floppies are casually left in floppy drives which increase the chance of spreading boot sector viruses. Patent 6550007 suggests alerting a user about the presence of a floppy disk in the drive before trying to boot from the floppy. This method enables the user to remove the floppy disk from the drive if he does not intend the computer system to boot from the disk (Principle-23: Feedback, Principle-9: Prior Counteraction).

Principle-24: Intermediary

- Most viruses come from external networks through network connections. One of the techniques to prevent such viruses is to put a firewall or proxy server in between the user computer and external network that can detect and prevent unwanted connections.
- Generally the emails are stored in an encrypted form in an email server and a virus scanner cannot access the individual attachments of the emails stored in an email server. Patent 5832208 suggests placing an agent between the mail server and the anti-virus program (Principle-24: Intermediary). The agent detaches the attachments and forwards them to the anti-virus application for scanning.

Principle-25: Self Service

- Auto protecting and auto healing features of Antivirus software-The residential component remains active in the memory and protects the system from virus attacks on real-time as soon as they are found (Principle-20: Continuous action, Principle-25: Self Service).
- If the programs were capable of undergoing a self-test to determine whether they have been modified then that would prevent executing infected programs.
- There should be a method of detecting infected machines and isolating them in a network automatically (Principle-2: Taking out, Principle-25: Self Service) so that the infected machine wont spread infection to other computers.
- The job of analyzing virus characters and extracting virus signatures are tedious jobs. This job can be expedited by using automated techniques.
- The self-running feature of the anti-virus program can run automatically at a pre-scheduled day and/or time, such as during nights or in holidays when the computer is not used.
- Self-updating features of the anti-virus programs to connect the user's computer to the anti-virus developer's site and download the updated virus definitions from the developer's website.

Principle-26: Copying

- Often a virus scanner puts excessive load on a computer that leads other programs to run slow. We want to scan our machine but don't want to reduce the performance of our machine. One solution is to copy all the files to a different machine and scan the files in the second computer (Patent 7644352) (Principle-2: Taking out, Principle-26: Copying).
- It is necessary to execute the encrypted viruses in order to see their decrypted code. But executing the virus code can lead to disastrous consequences. One solution is to execute the suspect code in a virtual machine. The virtual machine mimics the system functionalities and the virus gets fooled to execute within the virtual machine (Principle-26: Copy). If the decrypted part of the suspect program is found to be having virus code then the program is treated as infected.

Principle-27: Cheap and Disposable

- The emulation techniques create a virtual machine to run the suspect programs. If the activities of the suspect program are found to be really dangerous the program is terminated and treated as a virus. Even if the virus infects the virtual machine, it does not become a concern as the whole virtual machine is terminated and initialized after every detection.
- Patent 7996901 discloses detecting email viruses using hypervisor technology. The hypervisor opens a second operating system (or donor operating system) in order to open and scan the emails. This second operating system (or "donor OS" or "scratch OS") works as a scratch pad. Once the email activities are complete the "scratch OS" is discarded (Principle-27: Cheap and disposable). This way the user operating system encounters no damage.

Principle-28: Mechanics Substitution

- The metamorphic viruses are not detected by signature scanning as they change their viral body in every infection. Patent 7739737 suggests to compare the "function signatures" that describes the function of the malicious code instead of the conventional method of comparing "strings of codes" (Principle-28: Mechanics Substitution).

Principle-29: Pneumatics and Hydraulics

Principle-30: Thin and Flexible

- In a network environment it is better to scan the files in a central server instead of scanning in each individual machines. But sending each file to the centralized server for scanning would consume excessive bandwidth. Patent 7152164 suggests to send only the identifications of the files, such as, source URL, content type, size, date etc. along with checksum, which are tiny in size and require substantially less time and bandwidth (Principle-30: Thin and Flexible).

- The worms send probe packets through network for propagation and self-replication which is often detected by a traffic anomaly detector. In order to escape from traffic anomaly detection some stealth worms try to keep the signal–to-noise ratio (SNR) very low (less than 0.01%) by sending very less number of packets.

Principle-31: Hole

- In a stream scanning, the scanning of data may take slightly more time than downloading the data which may allow the last part of the infected file to get downloaded and cause danger. To avoid this problem, Patent 6088803 suggests feeding time gaps artificially between each individual segments and withholding the last part of the file. In other words the delay required for scanning is distributed and fed in between individual packets or segments (Principle-31: Hole, Principle-8: Counterweight, Principle-1: Segmentation).

Principle-32: Color Change

- Patent 7089589 teaches to use a bait server to detect viruses in a network. The address of the bait server is not published so that the clients in the network have no reason to access this server for any purpose (Principle-32: Color Change). But the virus-infected computer will send random probe packets to explore vulnerable systems. So any client attempting access to the bait server will be deemed as infected.

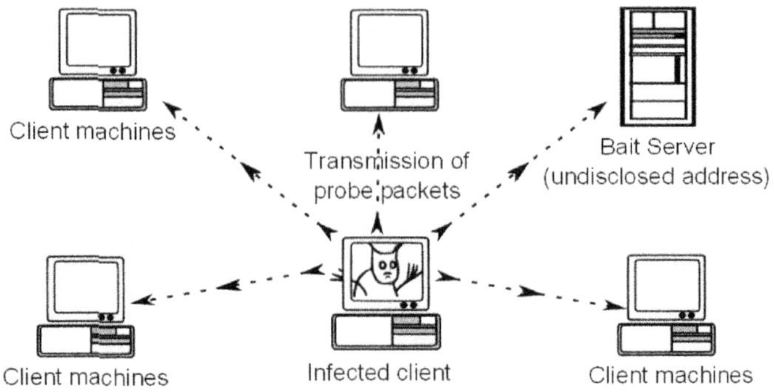

Detection of Infected Client by Bait Server

Principle-33: Homogeneity (Compatibility)

- Generally viruses are platform dependent and viruses created for one platform cannot spread in another platform. This knowledge can be used to keep safe backups. For example, Windows backups can be kept in Linux systems and Linux backup can be kept in Windows Systems (This is **Reverse** application of Principle-33: Homogeneity).

- When an infected document is edited by the user the virus code inside the document may change by insertion of white-space characters. Although the code is not detected by its signature it can still be dangerous. Patent 6230288 suggests to transform all the white space sequences in the file as well as the white spaces in the virus signature to one single format before scanning so that the altered virus code can be located with more probability.

Principle-34: Discard and Recover

- It is difficult to determine whether a modification is genuine or done by virus operation. By the time the virus operation is known with certainty the virus would have done its damages. Patent 6073239 suggests a method which intercepts a write operation and backs up the program in a different location. If the modification is determined to be virus made, the method undoes all modifications that the virus may have made to the program and recovers the original from the backup (Principle-26: Copying, Principle-34: Discard and Recover).

⇨ Infection in the boot sector implies changes in the boot record and no change in the boot record indicates no infection in the boot sector. Patent 6092161 allows a boot partition to be written without limit during a session. However, at the start of a new session, all the changes to the partition are undone and the partition is restored to its original state (Principle-34: Discard and Recover). That means, even if a partition is infected during a session it becomes virus-free again at the start of the new session.

Principle-35: Parameter Change

⇨ It is necessary to prevent an infected file from being used. US Patent 7293177 provides a simple solution of "locking" the infected files. When a file is found infected the method leaves the file as open and non-sharing. This status of the file does not allow other applications running on the computer to operate on the file.

⇨ There should be a method of scanning files in a network environment so that the same files need not be scanned again and again in every workstation. For example, the scanned files may be marked as "checked ok" or certified as "virus free" so that other users/ systems in the network trust the files to be "virus free" without scanning it again.

Principle-36: State Change and Conversion

⇨ When a MS Word document of an older format is opened by a newer version of MS Word application, the document is automatically converted to the new version along with the macro viruses. This leads to creation of multiple versions of the same macro virus. There is a technique used to detect all these versions of macros by using only a single signature. Before comparing the virus signatures, the macro formats are first converted to a canonical form and the detection is done on the canonical form (Principle-36: Conversion). This method eliminates the need for maintaining and comparing different signatures for different formats of the same macro virus.

⇨ When an anti-virus does not have the knowledge of disinfecting a file it stores the file in a separate directory for possible disinfection in future. But this leaves a possibility that the user runs those files to infect the computer. Hence some anti-viruses rename those files, change their extensions and encrypt their content to prevent those files from being used.

- As many viruses target to attack the anti-virus programs there is a need to protect the anti-virus from such attacks. Patent 7640583 suggests using polymorphism to obfuscate anti-malware files, such as, changing file names, altering the size and signature of the anti-malware files randomly in order to hide the anti-malware program from the viruses (Principle-15: Dynamize, Principle-36: State Change and Conversion).

- Patent application 20080141375 suggests to archive all the non-recently used objects into a non-executable format and omit them from periodic scans (Principle-36: State Change and Conversion). When there is a request to use any archived object, the archived object is converted to a non-archived state and virus scanned before made available to the requester.

Principle-37: Expansion

- Although metamorphic viruses can reorganize and change their viral body, they perform the same large-scale actions, independent of the code in their viral body. Hence, by coalescing small-scale actions into large-scale actions or meta-heuristic events, it is possible to circumvent the power of metamorphic viruses (Patent 7231667).

Principle-38: Enrich/ Improve Quality

- As the method of signature scanning depends on pattern recognition, better and improved methods of pattern recognition can be used in order to speed up the scanning process.

Principle-39: Calm (Inert Atmosphere)

- If a virus infection is found in a MS Word file, open the file in WordPad instead of MS Word. As WordPad does not support Macros, opening the infected Word file in WordPad will be safe and no macro virus will execute.

Principle-40: Composite

- Applying multiple methods of virus detection, such as, signature based detection and behavior based detection etc. by a virus scanning application may help detecting a virus that is not detected by one single method.

INVENTION-3: Using a large set of signatures and flags to avoid false positives in detecting a virus

The conventional approach uses single, specific signatures to detect viruses, i.e., one virus- one signature. But this method leads to mistakes in identifications and false positives.

Patent 6338141 (invented by Wells, assignee CyberSoft Inc, Jan 2002) discloses a relational anti virus engine (RAVEN) which uses a large relational set of signatures and flags to detect any given virus. Depending upon file type the relational set may contain over 30 different signatures and flags for a single virus which ensures precise identification. The virus detection data includes a set of traditional signatures, non-traditional/ extended signatures (like, FileSize, FileType, JumpCount, NoiseLevel, FileCRC etc.), heuristic flags and other information about the file which allows RAVEN to verify infections with high degree of accuracy and avoids possibility of false identifications (Principle-40: Composite).

Chapter 8.

Applying S-Fields and Inventive Standards for Virus Detection

8.1 Explaining basics of S-Field Models

S-Fields are graphical representations of technical systems. Each S-Field consists of minimum three items, two elements (or substances S1 and S2) and an action (or Field F). An element (or substance) can be anything, a computer or device or product or software or operating system or tool or human being that is supposed to be developed or improved or processed or measured or changed. An action (or Field) is an energy or force (chemical, thermal, mechanical, gravitational, electrical, electromagnetic, audible etc.) which acts upon the element (or substance) to produce some effect.

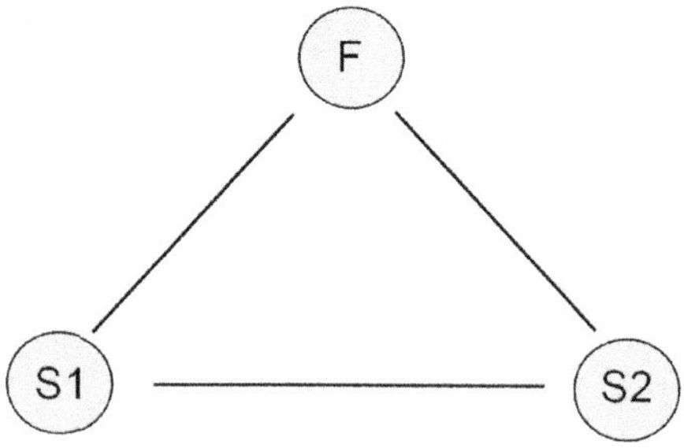

A basic S-Field Model

S-Fields are useful particularly when there is no contradiction visible in the system. There are some situations where there is no parameter to be improved but still there is a problem to be solved. Element-Actions (or S-Fields) help modeling a technical system. "S-Field is a model of Minimal, Functioning and Controllable technical system" (Yuri Salamatov).

Although some of the conventional action (or Field) types, such as, chemical, Magnetic, Gravitational etc. are not useful in software environment, the concept of "elements and actions" (or Substances and Fields) remains applicable. However, the terms "substance" and "field" are confusing in English which should rather be called as "elements" and "actions" for better understanding. Although I prefer to use the term "Element-Action" in this book instead of "S-Field" I use both the terms for easy understanding of people who are already acquainted with the term "S-Field". From my research, some new types of elements (or substances) in Software/ IT environment are data, files, storage devices, networks, Internet, computers, devices, operating systems etc. Similarly the new types of actions (or fields) in Software/IT environment are triggers, digital signals, messages, broadcasts, compilations, interpretations, viral infections, compressions, encryptions, conversions etc.

A basic Element-Action (or S-Field) diagram should have good relationship between all its three components. If there is an absence of an element or an action then the problem may be solved by adding the missing element or the missing action. On the other hand if there are insufficient or harmful or undesirable interactions between its components, or there are detection or measurement problems or other such problems then the problem may be solved by applying the 76 Inventive standards.

In our context of computer viruses, we have a computer (S1) which is infected by virus (F). It is confusing whether to consider the virus as an element (or Substance) or as an action (or Field). In my consideration virus as a computer program should be considered as an element (substance). But virus as an execution of malicious code should be considered as an action (or Field).

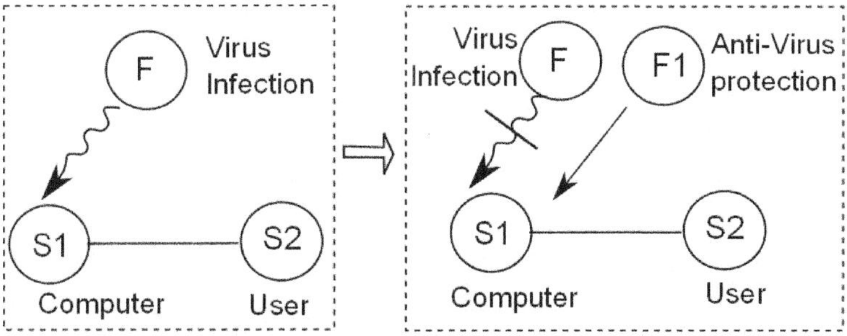

Element-Action (or S-Field) diagram showing
anti-virus protection against the harmful effects of Virus

In the above Element-Action model, the left side represents the problem model and right side represents the solution model. In the problem model we have a computer having negative effect (wavy line) from the virus. The double arrow in the center represents a transition from the old system to a new system. In the solution model we introduced an additional action (or Field) anti-virus, which neutralizes the negative effect of the virus on the computer. There can be several types of problem models and solution models, even many times more than described in conventional TRIZ books, which is beyond the scope of this book.

8.2 Using Inventive Standards for virus detection

Inventive Standards are like Inventive Principles that are used to solve standard problems or the problems that fall within the scope of generic problems. While the Principles are mostly used to resolve the contradictions, the Inventive standards are mostly used to solve problems when they are detected through Element-Action (S-Field) Modeling. While solving problems by Inventive Standards, there is no need to find a contradiction. The standards can be used in various situations such as to improve a system where there is no perceivable contradiction or to remove an undesired interaction between two elements (or substances or subsystems) etc.

There are 76 Inventive Standards divided in to 5 classes. Most of the Standards are applicable in improving our anti-virus system. Class-1.1: Construction of Element-Actions is useful for general improvement of anti-virus systems. Class-1.2: Destruction of Element-Actions is useful for removing "harmful" or "undesirable" interference of the virus. Class-2: Development of Element-Actions helps improving an anti-virus system. We will not describe all the Standards in this book (as that is being prepared as a separate book by the author) but we will present the relevant standards wherever applicable throughout the content of this book.

In this chapter we will discuss only "Class-4: Detection and Measurement Standards" which is useful for detection and measurement of anything, such as, viruses. As computer viruses are not directly visible the anti-virus researchers generally apply various techniques to detect them. While the clever viruses apply various stealth techniques to escape the detection techniques the anti-virus researchers must improve their scanning and detection techniques in order to detect the stealth viruses. Let's apply the Inventive Standards in Class-4 to improve our virus detection and measurement system.

8.3 Group 4.1. Applying alternative ways to avoid measurement and detection

Standard 4.1.1. If a problem involves detection or measurement, change the problem in such a way so that it will not need any detection or measurement.

- ⇨ Instead of detecting presence of viruses, better use a virus-proof Operating System or virus resistant Operating System so that there is no need of detecting viruses.
- ⇨ Instead of detecting presence of boot sector viruses, better use a ROM based booting so that there is no possibility of boot sector infections and therefore no need of detection.
- ⇨ Instead of checking macro viruses in Microsoft Word files better use .pdf files which are not subject to virus infection.

Standard 4.1.2. If it is not possible to avoid detection or measurement then detect the properties in a copy of the original object.

This Standard has some similarity with Inventive "Principle-26: Copying" as the detection is undertaken on a copy of the original object. The following invention is a good example.

INVENTION-4: Reducing scan load by scanning the data copied to another machine

Scanning of large number of files against large number of possible viruses consumes significant system resources and makes the computer slow. There is a need to solve this problem.

Patent 7644352 (invented by Grupe, assignee- McAfee, Inc., Jan 2010) suggests transferring data from the source computer to a second computer for scanning (Principle-26: Copying). The scanning computer scans the data and creates a log of suspicious files. The log file is then transferred to the source computer and the source computer scans only the suspicious data identified in the log file. This method avoids the need for a complete scan in the source computer thereby saves scanning time and load on the main computer.

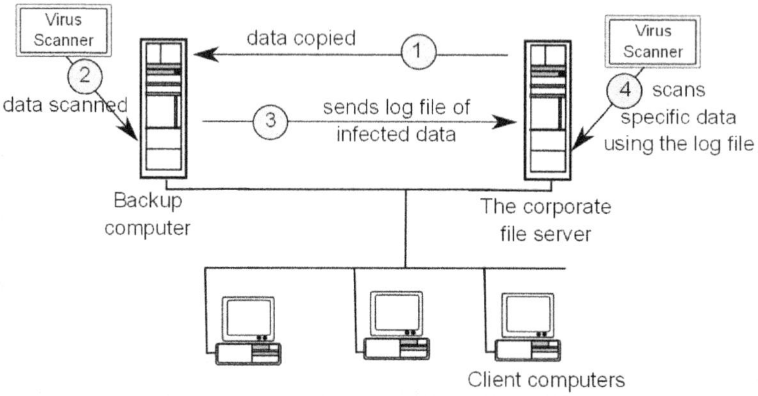

This invention is an example of applying Inventive Standard 4.1.2. which says "If measurement and detection is not possible in an object then measure a copy of the object." In our case scanning (measuring and detection) of viruses was not possible on the main computer because the main computer did not allow the scanning load. The invention implemented the scanning (measurement and detection) in the backup system which indirectly detects the infections on the main system. (Note: This is also an example of Inventive Standard 1.21, as the harmful effect of the scanner on the main computer is eliminated by introducing a backup computer.)

Standard 4.1.3. If it is not possible to avoid the need for measurement, and it is not possible to measure a copy of the object, then transform the problem into a problem of successive measurement of changes.

➪ Traffic anomaly based detection- when the worms self-replicate by sending probe packets to other elements in the network or communicate with each other; the network traffic pattern is affected. When a traffic detection program finds anomalous traffic that is different from the normal business pattern of the user then it suspects the presence of a virus.

8.4 Group 4.2. Synthesis of Measurement Systems

Standard 4.2.1. If a system is not easy to detect or measure then identify a different action (or Field) which is easily detectable and which is related to the parameters we need to detect or measure.

➪ Patent 8151073 suggests detecting viruses by analyzing hard disk LED activities. The invention compares the actual loading time of files with the expected loading time. If the actual loading time is longer than the expected loading time then a virus is suspected and an alarm is triggered. This method is a good example of TRIZ Inventive Standard 4.2.1. In this case, although a stealth virus is not detectable the invented method measures another detectable parameter (i.e., the LED activity) that is linked to the virus activity.

⇨ Detecting encrypted virus by its decryptor- as the viral body of the encrypted virus is encrypted, it is not visible to simple scanning. Decrypting the viral body is neither easy nor safe. But the virus can be detected by the signature of its decryptor that remains unchanged in every infection of the virus.

⇨ Behavior based malware detection- which considers any variation from the normal behavior of a program as suspicious. Although the presence of a malware is difficult to detect, the behavior of a program can be detected. This method is used in behavior analysis. For example if a program attempts to format a disk or requests a low level disk access or modifies system files or executable files, then the behavior based anti-virus program doubts about presence of a virus.

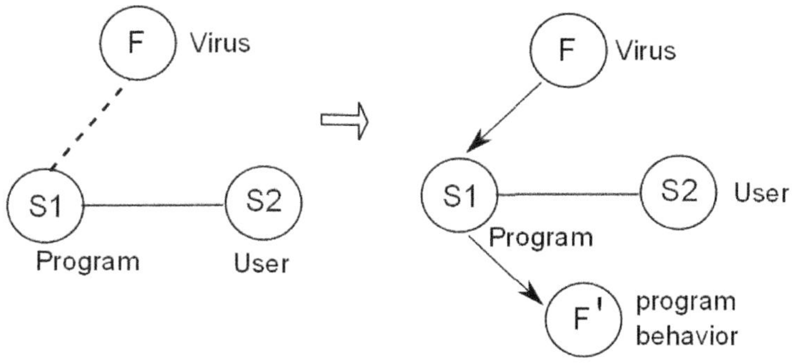

Detecting Program Behavior in Behavior Monitoring

⇨ Patent 7512982 shows the possibility of detecting computer viruses in a computer by looking at the presence of irregular data (Inventive Standard 4.2.1). As the virus infections in a computer network results in various irregular data, the invention uses a mechanism that collects irregular data and processes to find whether the irregularities represent a possibility of computer virus.

INVENTION-5: Detecting metamorphic viruses by using register signatures

As the metamorphic viruses change the instructions in their viral body with each infection they are not detectable by conventional methods of signature scanning. Patent 7409717 (invented by Peter Szor, Assignee- Symantec Corporation, Aug. 2008) uses a virus detection system (VDS) which uses register signatures to detect metamorphic and other types of viruses.

According to the method the virus program is executed in a virtual machine having a virtual processor, virtual memory and virtual registers. During execution of an infected program the virus has to store different values in the virtual registers. The method analyses the register values to decide whether the file contains any malicious code.

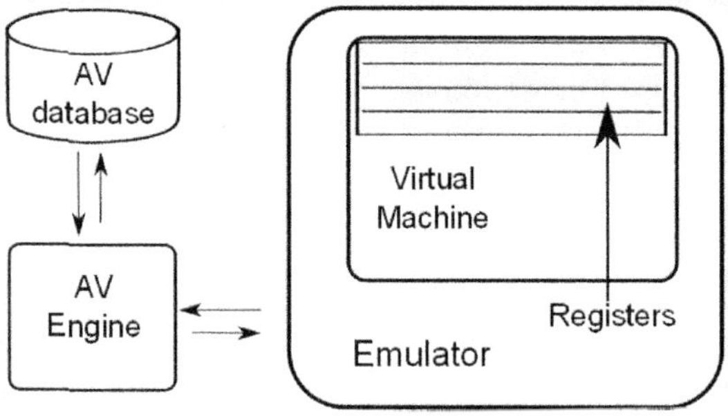

Virus Detection System (VDS)

This is a good example of inventive standards 4.2.1. As it is not possible to detect the metamorphic viruses, we have to find another parameter in the system that is measurable and at the same time linked with the activities of the virus. The Element-Action model of the problem looks as below.

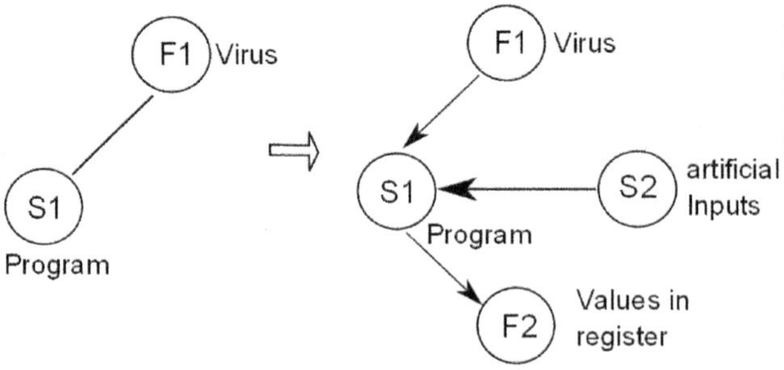

Detecting Metamorphic Virus by using
Register Signatures - Standard 4.2.1

The invention finds that the register values (i.e., outputs) are dependent upon the input values. Even the code-altering metamorphic viruses produce specific register values when given a specific set of inputs. The register values are then examined by a virus reporting module whether they contain any register signature stored in the virus database module. If a register signature matches then the selected file probably contains a virus.

Standard 4.2.2. Include an easy to detect element (or substance) in the system to form an Internal or External Complex S-Field

This method suggests introducing some additives to the present element (or substance) (thereby making an internal complex S-Field) or introducing a new external element (or substance) (thereby making an external complex S-Field) to help detection and measurement. The following is an example of internal complex measuring S-Field that helps detecting virus infections.

INVENTION-6: Feeding diagnostic objects during compilation to detect virus infection

Ideally a computer file/program itself should say whether it is infected or not. For example there should be something in the file that should show changes when the file is infected. But normally there is nothing in a file that shows an infection so easily. By applying Inventive Standard 4.2.2, we can insert some detectable parameters into a file that shall show up changes when infected.

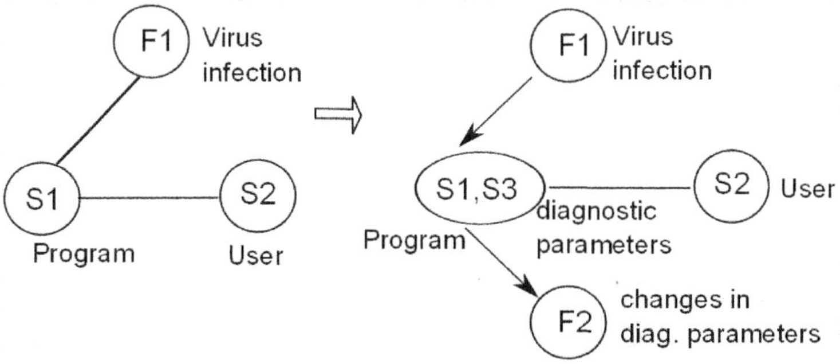

Feeding Diagnostic Objects into Programs
for Detecting Viruses - Standard 4.2.2

Patent 5881151 (invented by Yamamoto, assignee Fujitsu Limited, March 1999) suggests to feed some diagnostic objects to the program at the time of compilation. The diagnostic objects include program size, Checksum, Revision Information, Disk Address, Object Program etc.

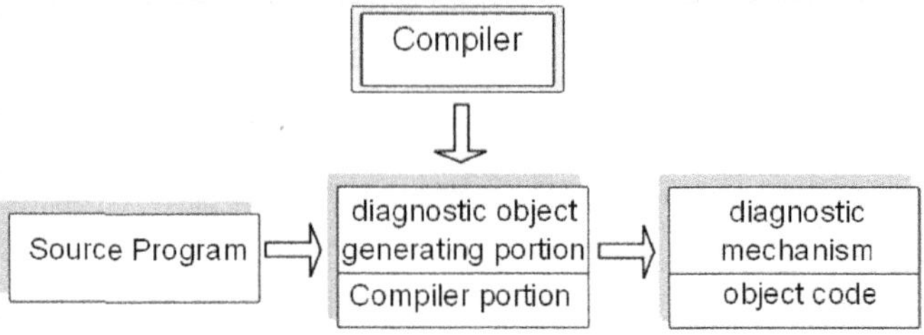

Inserting disgnostic objects in the program during compilation

When the program is infected with a virus its diagnostic parameters (such as, program size, checksum etc.) changes. When a difference is found between the original parameters (fed inside the program) and actual parameters (checked during detection), the method easily diagnoses that the program is infected. This method detects an infection quickly without waiting for obtaining virus signatures or definitions from external sources.

⇨ Deploying anti-viral viruses is also a similar example that creates an external complex SFM to help measurement. When the anti-viral virus infects or is infected by bad viruses its parameters are changed which informs about the presence of bad viruses.

INVENTION-7: Using counter viruses for detecting viral replication

Patent 6813712 (invented by Luke, assignee International Business Machines Corporation, Nov 2004) provides a beneficial counter virus for detecting virus infection in a computer system.

The counter virus attaches itself to other files for replication just like other viruses. But the counter virus maintains a predetermined population level by self-destructing or infecting other files depending on the population level. In this way the population is maintained unless the counter virus infects another (unauthorized) virus, in which case the replication mechanism of the unauthorized virus overcomes the population control mechanism of the counter virus. This resulting increment in the population reveals the existence of the unknown virus.

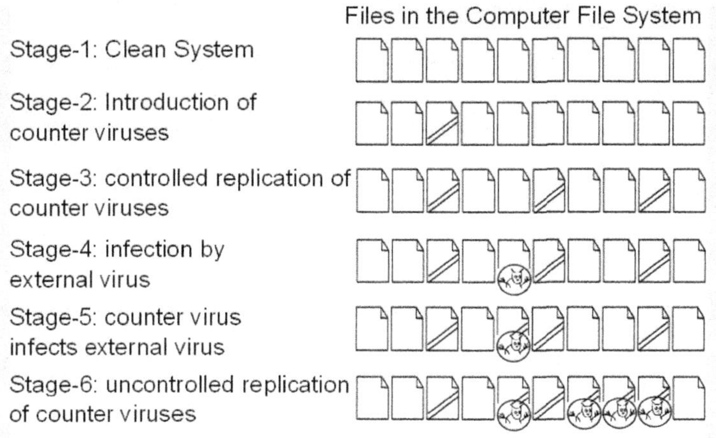

Virus detection by
uncontrolled repliation of counter viruses

This invention can be viewed from a perspective of Inventive Standard 4.2.2 which says that, if a system does not provide detection or measurement, we can solve it by transiting to an internal or external complex measurement SFM. In the previous example we had created an internal complex measurement SFM by adding diagnostic parameters into the programs. In the current example we are creating an external complex measurement SFM by introducing anti-viral viruses into the system (which are external to the program unlike the diagnostic parameters which were internal).

⇨ One of the difficulties to detect the viruses is that they are very small in size such as in bytes. Patent 5684875 (invented by Hans Ellenberger, Nov 1997) discloses a polymorphic protection method that encourages the virus writers to increase their code size. When the size of the viruses increases they are easily detected. (Inventive Standard 4.2.2. Add something in the element or. substance to help detection).

Standard 4.2.3. Introduce an easily detected additive in the external environment to detect and measure the effects on that additive

⇨ Deploying baits, traps, honey pots (such as bait computers, bait servers, bait ports, bait packets , bait files etc.) in a network to detect presence of viruses (Inventive Standard 4.2.3.). The baits work secretly and keep providing information about harmful viruses. While the parameters of viruses are difficult to detect and measure, the parameters of baits and traps are easy to measure as they are specially created for that purpose.

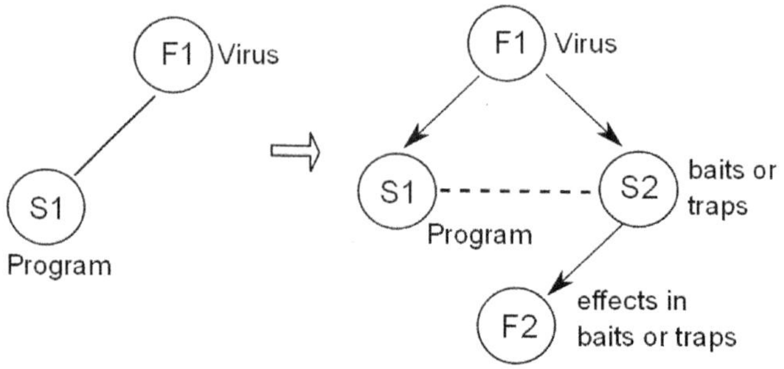

Deploying baits or traps
for Virus Detection - Standard 4.2.3

➯ Patent 8181249 (invented by Chow et al, assignee- Alcatel Lucent, May 2012) detects worms by sending bait packets. It is expected that the compromised hosts when receive the bait packets will try to probe the sending hosts. This behavior of the worms would reveal their presence.

INVENTION-8: Identifying the offending clients in a network by using a promiscuous bait server

Patent 7089589 (invented by Chefalas et al., assignee Lenovo (Singapore) Pte. Ltd., Aug 2006) suggests to introduce a bait server, wherein the bait server's address is not published to the clients in the network (TRIZ Principle-32: Color Change). As the bait server's address is not published no system should try to access the bait server in normal situations. Hence, any attempt to access the bait server would indicate the presence of a virus on the system that is attempting the access.

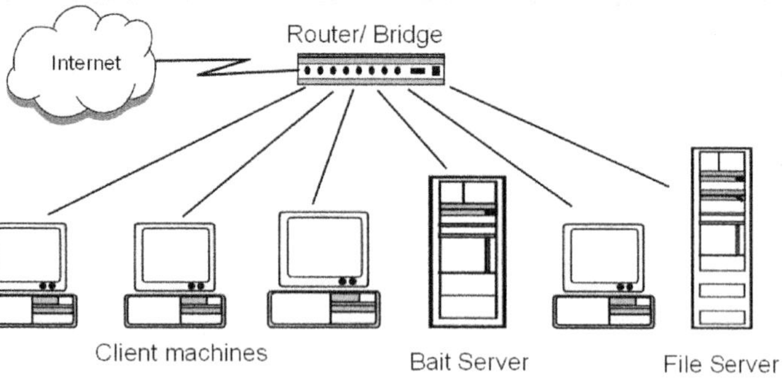

Deplyoing a Bait Server in a Network

Unlike conventional methods the approach here is not to search for the infected system; rather whichever system tries to communicate with the bait server is identified as the infected system. Thus the bait server automatically identifies the offending client (TRIZ Principle-25: Self service), directs the local server to disconnect the offending system from the network (TRIZ Principle-2: Taking out) and notifies the network administrator to take appropriate action to disinfect the offending client.

⇨ How to detect the computers in a network that don't have adequate security measures or which are not configured according to the network security policy? Patent 6205551 (described later) suggests inserting a probe to detect such computers in a computer network. The probe is configured as a Trojan horse. If any client computer has insufficient security then the probe (Trojan horse) will get into the computer and execute a security alert indicating that the client is vulnerable to a security breach.

Standard 4.2.4. If it is not possible to introduce additives in the external environment then change something that is already there in the environment so that the effects in the environment can be detected and measured

This method suggests using the existing environment for detection and measurement by changing something that is already there in the environment. For example, the following invention detects presence of viruses by analyzing changes in registry entries and/or file attributes. If the number of changes exceed to a threshold then the method suspects a virus infection.

INVENTION-9: Detecting viruses in a network by analyzing changes in file attributes

Patent 7779474 (invented by Garbow, et al, assignee- Trend Micro Incorporated, Aug 2010) discloses a method of detecting virus in a network by analyzing the changes in registry entries and/or in file attributes.

According to the invention, a watch controller program in the client computers take a count of events when a new file is added or an attribute of a file is changed or a registry entry is added, changed or deleted. The watch controller sends these events to a monitor in the network. The information may include the name of the file or entry, date of creation or modification, file type, size, modifying entity and other appropriate data.

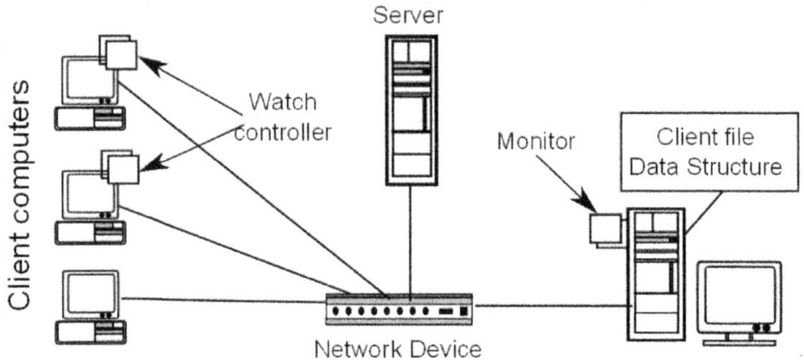

A monitor taking control of changes in the attributes in client computers in a network

When such notifications exceed to a threshold, the monitor suspects virus infection and sends warning to the watch controllers in the clients. The warning may prompt the clients to delete or rename the file or registry entry, or run an anti-virus program, or quarantine the file or registry entry, or issue a message etc.

➪ Detecting the source of virus-epidemic based on connection strength co-efficient (Patent 7743419)- the connection strength is calculated by the number and quality of connection channels between different geographical locations. This can detect the location of network worms during early stages of their outbreak.

8.5 Group-4.3. Methods of Improving Measurement Systems

Standard 4.3.1. Make use of physical effects or other effects present in the system to help the measurement

Standard 4.3.2. If changes in the system cannot be detected then introduce resonance vibration in the system such that the resulting frequency can be measured

Standard 4.3.3. If resonance vibration cannot be introduced in the system then use a subsystem or something that is already there in the environment and measure the changes in its frequency to make the measurement

INVENTION-10: Detection and prevention of virus outbreaks

The conventional signature scanning and heuristic scanning cannot detect new viruses or new types of viruses having new behavior. There is a need to detect and control the outbreak of new viruses.

Patent 6886099 (invented by Smithson, et al., assignee Networks Associates Technology, Apr 2005) detects virus outbreaks by measuring certain measurement parameters from the external environment such as, “how many e-mail messages are sent having an identical message title”, “how many emails are sent with identical file attachment”, “how many emails are sent having attachments of a given type”, “how many emails are sent having attachments of executable files”, and “the overall email throughput within the computer system”.

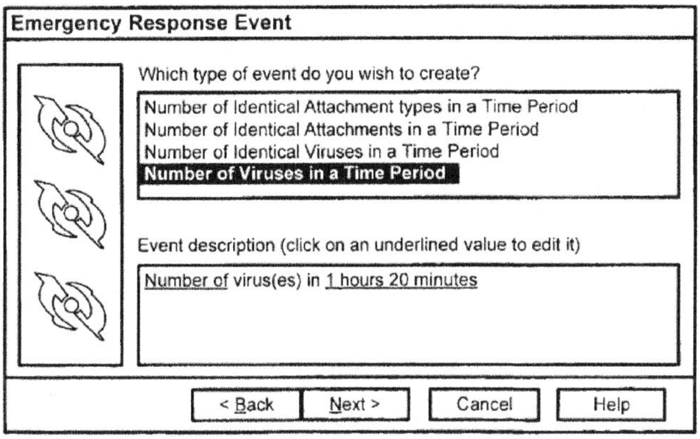

According to the invention, if the selected measurement parameters cross a respective predetermined threshold level, within the given measurement period, the system signals the outbreak of a computer virus.

This is a case of standard 4.3.3, which says if it is not possible to directly measure the change, the state of the system can be determined by a change in the natural frequency of the external environment connected with the system.

Group 4.4. Introduce ferromagnetic elements (or substances) either in the system or in its surroundings, and use a magnetic action (or Field) to help detection and measurement

8.6 Group 4.5. Evolution of measurement systems

Standard 4.5.1. Efficiency of measurement may be improved by using evolutions in the line of mono-bi-poly transitions

➪ For example the efficiency of measurement may be increased by following the mono-bi-poly trend which says using multiple scanning techniques like signature scanning, integrity checking, heuristic scanning, HMM#, data mining## etc. is more effective than using one single technique like signature scanning.

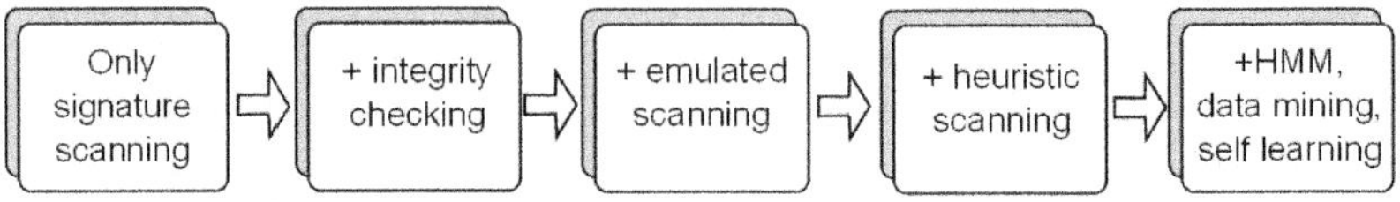

Trend - Mono-Bi-Poly Transitions

➪ If a malware has taken control of the OS then an integrity checker may not work because the suspect OS may report manipulated file properties. Patent 7627898 suggests obtaining file properties through more than one methods and compare. The detection system may compare the reported properties generated by a high-level scan with the reported properties generated by a low-level scan using the same suspect operating system. This comparison can identify if a malware has changed the behavior of the high level commands but has not modified the behavior of low level commands (Mono-Bi-Poly Transitions).

HMM (Hidden Markov Model) is a statistical technique where the states remain hidden, only the outputs dependent on the states are visible.

Data mining is a method of detecting patterns in large amount of data and using these patterns to detect future instances of similar data.

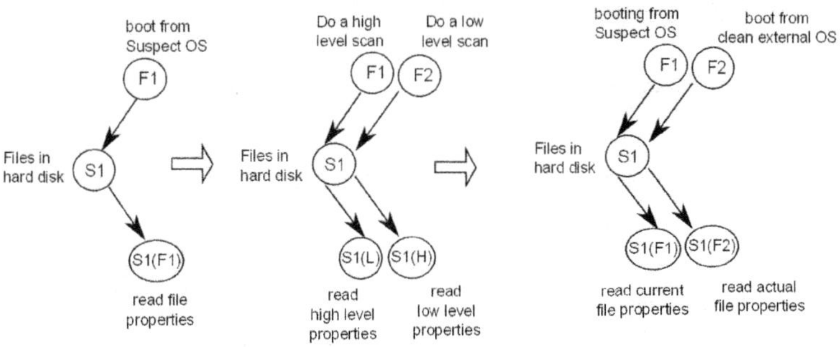

Getting file properties through one, two and more methods

For more reliable detection, the system may initially boot from the suspect OS to get current file properties and then subsequently boot from a clean external OS to get the actual file properties. If a comparison shows any difference then the suspect OS is deemed to be infected. (Note: The trends of evolution are discussed in detail in the next chapter.)

Standard 4.5.2. Measurement systems evolve in the direction → measuring a function → measuring the first derivative of the function → measuring the second derivative of the function etc.

Some of the 76 Inventive Standards are not useful for Software problems; particularly those which are based on thermal and magnetic Fields. As they are originally developed for technical/ mechanical Domains they need to be suitably modified in order to be applicable in other Domains. As we saw in this chapter, the Standards of class 4 are quite useful for detection and measurement of viruses in a system. The applications of many other Standards are illustrated in other examples throughout the book.

Chapter 9.

Trends in the Evolution of Viruses and Anti-Viruses

9.1 The philosophy of Trends

According to TRIZ, every system, product and process evolve over time. They start with an infancy, go through their youth and reach to a maturity. Altshuller finds four periods of a system, viz., selection of parts for a system, improvement of its parts, dynamization of the system, self-improvement of the system (Altshuller, "And Suddenly the Inventor Appeared"). This knowledge helps us predicting the future stage of the system thereby enabling us to make new inventions. New inventions help a system to grow in its desired direction. The philosophy of evolution is based on the following axioms.

- ✓ Evolution is a natural, continuous and inevitable process. We can accelerate or decelerate certain stages of evolution but we cannot stop evolution.
- ✓ Evolution is a desirable phenomenon as higher evolution leads to better products with higher efficiency.
- ✓ The evolution always moves towards the ideal stage of a product. Telling differently every stage of evolution carries a product one step towards its ideality.
- ✓ Not only the system but also the super-system and sub-systems evolve to reach their ideal stages. However, the evolution of every system or subsystems is not even.

- ✓ Sometimes during the process of evolution some systems or sub-systems merge with other systems or super-systems and thereby disappear.
- ✓ Sometimes new systems and/or subsystems are created to introduce new functionalities into the product during evolution.
- ✓ Two contradictory trends in an evolution lead to a class in future and a solution in due course of time.
- ✓ Analysis of a large number of high-level inventions shows that there are some laws that govern these patterns evolutions. The patterns of evolutions can be different for different systems.
- ✓ We can predict the future of technological systems, products and solutions by applying the trends of technology evolutions.

Like Inventive Principles and Inventive Standards, the Trends of Evolution are also derived from a large number of empirical observations of technical samples. Like other techniques of TRIZ the theory of Trends also move from specific observation (of evolution of individual products/ systems) → generalization (finding laws governing the Trends of Evolution) → generic solution (application of Trends of Evolution) → specific solution (predicting the future of a product in the line of evolution).

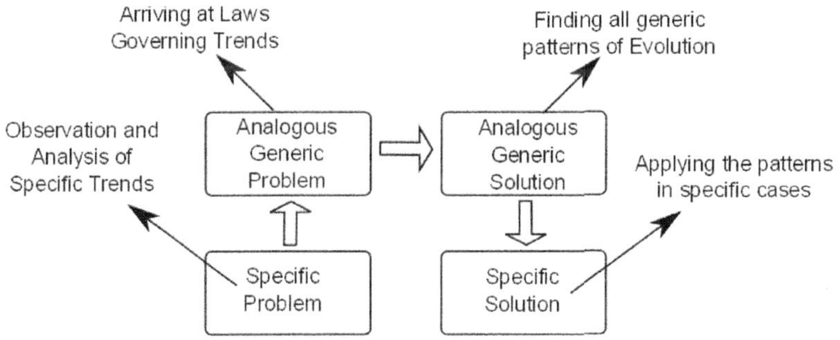

The TRIZ Approach and Trends

According to TRIZ the same set of trends are repetitively applied in all the evolutions again and again. Hence, use of the trends can give us valuable clue about the future stages of a product or system.

9.1.1 Application of Trends of Evolution in Software

"Trends of Evolution" is a powerful tool for technical problem solving, forecasting and designing. As the "theory of trends" is meant for all manmade systems it also works perfectly for software and IT systems. Like mechanical systems the evolutions are also inevitable for software systems. The software evolutions also follow certain patterns whether we know them or not. During evolution, some systems evolve in opposite directions, which result in extinction of weaker systems and emergence of new powerful systems.

As the problems are related to specific systems, it is interesting to observe that many new problems are automatically created and many old problems are automatically vanished because of the changes that take place during the process of evolution. For example;

- The text based user interface was replaced by graphical user interface (GUI) and the text based operating systems like DOS was replaced by GUI based operating systems like Windows. These changes in the system during the process of evolution led most DOS based viruses to see their grave.
- Growing usage of computers led to growing demand for storage space. This led to production of higher capacity storage devices. This resulted in obsolescence of floppy disks and floppy drives. These changes in the system led to extinction of many viruses that were specifically created around usage of floppies.
- The growing need for information sharing led to interconnecting computers through networks. The increasing popularity and usage of Internet has boosted the virus writers to create more viruses/worms for the Internet. The line of evolution is moving from floppy based viruses to →computer-based viruses to →network based viruses to →Internet based viruses.
- Increase in the Internet bandwidth has not only made communication faster but also made virus outbreaks easier than ever. The future days may see more sudden and virulent virus outbreaks through Internet.
- The IT industry is moving towards information openness. While the earlier techniques were mostly proprietary and confidential, the current techniques involves many patents and publications. However there are still a lot of confidential tricks involved in anti-virus techniques which are expected to be more open in future.

9.1.2 Laws governing the Trends of Evolution

According to TRIZ the Trends of Evolution are governed by some laws. It is important to know these laws as this knowledge can help us understanding and applying the trends more accurately. The following are the laws governing the trends of technology evolution.

- Increasing degree of Ideality- Every system moves towards its ideal final stage. In other words, every stage of evolution moves a system one step closer to the ideal system. Hence a future stage of a product has to be more ideal (e.g., intelligent, faster, automated, more powerful, more functionality etc. requiring less cost, less maintenance, less failure, less energy consumption etc.) If we know the characteristics of the Ideal product then all the imaginary interim stages can be forecasted as the future stages of evolution of that product.

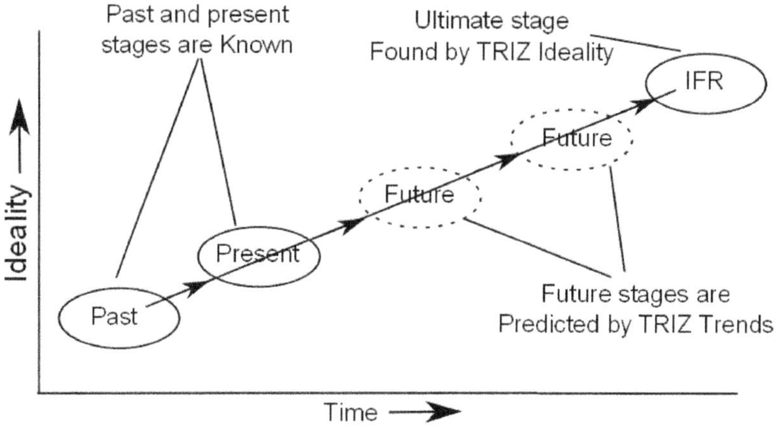

Prediction of future stages using Trends

- Increasing main useful function (MUF)- all improvements of any product or system revolve around its MUF and ensure that the MUF is improved in every stage of evolution. For example, the main useful function of an anti-virus program is to protect the computer from viruses.

- Moving from complicated system to simplified system- although systems become complicated in short term, they cannot go beyond a certain level of complicacy. When a system becomes over complicated it is divided into smaller systems or replaced by simpler systems.

- Increasing completeness and non-uniformity of evolution- every technical system consists of subsystems like engine, body parts, control system etc. Every part of the system evolves to reach their ideal stage. But every part of the system doesn't evolve uniformly.

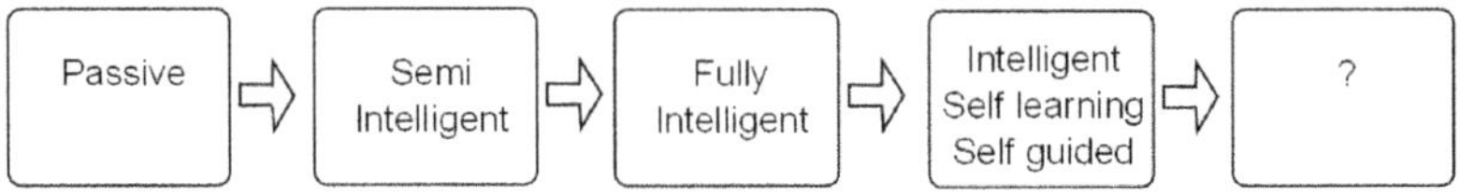

Trend - Increasing Smartness/ Intelligence

- Division and merging of systems- generally larger systems are broken into smaller systems or subsystems. This way the number of subsystems is increased. But then the redundant subsystems are eliminated which reduces the number of subsystems. But again new components or subsystems are added to introduce new functionality, which increase number of subsystems. Again subsystems get merged with co-systems or super-systems which reduces their number. The process continues in cyclic order.

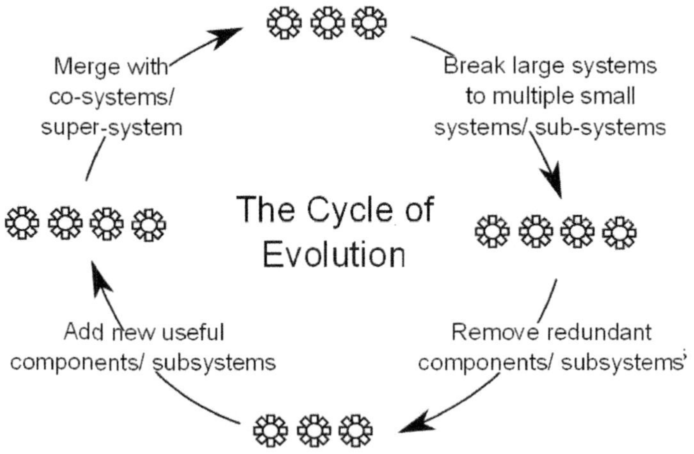

Continuous Repeatition of Addition, Removal, Division and Merging

- Evolution from macro to nano: larger components are replaced with smaller components and smaller components are replaced with micro components, which makes a system smaller and lighter. But the system again becomes larger when new sub-systems are added for including new functionalities and the process continues in cyclic order.

- Increasing degree of dynamization and automation- systems of rigid structure move to dynamic and flexible structure in order to improve performance. Manual system become automated and automated systems become self-controlled.

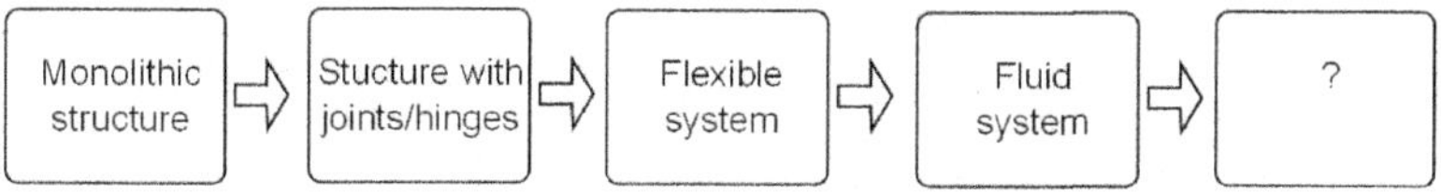

Trend - Increasing Dymamization

Trend - Increasing Automation

- Increasing degree of coordination- better coordination improves harmony between sub-systems and improves performance of the system. Thus every stage of an evolution witnesses better coordination between the subsystems in a system.

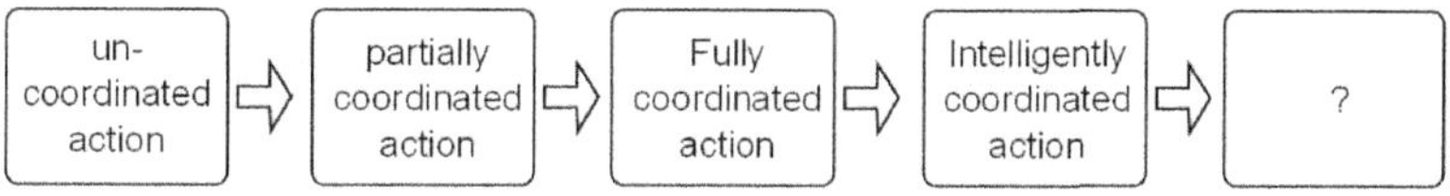

Trend - Increasing Coordination

The above are the laws governing the trends of evolution. Almost all the trends are governed by the above laws except some exceptional cases. The actual number of patterns in the evolution are neither fixed nor known, they are still under development by different TRIZ researchers. Besides the patterns in one field (say mechanical or electronics) can be somewhat different from the patterns in another field (say social or economic).

9.1.3 How to use the Trends of Evolution

Trends of evolution are used to predict the future stages of a product. This is useful mostly in product designing and sometimes in problem solving. When we don't know any trends we take random decisions by trial and error that may fail. But when we know the trends of evolution we take decisions in the right direction. This is like knowing the movement of the your opponent in the chess of in advance. If you can well predict the movements of your opponent there is a fair chance of winning the game.

When you know the trends of technology evolution you can foresee the shape, size, height, weight, look, function, feature and many characteristics of your future product. If you know so many things about your hypothetical future product it is more likely that you could design the right product. If you had not known anything about your future product you would have thought in random directions landing in chaos and futility.

When we know the trends, Ideality and main useful function we can confidently forecast the future stages of our product. For example, if our design is closer to the ideal final product and improving the main useful function then we can say that our design is in the right direction.

The patterns are derived from the life cycles of the products. The life cycles are represented by s-curves. The four main stages of S-curve are infancy, rapid growth, maturity and old age. The study of trends helps us predict the maturity of the current s-curve and find a new s-curve to extend the life of the product.

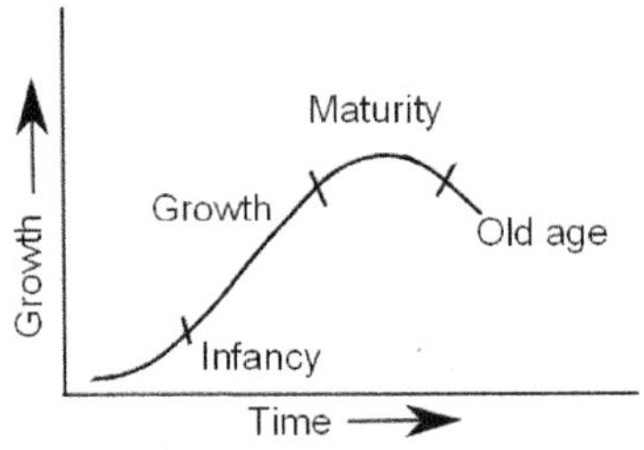

S-Curve

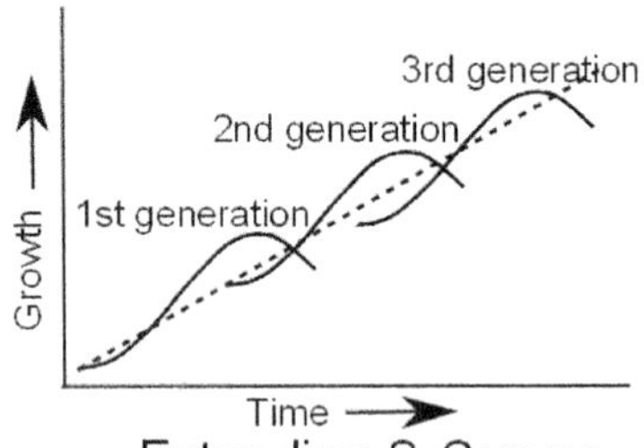

Extending S-Curves

Besides the trends of evolution can explore the undiscovered customer needs of the future. This helps us to build the next generation products that are more appropriate and advanced. Better products become more successful and bring us more competitive advantage.

9.2 Trends in the evolution of Computer Viruses

Viruses are also products like anti-viruses. They too use computer technology. They too have a life cycle. They too go through the process of evolution. It is important to know the evolution of viruses in order to foresee the features and functions of the future viruses. The knowledge of future viruses can guide us to develop the future anti-virus. Let's have a look at the trends of evolution of computer viruses.

A- Moving towards Ideality

Increasing functionality and capability

Virus must replicate	+ escape from detection by anti-virus programs	+ attack and paralyze the anti-virus and OS	+ send valuable data to the virus creator	+ all good's for the creator and all bad's for the user

In theory the viruses could evolve to a level where a virus would be able to export a polymorphic or metamorphic engine of itself for use in another virus or worm. Similarly, viruses would be able to exchange trigger routines and appear in newer combinations. This sounds superficial but the technology is out there to support these kinds of models[#].

Improved technology

Stealth techniques like encryption	+ Metamor-phism- self modifying techniques	+ Anti-emulation techniques	+ Anti-heuristic techniques	+ Totally flexible and totally undetectable

Floppy based viruses	Computer based viruses	Network based viruses	Internet viruses, spreading to mobile devices	Viruses everywhere?

[#] Peter Szor, "The Art of Computer Virus Research and Defence"

B- Transition from one to many

Increasing number of viruses

Few hundred viruses in eighties	Few thousand viruses in nineties	About a million viruses at present	More number of viruses in future	Uncountable number of viruses

Increasing number of sources and channels

Released through one channel from one source by the creator	Release through multiple channels by the creator	Multiple versions released through multiple sources and channels	Multiple versions by multiple people through multiple sources and channels	→

Increasing methods of infection

File virus (affecting only file)	Multipartite virus (infecting files and boot sector)	Multipartite worms (extending through network)	→	Using various methods/ channels for infection

Infecting increasing types of files

Infecting only to executable files	Infecting Microsoft office files (by macro viruses)	→	Infecting pdf, jpg and other inactive files	Infecting all possible types of files

C- Increasing complexity

Increasing complexity in stealthiness

Simple virus	Multipartite virus	encrypted virus	metamorphic virus	Totally undetectable virus (?)

Increasing complexity in virus structure

Encrypted viruses	Encrypted+ Oligomorphic viruses	Encrypted+ Polymorphic viruses	Metamorphic viruses (mutating virus code)	Mutating its own code and code of the host program

If the virus can mutate the code of the host program then it will generate innumerable number of virus forms. The whole computer may change and the user may still be able to work, a complete nightmare for any anti-virus.

Extension of Metamorphism

Metamorph-ism under DOS environment	Metamorph-ism under Windows	Metamorp-ism under every platform	→	Metamorph-ism everywhere
Metamorph-ism in file infector viruses	Metamorph-ism in macro viruses	Metamorph-ism in worms and other viruses	→	Metamor-phism in every type of virus

D- Increasing Dynamization

Spreading of Viruses from computers to Networks to Global

Stay within one computer	Spread to other computers in the LAN	Go out of LAN to spread through the Internet	Spread through multiple methods and multiple channels	Spread across the whole world

Increasing flexibility in structure

Static viral body	Dynamic decryptor & static body (Polymorphic virus)	Random polymorphic virus	Totally Dynamic body (Metamor-phic virus)	Code building virus (forming out of the host program)

Increasing speed of Infection

Slow moving viruses	Fast moving viruses	Moving through emails and Internet	Very fast moving viruses causing viral outbreaks	Viral explosion ?

E- Increasing Smartness/ Intelligence

Increasing capability to escape detection

Simple virus - no intelligence to escape scanning	Intelligence to escape signature scanning	Intelligence to detect emulated environment and escape emulation	Intelligence to escape heuristic scanning	Intelligence to escape any type of scanning and detection method

Increasing knowledge about other viruses

Does not recognize other viral infections	Recognizes patterns of its own infection to other files	Recognizes infection of other viruses of same family	Recognizes infections of viruses of other families	Recognizes infections of all types of viruses, worms, rootkits etc.

The intelligence of a virus to recognize other viruses can help it to coordinate and collaborate with other viruses. The trend of increasing knowledge about other viruses indicates a possibility of increasing inter-virus coordination in future. Think of a future possibility when viruses of same family or of different families talk together to launch a coordinated attack on a computer or on an anti-virus system!

Improved infection strategy

Infection by Replication of viral code	EPO (Entry Point Obscuring) infection	→	→	Building viruses out of the host program

Entry point obscuring viruses don't change the typical entry points of the host programs. Instead they change the program code somewhere in such a way that the virus gets control.

Code building is a technique to scan the availability of the virus codes in a host program and then integrate those codes to build the virus. This is a fantastic example of using TRIZ Resources. The code-building virus, instead of having its own separate code, can build a virus out of a genuine program or available codes on a computer.

F- Increasing coordination

Coordination between viruses

Simple Trojan horses	Trojan horses creating back doors	Rootkits protecting backdoors from detection	Capability to understand and communicate future viruses	Coordination between viruses created by different virus writers

Communication between viruses

Worms communi-cating between themselves	Worms communi-cating between different computers	Different types of worms communi-cating between themselves	Simple Worm communi-cation Protocol (SWCP)	Communi-cation between any type of worms/ viruses/ malware

Merging of functionalities

Trojan horse	Trojan with a dropper	Trojan with a rootkit	Trojan with a backdoor	Trojan with a rootkit and backdoor

Some recent viruses are capable of coordinating with each other (although to limited extent). For example, some viruses are being bundled with "rootkits". The rootkits replace the standard operating system tools with altered tools and provide safe shelter to the viruses by helping them to remain hidden and undetected.

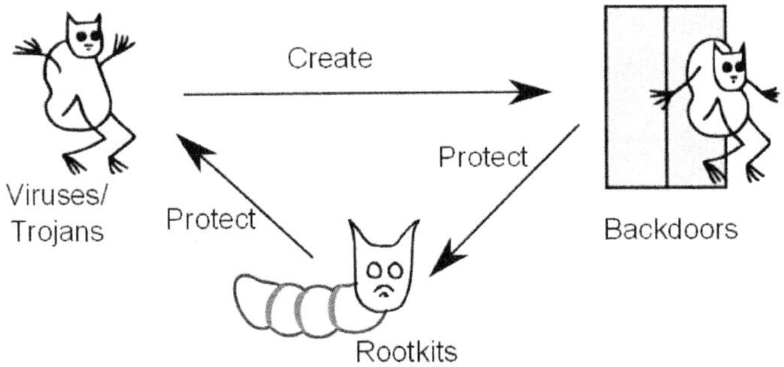

More coordination between the viruses is more likely to be seen in future. Some viruses will intentionally create very minute alterations in a system that is difficult to detect but sufficient to create security holes for the future viruses. (An example of TRIZ Principle-10: Prior Action). The future generations of those viruses are expected to exploit those security holes to control the system and cause new type of harm.

H- Increasing automation

Increasing automation in creating viruses

Writing code for a new virus from scratch	Copy an existing virus and modify the code	Use a virus creation tool or virus construction kit	Automated creation of new viruses by viruses themselves	Creating new breeds by mating one type of virus with other

The future viruses may be capable of creating new breeds by mating one type of virus with other, similar to male female conjugation in biological reproduction system.

Increasing automation in transfer of viral code

Carrying infected floppy or media by humans	Movement of infected files by email/ downloads	Automated sending of viral code through emails	Automatic transfer of viral code by worms	→

Increasing automation in triggering an infection

Executing infected file by double clicking the executable	Clicking the zip file or email attachment	Just clicking ok for an infected download	Drive-by Infection without user's confirmation	Pushed infection

Thus we see that the future viruses are going to be more smart and intelligent. They will have multiple complex functions and power to escape the current detection techniques. The future may see more "Trojan horse" type of viruses, because they are not only difficult to be detected but also fully capable of doing anything on a computer. They can open backdoors, transmit confidential data, format the hard disk and can even create new viruses. The future may see more drive-by infections and infections by pushed technology. There is a possibility that the viruses can do virtually anything that is possible on a computer.

9.3 Trends in computing environment

As we discussed earlier every system is evolving for maturity. This is true for viruses, anti-viruses and even for their super-systems such as hardware, software and operating systems. For example, according to Moore's law (Moore was the co-founder of Intel) the CPU speed doubles in every two years. The capacity of a computer in terms of memory, storage and processing increases exponentially in each generation.

The evolution of every system or subsystem has impact on its adjacent systems. While evolution of anti-virus system has impact on its adjacent systems, the evolution of its adjacent systems also has effect on the anti-virus system. For example, improving the speed of a processor will automatically improve the speed of virus scanning. Similarly popularity of mobile devices will attract virus creators to create viruses for such devices. Some relevant evolutions in the computing environment are as follows.

Increasing user awareness

Virus unaware users	Virus aware users	Virus and anti-virus aware users	Virus and anti-virus educated users	Fully educated users

User awareness can prevent virus infection through various hygienic habits. For example, a smart user can recognize the social engineering techniques used by virus emails. Let's examine a suspicious mail with a .zip attachment that came to my email address (below).

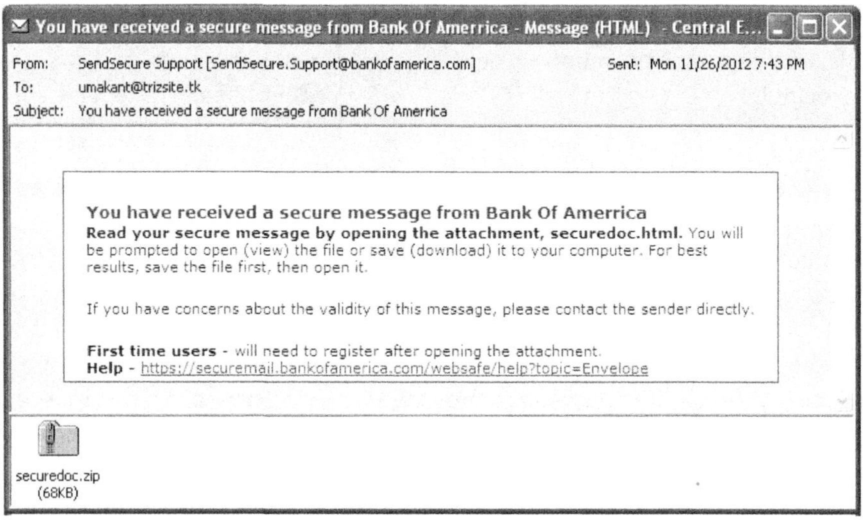

The above email looks like a genuine email. But I could know it to be a malicious mail using some heuristics. For example, (i) I have no account or transaction with Bank Of America, (ii) the Help link given in the mail does not internally point to bankofamerica.com but to a very different URL, (iii) I don't use the above email but a different email for financial purposes etc. But if I had an account with this bank and if I had used the same email address for this bank then the email might have succeeded to fool me and make me open the attachment.

Improvements in operating systems

OS with known flaws for virus attack	OS with patches and updates for known flaws	OS with unknown flaws	OS with prevention for unknown flaws	OS with no possible flaws or vulnerability

As we have discussed in Chapter-3, the loopholes in the operating system is one of the important reasons of virus invasion. The trend of evolution shows better operating systems with fewer flaws and therefore indicates lesser chances of virus proliferation.

Increasing speed of processor

The old x86 processors	Pentium processors	Pentium Dual processors with GHz	→	→

The increasing speed and capacity of the computer hardware reduces the negative effect of anti-virus software on system performance.

Increasing capacity of data storage

Hard disks (MBs)	Hard Disk (GBs)	Network storage devices (TBs)	→	→

Floppies 1.2 MB	CDs 700 MB	DVDs 4.7 GB	HD DVD 15-30 GB	Blu-ray 50 GB

Reduced usage of floppies has greatly eliminated *boot sector viruses* that were predominantly spreading through floppies. There are many such trends in the computing and software technology, which has natural effects on both virus and anti-virus systems.

9.4 Trends in the evolution of anti-virus

The evolution of computer hardware and software technology paves the path for more powerful software and user friendlier interfaces. The anti-virus system also evolves along with its co-systems and super-systems. Let's discuss some useful trends in the evolution of anti-virus programs.

A- Moving towards Ideality

It may be useful to go back to the earlier chapter on "Ideality" and repeat the IFRs of an anti-virus system because the future anti-virus programs must strive to be closer to the ideal anti-virus and strive to achieve the following IFRs as much as possible.

IFR The anti-virus should not allow any virus to enter into the computer. Even if a virus enters it should be detected and destroyed as soon as possible.

IFR The anti-virus program should be available free of cost or at least at low price. The upgrading or renewal charges should be minimal.

IFR The anti-virus program should be easy to install and easy to maintain. The anti-virus program should scan at very fast speed without consuming high amount of system resources... etc.

Note: Although the ultimate goal is a "no virus" environment, it is not possible to achieve unless there are substantial changes in the super-systems. Hence the future anti-viruses can be predicted to achieve a higher degree of IFRs and ensure a "reduced virus environment" or a "controlled virus environment".

Increasing Accuracy of Detection

Less false positives and false negatives	→	→	No false positive or false negative	Exact detection of all the viruses

Increasing Openness of Systems

Secret techniques	Patented techniques + proprietary techniques	Patented + publicly documented + proprietary techniques	→	Fully open (either patented or publicly documented)

Open systems (like Linux, GNU projects etc.) are less vulnerable as so many people scrutinize their codes that the faults are likely to be discovered by somebody or other.

B- Transition from one to many

Increasing methods of scanning techniques

Only signature scanning	+ Integrity checking	+ Emulated scanning	+ Heuristic scanning	→

The above is applicable even for specific techniques. For example,

Static heuristic scanning	Static + Emulation = dynamic heuristic	Static + Dynamic heuristic = hybrid	+ Data mining + automatic learning = Intelligent systems	Fully intelligent Expert systems

Increasing number of virus signatures

Hundreds of signatures	Thousands of signatures	100,000 or more signatures (50-100 MB signature file)	More signatures, larger signature file	More ?

There are two intersecting trends, one is increasing number of virus signatures and another is increasing speed of scanning. This contradiction will pose more and more challenges for anti-virus developers in future.

C- Increasing Complexity

Evolution of signature scanning

Simple scanning of virus signatures	Signature scanning with wildcard characters	Signature scanning in emulated environment	Signature scanning with dynamic heuristic scanning	→

Evolution of heuristic scanning

Static heuristic scanning	Static heuristics + code emulation = dynamic heuristics	Static heuristics + Dynamic heuristics = hybrid techniques	Artificial intelligence/ second generation heuristics	→

Complex scanning strategies

Off access scanning	On-access scanning, stream scanning	Emulated scanning, heuristic scanning	→	→

D- Increasing Dynamization/ Speed

Improving on-access scanning

Off access scanning	Resident scanning or on access scanning	Stream scanning	Network traffic scanning	→

Improving speed of scanning

Full scanning	Partial scanning, and priority scanning	Scanning only by specific test drivers, no duplicate scanning	Improved scanning techniques	→

This trend of improving speed of scanning is contrary to the trends like increasing number of virus signatures and increasing methods of scanning techniques. This situation will pose more and more contradictions for all times in future.

Smart update

Full update of AV database and program	Differential update of AV database, full update of AV program	Smart update of AV database and AV program	→	→

E- Increasing Smartness/ Intelligence

Intelligent scanning methods

Signature scanning	Wild card scanning	Scanning with emulation techniques	Heuristic scanning + emulation	Self built and self learning heuristics

Minimal scanning

Scanning the complete file	Scanning only vulnerable area, such as, begin and end	Scanning only if not scanned earlier	Scanning files only if modified after previous scanning	→

Smart scanning

Scanning on demand	Scanning during off hours	Start scanning only when user stops working	Using only as much free processor is available	→

F- Increasing coordination

Increasing coordination with other programs around

Anti-virus programs + OS	+ Firewalls / gateways	+ Anti-spyware	+ Sandboxes / emulators	→

Increasing coordination between anti-virus programs

Hostility between anti-virus programs	Installing multiple anti-virus programs but no coordination	Some coordination between anti-virus programs	Complete collaboration between multiple anti-virus programs	→

INVENTION-11: Simultaneous execution of multiple anti-virus programs

Currently different anti-virus programs are hostile to each other and installing multiple anti-virus programs lead to scanning loops and deadlocks. There is a need to utilize the power of alternative anti-virus programs and compensate each other's deficiencies.

Patent 8171552 (invented by Chang, assignee- Trend Micro, Inc., May 2012) discloses a method of "Simultaneous execution of multiple anti-virus programs" without suspecting each other and without causing deadlocks.

According to the invention the anti-virus programs run in a layered model of drivers. The anti-virus programs are installed as upper filter drivers in the layered model. The driver stack remains common to all the anti virus programs. The first filter driver associated with the first anti-virus program scans the target file and transmits a request to the second anti-virus program.

H- Increasing automation

Automation in extraction of virus signatures

Manual extraction by anti-virus experts	Use of semi-automated tools	Automated tools for virus extraction	→	→

Automation in updating virus signatures

Automatic reminder	Automatic connection to the distributor's website	Automatic downloading and self configuration	→	→

The anti-virus technology is including more and more automations which is going to reduce human intervention. But many things are yet to be automated, such as, automatic generation of heuristics to differentiate an infected file from a good file etc.

Chapter 10.

Overcoming Limitations of Signature Scanning

10.1 What is signature scanning

When the viruses infect the executable files they copy their viral code to the files they infect. Thus the malicious code of the virus is included in the target file during infection. These types of viruses can be detected by searching their "signatures" in the infected files.

A virus signature is a sequence of bytes that may be found in a virus program code but unlikely to be found in elsewhere. A signature is very carefully extracted from the virus code. Extracting a "virus signature" is a skillful job and generally done by an anti-virus experts.

10.1.1 How does signature scanning work

After extracting the signature of a virus, the signature is stored in a signature database. The anti-virus program uses the signature to scan a target program, such as, executable file, boot record or spreadsheet etc. If the signature is found then the target program is deemed infected.

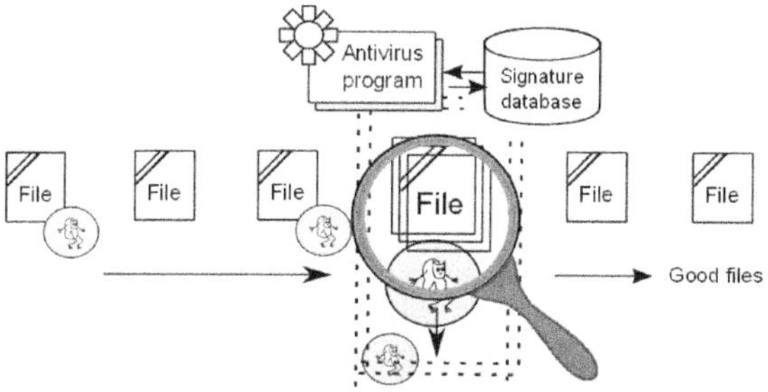

Signature Scanning by Anti-Virus Programs

10.1.2 Types of signature scanning

Signature scanning may be **simple signature scanning** or **generic signature scanning**. Simple Signature Scanning uses exact signature of specific viruses for scanning. Although this is a simple and sure sort method, this can detect only the known viruses whose signatures are already extracted and included in the virus signature database. It cannot detect unknown viruses or unknown variants of a known virus although the differences between their signatures are very minor. This deficiency is taken care by a generic signature scanning.

A generic signature uses a signature pattern found in a family of viruses (instead of specific signatures found in individual viruses). The generic signatures use various wildcards which can detect all the variants of a virus family. This is a quicker method as one generic signature (or wildcard) can detect many/ all viruses belonging to the same family. This method is also capable of detecting new and future viruses which bear the same pattern. This method works well because most viruses are not originally programmed rather created by modifying the code of previously existing viruses. In such cases a lot of similarities are found between the main virus and its variants. As various heuristics are applied to build a generic signature, the generic signature scanning is sometimes called as heuristic signature scanning.

10.1.3 Advantages of signature scanning

Signature scanning is the most popular method of virus scanning and is adopted by almost all anti-virus programs. The main advantages are:

- Simple logic – if a signature is found in a file then the file is deemed to be infected otherwise not.
- Requires no complicated engine - a simple search engine is capable of detecting the virus. As the engine is simple it consumes less memory and system resources.
- A large number of viruses (about 80%) can be detected by using this method.
- This can detect encrypted viruses too. Although the encrypted viral body does not bear any signature (because it is encrypted with different encryption keys) the decryption routine is generally static and is detected by signature scanning.

- Signature scanning is also used in heuristic methods and emulated environments.

10.1.4 Limitations of signature scanning

Although signature scanning is the most popular method of detecting viruses it has the many limitations. Signature scanning is a reactionary method. It can detect a virus only after the virus is released and has infected some computers. A typical cycle of detecting a virus through its signature is as below.

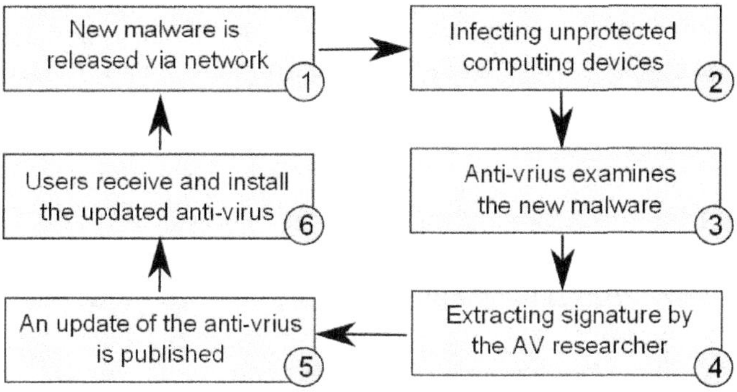

The cycle of scanning new viruses

- Hence signature scanning allows the new virus to infect some computers until the virus is caught and analyzed by the anti-virus software provider. Because the steps of signature extraction, signature distribution and signature scanning are time consuming steps, there will always be a time lag (from several hours to several days) between virus creation and virus detection.

- Difficulty of extracting virus signatures and viral characteristics - extracting virus characteristics is a skillful and time consuming job usually done by the human experts. Any mistake in extracting virus signatures and viral characteristics can lead to omission of viruses or detection of false positives during scanning.

- The worst drawback of signature scanning is that it cannot detect any new virus whose signature is not there in the signature database. Hence, this method always remains one step behind the viruses.

- Besides the user has to update the signature database regularly in order to deal with the latest viruses. There are many obvious problems in distributing/ updating virus definition databases for millions of anti-virus users.

- Excessive time and system resources required for scanning – as hundreds of viruses are created on every day; the size of virus definition files continuously increases. Scanning files with all these signatures requires abundant time and resources.

- Often the virus definition files and scanning engines are platform dependent. After extracting the signature, the vender has to make the same update available for each different platform or operating system.

- Signature scanning cannot detect polymorphic and metamorphic viruses. These types of viruses change the code of their bodies on every infection and don't have any specific signatures of their own.

- As there is competition between anti-virus venders, there is no agreement on virus names or signatures. The same virus may be called differently and detected by different signatures by different anti-virus developers.

10.2 Applying TRIZ to improve signature scanning

The signature scanning still remains the most widely used method of detecting viruses. The earlier form of simple signature scanning has gradually evolved to a quite advanced and powerful scanning today. Many improvements have been made in signature extraction, distribution and pattern matching techniques.

- ⇨ The simple "virus signatures" are often replaced with wild cards in most cases. Wild cards use strings like "??05 22D3 8BC5 235C" where "??" stands for anything in first two bytes. Wild card searching is very powerful and often catches new and unknown viruses of the same old family (Principle-6: Universality, Principle-35: Parameter Change).

- ⇨ Many techniques are also used to speed up virus scanning. For example, some scanners scan only the vulnerable area of the file (such as the beginning and the end of the file) and not the entire file (Principle-21: Skipping).

As the number and complexities of viruses are increasing, there is a need for continuous improvement of signature scanning. But the question arises which aspect of signature scanning needs to be improved. This question can be well addressed by analyzing the subsystems of the signature scanning system, finding the main useful function (MUF) and finding the Ideal Final Result (IFR) for each subsystem.

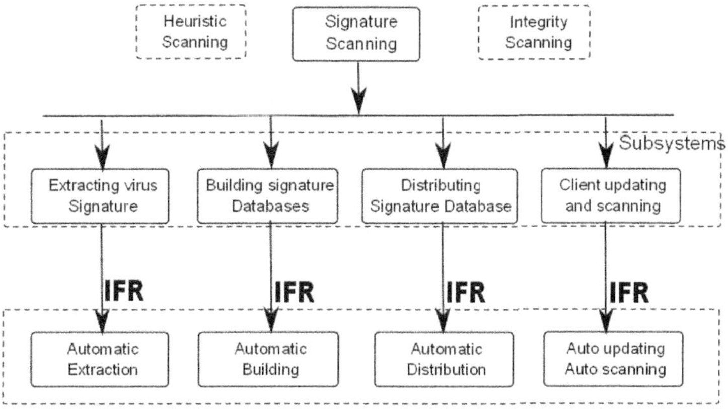

Development of sub-systems of Signature Scanning

The above diagram shows different sub-systems of signature scanning, such as, extracting virus signature, building signature database, distributing signature database, updating and scanning at the client machine. The development of signature scanning requires improvement of all its subsystems. Ideally each of these functions should be automated (Principle-25: Self Service).

- ⇨ Applying the trend of Increasing automation- Ideally there should be an automated system to extract virus signatures. The signatures should be automatically delivered to all the users immediately. And the files should be automatically scanned with these latest signatures.

- ⇨ Applying the trend of Increasing Ideality- Minimum volume of scanning should be done for maximum extent of virus protection. The IFR of signature scanning is to get all the benefits of signature scanning without suffering from any of its disadvantages.

Other methods of improving different aspects of signature scanning are illustrated below.

10.3 Overcoming the difficulty of extracting virus signatures

Extracting virus signature and virus characteristics is a highly skillful job usually done by the human experts in anti-virus laboratory. The anti-virus expert must have knowledge on various languages and programming environments. The boot sector viruses are written in assembly languages where as most windows viruses are written in c/c++ or Delphi or VB or VBA or even in JavaScript. The researcher must understand all these languages including internal functions of the operating systems. Any mistake in extracting virus signatures and viral characteristics can lead to omission of viruses or detection of false positives during scanning.

Ideal Final Result:

IFR There should be a method of automatically extracting virus signatures and characteristics from the virus code.

IFR The signatures should be extracted only once and shared by different anti-virus venders for different anti-virus programs.

Possible solutions:

- Automated signature extraction- the job of analyzing virus characters and extracting virus signatures can be expedited by using automated techniques (TRIZ Principle-25: Self Service). Human researchers may analyze the code only if a potential virus is unable to be handled by the automated systems.

- Automation in differentiating genuine program code, junk characters and virus code. Patent 5440723 (by Arnold et al.) discloses a method of automatic extraction of malware signatures and using the extracted signature for scanning subsequent infections of the system or network. Patent 5452442 (by Kephart) also discloses a statistical technique for automatically extracting signatures from the machine language code of a computer virus.

- While viruses are detected at the clients' machine the signatures are extracted in the anti-virus laboratory. The method may be reversed as to extract virus signatures directly in the client machine and later send them to the repository of anti-virus laboratory (TRIZ Principle-13: Reversing).

- Creating a new super-system above the signature scanning system (or above the anti-virus system as illustrated in chapter-3) can take care of collecting new virus data, extracting virus signatures and building the virus signature database. This can eliminate the duplicate works done by each anti-virus vender.

10.4 Reducing time lag between virus creation and detection

The method of signature scanning creates substantial time lag between virus creation and signature distribution. Before the newly found signatures are distributed the anti-virus users world wide, a new virus gets enough time to spread and cause damage. For example, the ILOVEYOU virus could spread very fast in year 2000 to infect millions of computers only in a few days. The method of signature scanning is not useful to control new viruses or tackle virus outbreaks.

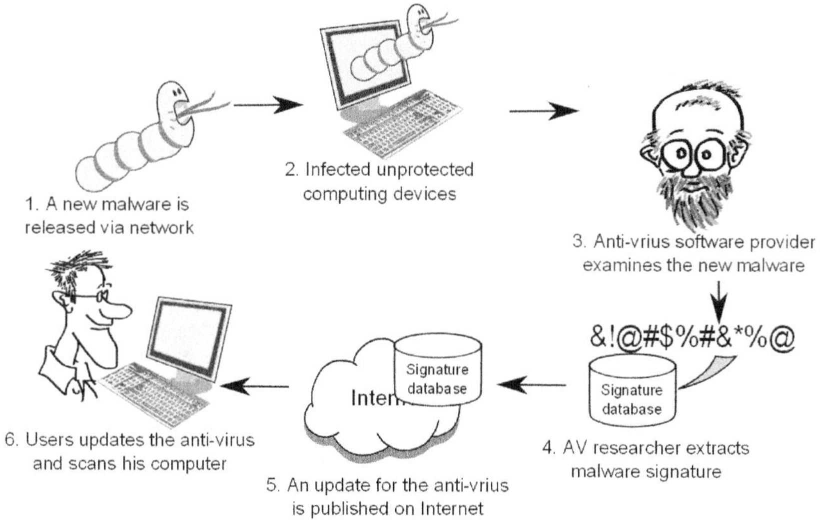

Too many steps between Virus creation and Virus detection

For example, when a new virus appears, the infected file is first sent to an anti-virus company. Then the anti-virus experts in the anti-virus company analyze the infected file and find the pattern or "signature" of the virus. Then the signature of that virus is updated in the signature database of that anti-virus software and distributed to the customers of that anti-virus software. Then the customers scan each individual file to find the signature of that virus.

Contradiction:

Contradiction	*If the vendor performs more comprehensive internal testing of the virus signatures then there will be a delay in releasing the signature database. On the other hand if the vender releases the signatures without sufficient testing then that may lead to false positives. The vender wants to release the signatures fast but doesn't want to take the risk of false positives.*

Analysis:

Improving Parameter: Reliability

Worsening Parameter: Loss of Time

Ideal Final result:

IFR There should be no (or minimum) time gap between virus creation and signature distribution.

Possible Solution:

- The time of discovering new viruses may be reduced by implementing a method of automatic submission of new virus instances by the client machines (Principle-23: Feedback, Principle-25: Self Service).
- Reduce the number of steps between virus creation and virus detection (Principle-21: Skipping). For example, building signature database directly in the client machine.
- Another option is to use an online scanning service provided by an anti-virus company and scan your computer remotely (Principle-17: Another dimension). This method allows clients files to be scanned always with latest signatures.

INVENTION-12: Automatic building of virus detection and cleaning routines

Patent 7234167 (invented by Teblyashkin, et al., Assignee- McAfee, Inc. Jun 2007) discloses a mechanism of automatic building of virus detection and cleaning routines (Principle-25: Self Service).

The method first compares the infected copy of the files with the non-infected copy of the same files in order to identify the characteristics of virus carrying portions. Then fingerprint generation logic automatically generates the fingerprint for the computer virus detected. The method also generates the virus removal data automatically. If the virus is encrypted then the method uses decryption techniques to recover the signatures. If the virus disguises itself then the method emulates the execution of the infected program until the viral code is detected. This method of automatic generation works successfully in most cases.

INVENTION-13: Quick releasing virus signatures without taking the risk of false positives

Patent 7290282 (invented by Renert, et al., Assignee- Symantec Corporation. Oct. 2007, extended in Patent 7757292, July 2010) discloses a method of quick releasing virus signatures without taking any risk of false positives.

The invented method releases the virus detection technique including a constraints module to all the clients. The constraints module is a special module which allows specific clients to test the new heuristics and provide test reports to the software server. The module contains the names of which heuristics to be tested, which subset of files to be tested and who are the clients to test.

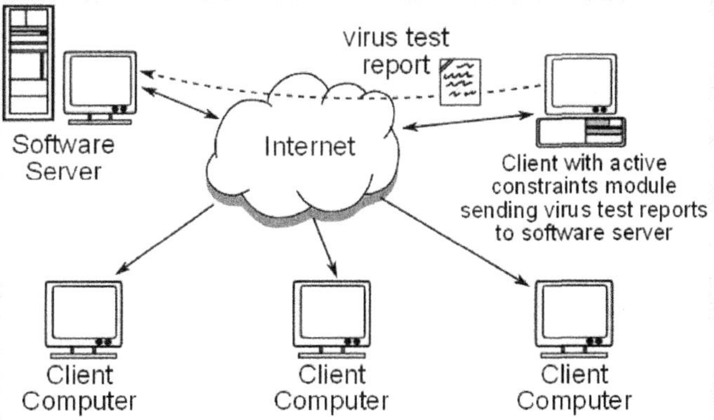

Collecting virus test reports from Clients

The client computers evaluate the virus definition constraints and provide feedback to the vender or administrator who monitors at a software server (Principle-23: Feedback). If more false positives are found in the feedback then the administrator modifies the constraints and re-release to the clients (TRIZ Principle-35: Parameter change). Once the virus detection technique is ready for wide release, the technique is circulated to all the clients.

- Conventionally the anti-virus vender has to track new viruses by information voluntarily submitted by computer users. But most users don't feel the need of reporting virus information to the anti-virus company. Hence, virus researchers don't get timely reports on recent viruses. Patent 7310818 (invented by Parish, et al., Assignee- McAfee, Inc., Dec. 2007) suggests to use a special data collection server in order to receive virus scan results which stores them in a database and updates in the publisher server at specific intervals.

- Patent 7516489 (invented by - Lahti, Assignee-F-Secure Oyj, Apr. 2009) discloses a method of scanning emails with latest virus signatures. According to the invention the anti-virus application is installed at the email gateway of the network. When a new virus is detected by the anti-virus provider, the anti-virus provider sends a notification to the anti-virus application on the gateway. In response to that, the anti-virus application stops scanning and holds the emails in a temporary buffer until it receives the newly discovered signatures from the anti-virus provider. After getting the new signatures, the application resumes scanning the previously buffered emails with the latest signatures.

10.5 Reducing the time and resource required for scanning

The number of viruses increases on a daily basis. At the same time the average disk space per computer has increased to hundreds of gigabytes. With thousands of virus signatures and large volumes of data storage a complete disk scan very often extends to several hours.

- The other disadvantage of virus scanning is that it consumes significant amount of system resources and adversely affects the performance of the system. The user feels irritated with prolonged scanning and often stops such scanning operations.

- Besides, an on-access scanner must finish scanning at a very high speed and pass the handle to the user application within a very short time. If the scanner takes longer time because of large size of the program or large signature database or poor scanning methods then the user application may lead to a timeout error. (More on on-access scanning is in Chapter-16 and on speed of scanning is in Chapter-16).

Contradiction	*If a virus scanner includes less number of signatures then some viruses may escape scanning. On the other hand if it includes all possible signatures then the scanning process will take very long time. We want to run more algorithms in order to detect all viruses with full certainty, but at the same time we don't want the scanning to take long time.*

Analysis of Contradiction Parameters

Improving Parameter: Volume of data processing

Worsening Parameter: Loss of time

Ideal Final result:

IFR A typical virus scanning of a file should take no (or minimal) time.

IFR A virus scanning operation should not impact system performance.

IFR The file should be available to the user even before on-access scanning is finished.

Possible Solutions:

- Keep the file scanned beforehand (TRIZ Principle-10: Prior Action) in order to avoid the need of on-access scanning. But the time between file scanning and file opening should be short enough to avoid any chances of infection.

- Once a file is scanned to be virus free, it should not be scanned again and again repeatedly in subsequent scanning sessions unless the file is found to be modified (TRIZ Principle-21: Skipping).

- Scanning the whole file for virus signatures takes long time. One method is to look for changes only in the beginning and at the end of the program code that are generally changed by the viruses and skip the rest of the file (TRIZ Principle-21: Skipping).

It is found that reading a file from the disk takes as much time as scanning the file. Patent 7036147 teaches to use two separate threads for the scanner, one thread for reading data from the disk and another thread for scanning the pre-read data. Both the threads are executed in parallel for accelerated scanning. **Limitation**- this method, although increases speed, can consume more resources.

INVENTION-14: Using Tree Patterns to search virus signatures

The conventional virus scanning involves scanning for each individual virus signature one after the other. But this is a slow method. There are many advanced methods of database searching available in the prior art, which can be effectively used for virus scanning.

If we apply Inventive standard 1.1.2, we find that we have a scanning engine (S2), which has insufficient interaction with virus definition database (S1). The Inventive Standard suggests to introduce an additive to either of the elements (or substances) to improve the interaction.

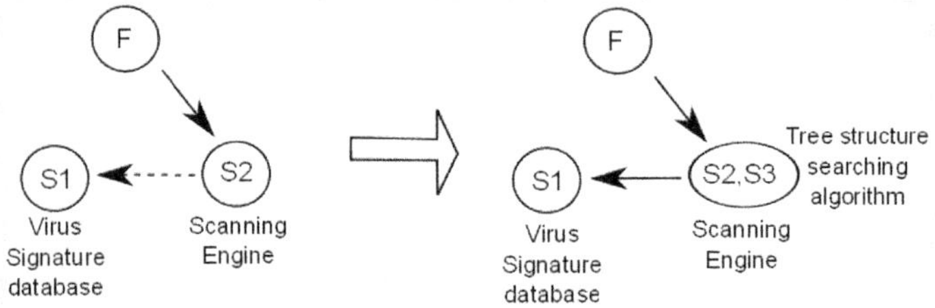

Standard 1.1.2

Patent 6980992 (invented by Hursey, et al., assignee McAfee, Dec 2005) suggests to utilize tree-structure database searching techniques to improve seed of virus scanning (TRIZ Principle-38: Enrich).

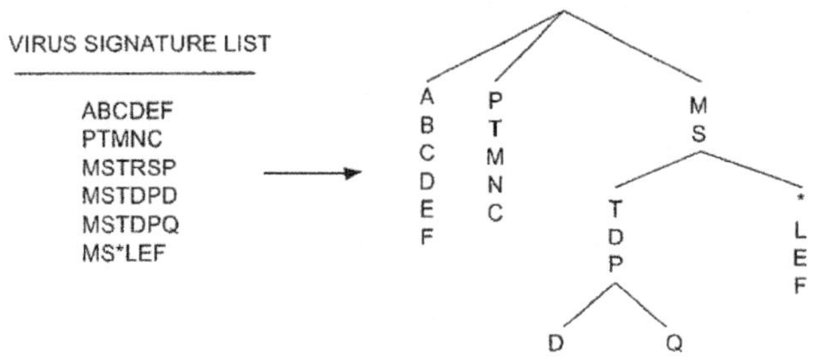

According to the invention the list of virus signatures is combined into a tree of virus signatures. In a tree-based system the index is organized in a tree structure having a head node on the top and multiple branch nodes under the head node (TRIZ Principle-17: Another Dimension). By this design, the efficiency of the virus signature recognition is improved since similar portions of the virus signatures need not be compared with the data more than once

⚒ Patent application 20080141375 (by Amundsen, June 2008) suggests to archive all non-recently used objects into a non-executable format (TRIZ Principle-36: State Change and Conversion). These archived objects are omitted from periodic virus scans. When there will be a request to use any archived object, the archived object will be converted to a non-archived state and virus scanned before made available to the requester. The scanning becomes faster as all these archived objects are omitted from periodic scans.

10.6 Advanced methods of Signature Scanning

The conventional signature scanning looks for exact signatures of specific viruses. This method is slow and time consuming. Gradually the method has gone through many improvements.

✓ Using fewer signatures for more viruses- Wildcards were introduced in signature strings. For example, the signature "??0A 45A9 8BC1 219A" indicates that the wildcard "??" can contain any byte (TRIZ Principle-6: Universality). Wildcard searches are also effective in scanning encrypted and polymorphic viruses.

✓ Early methods were scanning the entire file for virus signatures. But this was taking a long time to scan. Improved scanners scan only the vulnerable parts, such as entry points of the file, which made scanning much faster (TRIZ Principle-21: Skipping).

✓ While an exact identification scanning is more precise in detecting specific viruses to its drawback it takes long time. A nearly exact identification scanning overcomes this difficultly to achieve higher speeds in scanning. Nearly exact identification cannot accurately tell the name of the specific variant of a virus, but it is good enough to differentiate an infection from a good piece of code (TRIZ Principle-16: Partial or Excessive Action). (More methods of speed scanning are discussed in chapter-17).

INVENTION-15: Using fuzzy scanning system to randomly change virus definition files

Although the virus scanners and signatures are created for general computer users, the same tools are also available to the virus creators. The virus creators use those tools to test their viruses and modify their codes until they remain undetected by the signature scanner. This way the virus scanners help the virus creators to create new viruses that are not detected as variants of known viruses.

Contradiction	*The virus scanners and virus definition files should be available to the common users for scanning of viruses. But the same should not be available to the virus creators as they can misuse it to create viruses having new type of signatures. In other words, the anti-virus program should detect viruses in user machines but should not detect viruses in virus creators' machine.*

Patent 7284273 (invented by Peter Szor, Assignee- Symantec Corporation, Oct 2007) suggests to use a fuzzy logic to randomly change the virus definition files for different machines. For example, if there are 500 strings, 5 of those 500 strings are selected randomly for one machine and other 5 are selected randomly for another machine. This way the virus search strings will not be same for all the machines.

In this method, when the virus writer tests his virus on one computer as undetectable he will assume that his virus will also be undetectable on other computers and releases the virus. But the virus will be detected on other computers by other mutated virus definition files. Thus the unknown virus variants are quickly detected preventing them to be widespread.

INVENTION-16: Method and apparatus to detect malicious software

Although simple obfuscation may be defeated by more complex search instructions, complex metamorphic viruses may evade these sophisticated detection systems by changing the obfuscation specifics.

Patent 7739737 (invented by Christodorescu et al., assignee-Wisconsin Alumni Research Foundation, Jun 2010) suggests comparing the "function signatures" in the malicious program instead of comparing "string of codes" (TRIZ Principle-28: Mechanics Substitution).

The high level "function signatures" describes the function of the malicious code which can detect the new variants of a virus even if their "code strings" are different. This functional analysis is done by converting varying expressions into a standardized form prior to application of signature analysis.

Chapter 11.

Rise of Generic Detection Methods

11.1 Drawbacks of Specific Detection Methods

The methods of virus detection are often classified into specific methods (which detect specific viruses or specific types of viruses) and generic methods (which detect a virus of whatever type). A signature scanning is a specific method, whereas, integrity checking, heuristic scanning, behavior monitoring etc. are all generic methods.

The specific methods like signature scanning try to detect a virus only after the virus is created and circulated. This method fails seriously as it allows viruses to flourish till their signatures are extracted and distributed to the users. If the anti-virus developers depend only on this method then they will always remain behind the virus creators. The other drawbacks are:

- The number of viruses doubles almost in every 9 months. This situation keeps on increasing the size of virus definition database.
- Many existing viruses are just modified to create dozens of variants having slightly different strains. A specific scanning requires separate signatures extracted for each of these breeds.
- The specific methods demand continuous burden of distributing virus definition files to millions of anti-virus users.
- The specific methods are incapable to detect new and unknown viruses. They are incapable to detect polymorphic and metamorphic viruses.
- Some viruses may target at a specific organization or company. As those viruses will never spread outside the target location it is difficult to develop specific methods for those viruses.

Ideal Final Result

IFR The virus detection method should be capable of detecting any type of virus, known or unknown, old or new, past or future.

IFR The method should work for any types of viruses including hidden viruses, encrypted viruses, polymorphic and metamorphic viruses.

The generic methods of virus detection have been developed in order to overcome the above limitations of specific scanning and try to achieve the above IFRs.

11.2 Generic Methods of Virus Detection

The generic methods don't depend upon exact signatures rather follows various other methods to detect an infection. For example, the heuristic methods examine the code of the target program to determine whether it appears to be virus-like. There is not any single method called as generic method. All those methods, which are capable of detecting both known and unknown viruses, fall into the category of generic methods (TRIZ Principle-6: Universality).

Some Popular Generic Methods

- **Generic signature scanning or wildcard scanning**- which uses wildcard characters like "??" inside typical signatures to match with any possible characters in those positions. This method detects multiple viruses belonging to a family that falls within the scope of the wildcard. Limitation- the wildcards may not always work, as the future viruses of the same family may not necessarily fall within the scope of the given wildcard.

- **Integrity checking**- which compares the original file (or its "snapshot" or "fingerprint") with its backup to verify whether they match or not. If they match then the files are unmodified and therefore deemed to be uninfected. If they don't match then the anti-virus program uses artificial intelligence to determine whether the modification is "virus-like" or user-induced. (We will discuss more on integrity checking in the next chapter).

- **Behavior monitoring** – tries to detect a virus type activity, such as, attempts to format a disk, low level disk access, modification of executable files etc. The behavior blocker is a TSR program that monitors each program since they are loaded on to the memory till they finish their execution. If it detects any virus like activity then it immediately flags the activity and warns the user. Depending on the user's feedback the program is either allowed to continue or terminated from execution. The method monitors how programs act and not how they are built.

- **Heuristic scanning** – uses a large number of features called "classifiers" or "heuristics" that could be present in virus-infected files. Each heuristic feature carries a weight. If the total weight of all the heuristic features exceeds a pre-determined threshold then the code is deemed to be infected. (We will discuss more on heuristic scanning in Chapter-15).

- **Using Authenticode**- which verifies whether the downloadable code has been digitally signed by a reputed organization like "Verisign". If the program is not signed by a reputed organization then it prompts the user "This is trying to install program xyz which is not digitally signed. Do you want to install this program?" and acts according to user feedback. This method protects the user from downloading/ installing unreliable programs from Internet. **Limitations**: however an authenticode is poorly understood by common users. Besides, the program name and source in the alertbox can deliberately written in a way to confuse the user.

- **Using network behavior anomaly detection**- is useful to detect worms, email viruses and network viruses. When the worms and network viruses use the network bandwidth for their purposes the normal traffic pattern is affected. Analyzing network traffic can show anomalies like "packet anomaly", "protocol anomaly", "traffic anomaly" etc. and provide important information about presence of worms and network viruses. (More about worms and network viruses in Chapter- 23).

- **Using traps, baits and counter viruses (or anti-viral viruses)**- this concept is similar to the real-life baits and traps used to catch animals like rats. Each of these tools are interesting in its implementation and work secretly to provide information about harmful viruses. (We will discuss more about this concept in Chapter-13)

- **Using reputation data**- the reputations of individual hosts are maintained by a reputation server by analyzing the log files maintained by firewalls, routers, proxy servers, gateways etc. The reputation score represents whether a host or website is trustworthy or not. The malware analyzer on a client machine checks the reputation score of the target host and alerts if the score is rated to be malicious (Patent 7882542, Patent 8019689).

- **VICE (Virus Instruction Code Emulation)**- Jie-Sheng Lee et al. describes a method called "Virus Instruction Code Emulation" (or VICE) to detect viruses based on their behavior. The method uses the virus behaviors collected from the experiences of virus experts. The VICE has two components, an emulator and a knowledge based virus analyzer. The emulator emulates the viral code and sends the events to the analyzer. The analyzer checks whether the events are like "Int 21 hooked", "Open a File", "Write a File" etc. are suspicious or not. Thus VICE detects the viruses based on their behaviors and not on patterns. As the viral code is emulated in a virtual environment there is no fear of infection to the actual computer.

- There are many generic methods which strive to detect the presence of viruses and other malware. Because of the limitations of signature scanning, more and more research is being done on generic methods.

Advantages of Generic Methods

- No prior knowledge of individual virus signatures required.
- Can detect viruses whether they are known or unknown. Can detect future viruses which are not yet born.
- No need to download signature databases periodically.

Drawbacks of generic methods

- There are too many methods of detection falling under generic category. Many of them are either weak or not properly developed.
- The generic methods of virus detection are somewhat less certain than signature based detection for specific known viruses, they are likely to generate more false positives.
- There are many possible features of an infected file. It is difficult to decide which features to consider as virus classifiers in order to determine an executable whether "infected" or "not-infected".

- The generic methods cannot detect virus names and infection types so clearly as a signature based detection. If the infection pattern is not exactly known, repairing of the infected files is not possible.

11.3 Improving Generic methods of Scanning

The generic techniques are very impressive as they don't depend on virus signatures and don't require users to update signature database from the anti-virus developer's website. They can detect a future virus without even knowing about the virus. Although the concept of generic scanning sounds very impressive, the current age generic methods have not been able to replace the conventional signature scanning because of their less accuracy in detection.

There have been continuous efforts to improve the generic scanning methods to make them more accurate and to reduce the number of false negatives and false positives. There are continuous efforts to make them intelligent and adaptive by using "learning" techniques.

Ideal Final Result

IFR Ideally a generic method of virus scanning should give accurate results and should not raise any false positive or false negative.

Possible Evolution of Generic methods

- The file may contain certain smart materials (like, fragile watermark) which should reveal about the infection.

  Fragile watermarking- Generally a software watermark embeds the copyright protection and authentication information inside a program code. A fragile watermarking technique is very sensitive to any modification including virus infection. Zuwei Tian et al. ["A Scheme of PE Virus Detection Using Fragile Software Watermarking Technique"] suggest a technique where first a watermark (W1) will be calculated based on the embedded algorithm. Next the embedded watermark (W2) will be extracted from the resources section of the PE. Finally both W1 and W2 will be compared. If there is no difference then the file is not infected, otherwise infected. This method close to our IFR we described in the earlier chapter that says "ideally the file itself should say whether it is infected or not".

- ⇨ The poor generic methods are to be discarded and better generic methods are to be improved further to get promising result.
- ⇨ Further development of sub-systems- there is enormous scope to improve generic methods like heuristic scanning. Heuristics are applied in various methods, such as in signature scanning, network scanning, emulation and others. (More on heuristics in Chapter-15).

We will continue discussion on some of the popular generic methods in the following chapters and see how TRIZ can be useful in improving them further.

Chapter 12.

Improving Integrity Checking

12.1 What is Integrity checking

Integrity checking is a method that detects a virus infection by verifying the "integrity" of a file. An integrity checker generally keeps a small "checksum" or "hash value" or "snapshot" or "fingerprint" of the uninfected programs (such as, executables, boot records etc.) in a secured location in the beginning when they are presumably uninfected. During integrity checking, the integrity checker recalculates the new fingerprints of the programs and compares those with their original fingerprints. If both the fingerprints match then the files are assumed to be unmodified and hence deemed to be uninfected. If they don't match then the anti-virus program has to use further intelligence to determine whether the modification is "virus-like" or user-induced.

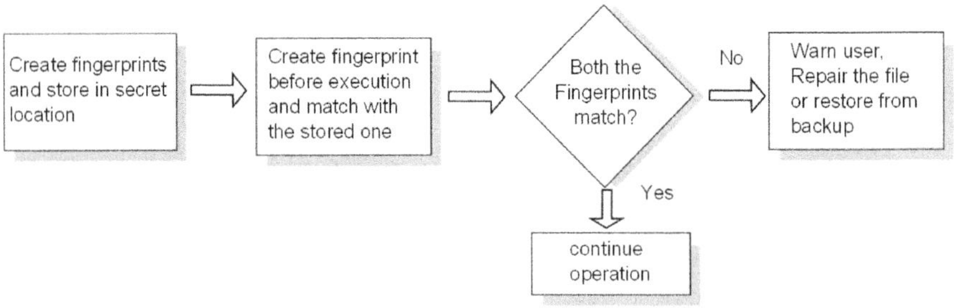

Steps of Integrity Checking

The method of Integrity checking works because the viruses must make changes to their host programs in order to infect. In other words, no virus can infect a program without modifying its code. Hence, the hash of the infected file has to differ from that of the infected file.

Advantages of integrity checking

Integrity checking is a generic method of virus detection. It is not dependent on virus signatures. It can be used to detect any kind of viruses, including new and unknown viruses. Besides passing through an integrity check is much faster than passing through a signature scan. As with signature scanners, integrity checkers can also be used to check the entire disk or can be used for on-access scanning to check each program that is about to be executed.

Application of integrity checking

The method of integrity checking is adopted not only by the virus scanners but also by other security systems. Some CMOS BIOS systems have a setting to monitor the changes in boot records. Windows XP and later systems do an integrity check of their system files during booting as part of their System File Checker (SFC) mechanism. Many advanced operating systems keep a backup of their core system files in secrete locations and role back the files when found damaged or infected.

12.2 Methods of Implementing Integrity Checking

The integrity checker keeps the details about each executable file on the system, such as, COM, EXE, SYS files. Some integrity checkers even maintain the details of DLL, DRV, OBJ, LIB, OVL and other user-defined extensions too.

The integrity checker works in two phases. In the first phase, the integrity checker calculates a checksum for each file and stores in a database. In a second phase when any of these files are accessed, a TSR (memory resident integrity checker) calculates the checksum of the file and compares with the checksum stored in the database. If the checksum values are same then the program is allowed to execute. On the other hand, if the checksums are different then the user is issued a warning about a possible infection.

Parameters of Integrity Checking

Integrity checking is based on the assumption that a virus, in order to infect a file, has to modify it. In other words, there can be no infection without modification. In other words, if there is no modification then there is no infection. Therefore, the integrity checker tries to check whether a file is modified or not by verifying different parameters including:

- **Verification of file/program size**

  This method stores the original size of the object program translated by the compiling portion. Then it compares the execution size of the object program with the original size. If they coincide with each other, then the file is deemed as uninfected otherwise suspected of virus infection.

- **Verification of checksum or fingerprints**

  This method stores the checksum of the original object program translated by the compiling portion. Then it compares the checksum of the object program with the original checksum. If they coincide with each other, the process is continued otherwise suspected of virus infection.

- **Verification of CRC code**

  The CRC (cyclic redundancy check) code is usually a two-byte or four-byte number that is computed from the content of the file. For each and every file to be protected, a unique CRC code is derived and then stored in a special file. At a later time, a CRC checker computes a new CRC code and compares with the stored CRC code to determine whether those files have been altered. **Disadvantage**- CRC codes are not very strong and can be tricked by intelligent viruses. A cryptographic hash is more suitable to detect intentional modification of data.

- **Verification of MD5 hash or SHA hash**

  MD5 hash is a cryptographic hash function that creates a 128bit (or 16 byte) hash string which is considered to be too strong to be broken. This hash is widely used in various security applications including integrity checking for virus scanning. **Limitation**- during recent years some attacks are reported on MD5 hash and this is not considered as absolutely secured any more.

  SHA (Secured Hash Algorithm) is another cryptographic hash generating standard designed by US National Security Agency and adopted by NIST "National Institute of Standards and Technology" as the standard for Digital Signature Algorithm. There are four SHA algorithms (SHA-0 through SHA-3). SHA-3 is the recently improved standard announced in 2012.

- **Verification of revision information**

  This method stores the revision information (such as date and time of updating, version number etc.) of the original object program. Later it compares the actual revision information with the original revision information. If they coincide with each other, the process is continued otherwise the program is suspected of virus infection.

- **Verification of disk address**

  The disk address indicating the place, in which the object program translated by the compiling portion is stored, is compared with the disk address of the object program loaded and executed as an operating system or a program for the computer. If they coincide with each other, the program is deemed to be uninfected and the process is continued.

- **Verification of object program**

  The original object program, which was translated by the compiler to produce the executable, is compared with the loaded object program. If they coincide with each other the process is continued. If they don't coincide with each other the program is deemed to be infected and the process in interrupted. Some methods also use verification of object program by using compression and decompression.

- **Verification of complete files**

  Two copies of the files (intended to be protected) are stored in two different places, one in the normal storage, and another in a write-protected storage. The files are compared during startup or whenever there is a need for a virus check. If any of the files in normal storage is found to be infected the original copies are recovered from the write-protected storage. **Disadvantage**- (i) additional space and effort for file storage, (ii) longer time for comparing complete files,

12.3 Limitations of integrity checking

- Integrity checking is of no use if the computer is already infected at the time when the programs are first fingerprinted. In such situations the computer will be inoculated with virus-infected files and create a safe haven for viruses to infect other programs.

- Comparing the checksum or CRC is effective if the program is stored in the hard disk. But if a program is read or executed from a floppy or CD or pen drives then the method does not work. As the uninfected fingerprints are not available for files in floppies or CDs or other external disks, the checksum method cannot detect whether the files residing in the external media are infected or not. Similarly the integrity checker does not work for the programs transferred from one computer to another in a computer network.

- Many different files may yield the same hash value. If by chance the hash of infected file matches with the hash of the original file then the infection will go undetected. Alternatively a virus developer may gain sufficient knowledge on the hash calculation formula and develop the virus accordingly.

- When a change in a program is detected by integrity checking, it is often difficult for the antivirus program to determine whether the change was induced by a virus or induced by a user. For instance, the user may genuinely modify a program or update a program by installing a new version or copying an updated file – which may lead to a false positive. Even if the antivirus program may ask the user to take a decision in this regard, many users may not be knowledgeable enough to determine whether the changes are genuine or virus induced.

- Integrity checking is suitable only for the files that never change over a period of time. The method does not work for documents or data files which are frequently modified by the user. Besides the method is not suitable for the whole disk, as that would require a lot of backup storage space. Moreover, comparing large files with their stored copies can take long time.

- The files or fingerprints stored in the write-protected partition of the hard disk may not be adequately secured. It is possible that a virus breaks into the write-protected disk and infects the secured copies or fingerprints. In that case the integrity checker fails to detect any infection.

- Generally an integrity checker issues warnings in case of disparity of checksums. This method becomes annoying in software development environments where the executable files are altered on a regular basis during every compilation.

- There are some viruses which target on integrity checkers and try to confuse the user to allow modifications to a file. When the user allows the changes to the executable file, the infections are also allowed and added to the database.

- Sometimes the virus authors target the integrity database and try to delete or modify the integrity database in order to avoid detection. If the integrity checker recreates the deleted integrity database, it has to calculate checksums of infected files.

- Some viruses use "stealth" techniques to bypass file reads thus fooling the integrity checkers which believe that the checksums remain the same.

- There may be a rootkit which conceals the running processes, files or system data from the operating system. When the scanner gives a "openfile" command, the rootkit may intercept and return a "file missing" error or return a wrong file. In such case the anti-virus tool may fail to check for virus infection or check with a copy of the original file to report no infection.

- Integrity checkers can detect an infection but they cannot prevent any infection. Besides they cannot give any details about the infecting virus and infection pattern. It is often not possible to repair infections without knowing the nature of infection.

12.4 Improvements in Integrity checking

As we saw above, although integrity checking is a faster and guaranteed method, it has several limitations. It is necessary to improve the features of an integrity checker in order to overcome the above limitations.

- If the backup files or hash values are stored in the same hard disk or same volume the viruses may infect those files too. Hence it is advised to store the hash values in a separate disk or volume with restricted access (TRIZ Principle-2: Taking out).

- The above problem can also be solved by using a separate additional hardware (memory chip) to store backup files or hash values. (TRIZ Principle-2: Taking out). As the hardware is becoming cheaper, this solution gives better guaranty at less additional cost.

- Better file comparison algorithms can compare complete files even at high speed. (TRIZ Principle-28: Mechanics Substitution). As the storage space is becoming cheaper this can be a viable solution.
- Compare the file properties reported by the suspected operating system with the file properties reported by a clean operating system (Patent 7627898 below).
- Compare the file properties reported by a high level scan with that reported by a low level scan for accuracy (Patent 7627898 below).
- A normal CRC code may be tricked or manipulated by a virus. Using a "cryptographic" hash or "collision resistant" hash or "collision-intractable" hash or "collision-free" hash is more reliable for better security and reliability (TRIZ Principle-38: Enrich).

INVENTION-17: Preventing virus infection by using WMR partition

Some methods propose to make the system folder or boot partition "read only" in order to protect them from virus infection. But Microsoft Windows requires many files in "\windows" directory to be written to. Hence making the boot partition "read only" can cause the system to halt.

Contradiction	*We want to make the boot partition "read only" in order to protect it from virus attack. But we don't want to make it "read only" as it halts the computer because of incompatibility with Microsoft Windows operating system and some other application programs.*

Patent 6092161 (invented by White et. Al, assignee Arendee Limited, July 2000) suggests to designate the boot partition (and optionally other partitions too) as a WMR (Write Many Recoverable) partitions. When data is written to WMR partition, the updated data is stored in a new location without overwriting the previous information. A system reset discards all changes and returns the WMR to its original state.

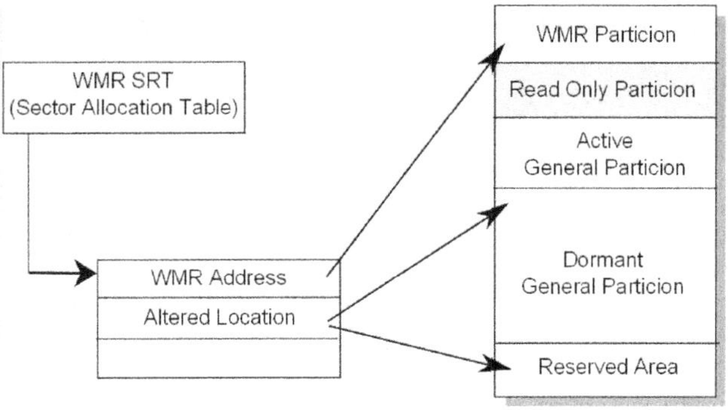

WMR Partition, Patent 6092161

According to the invention the boot partition is permitted to be written to without limit during a session. However, at the start of a new session, all the changes to the partition are undone and the partition is restored to its original state. In other words, if a partition is virus-free during startup, it will remain virus-free at the start of each new session (TRIZ Principle-34: Discard and Recover).

This method solves the above contradiction by making the boot partition "read only" (by protecting its original information and recovering at the beginning of every new session) and by not making it "read only" (by allowing any information to be written to the boot partition without limit during a session).

INVENTION-18: Detecting virus infection by comparing a file with its archive copy

Patent 7043634 (invented by Wolff, et al., assignee McAfee, May 2006) suggests to create an archive copy of the whole file at the time when the file is created. Later when the active copy is accessed the entire file is compared with its archive copy. The comparison takes minimal time as the invention discloses a faster method of comparing large files.

The invention also prefers to store the archive copy in encrypted form or in a PGP disk for better security (TRIZ Principle-36: State change / Conversion). The archive may also be stored in a different part of the disk or in a separate disk for better security (TRIZ Principle-2: Taking out).

INVENTION-19: Detecting Trojan horses and Viruses by comparing the hash value of a system with a previously computed trusted hash value

Most prior art anti-virus systems do not protect against attacks by Trojan horses. There is a need to detect unauthorized applications like Trojan horses prior to provide security data from a trusted store.

Patent 7526654 (invented by Charbonneau, Assignee- Nil, Apr. 2009) suggests to store a trusted hash value that is representative of a trusted state of the computer. Then the computer determines the hash value of the current data stored in the memory and compares the new hash value with the predetermined hash value. If the two hash values are found to be not identical, then the trusted group of applications sends a lock command to lockout the un-trusted application.

Invention-20: Detecting infection of suspect Operating System by comparing files with a clean Operating System

Sometimes backdoors and key-loggers steal confidential data from a computer. Checking the presence of an open port may not work as the backdoor may open the port only on specific times. Even integrity checking of files may not work as the malware might have taken control of the operating system.

Patent 7627898 (invented by Beck et al., assignee- Microsoft Corporation. Dec 2009) discloses a method of detecting the possible infection of an operating system by comparing its properties with the same reported by a (different) clean operating system. The system initially boots from the suspect operating system and records the file properties and then boots from a clean external operating system and record the properties. If there is a significant difference, such as an actual file is not reported by the suspect operating system, then the suspect operating system is deemed to be infected.

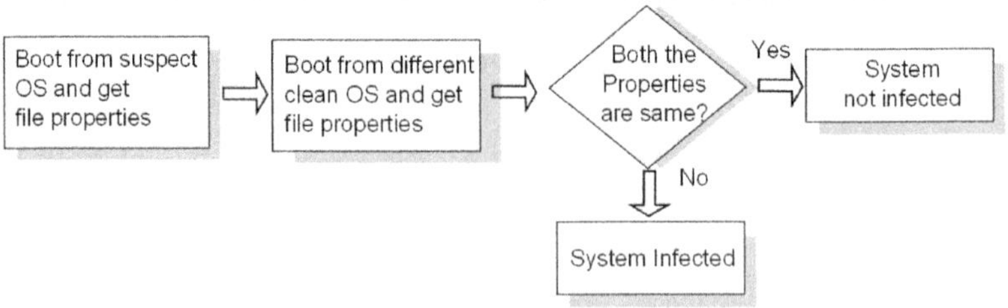

Detecting Infection by booting through clean OS

This is an example of Inventive Standard 4.5.1 which says efficiency of the measurement system can be increased by forming a bi or poly system. In the normal detection system there is only one (i.e., suspect) operating system. This invention uses the output of two operating systems, viz., the suspect OS and different clean OS.

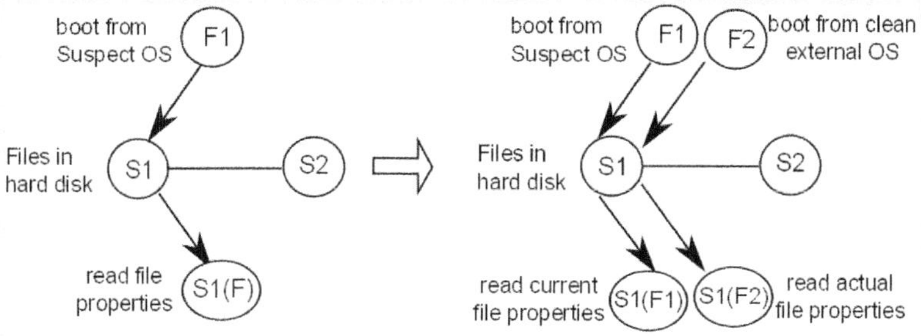

Boot from two different OS to detect differences in file properties

The invention also suggests another alternative. The detection system may compare the reported properties generated by a high-level scan with that of a low-level scan using the suspect operating system (TRIZ Principle-35: Parameter change). A high-level scan collects file properties using high-level functions such as APIs to the system registry. A low level scan collects file properties using low-level functions such as by reading disk sectors. This comparison can identify if a malware has changed the behavior of the high level commands but has not modified the behavior of low level commands.

Patent 7752667 (invented by Challener et al., assignee- Lenovo (Singapore) Pte Ltd., Jul 2010) suggests to create file signatures during file modification for rapid scanning. The method creates a file signature each time a file is modified (i.e., with each "file write" to that file) and stores the signature into the file attributes (file header) along with date and time of creation. During scanning the method checks to ensure that the file signature is secure and is valid and up to date. Only if the file signature is not valid and up-to-date the virus scan program creates a new file signature at the time of the running of the virus scan.

INVENTION-21: Anti-virus method based on a security chip

Prior inventions propose to keep backup of critical system files in a HPA (Host Protected Area) of the hard disk. But this is not safe because there are possibilities of an HPA being attacked. Patent 8132257 (invented by Li, et al., assignee- Lenovo (Beijing) Limited., Mar, 2012) suggests to store the key files such as, BIOS code file, MBR code file, the hash values of operating system files and other important files in a security chip.

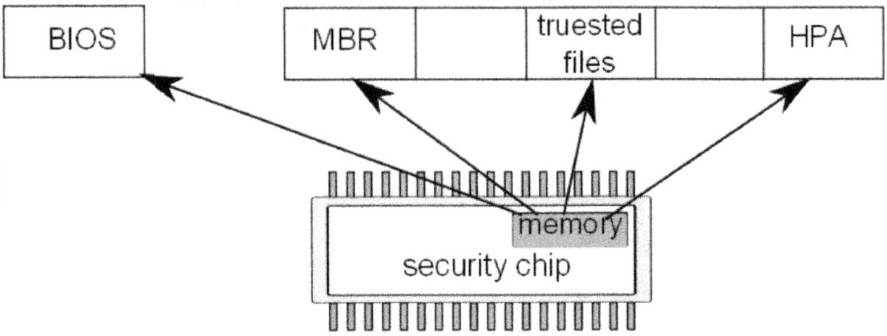

Storing critical data in a security chip

According to the invention, when the computer is powered on, the control program verifies the integrity of the system control program with the hash value stored in the memory of the security chip. If all the files are found alright then the computer is started otherwise the damaged/ infected files are retrieved from the backup.

Here we can make a reference to the inventive standards. According to Inventive Standard 1.2.1 and 1.2.2, if harmful effects appear between two elements (or substances S1, S2) the problem can be solved by introducing a third element (or substance) between them. The element (or substance) can be a new element (or substance S3) or a modification of the existing element (or substance S1' or S2').

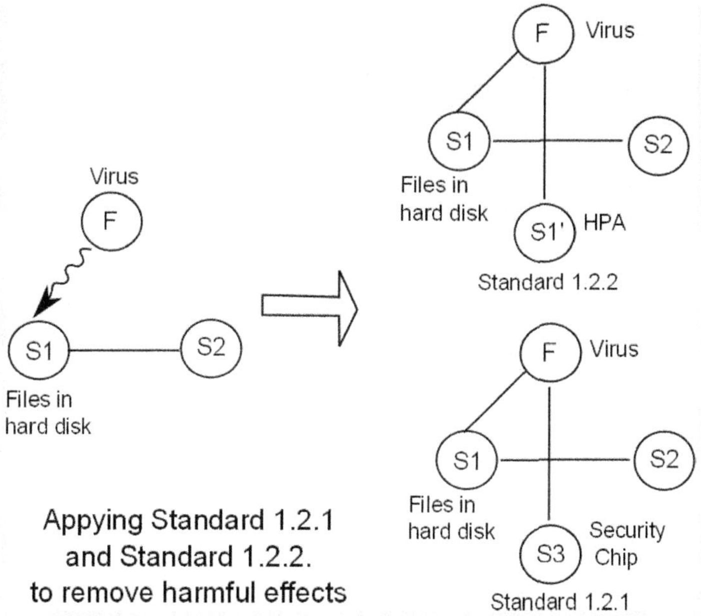

Appying Standard 1.2.1
and Standard 1.2.2.
to remove harmful effects

In this case the virus has a negative effect on the data storage. One option is to create a protected storage (HPA) is by modifying the same element (or substance, i.e., hard disk). Another method is to introduce a new element (or substance, i.e., security chip) which provides protected storage.

🛠 While the approach of "trusted computing" stores critical data in a secured place it requires an additional hardware. Ideally we should get the benefits of an external chip from the same existing hard disk without buying a separate chip (IFR). Patent 8239959 (invented by Gellerich, assignee- International Business Machines Corporation, Aug, 2012) suggested converting a portion of existing computer memory to write-protect mode to prevent file manipulations by virus infections. This portion of hard disk is made inaccessible from the host operating system. This is made to be exclusively operable only from outside the computer's operating system. As this portion of memory is not operable from inside the operating system, it remains safe even if the computer is infected by a virus.

INVENTION-22: Locating positions of virus infections by using cryptographic hashing

Although an integrity verification detects a virus infection it fails to indicate the exact location of virus infection. It is necessary to localize the virus for cleaning of the file.

Patent 8191146 (invented by Di Crescenzo et al., assignee- TTI Inventions C LLC., May, 2012) suggests a cryptographic hashing for localizing viruses in a host file. A cryptographic hash function returns a fixed-size, such as 128 or 160 bit hash for the file. This method is also called a "collision resistant" hash function or "collision-intractable" hash function or "collision-free" hash function.

FIG. 3

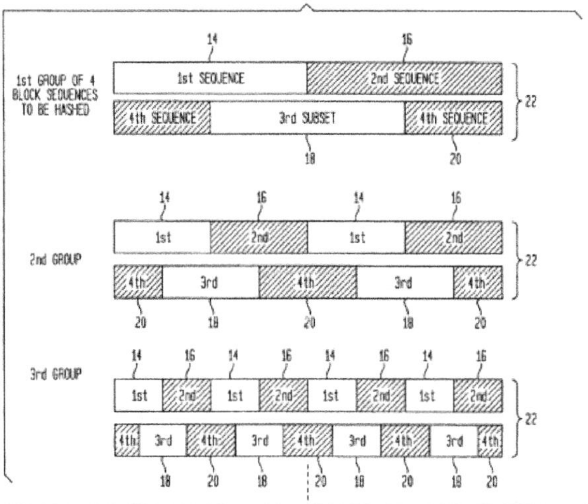

The method compares the uninfected hashes of the host file to that of the infected hashes to detect a location of virus infection. The method is also fast as the hash functions are not too longer than the conventional hash functions.

Chapter 13.

Using Baits, Traps and Counter Viruses

13.1 Introduction to Baits and Traps

While most of the anti-virus methods try to prevent viruses from being active some other methods follow a very different approach of inviting the viruses and encouraging them to be active. When the viruses become active and show their behavior the detection program uses a trap to contain the virus. In this approach the anti-virus takes secret and deceptive steps. For example, it keeps its presence confidential and address undisclosed. This method is adopted by baits, traps, honeypots and counter viruses.

Baits

Baiting is a technique to catch a virus when the virus tries to interact with baits. Baits can be of different forms such as bait files, bait servers etc. The bait files are created or modified or executed or opened in order to attract the resident viruses to infect them. When the virus attempts to infect or modify the bait files the infection is detected. Similarly bait servers adopt various techniques to detect the movement of malicious packets in the network in order to detect the infected computer.

Traps

A trap is a tool that resides in memory and monitors any suspicious activities such as writing to boot sector etc. A well-written trap should be able to detect virus behaviors and protect the computer from infection. Baits and traps are used to deceive the viruses and attract them. When the viruses start showing their behavior they are detected and caught.

- **Honey pots**

  A honeypot uses a similar technique as baits and trap. It is an undisclosed device deployed in the network. There are different implementations of a honeypot depending upon its purpose and operating platform. It can be implemented in a server or workstation or even an embedded device. The device has an IP address (so that it can be communicated) but it is not assigned any useful role or function in the network (so that no computer has any reason to communicate it). Under this condition all packets sent to the honeypot are considered as unsolicited and suspect. A careful analysis can differentiate between the harmless packets (such as broadcast, packets network administration or web-crawler requests) and harmful packets (such as viruses, worms or other exploitation codes).

- **Counter viruses**

  A counter virus is a beneficial virus created to detect and remove the harmful viruses. It has all the features of a virus, but instead of doing harm to the user it is engaged in detecting and attacking the harmful viruses. There are several implementations of a counter virus. For example, it may look for the presence of one specific virus and remove that virus. Alternatively it may look for all types of viruses in general and take control of them.

13.1.1 Advantages of applying these methods

All the above methods including baits and counter viruses are generic methods. So they have all the advantages of generic methods.

- Being generic methods they work for all types of viruses, known and unknown, old and new.

- While the conventional anti-virus mechanism catches viruses only after they enter into the system and often after performing their intended activity, these methods are competent even to detect viruses much earlier.

- These methods are useful to detect stealth and complicated viruses which are not detectable by other means.

13.1.2 Disadvantages

- Baits and traps cannot fool all types of viruses. There are intelligent viruses which recognize baits and traps and avoid them.

- Anti-viral viruses or beneficial viruses, although very attractive in concept, cannot solve the virus problem. Firstly, when there will be many beneficial viruses, they will look suspiciously to each other. Secondly, they will also consume memory and processor like any other harmful virus. Hence, too many of beneficial viruses can cripple a computer.

13.2 Inventions on implementing Traps and Baits

There are many improvements on baits and traps that intelligently study the virus activities and detect them when they show off their behavior. This is a very interesting method as it is based on fooling or deceiving the harmful virus. The following are some inventions on these techniques.

INVENTION-23: Creating a virus trap by introducing a foreign operating system

The conventional anti-virus programs detect viruses only after they enter into the target computer system. It will be better to detect and eliminate all types of viruses, old and new, before they can enter into a computer system.

According to Inventive Standard 1.2.1, 1.2.2 and 1.2.3, if there is a harmful interaction between two elements and there is no need to maintain a direct contact between the elements, the problem can be solved by introducing a third element between them. This concept is applied in a trap or honey pot or virtual machine or virtual operating system which can either absorb or neutralize the effects of the virus.

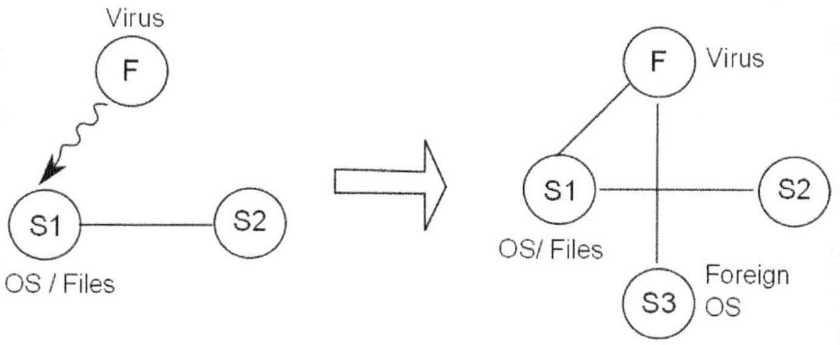

Introducing a third substance to remove harmful effects
Standard 1.2.x

Patent 5842002 (invented by Schnurer et al, assignee Quantum Leap Innovations, Nov 1998) discloses a virus trapping device by introducing a foreign operating system i.e., different from the operating system intended to be protected. The foreign operating system ensures safety as the viruses are typically platform dependent and cannot harm the foreign OS (reverse application of TRIZ Principle-33: Compatibility).

The foreign operating system is used to emulate the host computer system. The environment fools a computer virus to think as if it is present on its intended target system (TRIZ Principle-26: Copy).

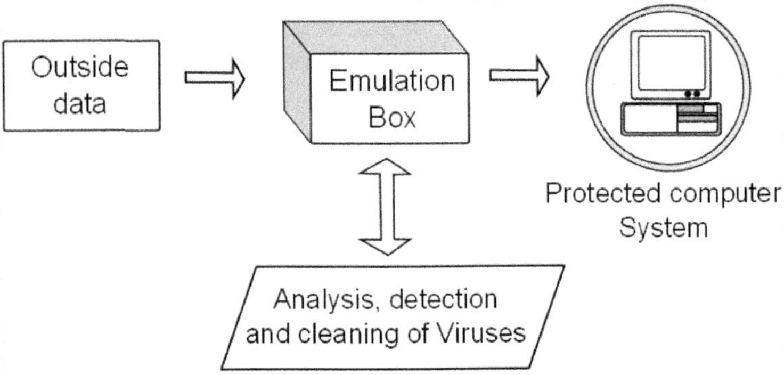

Emulating incoming data through foreign OS
Patent 5842002

Contrary to the conventional defensive strategies, this method follows an offensive strategy by encouraging a virus to perform its intended activity (TRIZ Principle-13: Reversing). When the virus starts its disruptive behavior within the simulated host computer system it is caught and removed. Thus the invented method removes the virus from the data stream before it is delivered to the host and makes any damage.

Patent 6931552 (invented by Pritchard, et al., Aug 2005) suggests to place a "sacrificial computer" in between the host computer and internet. Thus no computer can access the host computer directly from outside without going through the virus trap. The virus trap computer is a fully functional computer with capability to access the Internet. When the trap computer detects any virus or unauthorized access it erases all the data along with viruses and installs a clean version of operating system. **Limitations**: the virus trap must install an anti-virus to have capability to detect a virus.

In earlier chapter on Ideality we found that ideally the file itself should say whether it is infected or not. Is there already anything in a file which actually changes to speak out that the file is infected? If there is nothing already in the file can we insert anything into the file that can give an indication of a virus infection? Patent 5881151 (described earlier in Chapter-8, Inventive Standard 4.2.2) suggests to feed some diagnostic objects (such as program size, checksum, revision information, disk access, object program etc.) to the program at the time of compilation. When the program is infected by a virus its diagnostic parameters changes which indicates an infection.

INVENTION-24: Using bait address to detect probe packets

Worms self-replicate by sending network packets to unguided elements of the network. There is a need to detect stealth and intelligent worms whose SNR (Signal to Noise Ratio) is very low to be detected by traffic analysis. Patent 8181249 (invented by Chow et al, assignee Alcatel Lucent, May 2012) discloses a method of detecting worms by enticing them to send scan packets to one or more bait addresses.

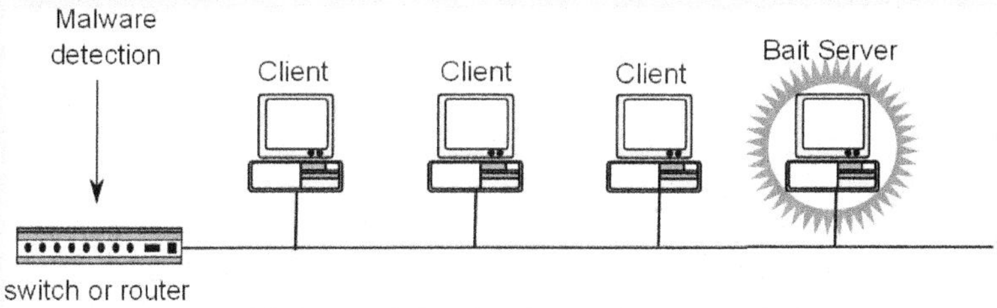

Malware detection by analysing packets going to the bait address

The method allocates one or more ports of a router or switch or other network node as bait addresses. Then it does a "sting" operating by sending outgoing bait packets and identifying compromised hosts that targets the bait addresses for scanning and sending probe packets. This technique allows reliable identification of stealth worms that send scan packets even at a very low rate.

13.3 Inventions on beneficial or counter-viruses

The concept of beneficial virus is like that of Robin Hood. Like Robin Hood was robbing the rich and helping the poor, the beneficial virus is built with an intention to attack the wicked virus and help the innocent users. The idea is to use the same virus technique to catch or destroy the viruses.

- Patent 6813712 (illustrated earlier in Chapter-8, Inventive Standard 4.2.2.) discloses a beneficial counter virus agent for detecting viral infection. This beneficial counter virus use virus-like techniques to attach itself to other files for replication. But it maintains a predetermined population level by repeated self-destruction and file-infection. When a new (unauthorized) virus infects the computer, the population of beneficial virus increases which reveals the existence of the unauthorized virus.

INVENTION-25: Repairing infected computers by modifying the code of same viruses that infected the computer

Patent 7512808 (Anti-computer viral agent suitable for innoculation of computing devices, invented by - Liang, Assignee-Trend Micro, Inc. (JP), Mar. 2009) discloses a method of inoculating virus infections by anti-computer virus agents. The invention creates an anti-computer virus agent by parsing and modifying the code of the same virus that caused the infection (TRIZ Principle-22: Turn Harms to benefits). The modified virus detects whether a client computer is infected with that virus. In case of infection it performs a reverse action for cleaning and repairing of the damage done to the client device. As the virus knows what alterations it does, it uses that knowledge to undo the alterations.

Chapter 14.

Improving Emulation Techniques

14.1 Rise of the Technology War

With the improvement in virus detection technology the older generation viruses had serious problems to survive. Hence the virus creators had to improve the anti-detection capabilities of their viruses. They implemented various methods to achieve one of the most crucial Ideal Final Results of the viruses, i.e., to make the viruses totally undetectable.

The most powerful techniques the viruses use to escape scanning are encryption, polymorphism and metamorphism. The encrypted virus has an encrypted body and a decrypting routine that decrypts the viral body before execution. Then the virus code makes a new infection and encrypts the code of the new infection with a new encryption key. Thus there is no common string in the encrypted virus and therefore no signature. The polymorphic viruses not only have different viral bodies in each infection but also use mutation engines to change their decryptors in every infection. Metamorphic viruses are even worse to leave nothing common in any infection thus making it untraceable by signature scanning.

14.2 The problem stealth viruses

As the encrypted and polymorphic encrypted viruses have encrypted viral bodies, which change in each infection, their bodies don't' have any signature and hence cannot be detected by signature scanning. But simple encrypted viruses can be detected by the signature of their unchanged decryptor routine. This weakness of the simple encrypted viruses is overcome by polymorphic encrypted viruses whose decryptor also changes in every infection thus leaving no common piece of code between two generations of infection.

But one of the weaknesses of the encrypted viruses is that the virus cannot execute in its encrypted form. Hence the encrypted viral body has to be decrypted before its execution. That means the virus must show up its body before it can cause an infection and the body of the virus can be seen in the memory (RAM) during execution. But there is a problem in reading the virus code from the memory. By the time the anti-virus reads the decrypted viral code from the memory the virus would have already infected the computer.

Contradiction	*The decrypted viral body can be read from memory during runtime. But if we run the infected program to see its viral body then we may well damage our computer system. We want to run the infected program to see its decrypted viral body, but we don't want to run the program as that will infect and damage the computer system.*

Analysis

Improving Parameter: Reliability (of scanning)

Worsening Parameter: Security (Risk of getting infected)

Ideal Final Result

IFR Ideally we should be able to detect the viruses even from their encrypted viral body.

IFR If the above is not possible, at least there should be a method of decrypting the body of the encrypted viruses without running the virus-infected file.

IFR If the above is not possible at least there should be a method of running the infected file without causing damage to the computer. This method is possible though code emulation.

14.3 What is Code Emulation

Code emulation is a technique of running untrusted programs without taking any risk of damaging the computer. In code emulation, the anti-virus software simulates a virtual machine and executes the viral code inside the virtual machine. The virtual machine takes all attempts to mimic the system functionalities so that the virus cannot differentiate between the real machine and virtual machine and executes its code in the virtual environment. During its execution the decrypted parts of its body are found in the virtual memory and caught by the virus scanner (Virtual machine uses TRIZ Principle-26: Copying, Dissolving the virtual machine on each infection uses TRIZ Principle-27: Cheap and Disposable).

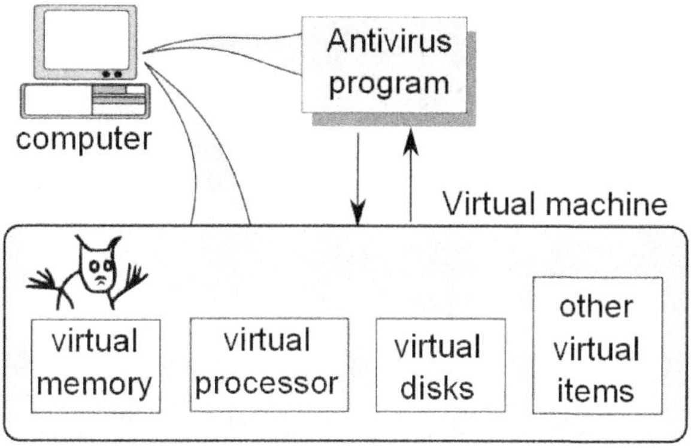

Scanning encrypted viruses through emulation

This method is also called as Generic Decryption (GD) technology. When the decryptor of the polymorphic virus decrypts the viral body the GD scanner detects the virus by searching through the virtual memory of the virtual computer.

This method is similar to sandboxing. Sandboxes are virtual subsystems of the actual operating system. The programs running in sandboxes get access only to a copy of all the information available on the computer. Conventionally the sandbox technique is used to place anonymous FTP services in Unix environment. Even if an intruder manages to gain access to the server, he cannot break the sandbox to gain access to any critical system data. The same technique is used for detecting viruses and malicious programs. When the viruses and malicious programs attempt to make any changes they make them only in the replica of the original data which are all discarded after the operation is over.

The techniques of Code Emulation

Virtual machines emulate a complete copy of the host computer having virtual memory, virtual processor, virtual disk and all virtual resources. The malicious code is allowed to run inside the virtual machine or sandbox without having access to the actual programs in the host system. The code emulator includes a code reading mechanism and a decision mechanism. During emulation the execution stops at certain break points and the code reading mechanism tracks the active instructions in the memory. If the code is found to be containing virus signatures the emulation is terminated. If the code has no viral signatures the decision mechanism decides whether to continue further emulation or not.

Advantages of Code Emulation

This is a powerful technique particularly for dealing with encrypted and polymorphic viruses. As the virus gets no access to the actual machine, the actual machine remains safe. The infections to the virtual machine are reset by dissolving the virtual machine. Even this method is useful to monitor the behavior of metamorphic viruses at the time of their execution.

Disadvantages of Code Emulation

Although CPU emulation is a powerful technique used for detecting virus-like operations it has the following problems and limitations.

- Some intelligent viruses recognize that they are examined in a virtual machine and don't show their viral behavior. For example, the network functionality in a virtual machine is lesser than a real machine. The virus may use this test and try to read some data from other computers in the network or from the Internet. When it fails to access the desired location, the execution flow may change. Thus, code emulation may not detect viruses that exploit network services.

- Some cases may require extensive emulation before the virus-like operations occur. For example, if a virus gives loop command million times before executing a "file open" operation, the processor remains busy to operate that loop command. Excessive load on processor may drastically slow down the performance of the anti-virus program and of the computer.

- Load on disk space- Code emulation may need enormous disk space while decompressing specially created compressed files thereby leading to out of space error.

- Many viruses use anti-emulation techniques. For example, some viruses don't activate immediately. They activate only when certain arbitrary conditions are met like a particular date (such as 13th of a month). If this condition is not met during code emulation the infectious behavior of the virus will not be detected.

- While it is easy to emulate a DOS machine on Windows platform, it is extremely difficult to emulate the complexities of Windows environment on a Windows platform. Extending a good emulator inside a scanner can take a lot of system resources.

- The CPU emulation program may emulate a version of the CPU that is different from the version of the CPU in the computer. For example, 8086 CPU instructions may vary slightly from 80x86 instructions and Pentium CPUs. Similarly instructions on x86 will vary from VAX or Macintosh. Emulating all versions of the CPU by the scanner may be too difficult. Besides if the virus finds different CPUs in a sort span of time it can well guess it to be an emulation. **Solution**- one solution is to check the version of the host machine and emulate only that version. **Drawback**- the incompatible virus intended for a different version will escape from detection. Although it will not infect the host machine, it will remain alive and infect other machine when transferred.

- Some "non-deterministic" events cannot be fully duplicated by the scanner's CPU emulator. For example, an I/O port value may change during a program's operation. A virus may take advantage of this event by reading the I/O port value (and check if the port value is 55) and decrypt itself only if the value (is same as 55) corresponds to a real machine. **Possible solution**- Patent 5964889 proposes a "fault manager" to prevent the viruses from using anti-emulation techniques to evade from emulation based scanner. The fault manager examines the opcode of the instructions when a "fault" is triggered and uses a fault handler to continue execution of the virus for further investigation.

- The emulation method may not work well for memory resident programs. A dynamic heuristic antivirus program begins emulation at the main entry-point of a target program. However, the infectious viral code of a memory resident virus is not reached via the main entry-point of its host program. Instead, the infectious viral code is executed only when the interrupt into which the virus is hooked is called may be by a different program other than the infected host program.

- Most CPU emulators execute only a limited number of instructions in order to decide whether or not a file is infected. If the emulator emulates more instructions the user have to wait for longer time. A virus may take advantage of this and may use large number of "do-nothing" instructions and "dummy loops" in the instructions and avoid detection unless the scanner emulates a large number of instructions.

So, even if the emulated environment protects the actual machine from infection the infectious viral code may not be reached and thus the suspicious viral operations may go undetected.

14.4 Improvements in emulation techniques

The emulators must emulate sufficient amount of code so that a virus infected portion of the file is decrypted. But emulating too much code can be time consuming and confusing. Some of the improvements required to overcome the above limitations of emulation are as follows.

- If the emulator emulates only for the current processor then the files infected on a different processor (and later transferred to this system) will not be detected. On the other hand emulating each file for each pre-fetch queue size will be wasteful and time consuming. Patent 5765030 (by Nachenberg et al.) suggests to emulate files with a variable pre-fetch queue sizes so that the viruses of different processor architecture are detected through minimum number of emulations (TRIZ Principle-15: Dynamize).

- The emulation may be as perfect as possible to show all characters of an actual machine including hardware emulation and internet emulation in order to avoid anti-emulation techniques applied by viruses.

- The emulation technique should be intelligent to detect unnecessary loops in virus codes and avoid executing those codes. Besides the emulator should be intelligent to avoid decompressing intentionally created compressed files that requires huge processing time and disk space.

- It is not necessary to do a complete emulation to see the completely decrypted viral body. The advanced scanner can check the virtual machine's memory whether the decrypted part is long enough for identification of the virus. While the viruses employ anti-emulation techniques to fool emulated hosts the advanced emulators should aim at detecting virus code with minimal emulation.

INVENTION-26: Protective Virtual Machine with network/ Internet access to detect viruses

Many virus programs relating to emails and external communications may not run effectively in a virtual machine without having an Internet connection.

Patent 7493654 (invented by Bantz, et al, Assignee-International Business Machines Corporation, Feb. 2009) discloses a virtualized machine having an interface to Internet. The malware is allowed to pass into the virtual machine without obstruction. All communications between the host computer and the internet is mediated by the PVM (protective virtual machine).

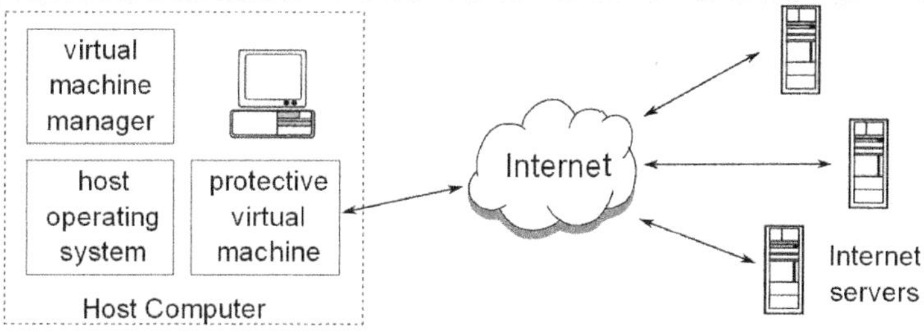

Connecting to Internet through Protective Virtual Machine (PVM)

This mechanism is useful for scanning of emails. Once the email is processed in the virtual machine, the entire PVM is destroyed and recreated for the next email message that needs to be processed (TRIZ Principle-34: Discard and Recover). Thus any harm that might have been caused by trojans, spyware, and registry changes etc. are completely discarded when the environment is recreated and the main operating system is not affected.

Some programs may require full emulation of the environment including hardware and Internet. Failing to read data from Internet may change the execution flow and never reach the desired malicious code. To avoid this problem some emulators point to some particular key point in the computer and then emulate the computer code just from that point (TRIZ Principle-21: Skipping). (Note: Key points refer to known elements of computer code, such as, malware signatures). This method results in faster and more efficient emulation.

INVENTION-27: Detecting malware by back-stepping the program code inside the emulated system

Patent 7739100 (invented by Muttik et al., assignee- McAfee, Inc. Jun 2010) discloses a faster emulation by stepping back upon detection of a key point. The method first searches for known elements of computer code or suspected program code called as key points. Then the execution does a stepping back of few bytes to few hundred bytes (TRIZ Principle-13: Reversing).

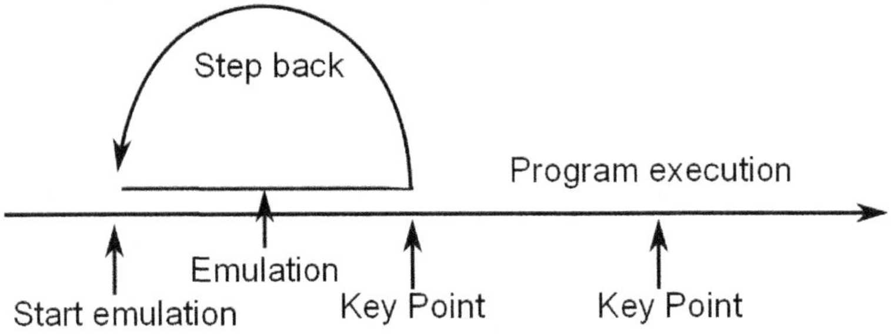

Stepping back at key point
Patent 7739100

From the stepped back position the method does an emulation till it reaches the key point. The results of the emulation is compared with a malware database to find the presence of any matches. If no matches are found then the method may be repeated for a plurality of key points.

Chapter 15.

Improving Heuristic Analysis

15.1 What is heuristic analysis

Heuristic scanning is another method of virus detection that is neither signature based nor integrity based. Heuristic based scanning is a method that examines the pattern of code and the behavior of a suspect program (whether executable file, boot record, or document file with macro, or whatever) to check whether they look to be virus-like. If the pattern of the code or behavior looks to be virus-like then it flags the program as a possible virus and takes other courses of action.

The term "heuristic" means discovering by self-learning methods or by experimental methods or by trial and errors or by loosely set of rules. In heuristic programming the rules are drawn from experience. The heuristic analysis is applied in the same way a human expert would analyze a system. The decisions are taken in the same way as a human expert would have taken that decision. Heuristic programming is used in applications of artificial intelligence and in expert systems.

As we saw that the conventional signature scanning is totally ineffective for polymorphic and metamorphic viruses the heuristic methods are applied to find an approximate solution. Although various heuristic methods were implemented in virus detection since old days, the recent heuristics include more sophistication and intelligence.

How does it work?

Heuristic systems are expert systems which are built to replace the job of human experts in the specific field. The knowledge and rules of the experts are translated to the terms that a computer can understand. The computer applies artificial intelligence in the same way a human would have applied his intelligence.

A heuristic engine detects the commands within a program that are not found in typical application programs, such as, the replication mechanism of a virus, the distribution routine of a worm or the payload of a Trojan. If the target program's code appears virus-like, then the scanner reports a possible infection.

Heuristic methods depend upon meta-heuristic analysis such as pattern matching, automatic learning, environment emulation, neural networks, data mining and other methods. Meta-heuristic methods are useful when there is no logical or heuristic method available to solve a problem. Meta-heuristics are not direct solutions to a problem. They are just general ideas or broad strategies which can probably be useful to solve a problem.

Examples

- ⇨ For example, the heuristic scanning methods scan the critical areas like the beginning or end of the program first. If the signatures are found in the beginning of the program there is no need to scan the whole file. This process saves time and system resources.
- ⇨ Similarly the heuristic methods advise to scan boot sectors for boot sector viruses and executable files for file viruses. There is no point scanning executables for macro viruses or boot sectors for file viruses. This technique saves time and system resources without compromising security.
- ⇨ Often the viruses mark the already infected files with some kind of marker to avoid multiple infection. If the heuristic algorithm can make use of this infection marker it can know whether a file is infected or not.

Advantages

- Being a generic method it does not depend on specific virus signatures. The user need not update virus signatures on a day-to-day basis.
- It can detect unknown viruses and even future threats whose signatures are not yet known. It is very effective to detect variants of existing virus families.

- Because the heuristic technique does not use integrity information, it does not require the fingerprints of programs to be saved in a separate secured place.

- The heuristic scanning intend to detect viruses before they execute themselves and cause damage.

- Heuristic scanning is useful to verify the results obtained from other methods like signature scanning to increase accuracy.

Disadvantages:

- As there is no exact method of defining a virus-like code or virus-like behavior the method may not identify some real viruses or may identify false positives.

- Some heuristics (especially behavior blockers) show a lot of warnings and ask for user feedback. This method requires advanced level of users and are often irritating for common users.

- The heuristic scanners often display a generic name of the virus and not the exact name. The exact virus may be a new virus of the same family or a different virus with similar behavior. That way different scanners may show different names for the same virus.

- The heuristic scanning can analyze viruses written in assembly language, but cannot analyze viruses written in high-level languages like C, Pascal or BASIC. This is because the compiled code for high level languages are extensive and complex.

15.2 Types of heuristic analysis

Heuristic methods can be static or dynamic. Static heuristics is based on the analysis of file formats and the code structure of virus fragments. Dynamic heuristics uses code emulation. The virus codes and virus operations are observed under a simulated processor and operating system. Thus the primary difference between these two detection schemes is that the dynamic method uses CPU emulation while the static method does not.

15.2.1 Static heuristic detection

In static heuristic virus detection, the antivirus program searches the instructions of a target program for sequences of instructions that perform operations typically used by viruses. Unlike virus signatures, these sequences are not designed to be specific to a single virus. Instead, they are meant to be as general as possible in order to detect the operation of many different viruses.

A typical heuristic scanner first narrows down the search by determining the most likely location of a program to find a virus. Then it analyzes the code to determine its likely behavior upon execution. The common heuristics are;

- ⇨ If there is any inconsistency in the location of Entry point
- ⇨ If there is any suspicion with section characteristics
- ⇨ If there is any inconsistency in size calculation
- ⇨ If there is a corrupt relocation table
- ⇨ Using NGrams or consecutive binary sequences inside a program code. Generally the NGrams of benign software are different from the NGrams of malicious software.
- ⇨ Relationships among instructions within each basic block, which can be different for benign software and malicious software.

For example, if the static heuristic antivirus program finds a file open operation, followed by file read and write operations, and also finds a string "VIRUS" in the program, it may report that the file is infected by an unknown virus. Static heuristic detection is generally fast and often performed before CPU emulation.

Limitations of Static Heuristics

- Although static heuristic detection programs can be relatively fast, they may recognize only some of the numerous possible ways of various virus-like operations. For example, different viruses may open files by using different codes and different methods.
- The static heuristics has to look for a large number of different ways to detect the same operations. This involves various possible

permutations and combinations which may eventually become unmanageable.

- Although static heuristic methods can detect metamorphic viruses by targeting specific viruses, they involve complex algorithms and intense computation.

15.2.2 Dynamic heuristics

While static heuristic detects infection without running the suspected code, the dynamic heuristic detects the infection during execution of the suspected code. As running an infected code can be risky, the dynamic heuristic method uses code emulation which loads the target program into a software-based CPU emulator. When the target program is emulated, its virus-like operations are identified and catalogued. From this catalog of virus like operations, the heuristic algorithms determine if the target program looks like a virus.

Thus the method of applying heuristic techniques along with CPU emulation is called dynamic heuristics. This method is considered to be the most powerful method, which is capable of detecting almost all kinds viruses including encrypted and polymorphic viruses. This can also detect polymorphic decryptors that are not detected by static heuristics.

Advantages

- Most powerful method of virus detection
- Capable of detecting encrypted and metamorphic viruses
- As the viral codes are executed in the virtual computer there is no real damage to the host computer.

Disadvantages

- As dynamic heuristics uses code emulation it suffers from all the limitations of code emulation that is described in Chapter-14.

15.2.3 Hybrid or Combined techniques

As both static and dynamic heuristics has their own drawbacks, most modern implementations include both static and dynamic heuristic methods. The static heuristics has the advantages of faster detection but may not work in case of encryption or obfuscated program logic. On the other hand dynamic heuristic has greater scope of detecting all types of viruses when the viruses open up themselves within the simulated environment. However, CPU emulation is a slow process compared to static heuristic scanning. Besides some viruses are intelligent to avoid running in a simulated environment. Hence, both these techniques are not substitutes rather supplementary to each other. Most advanced scanners use both the techniques in their detection algorithm.

15.3 Evolution of Heuristic Detection

Some level of heuristic detection was prevalent in virus scanners since very old time. For example, the integrity checkers were showing a warning when the executable file was being changed. But the integrity checker was not aware whether the executable was changed because of recompilation or because of virus infection. Hence such types of warnings were irritating in a development environment.

While the first generation heuristics were developed on very basic rules, such as, peculiar file date and file stamps, strange headers etc. the second generation of heuristic scanners are much more sophisticated. While all the capabilities of the first generation scanners are retained many advanced heuristics are added, such as, code analysis, code tracing, strange opcodes etc. A modern heuristics includes artificial intelligence, self learning systems, behavior rules and even automatic creation of rules. Looking at various instances of the virus, the scanner learns which part of the virus can be altered and which part of the virus cannot. This learning of the intelligent scanner helps it to scan more and more variants of the same virus more confidently without leading to any false positives.

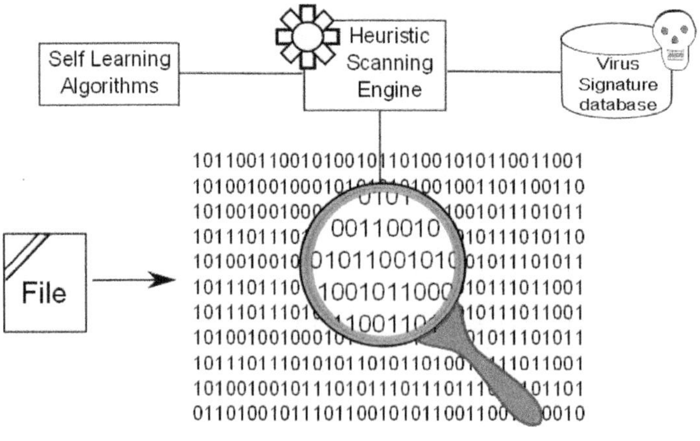

Heuristic Scanning by anti-virus programs

While a specific signature scanning searches for an exact matching of the signature of a known virus, a heuristic scanning scans for a possibility of a new virus threat. But a mere possibility cannot be said to be an infection. Hence, heuristic scanning methods generally consider a large number of heuristics and assign weights for each of them. Although one positive flag is not enough to decide a code to be virus like, when several flags show positive indications that crosses a threshold level the code is decided to be a virus with certainty. For example the behavioral flags in TbScan[#] are;

F- Suspicious file access, might be able to infect a file

R- Relocator Program code will be relocated in a suspicious way

A- Suspicious Memory Allocation. The program uses a non-standard way to search for and /or allocate memory

N- Wrong name extension- the extension conflicts with program structure.

S- Contains a routine to search for executable (.COM or .EXE) files

#- Found an instruction decryption routine. This is common for viruses but also for some protected software

E- Flexible Entry point. The code seems to be designed to be linked on any location within an executable file. common for viruses.

L- The program traps the loading of software. Might be a virus that intercepts program load to infect the software.

D- Disk write access. The program writes to disk without using DOS.

M- Memory resident code. The program is designed to stay in memory.

!- Invalid opcode (non-8088 instruction) or out-of-range branch

T- Incorrect timestamp. Some viruses use this to mark infected files

J- Suspicious jump construct. Entry point via chained or indirect jumps. This is usual for normal software but common for viruses.

?- Inconsistent exe-header. Might be a virus but can also be a bug.

G- Garbage instructions. Contains code that seems to have no purpose other than encryption or avoiding recognition by virus scanners.

U- Undocumented interrupt /DOS call. The program might be just tricky but can also be a virus using a non-standard way to detect itself.

[#] Frans Veldman, "Heuristic Anti-Virus Technology",

Y- Bootsector violates IBM bootsector format. Missing 55AA-marker.

Z- Exe/Com determination. The program tries to check whether a file is a com or exe file. Viruses need to do this to infect a program.

O- Found code that can be used to overwrite/move a program in memory

B- Back to entry point. Contains code to re-start the program after modifications at the entry-point are made. Very usual for viruses.

K- Unusual stack. The program has a suspicious stack or an odd stack.

According to Frans Veldman (the developer of TbScan) TbScan antivirus would have raised the following flags for the given viruses.

Virus	Heuristic Flags
Jerusalem/PLO	FRLMUZ
Backfont	FRALDMUZK
Minsk_Ghost	FELDTGUZB
Murphy	FSLDTMUZO
Ninja	FEDMTUZOBK
Tolbuhin	ASEDMUOB
Yankee_Doodle	FN#ELMUZB

Calculation of Heuristics

As a normal file may have one of the above virus-like characteristics a single heuristic is never determined as a virus. Only availability of multiple heuristics creates a virus alarm. Besides, each of the virus-like activities is assigned a weightage. After verifying all the behaviors the weightages are summed up to find whether the summed weightage exceeds a threshold. If the combined weightage exceeds the threshold then the program is deemed to be infected.

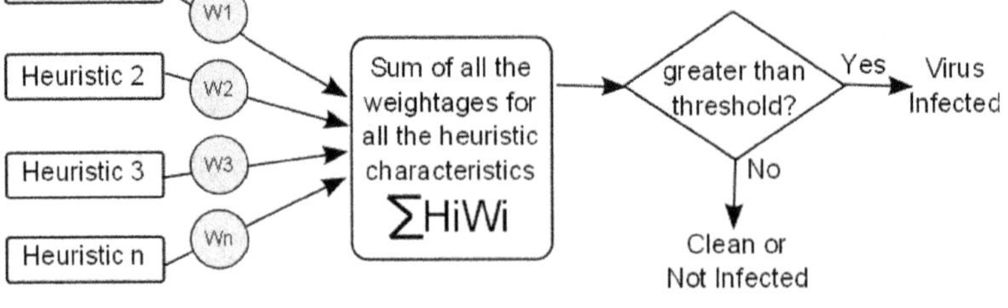

Decisions process in Heuristic Scanning

However, the threshold level may be adjusted to high or low to improve the accuracy and speed of scanning.

- ⇨ Highest level threshold- for exact identification or nearly exact identification. Minimum heuristics used.
- ⇨ Medium level threshold- a balance between speed and accuracy. Speed scanning with low risk of false positives.
- ⇨ Low level threshold- The scanner becomes more sensitive to detect most of the new viruses/malware. But the risks of false positives are increased.

15.3.1 Evolution of virus intelligence

However the virus creators are not easy to get defeated by such simple heuristics. They went further to use various stealth techniques and implemented polymorphism using mutation engines. A combination of these techniques enabled the viruses to remain invisible for the traditional signature scanners and even to simple heuristics. As the heuristic techniques were often documented and known to the virus creators they could become successful in implementing many anti-heuristic techniques in their viruses.

If we look at the trends of evolution in virus technology (Chapter-9) we find the following pattern of evolution. The stealth techniques of viruses gradually improve from encryption to metamorphism to anti emulation to anti heuristic as below.

Stealth techniques like encryption	+ Metamor- phism- self modifying techniques	+ Anti- emulation techniques	+ Anti- heuristic techniques	+ Totally flexible and totally undetectable

This method is same as described in TRIZ Inventive Standard 3.1.1 which says that the efficiency of a system can be improved by combining the system with other systems to form a bi-or-poly system. The method moves from simple to complex or one to many. The evolved new system is a combined system of encryption + metamorphism + anti-emulation + anti-heuristic techniques which is a perfect example of TRIZ Principle-40: Composite.

15.3.2 Integrating artificial intelligence with heuristics

As the encryption and polymorphism techniques became common with the viruses, the virus scanners had to adopt new technologies like code emulation where the anti-virus allows the viruses to execute inside a virtual machine. (We have already discussed about code emulation in previous chapter). The heuristic scanning in virtual machine with code emulation is called dynamic heuristic scanning.

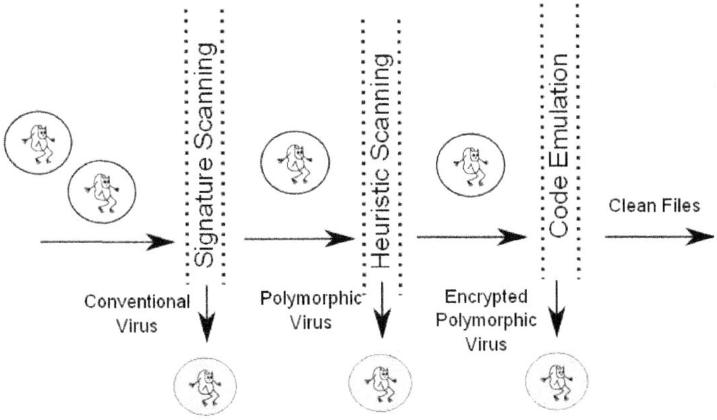

Steps of Scanning by Anti-Virus Programs

If we look at the trends of virus detection technologies in Chapter-9 we find the following transition of techniques from one to many. The later systems included a combination of multiple techniques.

Signature scanning	+ Integrity checking	+ Emulated scanning	+ Heuristic scanning	→

The same trend (TRIZ Inventive Standard 3.1.1) is also found in the development of heuristic scanning method. The earlier heuristic was implemented in combination with emulation to become dynamic heuristics → then both static and dynamic heuristic are combined to build hybrid system → then data mining and automatic learning are combined to build Intelligent systems → and moving towards a fully intelligent Expert system.

Static heuristic scanning	Static + Emulation = dynamic heuristic	Static + Dynamic heuristic = hybrid	+ Datamining + Automatic learning = Intelligent systems	Fully intelligent Expert systems

INVENTION-28: Combining Static and Dynamic heuristics to detect Polymorphic Viruses

Patent 5696822 (invented by Nachenberg, assignee- Symantec Corporation, Dec 1997) teaches to use both static heuristics and dynamic heuristics for detecting polymorphic viruses with more certainty (TRIZ Principle-40: Composite).

The invention includes a CPU emulation module, a static exclusion module, a dynamic exclusion module and data for known polymorphic viruses. First the static exclusion module examines the code. Then the emulation continues until all mutation engines have been flagged or until a threshold number of instructions have been emulated without resorting to "booster" or "stopper" heuristics. If the virus is detected from the partially decrypted file then it is not necessary to decrypt the static virus body fully.

Advanced heuristic techniques

The second generation (and third generation) heuristic techniques involve various advanced technologies, such as,

- ✓ Advanced behavioral analysis
- ✓ Considering a large number of heuristics (may be several hundreds) can result in a more reliable decision on infection.
- ✓ Assign proper weightage to each virus like activity. Every heuristic should not carry equal importance.
- ✓ Include rootkit heuristics (time based analysis)
- ✓ Generic unpacking, blocking and uncloaking techniques,
- ✓ TruePrevent techniques (Panda antivirus).
- ✓ IBM's anti-virus boot scanner.
- ✓ Symantec's bloodhound technology.

15.4 Improving Heuristic Scanning

With the improvement of dynamic heuristic scanning with artificial intelligence it seems there is no space left for the virus to hide. However, there is no limit to artificial intelligence and no end to improvement. The following are some important improvements on heuristic scanning.

- ✓ Heuristic scanning, so far as it is improved, is likely to raise a lot of warnings even for genuine programs thus leading a lot of false positives. A commonly accepted method is to combine multiple heuristics, such as, code anomaly detection, protocol anomaly detection and other heuristics to ensure correct decision.
- ✓ Combine multiple scanning techniques such as, signatures, wild cards, integrity checking, heuristics, code emulation etc. If both traditional methods and heuristic methods give the same results then the result may be correct. This method substantially reduces the false positives and false negatives.
- ✓ Automatic learning- lets the anti-virus to learn from its experience. This method reduces human effort and yields tremendous results.
- ✓ Scan as often as possible – a repeated scan can show the exact behavior of certain codes. As many viruses are slow performers, they may not expose their payload in early scanning.
- ✓ Creating signatures locally in the client machine and notifying to the central security server (Patent 8225405 below).

INVENTION-29: Automatic extraction of classifier data strings for generic detection of computer viruses

Generally it is difficult to construct classifiers that would distinguish an infected program from a good program. A human expert has to identify a number of features that could be present in many viruses in order to construct a classifier. There is a need to construct classifiers automatically.

Patent 5675711 (invented by Kephart et. Al., assignee IBM, October 1997) teaches to use "adaptive" or "learning" techniques from the domain of statistical regression and classification, such as, multi-layer neural networks. It also makes use of techniques available in other fields (like DNA or protein sequences) to construct virus classifiers. This method automatically extracts generic viral features from sets of infected and uninfected programs and automatically constructs a classifier that employs those features to distinguish between infected and uninfected programs (TRIZ Principle-25: Self Service). As the classifiers are constructed automatically the method save human effort and human expertise.

INVENTION-30: Detecting malware by identifying embedded pseudonyms and malware slang

Heuristic detection techniques can be more effective by detecting suspicious target words. Patent 7114185 (invented by Moore, et al, assignee- McAfee Inc. Sep 2006) recognizes the psychology of malware authors is that they often embed their signature in the form of a pseudonym to demonstrate their authorship or communicate a message to other malware authors through their malware. Identifying this embedded text within a computer file can provide a mechanism for detecting malware.

There are wide variety of words that may be indicative of a malware, such as, pseudonyms of malware authors, associated jargon/slang, phonetically equivalent words (e.g., cracks=krakz) etc. other patterns may be unusual mixes of upper and lower case characters in a single word, particular suffixes to words (e.g., ending with "z" instead of "s"). If any such words are found in a file, then the file may be considered suspicious. This method improves the effectiveness of the subsequent heuristic scanning. **Limitations**- however new types of suspicious activities may be included in the malware.

INVENTION-31: Virus detection using heuristic analysis

Patent 7231667 (invented by Jordan, assignee- Computer Associates Think, Inc.. Jun 2007) discloses a method of virus detection by comparing the chronological order of the heuristic events with the chronological order of a defined list of heuristic events.

Although Metamorphic viruses can reorganize and change their viral body, they perform the same large-scale actions, independent of the code in their viral body. Hence, by coalescing small-scale actions into large-scale actions (referred to herein as meta-heuristic events), it is possible to circumvent the power of metamorphic viruses (TRIZ Principle-37: Expansion).

The invention finds that the static heuristics systems discard a lot of very valuable information, e.g., the chronological order in which the heuristic data is being collected. The invention finds that this discarded information, if utilized properly, can be fundamental to a virus scanner's ability to distinguish between false positive results and true-positive results (TRIZ Principle-22-Turn Harms to Benefits).

- The virus programmers use various anti-heuristic techniques to avoid detection of their malicious code by static heuristics. Hence it is necessary to find additional reliable heuristics to detect computer viruses and other malicious codes. Patent 7418729 (Inventor- Peter Szor, Assignee- Symantec Corporation, Aug. 2008) discloses a method of detecting malicious code by tracking suspicious memory pages. While emulating the host file, the system tracks the host file's access of the virtual memory. If the program tries to access any address beyond the normal range the virus reporting module declares a potential virus.

- Microsoft has introduced a feature called System File Protection (SFP) in the newer versions of Windows. SFP checks the version number of the file and prevents the user from overriding critical files or deleting the protected system files that will cause instability on the computer. If the file is corrupted for any reason, SFP automatically replaces the file from a backup copy.

INVENTION-32: Heuristic detection of computer viruses

Patent 7478431 (invented by - Nachenberg, Assignee- Symantec Corporation, Jan. 2009) discloses a method of heuristic detection of computer viruses which is slightly different from Microsoft System File Protection (SFP).

The invented method provides a pre-populated database with version and hash information to the user. As the hashes are pre-populated it can detect even existing infections including future infections. While SFP works on an individual user's computer, this method can be used on any computer, such as an e-mail gateway, a file server, a desktop computer, or a back end infrastructure computer.

INVENTION-33: Detection of viruses by comparing the frequency distribution of program code

Patent 7519997 (invented by- Alexander Shipp, Assignee- Messagelabs Limited, Apr. 2009) detects virus infection by comparing the frequency distribution analysis of the program code with that of the expected distribution of a program created with the same compiler.

The invention analyzes the program files and determines which compiler was used to create that program. The method is based on the assumption that the programs created by a compiler follow a certain frequency distribution and if a program does not follow the expected pattern, may be suspected as infected.

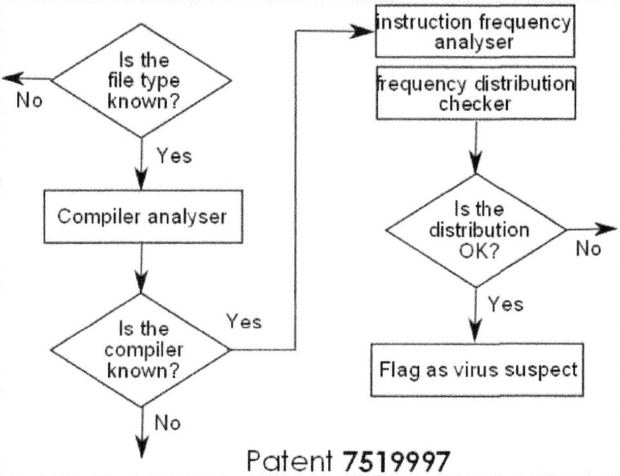

Patent **7519997**

After determining the compiler, the method reverse engineers the program (TRIZ Principle-13: Reversing) and performs a frequency distribution analysis of instructions found in the code to see whether it corresponds with an expected distribution for a program created with that computer. If the frequency distribution checker determines that the frequency distribution is sufficiently closely matching with the expected one, then the processing is discontinued, otherwise the file is considered as suspicious and flagged as possibly having a viral infection.

Sometimes the viruses are hidden in zip files and transferred as email attachments. Patent 7854007 (invented by Sprosts, et al, assignee- Ironport Systems, Inc., Dec, 2010) provides a series of heuristic tests to examine a message content and sender's reputation. The heuristics include name and type of file attachment to a message, size of the file attachment, the amount of similar file sizes attached to received messages, the amount of similar file names attached to received messages and the names of attachments of known viruses. Besides some heuristics are checked on the message sender, subject or body etc. Each of these heuristic has threat scores. When too many messages show higher threat parameters the situation indicates a virus outbreak.

INVENTION-34: Monitoring and detecting modification or removal of uninstaller programs by malware

Sometimes the malware is packaged with a standard installer to convince the user/scanner about the legitimacy of the program. After installation the malware deletes or damages the uninstaller so that the user cannot uninstall the malware. There is a need for detecting such type of installations and remove such malware from computer.

Patent 8099784 (invented by Chen et al, assignee- Symantec Corporation, Jan 2012) discloses a "security module" that will monitor and detect such types of installations performed on a computer. The invented security module ensures that the installation action installs the application along with an uninstaller for uninstalling the application. The method also intercepts and blocks if there is any attempt to remove or modify the uninstaller.

INVENTION-35: Easy future scanning of previously detected viruses through heuristic detection

Patent 8225405 (invented by Peterson, et al., assignee- Symantec Corporation, Jul, 2012) suggests to maintain a blacklist of virus signatures in the host computer. When a virus is detected heuristically a virus signature for the malicious code is created locally on the host computer and updated in the blacklist (TRIZ Principle-17: Another Dimension). This makes the subsequent detection of the virus easy by scanning the file using the locally created signature without going for an execution of the malicious code in an emulated environment.

The signature is then notified to the central security server. The central security server, based on a threshold number of notifications, decides whether to certify it as a signature and distribute that signature to the general public.

INVENTION-36: Heuristic method of recognizing similar viruses having different signatures

Patent 8250655 (invented by Malanov et al, assignee- Kaspersky Lab, ZAO, Aug, 2012) provides a heuristic method of rapidly recognizing similar (or slightly modified) viruses containing different signatures or byte sequences.

The method first divides the file into a number of pieces and then makes various calculations to find if any code of it corresponds to any known malware, such as, a Trojan horse or a virus or a rootkit or a worm. This method easily determines whether the received file is likely to be a modification of the known malicious file.

Chapter 16.

Overcoming Drawbacks of On-Access Scanning

16.1 Introduction to on-access scanning

The conventional scanning method scans the files when they are not in use. This method is called off-access scanning method. This is the popular scanning method which can be scheduled to run during off-peak hours, when the files will be most likely available to the scanning software. Although off-access scanning does a thorough scanning at the wish of the user and scans during convenient hours it has the following drawbacks.

- With the popularity of Internet and proliferation of file sharing, the conventional off-access virus scanning is not sufficient. By the time an off-access scanning is initiated many viruses can spread across many computers and do inconceivable damage.

- The off-access scanning can detect only after infection but they cannot prevent viruses from infecting.

On-access scanning has been developed to compensate the above drawbacks of off-access scanning.

16.2 Implementation of On-Access Scanning

In on-access scanning, as the name suggests, a file is scanned when an access is attempted to the file. The scanner works in collaboration with the access subroutines of the Operating System. The Operating System informs the scanner when a file access attempt is made. The scanner intercepts the file access and scans the file before it is allowed to be accessed by the requestor.

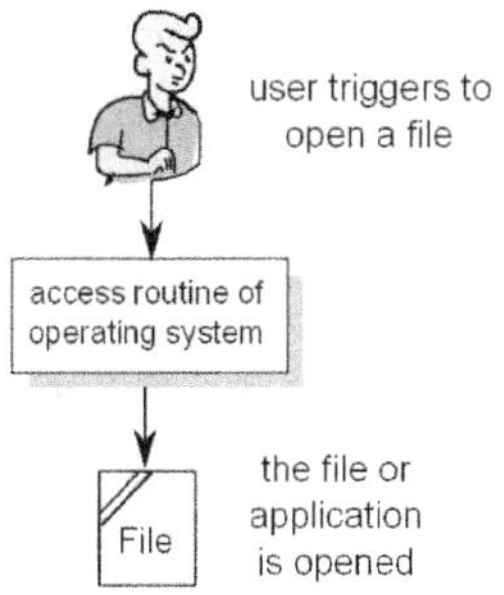

File access without scanning

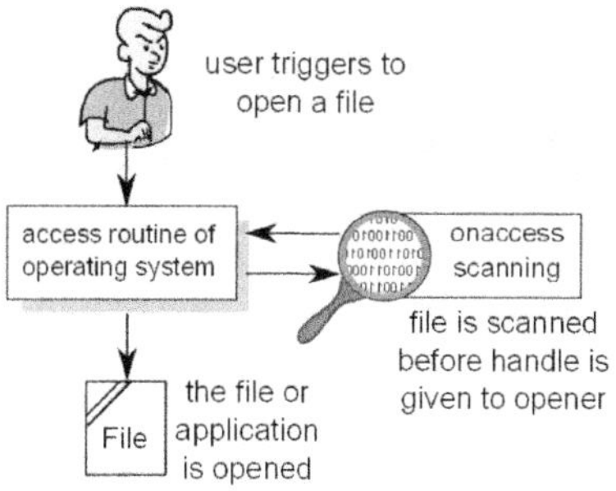

File access through on-access scanning

On-access scanning vs. off-access scanning

- On-access scanning scans only those files or sectors that are accessed unlike off-access (or on-demand) scanning which generally scans all the files in a computer.
- On-access scanning provides a real-time scanning during on-open, on-close, on-read, on-write, on-save and on-execution etc. while off-access scanning scans a file when given to scan.
- On-access scanners are TSR programs, which remain active at all times, unlike the on-demand scanners which start, scan and finish.
- On-access scanning generally does a less detail scanning compared to their on-demand counterparts.

Advantages of on-access scanning

- Scanning is done automatically just before a file is accessed and just before the file is closed. Hence, no need to wait for a human command to scan the file (as in off-access scanning).
- It not only detects infection but also prevents infection. When a virus infects a file it has to open and edit that file. As the on-access scans just before the file is accessed the infection is detected and the virus does not get scope to infect.

16.3 The Problems of On-access scanning

However, there are some problems with on-access scanning. Firstly it occupies some amount of memory continuously as it has to run as a TSR program. Besides it causes a quick surge in the processor load during scanning. A typical problem is balancing security against system overload as any imbalance may lead to either delay in file access or compromise in security. Some of the disadvantages are:

- As the file is scanned before it is allowed to be accessed, the requestor has to wait till the scanning is over in order to get access to the file. If the file is requested by another program, an overly delay to access the file may result in I/O error or other type of file-access errors.
- If the waiting time is too long then the user may believe that there is a malfunction with the hardware or software.
- As the on-access scanning has to finish within a short time it has to do a less detail scanning because of time constraints.
- During scanning on closing of a file, a virus may be detected after the virus code is already saved into the hard disk.

16.4 Overcoming the Problem of Delay in File Access

One of the most desired objective of on-access scanning is to maximize the security but without delaying file access beyond an acceptable limit. The method has to scan the file and release the handle to the requestor within a very short time so that the requestor (whether a human user or a software program) should not confuse or interpret it as a timeout error or an I/O error or other type of error. This problem may be presented in the form of following contradiction.

Contradiction

Contradiction	*We want to scan the files on a realtime basis when they are accessed so that an infection can be detected immediately during infection. But on-access scanning requires some scanning time and therefore delays the file access. We want to scan files during access but we don't want any delay in file access that would cause "file access error" or other confusions.*

Analysis of Contradiction Parameters

Improving Parameter: Security (of computer)

Improving Parameter: Reliability (of scanning)

Worsening Parameter: Loss of Time

Ideal Final Result

IFR Ideally the on-access scanning should take no time (or minimum time) for scanning.

IFR The on-access scanning should not detain the file for scanning.

Possible solutions

As we have discussed earlier in Chapter-3, many prior art techniques try to compromise on security and provide either more security or less security depending on other parameters. But TRIZ does not believe in compromising benefits. TRIZ tries to achieve all the benefits by solving the contradictions.

- Patent 6898712 (invented by Vignoles, et al., assignee Networks Associates Technology, May 2005) provides a plurality of anti-virus test drivers. As there is no point in checking an EXE file for a macro virus, the test engine applies only the specific test drivers based on a previously given classification to speed up scanning. (TRIZ Principle-2: Taking out, Principle-21: Skipping).

INVENTION-37: On-access virus detection actions based on process and file type

Patent 6931540 (invented by Edwards et al., assignee Networks Associates Technology, Aug 2005) suggests an on-access scanning based on the type of the files being accessed and the identified process. For example, executable files and macro files etc. are more likely to propagate virus than data files or image files and hence requires more security measures to be executed. This method allows for more efficient use of system resources while maintaining an appropriate level of security measures.

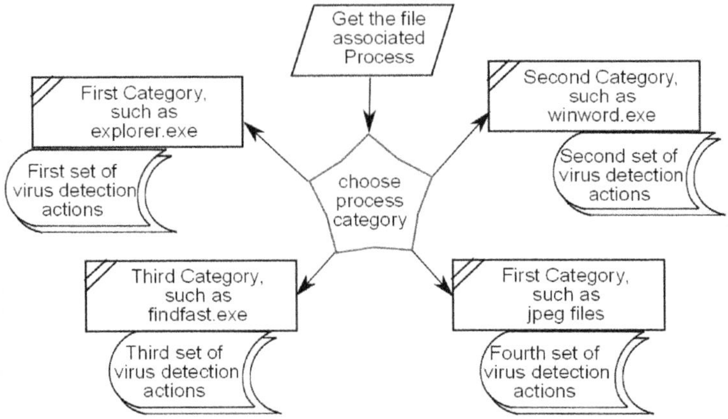

On-access detection, Patent 6931540

According to the invention, the processes associated with Explorer.exe and Iexplore.exe are put in a first category and a first set of virus detection actions is defined (which includes macro and program heuristics). The processes associated with WinWord.exe (high risk of virus propagating) are placed in a second category and a second set of virus detection actions is defined (that includes macros and macro heuristics). The processes associated with Findfast.exe (opens many files for indexing, but no risk of virus propagating) are placed in a third category and a third set of virus detection actions are defined (which includes no scanning). A fourth default category is defined for all other processes and a fourth set of virus detection actions are defined (that includes scanning files only with a recognized filename extension). Thus the first and second categories ensure that the security is heightened whereas the third and fourth categories avoid on-access scanning of too many files (TRIZ Principle-35: Parameter Change).

- Patent 6938161 (by the above inventors and assignee, Aug 2005) classifies the drivers in more detail such as email body scanners, email attachment scanners, on-access scanning agents, on-demand scanners, firewall scanners, network server scanners etc. and places them in a priority order when scanning.

- Patent 7251830 (invented by Melchione, Assignee- McAfee, Inc., Jul 2007) suggests to scan files based on two aspects of the system. The first aspect of the system may include the process adapted for accessing the files and the second aspect of the system may include the type of the files. The processes like reading or indexing has less vulnerability while processes like executing and editing has more vulnerability. This method allows more efficient use of system resources while maintaining the appropriate level of security.

INVENTION-38: Anti-malware scanning with variable scan settings

Many users don't like waiting longer than one or two seconds to check a file. But such a short period of time is not enough to test more than just a few rudimentary checks. There is a need to balance time and effectiveness of scanning.

Patent 7392544 (invented by Pavlyushchik, assignee- Kaspersky Lab, ZAO. Jun 2008) discloses a variable scan setting for scanning of executable files. Before executing a file the method first identifies whether the file is known or unknown. If it is a known file then it performs a signature check. If the file is an unknown file it performs a risk analysis and risk assessment.

The risk analysis is based on any of file source, file origin, file path, file size, whether the file is digitally signed, whether the file is a download utility, whether the file is packed, and whether the file was received from a CDROM. Based on the risk analysis and risk assessment it identifies certain algorithms and performs a malware detection on the file.

Other methods may be used to improve speed of virus scanning such as using a virus co-processor (Patent 8079084). More improvements on scanning speed are described in next chapter.

16.5 Overcoming Problem of System Performance

The on-access scanning is implemented on a real time basis to scan each file during every access. As a typical Microsoft Windows session may involve several file open/ write/ close sessions per second, an on-access scanning may generate huge processing load and degrade system performance. This situation becomes worse for computers having low processing power.

Ideal Final Result

IFR Ideally the on-access scanning should impose no processing load (or minimum load) on the processor.

Possible Solutions

INVENTION-39: Distributed processing of on-access virus scanning

Patent 7243373 (invented by Muttik, et al., Assignee- McAfee, Inc., Jul 2007) advises to follow a distributed processing approach for on-access malware scanning.

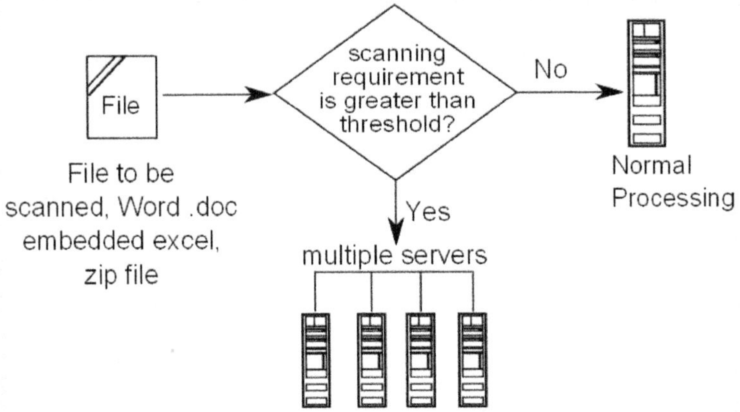

Distributed On-access Scanning
Patent 7243373

The invention first estimates the possible complexity of an on-access malware scan, depending on the file type (e.g., zip files or MS Word files embedding other files). If the estimated time is more than a predetermined threshold, then the scanning of the file is broken down to a number of independent tasks that may be delegated to different computers (TRIZ Principle-1: Segmentation). This method results in a faster completion of scanning because the computationally intensive scanning is distributed between multiple different computers.

INVENTION-40: Introducing an interval between file access and file scanning

Patent 7757361 (invented by Edwards, et al, assignee- McAfee, Inc. Jul 2010) that teaches to introduce an interval between the file access and file scanning. Instead of actually scanning the file before access, the file is just marked for scanning after an interval. As the scanning is not done immediately before file access, there is no surge of load on the processor. During this interval period other open, close and write operations requests are allowed to proceed. However, there is a risk of infection during this interval period.

Contradiction- The time interval for the scanning should be short enough for the viruses/ malware to do any harm to the computer, and should be long enough to follow the open/write/close cycle that is required by the application program.

The above contradiction is solved by setting a duration of interval based on file type, process type and other factors (TRIZ Principle-35: Parameter change). This method allows a reliable scanning and at the same time keeps the delay to acceptably short.

16.6 Overcoming the Problem of Scanning the Streaming data

While downloading streaming media from Internet servers, it is possible to get virus infection through the streaming data. There is a need to scan the streaming data but without compromising throughput efficiency.

INVENTION-41: Scanning streaming data guaranteeing a maximum delay

Patent 7203960 (invented by Painter, assignee- Trend Micro, Inc, Apr 2007) discloses a method of scanning streaming data without compromising the throughput efficiency.

The method scans a portion of the streaming data and compares the scanning time against the maximum scan time. (The maximum scan time is either predetermined or dynamically calculated depending on various factors.) If the estimated scan time does not exceed the maximum scan time, then the incoming data stream is scanned for computer virus. If a virus is detected the remedial action may include blocking the infected data stream, notifying the user about the virus etc. On the other hand if the estimated scan time exceeds the maximum scan time, then the data stream is transmitted without virus scan. Thus the method guarantees a maximum delay for scanning the streaming data.

Chapter 17.

Increasing Speed and Decreasing Load of Virus Scanning

17.1 Problems relating to the speed of scanning

According to Moore's law, the CPU speed doubles in every two years. Everything in the computing industry is increasing at an exponential rate including the processing speed, memory capacity, storage space, display resolution etc. Unfortunately, the speed of virus scanning has not been able to cope with the pace. Although the processing speed has substantially increased, a typical full scanning is still taking several hours for an average computer.

Moreover running an anti-virus consumes significant amount of system resources and affects the system performance negatively. An anti-virus loaded system takes more time to boot, more time to shutdown and runs slow while executing other programs. Because of this reason many users don't like to virus scan their computers unless so required. These two problems, i.e., speed and load are often interrelated. Increasing speed of scanning increases load on memory and processor. There is a need to improve the speed and reduce the load of virus scanning.

17.2 Analysis of problem environment

We have mentioned about this contradiction of "scanning speed and system performance" in Chapter-5. We will deal with this contradiction in more detail in this chapter. The contradiction is "We want the anti-virus to scan the computer, but we don't want it to affect the system performance". The improving parameters are "volume of Execution", "speed of execution", and worsening parameter is "Load on machine". An analysis of the system and its environment finds the following factors that lead to increase in scanning time and scanning load.

- Increase in the number and size of files
- Increase in the number of viruses and virus signatures
- Increase in the complexity of viruses
- Increase in the number of scanning methods or algorithms (such as number of heuristics)
- Need for a higher reliability in scanning
- Increase in the complexity of compressed files- scanning compressed files needs more time to uncompress the files before scanning.
- Repetitive scanning of the same files – either in the same computer or when transferred to other computers.
- Storing and accessing previous scan data (to avoid repetitive scanning) also takes time
- Weaker pattern matching logic can take more time
- A weaker processor takes more time to scan

Let's analyze the above factors to find which factors can be manipulated to improve the scanning time. At least one factor i.e., "reliability of scanning" cannot be compromised. The next important factors are "number and size of files", "complexity of files" etc. which prima facie seem to be totally dependent on the user and his working environment and not in the hands of anti-virus developer to be manipulated. But if we analyze further we can find interesting lights of solution.

- The number of files in the user computer may be more, but the number of files required to be scanned should be less.
- The size of the file may be large, but it may be possible to detect viruses by scanning only a small part of the file that is vulnerable.
- The files in the user computer may be complex, but there may be a simple method to scan the complex files.

Thus the factors, which initially appeared to be totally dependent upon user and his working environment, now look different. The factors, which appeared to be totally independent of the anti-virus program or anti-virus developer, now seem to be controllable. The number of viruses may go up but the number of signatures can be reduced (e.g., by using global signatures or by using generic methods of scanning). The number of signatures may go up but scanning time can still be reduced (e.g., by using specific type of signatures for specific type of viruses).

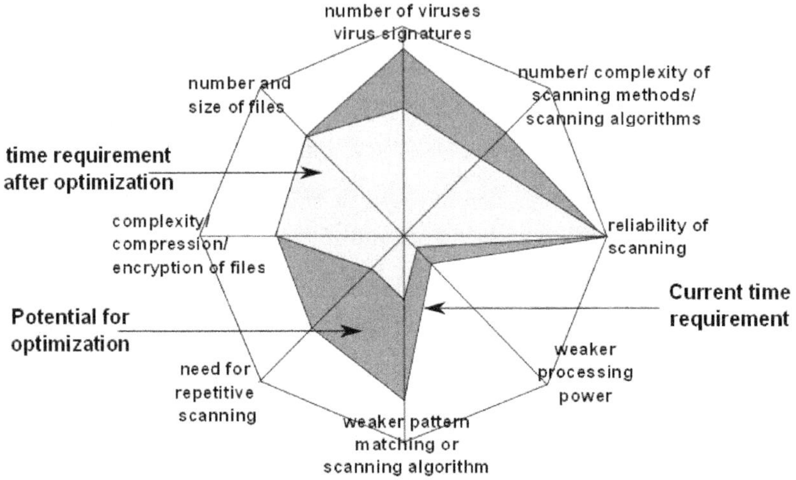

Optimizing Scanning Time

The other factors like "complexity of scanning", "pattern matching algorithm", "need for repetitive scanning" etc. are directly controllable by the anti-virus engine. There are techniques like "using cache for scanning", "scanning only the changed sectors", "using scanner cards", "using separate scan processor", "using virus co-processor", "scanning in a different machine", "smart scanning or intelligent scanning", "using faster databases", "using improved pattern matching" etc. which can improve the scanning speed without compromising the quality or reliability of scanning. Thus in the above paragraphs we found that most of the factors can be controlled by improving the anti-virus technology which can result in improving speed of scanning and reducing load on the machine.

17.3 Contradiction of number of files and scanning time

The time required for scanning is directly correlated with the number and size of files in the computer. This is because all the data has to be read from the disk in order to be compared against virus signatures. An average processor takes about 30 minutes for scanning each 10 GB of hard disk. Thus if the number and size of the files are more then a scanning can take proportionately longer time because of the processing and disk I/O requirement. One solution is to advise the users to reduce the number and size of files. But we don't want to curtail their productivity by imposing such kind of restrictions.

Contradiction

Contradiction	*We want to scan all the files in order to ensure that no infected file is skipped. But we don't want to scan all the files, as that would require long time to scan.*
	We want to increase the number and size of files in order to meet the growing need of our work. But we want to reduce the number of files (and their size) in order to have faster scanning.

Analysis of Contradiction Parameters

Improving Parameter: Volume of Execution

Worsening Parameter: Loss of Time

Improving Parameter: Volume of Data

Worsening Parameter: Volume of Execution

Ideal Final Result

IFR Scanning a minimum number of files should ensure full security.

IFR Scanning a small portion of a file should ensure the status of file whether infected or not

IFR Employing only a few methods or scanning only specific areas of computer (partial scanning) should give us full security

Possible solutions:

- One option is to scan only the executable file types (.exe, .com etc.) which are more susceptible to viral infection. **Drawback**: with the advent of complex structure of files many non-executable files also contain malware.

- We don't want to reduce the number of files or size of files, but we want to reduce the size of data to be scanned. The solution comes out soon. Advanced scanners don't scan the whole file for virus signatures. Depending on the file type, such as, .com or .doc, the scanners scan only those areas of the file that are more vulnerable and more likely to contain a virus which is much faster than scanning the whole file (TRIZ Principle-21: Skipping).

- Generally a disk cache is used to speed up reading data from a disk. A similar technique may be used to read the files from cache. **Limitations**: a standard caching mechanism does not help as the scanner still has to wait for the data to be read from the disk before it can be stored in the cache.

- Main memory and more vulnerable files may be scanned first with high priority and other files may be scanned later with low priority.

INVENTION-42: Save time by skipping the scanning of unmodified opened files

In the prior art method, an anti-virus first scans a file when the file is requested for opening. It allows the file to be opened only if the file is found to be free from any virus. Similarly, the anti-virus scans the file again when the opened file is requested for closing to ensure that the file is not infected when it was open.

Patent 6928555 (invented by Drew, assignee Networks Associates Technology, Aug 2005) suggests to avoid scanning of files unless they are found to be modified during the period when they were opened.

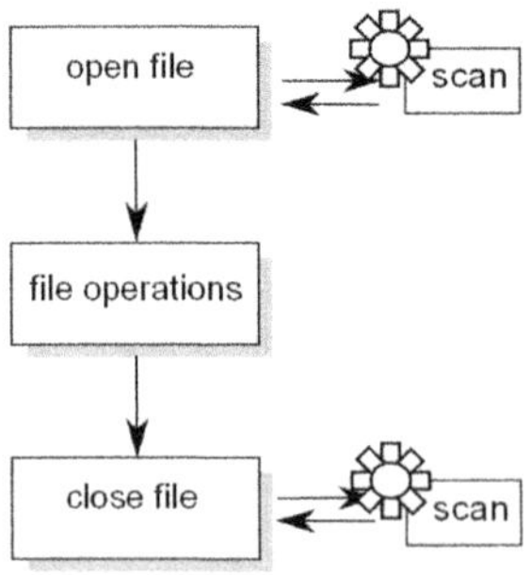

Prior art - 2 scans
once while opening and
once while closing file

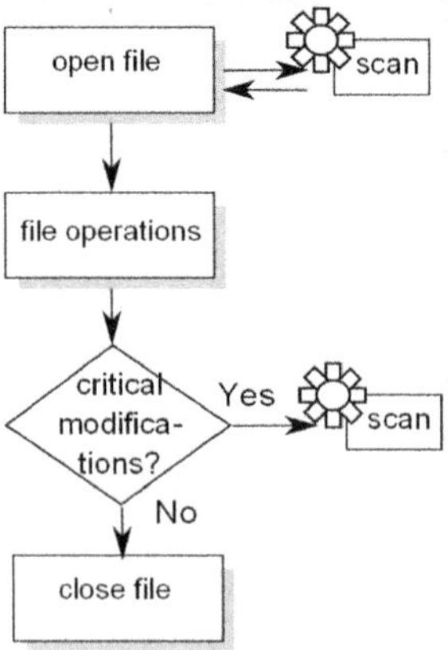

invented method
Patent- 6928555

The invented method does not scan a file just because it is opened for modification. The invention checks the "dirty cache buffer" of the Operating System to check whether the file has actually been modified after it was opened. If the file is found to be unmodified then the method considers the file to be clean and skips scanning of the file before closing (TRIZ Principle-21: Skipping).

INVENTION-43: Faster scanning by disk reading and virus scanning in two separate threads

The reading of the actual data to be scanned from the disk takes a lot of time. In a typical scanning session, as much as 40% of the scanning time is consumed by reading the data from the disk.

Patent 7036147 (invented by Hursey, assignee McAfee, April 2006) suggests to accelerate scanning by reading the data in a separate thread while the main thread is busy scanning the pre-read data.

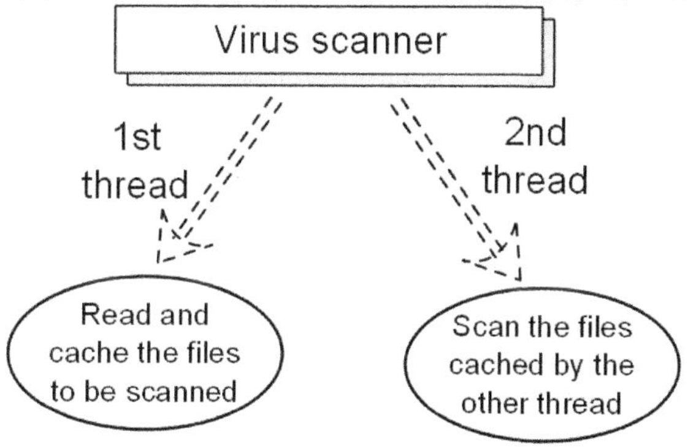

Reading and scanning files in separate threads

The invention executes two threads in parallel. The first thread is used to read the data from the disk and the second thread is used to scan the pre-read data (TRIZ Principle-1: Segmentation). The first thread is executed in parallel with the second thread in such that while a first portion of the data is being scanned, a second portion of the data to be scanned is being read and cached (TRIZ Principle-10: Prior Action, Principle-5: Merging). This method avoids the delay generally caused by the disk read operations.

INVENTION-44: Reducing files to be scanned by heuristically detecting viruses in executable code

Because of Internet and email, many files move from one computer to another. But scanning each of these files on every computer will be a repetitive work. Patent 7664754 (invented by Alexander Shipp, assignee- Symantec Corporation, Feb 2010) discloses a method of reducing number of files by eliminating known good files from scanning.

The method first identifies the known executables and matches their characteristics (or hash string such as MD5 or SHA5 checksum algorithms) with a database. If the hash string/ characteristics are unchanged then they are deemed to be safe and eliminated from scanning. If on the other hand the hash string/ characteristics are found to be changed then those cases are treated as extremely suspicious and most likely infected by viruses.

Patent 8028338 (Invented by Schneider et. al., Sep 2011) discloses a set of goodware characteristics which can be used to determine whether a file belongs to goodware. This method identifies the good files easily without scanning them for malware characteristics. As the number of good files are generally more than the number of infected files this method saves time by avoiding unnecessary scanning of malware characteristics in a large number of good files (TRIZ Principle-17: Another Dimension, Principle-21: Skipping).

17.4 Contradiction of number of signatures and scanning time

Anti-virus programs scan the computer files by comparing each file to a list of virus signatures. In such a situation, as the number of viruses increase, their signatures also increase and the required scanning time as well.

$$\text{Scanning time required} = \frac{\text{number of viruses X number and size of the file objects X number of detection methods}}{\text{Speed of processor}}$$

Ideal Final Result

IFR The number of viruses should not increase there should be no need to scan for each individual virus.

IFR One single signature or set of signatures should detect all types of viruses.

Contradiction

Contradiction	*If a scanner includes all available virus signatures then the scanning process will take very long time. On the other hand if the scanner does not include some virus signatures then there is possibility of some viruses being escaped.*

Analysis of Contradiction Parameters

Improving Parameter: Volume of execution, Reliability

Worsening Parameter: Loss of time

Possible solutions:

- If we look at the IFR and contradiction, the desired result can be achieved either by reducing the number of viruses or by reducing the number of signatures. But are there some representative viruses which can be scanned to vouch for other viruses? Can there be some special signatures (e.g., wild card signatures) which can be used to detect a large number of viruses in one go?
- One of the solutions to the above problem is to spread a scanning process over several sessions (TRIZ Principle-1: Segmentation). **Limitation**: this method does not reduce the total time required for scanning.
- Another solution is to do a partial virus scanning of the core elements like main memory, boot sector, file system etc. (TRIZ Principle-16: Partial or Excessive Action). A partial virus scanning is a fast mode virus scanning that is useful during boot time.
- Scanning only relevant types of viruses depending on the type of files thereby eliminating the scanning of irrelevant virus types. For example, a boot sector signature need not be used to scan a macro file. This method reduces the total number of search operations and reduces the scanning time.

INVENTION-45: Computer resource optimization during malware detection using anti-virus cache

As the virus-definition databases are quite large, it takes a long time to get loaded in to the memory and converted to the usable format during system startup and before each process of scanning. There is a need to reduce load on system resources.

Patent 7962959 (invented by Batenin, assignee- Kaspersky Lab ZAO, Jun 2011) suggests to use an anti-virus cache in a non-volatile memory or in hard disk. The anti-virus application periodically updates the cache when required from the anti-virus database (TRIZ Principle-24: Intermediary).

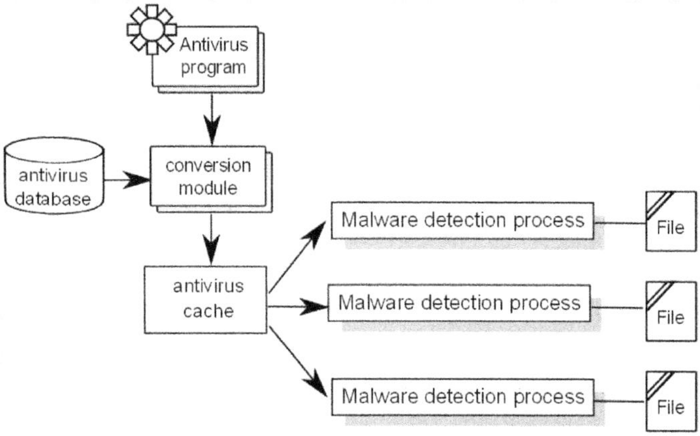

Using anti-virus cache, Patent 7962959

The executable code sections are also converted into platform-specific dynamic libraries stored in the antivirus cache. During execution the same anti-virus cache is shared and simultaneously accessed by multiple detection processes.

17.5 Contradiction of more reliable scanning and scanning time

The results of a scanning should be reliable and should raise minimum number of false positives or false negatives. In order a scanning to be reliable it must do various tests to confirm the existence or non-existence of a virus that requires more scanning time. Exact identification scanners, which use all the signature strings of a virus, are more reliable than nearly exactly identification scanners. But exact identification scanners take more time to scan. The situation leads to following contradiction.

Contradiction

Contradiction	*If the anti-virus program does not apply all the required methods of scanning it may lead to false positives or false negatives. On the other hand if it applies all available methods to confirm a scan result, then it would take more scanning time. We want a confirmed result on scanning but we don't want to give more time for scanning.*

Ideal Final Result

IFR One single method should be able to detect all types of viruses thereby eliminating the need for implementing multiple methods.

IFR Even if more methods are applied for scanning they should be very fast so that the scanning is finished within no time.

Possible solutions:

- Scanning more harmful viruses in order of priority instead of scanning all the viruses in one go. **Limitation**: This method can only reduce the damages caused by virus infection.

- Skipping irrelevant virus signatures can save time without compromising security. For example, there is no point in checking an EXE file for an embedded Word macro virus or vice versa. A file virus cannot infect a Word Macro in any way.

INVENTION-46: Classification and ordering of virus test drivers

Patent 6898712 (invented by Vignoles, et al., assignee Networks Associates Technology, May 2005) provides a classification of virus test drivers which may be used to apply only selected test for any given type of file. this method works fast as there is no need to apply all types of tests for all types of files.

	DRIVER TYPE				
FILE TYPE TO BE SCANNED	EMBEDDED HTML	MACRO	GENERAL	TROJANS/ WORMS	GRUNT
EXECUTABLE FILES			✓	✓	✓
DOCUMENTS	✓	✓	✓	✓	✓
E MAILS ATTACHMENT		✓	✓	✓	✓
E MAIL BODIES	✓				

FIG. 2

The invention also classifies the anti-virus test drivers in order of priority so that the higher threats and/or faster tests are applied first. An approximate order of priority for applying anti-virus drivers may be something like a test for a newly released virus, a highly infectious virus, a highly damaging virus, a common virus, a test that is quick to perform, an average threat level virus, a rare virus and a test that is slow to perform. However, the priority ordering may be dynamically altered depending on the file type and other factors (TRIZ Principle-15: Dynamization).

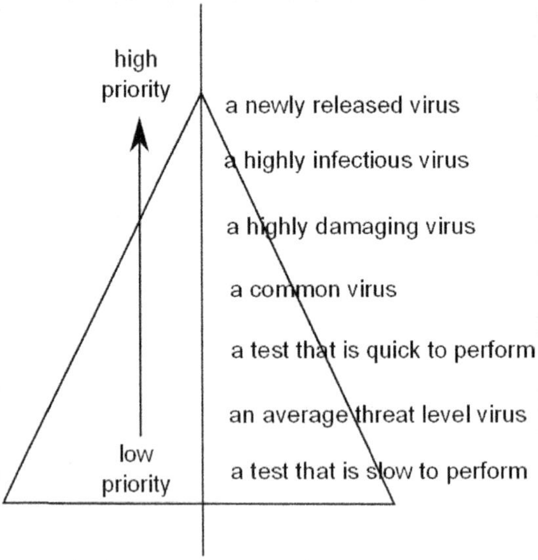

Priority of scanning

17.6 Contradiction of file complexity and scanning time

Certain types of files need more time to scan. For example, the email attachments are to be detached and the compressed files need to be decompressed before scanning. Complicated compression algorithm can take more time for decompressing files. Some viruses intentionally create complex nested zip files in order to fool the anti-virus. The anti-virus takes long time for decompressing those files and consumes huge system resources.

$$\begin{array}{c}\text{Time required for}\\ \text{decompression}\end{array} = Fn\left(\begin{array}{c}\text{Size of actual file, Complexity}\\ \text{of Compression algorithm}\end{array}\right)$$

Similarly when a file is encrypted it's not possible to trace the virus signatures in the encrypted code. There can be numerous types of compression and encryption. The situation is worse if the compression algorithm is more complex. The situation becomes even worse when the compressed/encrypted file is password protected.

Contradiction	*Encryption- The anti-virus program cannot scan an encrypted file because its content is scrambled. If the anti-virus decrypts the file using brute force then it will breach the privacy and confidentiality of the file.*
	Compression- It is sometimes necessary for people to use complex algorithms to reduce size of compressed files. But such type of compression requires complex scanning procedures and longer scanning time.

Ideal Final result:

IFR The compressed/encrypted files should have built-in virus resistance.

IFR The compressed/encrypted files themselves should indicate whether they are infected or not.

IFR The scanner should be able to detect viruses in a compressed/encrypted file without decompressing/decrypting.

IFR Even the most complex decompression/decryption should take very little time.

Possible solutions:

- When an anti-virus takes an abnormally long time to decompress a compressed file during scanning, some systems introduce a time-out in the scanning operation in order to help the anti-virus to come out from the scanning loop (TRIZ Principle-21: Skipping). **Drawbacks**- although this method helps the anti-virus to come out of a virus trap, it may terminate virus scanning in a genuinely slow and overloaded computer thereby compromising security.

INVENTION-47: Scanning file archives without decrypting and without decompressing

Patent 7797746 (invented by Fossen, et al, assignee- Fortinet, Inc., Sep, 2010) teaches a method of scanning an archive file without decrypting and without decompressing the content of the archive.

The invention first identifies the structure of an archive file and obtains some descriptive information for each of the contained files. Then the descriptive information for each of the files is compared with known virus signatures to determine if any of them are malicious. Thus the undesired computer files are detected in encrypted, compressed, password-protected and even in damaged archives without decompressing the archives.

- Patent 7802300 (invented by Liu, et al, assignee- Trend Micro Incorporated, Sep, 2010) teaches a method of detecting rootkits in file archives without opening it. The invented anti-rookit module compares the operating system kernel binary files to their loaded kernel file image in the memory to find a difference between them. If a difference is detected then it further verifies whether the modifications are done by rootkits. If the difference is due to rootkits, the kernel file image is restored to a known good condition to disable the rootkit.

INVENTION-48: Maximizing virus checking and minimizing redundancy in scanning compressed files

Often compressed files require recursive scanning and requires too much time and system resources. Patent 7979904 (invented by

Ramer, assignee- International Business Machines Corporation, Jul 2011) discloses a faster method of scanning compressed files.

The method decompresses the compressed files recursively to a directory using a decompression tool. If the files are decompressed without error then they are considered as uninfected and deleted. If any errors are ascertained, then the respective files are scanned by a virus-canning tool. Thus the scanning tool avoids checking the respective compressed files which were decompressed without error (TRIZ Principle-21: Skipping).

17.7 Methods of avoiding Repetitive Scanning

A typical anti-virus system scans the same files again and again repeatedly in every scanning session although most files have never been used by anybody in between the scans. Besides in a networked environment many files are copied them from one computer to another for sharing. Although the files were already scanned in their previous locations they are usually scanned again and again in every computer they are copied to. This process of repetitive scanning unnecessarily wastes a significant amount of time and system resources. It would be better to avoid repetitive scanning in order to save time and system resource.

Contradiction	*A scanning session scans through a large number of files although only less than 1% of the files have been used or altered. We want to ensure that the files we share are free from viruses but we don't want to waste time and resources to scan the files again and again when copied from one computer to another.*

Analysis of Contradiction Parameters

Improving Parameter: Volume of Execution

Worsening Parameter: Loss of Time, Load on Machine

Ideal Final Result:

IFR Only the infected files should be scanned and others not.

IFR Once a file is scanned and deemed to be virus-free it should not be scanned again unless found to be modified.

Possible solution:

- US Patent 5473769 (By Paul D. Cozza) discloses a method of avoiding repetitive scanning of the same objects. The method saves a set of parameters as AV state (such as the details of the last scan) in a database. The object is scanned only if the object is new or if the object is changed since its last scan. On the other hand the object is skipped from scanning if the object is not changed since its last scan (TRIZ Principle-21: Skipping)

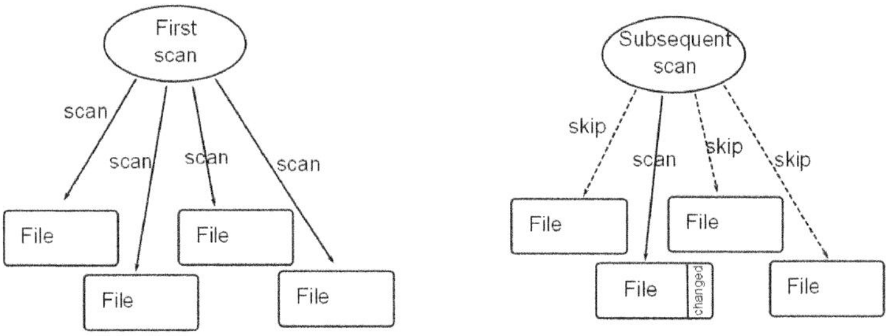

Skip repetitive scanning, US Patent 5473769

- Patent 6021510 (by Nachenberg) discloses an anti-virus accelerator which stores the hash value of each storage sector in a critical sectors file. During scanning it compares the hash value of the sectors with those stored in the critical sector file. A file is scanned only if any if its sectors fails to match its hash value with the stored value.

- Patent 6094731 (by Waldin et al.) suggests to store the hash values of each scanned sector of a file into a critical sectors file. When the file is transferred to another computer, the critical sectors file is also transferred along with the file. The recipient computer examines the critical sectors file and scans the file only if any of the sectors is found altered (TRIZ Principle-10: Prior Action, Principle-21: Skipping).

- Another method to avoid repetitive scanning is by certifying the data to be virus free. The scanner may certificate a file or email or other object to be virus free in order to avoid successive scanning in the same machine or in other machines (Patent 7107618).

INVENTION-49: Increasing virus detection speed by an improved method of storing the scanning state

The method of using the last scan information is effective only if the file is to be scanned against the same list of viruses. But if the signature database is updated then the last scan information must be initialized to get the benefit of the updated virus list, otherwise the files infected with newly added viruses cannot be detected.

Contradiction	*With the updated virus definition database, if the scanner ignores the last scan status and rescans the object against the new database, then the scanner does not get any benefit from the last scan status database. On the other hand if it skips the object without scanning, then it does not get the benefit of updated virus database and leaves the object possibly infected.*

Patent 6952776 (invented by Chess, assignee International Business Machines Corporation, Oct 2005) discloses a new method which checks not only the last scan status but also the last update status (TRIZ Principle-40: Composite). This method considers both the last scan status of the files and the last update status of virus definition database to get the benefit of both. This method of virus scanning requires less time than the conventional techniques, as the method does not always rescan even if the virus definitions have changed (TRIZ Principle-21: Skipping).

INVENTION-50: Fast virus scanning by storing last scan status in directory database

Although skipping the previously scanned files saves scanning time, storing and accessing the results of a previous scan can be a time taking process.

Contradiction	*If the AV state is stored in a cache then it will be fast to access, but it will remain for a short period, as the cache is volatile in nature. On the other hand, if the AV state is stored in a separate database, then the data can be stored permanently, but access will be slower. We want to store the AV state data permanently in a database but we don't want to make its access slow.*

Patent 6763466 (invented by Glover, assignee Networks Associates Technology, July 2004) suggested to store the AV state information in the unused fields of the directory database where the file system maintains information about each file. The invention tries to explore what **resources** are already available inside the system and utilize those resources (TRIZ- System Resources).

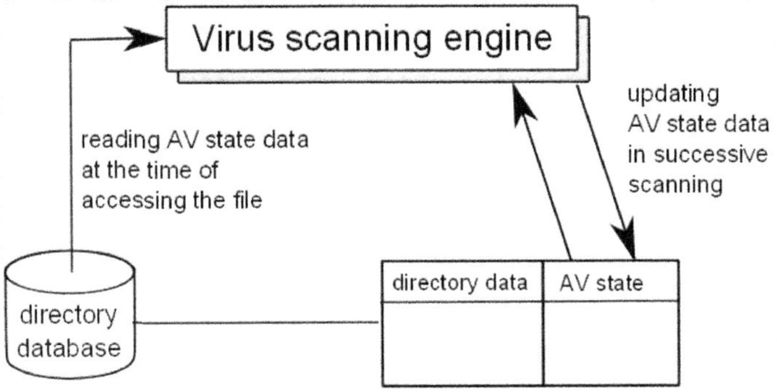

Storing AV state in Directory Database

This method of storing the AV state data is extremely fast as the anti-virus data for a file can be retrieved by the file system at the time when the file is being accessed by an application program.

- The above method of skipping "already scanned" files from subsequent scanning has one drawback. If a virus changes the status of an infected file as "already scanned" then the scanner would skip that file from scanning. **Ideally the anti-virus should be able to change the status of the file to "already scanned", but the virus should not be able to change the status (IFR).** This problem is solved by keeping the AV state data in a secured place which cannot be accessed by any virus. One method is to create a HPA (Host Protected Area) in the hard disk. Another method is to use a separate memory chip for secured storage.

- Patent 7401361 (invented by Freeman, et al., Assignee- Lenovo (Singapore) Pte. Ltd., Jul. 2008) follows a different approach by marking the changed sectors in a hard disk instead of marking the changed files. According to this method a protected archive bit is maintained for each sector on the hard disk. When a sector on the hard disk is altered, the sector is marked as "changed". The virus scanning software scans only these "changed" sectors instead of scanning all the sectors (TRIZ Principle-17: Another Dimension).

INVENTION-51: Pre-approving computer files to speed up virus scanning

Patent 7257842 (invented by Barton, et al, assignee- McAfee Inc. Aug 2007) suggests to maintain a list of specific known malware free computer files. During scanning the files in the user computer are matched with the corresponding malware free files by comparing a checksum. If a match occurs with any of the specific known malware free computer files, then the file may be pre-approved to be virus free without requiring further scanning.

INVENTION-52: Reducing scanning time by scanning only the changed sectors

Patent 7581250 (invented by Sitze, assignee- Lenovo (Singapore) PTE Ltd, Aug 2009) suggests scanning only the changed sectors of the hard disk in successive scanning instead of scanning the complete hard disk. While the objective of the invention is same as above, i.e., to skip the already scanned data, the method is completely different as it uses a physical sector based approach instead of a file-based approach.

The invention first scans all the sectors of a disk. Later it scans only those sectors in which the data is modified. This method is much faster, because in each scanning session, the method checks whether there has been any write operation to any sector of the hard disk. If there is any write operation then the specific sector is scanned otherwise the sector is avoided (TRIZ Principle-21: Skipping)

Patent 7155461 (invented by Miyata, et al., assignee- Hitachi Ltd, Dec 2006) suggests a method of eliminating unnecessary scans to accelerate file access. A file server and a scan server works cooperatively. The file server stores the last scan time of every file as file attribute information. If the last scan time of a file requested is later than the last update time of the virus pattern then the scan is omitted (TRIZ Principle-21: Skipping).

INVENTION-53: Avoiding repetitive scanning of duplicate files in a network

The same files are repeatedly scanned and repeatedly backed up in a network. There is a need to avoid this repetition to save time.

Patent 7398399 (invented by Palliyil, et al., Assignee- International Business Machines Corporation, Jul. 2008) identifies identical resources on different computers in a network by comparing the hash values for each resource. Once the identical resources are identified, the information is used for different purposes.

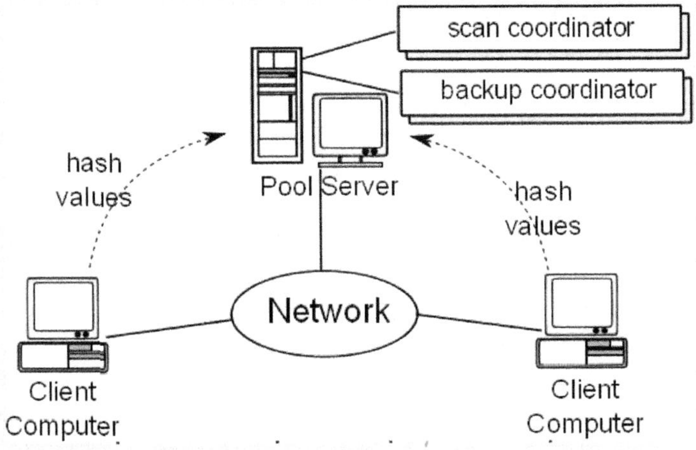

For example, if a resource is identical to its previous stage then a virus scan may not be required for the resource. Although a hash comparison does not indicate whether a file is infected or not, it determines whether a scanning is required or not. The same information is also used for managing backups as the identical resources may not be backed up again.

Conventional methods scan every opened files at the time when they are closed. Patent 7441274 (invented by Drew, Assignee- McAfee, Inc., Oct. 2008) suggests to skip scanning of an opened file at the time of closing unless the file is changed. When a file is requested for closure the method checks the operating system flag whether the file is modified or not. If the file is not modified since the time it was opened then the file is assumed to be not infected and not considered for scanning.

INVENTION-54: Storing the tracking of changed files in a secure storage to speed up virus scanning

Patent 7581252 (invented by Challener, et al., assignee- Lenovo, Aug 2009) and Patent 7581253 (Aug 2009) suggest to divide the storage into a scan area and a protected area. The scan area is used for storing the regular user files and the protected area is used by a security subsystem.

The security subsystem trustfully tracks the alterations of files and storage devices and stores the alteration data in the secured location. The security subsystem uses a memory that is inaccessible to any code executing from the operating system so that the no virus can change the data relating to the last scan status (TRIZ Principle-2: Taking out).

The invented method advises to scan the altered files or storage areas with a super-set of virus definitions (i.e., all viruses) and the unaltered files or storage areas with a subset of virus definitions (i.e., only the new viruses).

17.8 Improving database access and pattern matching

In both signature scanning and emulation, most of the CPU time is spent in matching the data against a set of signature strings that represent virus properties. As the number of viruses is increasing the commercial virus scanners have to maintain database of about a million virus signatures. Any weakness in the structure of database can significantly degrade the performance. Similarly a poor string searching or pattern matching algorithm can make the virus-scanning operation longer. Some of the techniques used to speed up virus scanning are as below.

- Smart scanning- the advanced scanners are capable of recognizing junk instructions and exclude them from scanning (TRIZ Principle-21: Skipping). For example, some viruses use mutation engines to change viral codes by inserting NOP and junk instructions. A simple signature scanning fails to detect these mutated codes. But a smart scanner skips NOPs and junk instructions and don't consider them as virus instruction bytes.

- Sometimes the virus codes are mixed up with white space characters (like space, line feed, tabs etc.) This may happen particularly when executable text files (such as batch files and script files like .ini, etc) are edited by an user. As a result a simple scanner fails to detect the virus signature. Patent 6230288 (invented by kuo et al., assignee Network Associates, May 2001) suggests to eliminate all additional whitespaces (TRIZ Principle-2: Taking out) and replace all whitespace characters in the file by a common whitespace character such as a space. Then the same transformation is also applied to the virus signatures. By uniformly transforming all whitespace sequences within both the virus signature and the file to be searched, a virus in an infected file is much more likely to be located (TRIZ Principle-33: Homogenous).

- While an exact identification scanning is more precise in detecting specific viruses it is quite slow. A nearly exact identification scanning if combined with checksums can achieve higher speeds and greater accuracy.

- Skeleton detection – invented by Eugene Kaspersky, the founder of Kaspersky anti-virus - The method reduces the searching zone by removing each instruction that probably does not belong to the virus code (TRIZ Principle-2: Taking out). This method is useful particularly in detection of macro viruses.

17.9 Compensating a weaker processor

The power of the processor is inversely correlated with scanning time. A better processor does faster scanning. Although the power of the processor is improving in each generation it is still not sufficient to cope with the multitude of new viruses and volume of data to be scanned. Let's find how to solve this problem.

Ideal Final Result

IFR The scanning should involve such algorithms that would put minimal load on the processor

IFR The processor should be so powerful that a virus scanning should take minimal time

IFR The load of scanning may be shifted to another processor/s so that there is no load on the main processor for scanning

Possible solutions

- An obvious solution is to upgrade the processor which will compensate the load (TRIZ Principle-8: Counterweight). **Drawback**: upgrading processor is an expensive solution.
- Another solution to reduce the processor load is by putting the anti-virus on the gateway. This will protect the system by scanning all incoming and outgoing files but will not affect the system performance (TRIZ Principle-2: Taking out). **Drawback**- It can check viruses coming from external sources but cannot check viruses coming through CDs, pen drives and other internal sources.
- Another solution to reduce processor load is by scheduling virus scanning during nights or on holidays when the user is not working. The self-running feature of the anti-virus program can run automatically at a pre-scheduled day and/or time (TRIZ Principle-20: Continuity, Principle-25: Self Service). **Limitation**- this is not useful for home computers which are used at anytime irrespective of any day of the week or any hour of the day.
- Another solution is to run the anti-virus when the system is running but the user is **not** working. Some modern anti virus programs can be scheduled to run when the system is left idle for certain time (TRIZ Principle-15: Dynamize, TRIZ Principle-25: Self Service).
- Yet another solution is to divide the scan load on multiple computers. Patent 7644352 (invented by Grupe, assignee- McAfee, Inc., Jan 2010) suggests to transfer data from the main computer to a second computer for scanning (TRIZ Principle-26: Copying). As the scanning is done on the second computer there is no processing load on the first computer.

INVENTION-55: Improving virus detection speed by using a virus co-processor

Patent 8079084 (invented by Huang, et al., assignee- Fortinet, Inc., Dec, 2011) suggests improving virus detection speed by using a hardware co-processor (called virus coprocessor).

The co-processor can be used for various types of Content Pattern Recognition (CPR) instructions, such as comparing string instruction, comparing buffer instruction, performing checksum instruction, seek instructions and test instructions etc.

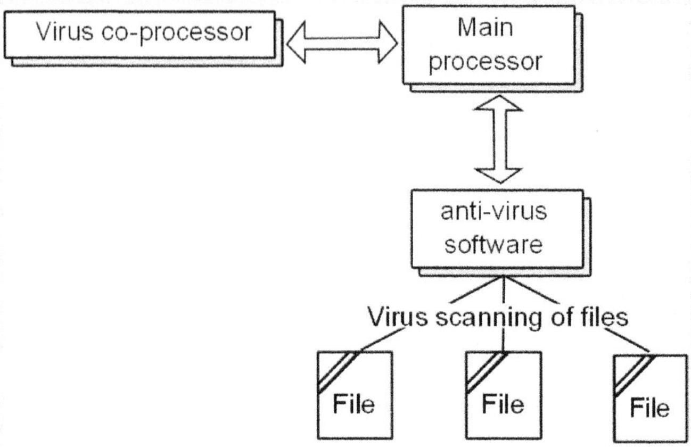

Using Virus Co-processor, US Patent 8079084

The memory of the virus co-processor is capable of communicating with the memory of the main processor so that the results of virus scanning are available to the main processor.

Chapter 18.

Improving Accuracy in Virus Scanning

18.1 The problem of false positives and false negatives

False positive is falsely and positively identifying a virus, i.e., an instance of wrongly labeling a benign program as malicious program. False positive is considered as a drawback of a virus detection method. Minor weaknesses of any virus detection method can lead to false positives.

In contrast, false negative is falsely identifying a virus to be benign, i.e., allowing a virus to go free and do its job. This is a serious limitation of anti-virus program. Both false positives and false negatives are equally dangerous and undesirable.

Ideally the virus detection program should not lead to any false positive or false negative. The rate of false positives and false negatives should remain 0 or very close to 0. Even a slightest increase in the rate is considered as undesirable.

18.1.1 Reasons for getting false positives and false negatives

Some methods of virus scanning are more susceptible to errors than others. Generally integrity checkers don't raise any false positives or false negatives. But integrity checking has a very limited scope. Although specific methods like exact signature scanning don't raise such mistakes they are not capable of detecting any new or unknown viruses.

The deficiency of the above methods led to development of many other generic methods to detect new and unknown viruses. Although these methods are capable of detecting unknown viruses they are more prone to errors and they fail to deliver accuracy in detection. Generally there is a positive correlation between the capability to detect new and unknown viruses and rate of false positives/false negatives.

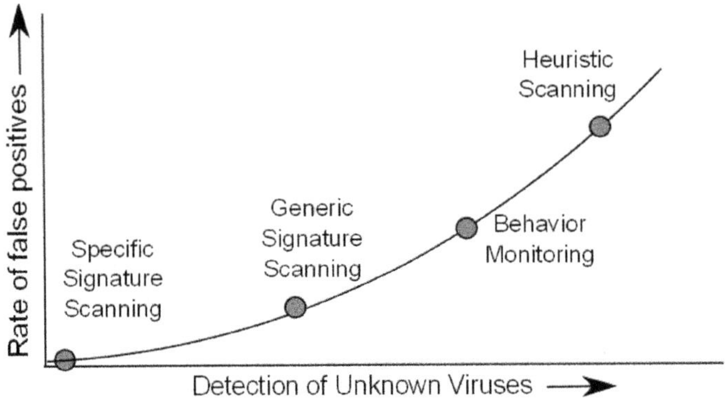

Correlation between
unknown viruses and false positives

For example, the heuristic methods can detect new and unknown viruses but they are more susceptible to false positives. This is because the inherent strategy followed by the heuristics are based on probabilistic methods and do not guarantee an infection. The possibility of errors in different methods is as below.

Methods of virus detection	**Chances of false positives**
Integrity Checking	NIL
Specific signature scanning	NIL – extremely low
Generic signature scanning	Low – Medium
Behavior monitoring	Medium – High
Heuristic detection	Medium – High
Network anomaly detection	Medium- High
Other Generic methods	Medium- High
A mixture of multiple methods	Extremely low

The errors in virus detection increase because it is extremely difficult to differentiate between the good and bad code. Any mistake in judgment can lead to false positives or false negatives. An anti-virus program searches only for virus signatures and not the complete virus code. Besides in many cases it searches for wild card signatures to speed up the operation. These situations lead to many false matches and errors.

18.1.2 What is the Ideal Final Result

While a traditional approach tries to achieve a right balance between false positives and false negatives a TRIZ approach looks forward to achieve the Ideal Final Result as below.

IFR Ideally the anti-virus should detect and prevent viruses with full certainty. The chances of error should be nil and the anti-virus should not raise any false positive or false negative.

However there are many contradictions in achieving the above IFR, which are presented as below.

18.2 Contradiction of tighter rules and false positives

It is very difficult to avoid both false positives and false negatives. If we tighten the set of virus detection rules we will fail to detect many viruses. On the other hand if we loosen the set of virus detection rules we will get more false positives.

Contradiction	*A virus scanner involves various sets of rules, whether signatures scanning or heuristic scanning. If the rules are tighter then, then it may miss many real viruses. On the other hand, if the rules are looser then it will detect many false positives. We want to detect viruses and not false positives.*

Possible solutions

- One option is to use slightly tighter rules but employ multiple rules and use multiple detection methods. The tighter rules will avoid false positives. Although the method will skip some genuine viruses the viruses cannot ultimately escape as they will be detected by other rules and detection methods.

- Patent 8239948 suggests to use multiple signatures of a virus and score all these signatures according to their likelihood to be found in non-malicious programs. Finally the candidate signature of the malware is decided based on such scores. As the signatures are pre tested to be unique, the chances of false positives are reduced.

- The heuristic scanners use a threshold level to determine whether a code is malicious or not. But this has a problem similar to above.

Contradiction	*If the threshold level is higher then many suspicious activities will be ignored. On the other hand if the threshold level is lower then it increases false positives. We want to increase the threshold to avoid false positives and decrease the threshold to avoid false negatives.*

One solution to the problem is to consider a large number of heuristics each having specific weightage. If the summed weightage exceeds a threshold then the program is deemed to be infected otherwise not. As the weightage is calculated by summing up multiple heuristic events the possibility of false positives or false negatives is reduced.

18.3 Contradiction of adequate testing of anti-virus software

Every product must go through a rigorous testing process before being released to the market. But there is a problem in testing anti-virus programs satisfactorily, as there are frequent updates in virus signatures and detection algorithms.

Contradiction	*If the vendor performs more comprehensive internal testing of the software update then there will be a delay in releasing the product. On the other hand if the vender releases the software updates without delay, then the testing remains insufficient and involves the risk of false positives and false negatives. The vender wants to release the updates fast but doesn't want to take the risk of errors.*

Possible Solutions:

- The anti-virus companies may adopt computerized techniques to fast extract signatures and employ automated methods for fast testing the software (TRIZ Principle-21: Skip, Principle-25: Self Service).

- Another option is to use an online scanning service provided by the anti-virus company and scan the computer remotely (TRIZ Principle-17: Another dimension). This method allows the client's files to be scanned always with the latest signatures.
- Patent 7290282 (invented by Renert, et al., Assignee- Symantec Corporation. Oct. 2007, also Patent 7757292, by the same inventors, Jul 2010) discloses to release the virus detection technique with a constraints module that which allows specific clients to test the new heuristics and provide test reports to the software server (TRIZ Principle-23: Feedback). If the server administrator (or vender) finds more false positives in the feedback then he modifies the constraints and re-release to the clients (TRIZ Principle-35: Parameter change). Once the virus detection technique is ready for wide release, the technique is circulated to all the clients.

18.4 Contradiction of scanning time and false positives

A slow scanning is irritating to most users. But a faster scanning may not be sufficiently reliable and may lead to more false positives or false negatives. In most cases there has to be a tradeoff between speed and thoroughness.

Contradiction	*If a thorough scanning is done using all the signatures and applying all the methods on all the files then the scanning will take enormous time and may not finish before the next scanning is due. On the other hand, if some signatures will be ignored or some methods will be omitted then the scanning may not be reliable. We want high speed scanning but don't want any errors.*

Many methods of improving speed of virus scanning are described in the chapter-17. All those methods of improving speed of scanning can be useful in solving this contradiction.

18.5 Methods of improving accuracy and reliability of scanning

Usually an anti-virus program generates an alarm signal when there is a reasonable suspicion. But suspecting a program before it causes any infection can lead to a false positive. But waiting for more time for hundred percent accuracy will allow the virus to do its intended damages. One solution is to use emulation techniques to run the virus in a virtual machine. We have already discussed about emulation techniques in Chapter-14.

- The traditional approach uses single, specific signature types to detect viruses, i.e., one virus - one signature. This method raises more false positives. Patent 6338141 proposes RAVEN detection system that uses a combination of multiple signatures and flags (up to about 70 different data items depending on the virus type). Using multiple signatures for each virus allows RAVEN to verify infections with a high degree of certainty and avoid possibility of false identifications.

- Sometimes the anti-virus finds that a system file has been modified but cannot determine whether the file has been modified by a virus or by the user. This situation leads to a contradiction. *If the program generates a virus alarm it may lead to a false positive. On the other hand if it ignores such a suspicious alteration then it may allow a virus to cause serious damages.* One solution to the above problem is to ask the user to take a decision whether the operation is genuine or not (TRIZ Principle-23: Feedback). **Drawback**: the user may not be adequately knowledgeable to take such a decision.

- Patent 8028338 (Invented by Schneider et. al., Sep 2011) discloses a set of goodware characteristics which can be used to determine whether a file belongs to goodware. This method reduces detection of false positives.

- Another option is to use second and third generation heuristics which are quite sophisticated having the capabilities of detecting stealth viruses and also capabilities of detecting with high accuracy (TRIZ Principle-28: Mechanics Substitution).

- Patent 7739737 (invented by Christodorescu, Jun 2010) suggests to compare the "function signatures" that describes the function of the malicious code instead of comparing "codes strings" which may vary in polymorphic viruses (TRIZ Principle-28: Mechanics Substitution). This functional analysis is done by converting varying expressions into a standardized form prior to application of signature analysis.
- Sometimes the scanning engine of the anti-virus is attacked by the viruses. Some viruses use "stealth" techniques to bypass file reads fooling the integrity checkers to believe that the checksums remain the same.

Chapter 19.

Updating Anti-Virus Programs and Virus Databases

19.1 The problem of updating Anti-Virus Programs

The progress in computing industry has led to rise of many different languages, operating systems and environments. As many of them are incompatible to each other an anti-virus program designed for one operating system will not work in another. Hence, the anti-virus vender has to develop separate programs for each operating system or operating environment. Besides the anti-virus developer has to add new features to their virus scanners in order to combat the advanced viruses. This process requires changes in the program code and recompilation of the new scanning engine. Updating scanning engines for each different platform becomes a real problem for the anti-virus developer.

19.1.1 Analyzing the Problem

If we analyze the problem of updating anti-virus program we find that it affects almost everybody in the computing industry.

Problems faced by Anti-Virus Developers

- The anti-virus developer has to change the code of anti-virus program and recompile it. This requires lot of programming, testing and documentation efforts.
- Sometimes the new product (or version) makes the old product (or version) obsolete. If the old product is totally replaced by the new product then and all efforts relating to the old product go waste.

- If the anti-virus developer wants to maintain the old products (or versions) along with the new product (or version) then it has to release virus information databases separately for all the products.
- As the scanning engines are often platform dependent the same updates have to be available for different operating systems, which requires a lot of testing and debugging overload.
- Each new product also involves a lot of ancillary activities like marketing, distribution, documentation, promotion and lot of administrative activities.

Contradiction

Contradiction	*The anti-virus developer wants to update the anti-virus engine in order to incorporate the enhanced capabilities. But the anti-virus developer doesn't want to go through the whole process of testing and debugging for every such update for each different platform.*

Analysis of Contradiction Parameters

Improving Parameter: Reliability, Productivity

Worsening Parameter: Ease of manufacturing, Ease of maintenance and admin

Problems faced by Network Administrators

- The network administrator has to download and install the new anti-virus product on the server and on individual hosts throughout the network. Downloading for each individual machine can consume a lot of network bandwidth.
- He has to learn the features of the new product and implement it properly in order to get the benefits of its advanced features.

Problems faced by Users

- The user has to download and install the updated program in order to detect the latest viruses and ensure security.

- The user has to learn the features of the new product in order to implement it properly.

Contradiction

Contradiction	*The user wants to get the benefits of the latest anti-virus product but he does not want the difficulties of downloading and installing the updated versions.*

Analysis of contradiction Parameters

Improving Parameter: Volume of data Transmission

Worsening Parameter: Loss of time, Ease of operation

In the second place, the same contradiction is converted to a physical contradiction where the same action "updating of virus database" is considered to be both useful and harmful.

19.1.2 Ideal Final Result

IFR Ideally the same anti-virus program should be able to scan all types of viruses for all operating systems for all times in future.

IFR The anti-virus programs should not require to be updated or should be automatically updated.

19.2 Solving problem of distributing Anti-Virus programs

Because of continuous research and development the anti-virus programs go through frequent modifications and updations. Many commercial anti-viruses come up with their updates almost in every quarter.

There are several methods of updating an anti-virus program in a client machine. One option is to download the new engine and replace the old engine with the new engine. Another option is to retain the old engine and update the patches. Another option is to retain the old engine and download the source code for the extensions of the scanning engine and compile/ interpret at the client machine. However each of the methods has its own disadvantages.

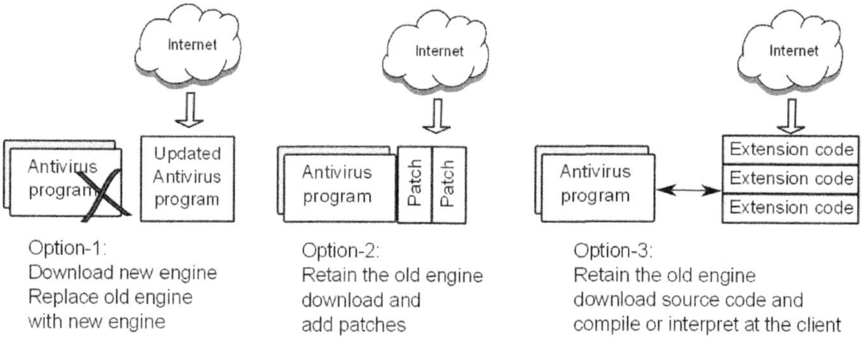

Methods of updating anti-vrius engines

Possible solutions

- All modern anti-virus programs implement automatic reminders to inform the user that the anti-virus engine has gone out of date and advise users to update the new engine available in the developer's website (TRIZ Principle-23: Feedback, Principle-25: Self Service).
- All modern anti-virus programs implement self-updating features to connect the user's computer to the anti-virus developer's website and automatically download the updates and patches and updates from the developer's site (TRIZ Principle-25: Self Service) of course after taking consent of the user.

INVENTION-56: Extending anti-virus functionality by including object code in the virus definition records

Upgrading anti-virus engines in corporate environments involve substantial administrative work. There should be a method for avoiding patches and updates.

Patent 6718469 (invented by Pak et al., assignee Networks Associates Technology, April 2004) suggests including virus detection instructions along with virus definitions in order to avoid separate patches for anti-virus engine.

ID	Name of Virus	Detection Section	Removal Section	C Language Extension

Virus definition record

According to the invention each record of the virus definition includes an identifier, a virus detection section and an extension sentence. The same anti-virus engine uses the source code extensions that are downloaded along with the virus data. This method enhances the capabilities of the anti-virus engine without modifying the engine by installing separate patches.

- One alternative to updating anti-virus engine is to implement web-based scanning which uses the updated engines and databases directly from the anti-virus company's website (TRIZ Principle-17: Another Dimension). VirusTotal (www.virustotal.com) is an online AV service which scans the uploaded file using more than 40 different AV engines (TRIZ Principle-40: Composite). All the engines are automatically updated on a real time basis (TRIZ Principle-15: Dynamize, Principle-25: Self Service) so that the scanning result is assumed to be up-to-date and accurate.

- Patent 7716736 (invented by Radatti, et al, assignee- Cybersoft, Inc. May 2010) provides a method of testing a file infection through a remote server (Principle-17: Another dimension). According to the invention a host is permitted to upload suspected files to a server. The server has two operating environments. The uploaded files are run in a separate operating system environment to check any infection. After the testing is over, the user is notified the results. In case the file was infected, the repaired file is made available to the user.

- Japanese Patent 2004-152251 discloses a method in which a server stores the latest version of security information such as virus definition files etc. which is used by the client computers in a network. **Limitations:** when many computers execute virus checks the load on the network increases which affects the communication speed of the computers.

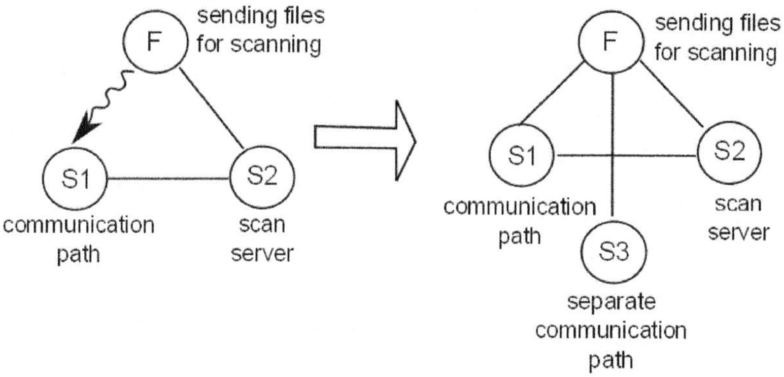

Appying Standard 1.2.3 to solve bandwidth problem

If we apply Inventive Standard 1.2.3, the harmful effects between two elements can be eliminated by introducing a third element (or substance) which absorbs the harmful effects of the action (or Field). The above problem is solved by introducing a separate communication path in the patent below.

INVENTION-57: Using a different communication path for virus scanning through a storage centric system

Patent 7788488 (invented by Nakatsuka, et al, assignee- Hitachi, Ltd, Aug, 2010) discloses a virus check server which scans client computers via a communication path that is different from the regular communication path. Therefore, a virus check executed by the virus check server does not lower the computer's communication speed or disk access speed. (TRIZ Principle-17: Another dimension).

Patent 7849508 (invented by Jung, et al, assignee- The Invention Science Fund, also patent 7917956, 7934260, 8146161, 8151353) also suggests a similar solution. It uses a bypass network connection, either logical or physical (including necessary hardware), to distribute anti-virus agent when the network is infected with viruses.

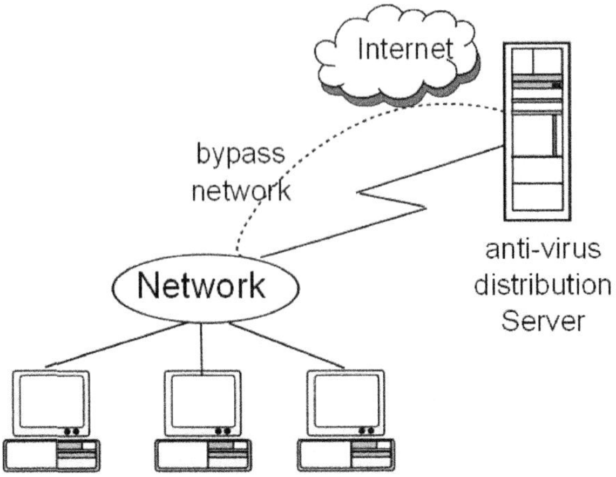

Using bypass network to distribute anti-virus

This method is useful in a multi network environment where one network is fully infected with virus and it is either not possible or not safe to use the network for distribution of anti-virus code. In such a case the second network is used for propagation/ replication of the desired anti-virus code.

🛠 Generally a computer has to complete the booting process and load all its drivers in order to check or download the anti-virus updates. But this method leaves a potential time for infection. US Patent application 20100132042 (by Wanchun Zhang, May 2010) suggests to use a second operating system during boot time to download an anti-virus update from a Internet based server. The benefit of this method is that the latest anti-virus software can be updated when the computer is started. If we use S-Fields to analyze this patent we get the following pattern.

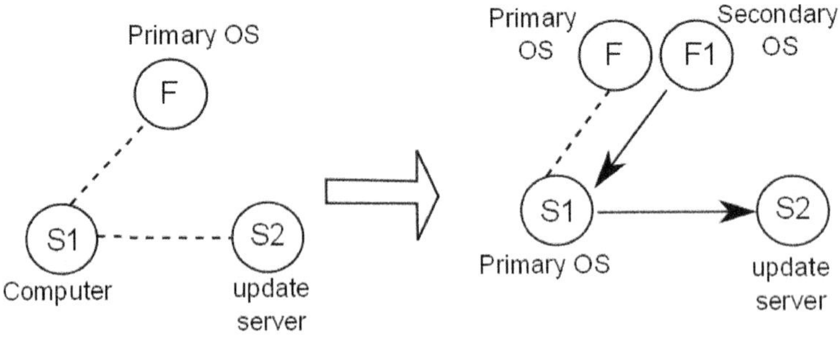

Using a second OS to download AV update

In the prior art there was a problem of accessing the update server on the Internet with the main operating system of the computer. This problem was solved by using a second operating system that downloads the anti-virus update at the time when the computer is booted from the main operating system.

19.3 Solving Problems of booting from Infected Computers

If a computer has an infected booting or an infected operating system it may not be able to boot from hard disk. Even if it boots it may not be able to connect the Internet to get the required anti-virus help. Even if it downloads anti-virus program/updates it may not be able to install it because of infected drivers. This situation causes user frustration and often leads to reinstallation of entire operating system, resulting in loss of data, time, money and effort.

19.3.1 Ideal Final Result

IFR Ideally the OS and booting program should never get infected

IFR If the OS is infected the computer should have alternative ways of booting to heal the infection

19.3.2 Possible Solutions

If we apply Inventive Standards we find that booting has no effect on the Primary OS because virus has negative effect on the Primary OS. This problem can be solved by adding a new element (or substance S3) such as a secondary OS or a secondary storage or both to boot the system and implement necessary anti-virus solutions.

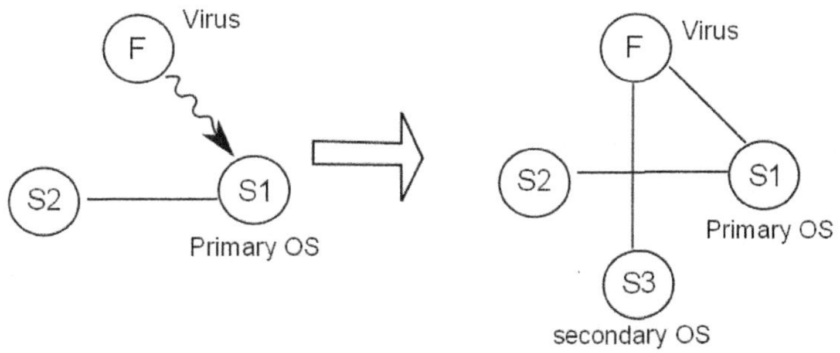

Adding a secondary operating system, Standard 1.1.3 and 1.2.2

INVENTION-58: Using a secondary OS to download anti-virus when the computer is already infected

Patent 7587765 (invented by Challener, et al., assignee- International Business Machines Corporation, Sep 2009) discloses a method of receiving the anti-viral program even when the client computer is unable to boot because of infection.

According to the invention, when there is an update available with the anti-virus server it notifies the client computer to download the update (TRIZ Principle-23: Feedback). The client computer is then shut down and re-booted by using a Wake On LAN (WOL) protocol. When rebooted the client computer applies a filter to disconnect the regular network and communicate only with the pre-authorized fix-server to download the anti-virus (TRIZ Principle-2: Taking out).

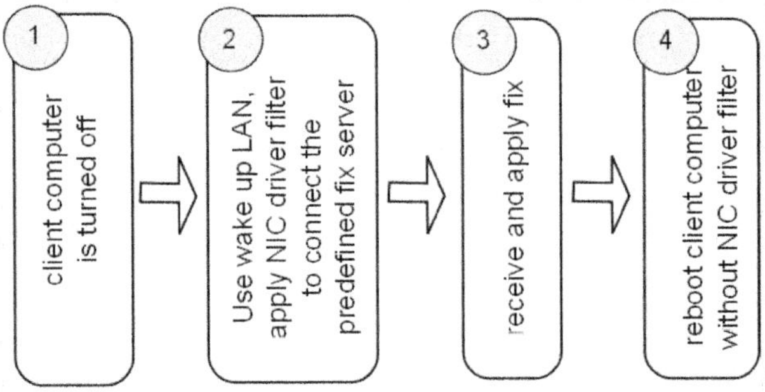

Steps to download anti-virus fix

If the primary operating system (OS) of the client system is infected, a secondary OS in the client computer performs the anti-virus download and execution. After the necessary anti-virus fix is downloaded and installed, the client computer is re-booted (without the filter) and allowed to connect other resources on the network.

INVENTION-59: Using a portable rescue device to disinfect the infected computers

Patent 7591018 (invented by Andrew Lee, assignee- Trend Micro Incorporated, Sep 2009) discloses a rescue device with solid state memory to disinfect a computer infected with virus.

According to the invention, the rescue device can be plugged in to an infected computer and do the necessary scanning and repairing without bothering about the condition of the original operating system.

The rescue device may be removable from the computer and reusable for update and/or upgrade over a computer network. The rescue device may comprise a bootable partition, a virus scanning engine and a virus pattern file.

There may be situations where the anti-virus is not updated and hence not capable of fully removing the viruses. Patent 7836500 (invented by Nason, et al, assignee- eAcceleration Corporation, Nov, 2010) discloses a method of getting custom scanning/ cleaning automatically from a server.

According to the invention, the scanner first determines the presence of a suspicious attribute resident to the computer. The scanner then automatically determines whether there is a need for a custom cleaner. If so then it automatically sends the information about the computer system along with information about the suspicious attribute to a server and requests for a custom cleaner. In response a custom cleaner is automatically created at the server and downloaded to the client and executed (TRIZ Principle-3: Local Quality).

INVENTION-60: Using a multi partition USB flash disk to recover infected computers

Patent 7930531 (invented by Chow et al., assignee- Super Talent Electronics, Inc., Apr, 2011) advises to use a multi-partition USB flash disk having multiple operating systems for recovering an infected computer.

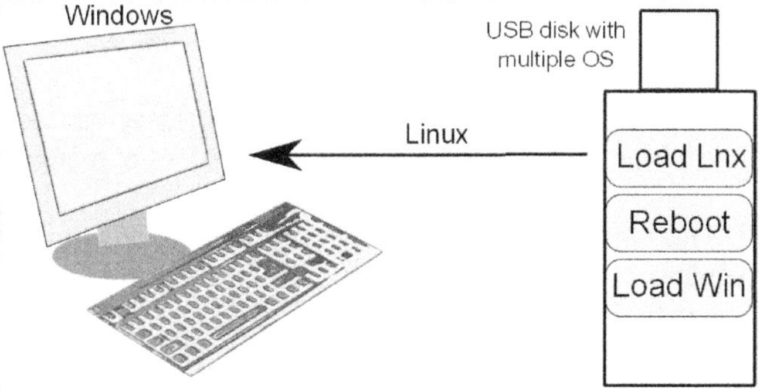

Booting with an alternate OS for virus scanning

When the host computer is infected the user will reboot the computer from the flash disk using a different or alternate OS image. As the viruses are platform dependent, the viruses executing in the primary operating system will not infect on the alternate operating system. Hence the virus removal programs in the alternate OS can help recover from a virus in the primary OS.

19.4 Solving problem of Updating Virus Definition Database

The virus definition database contains the signatures and other information about thousands of viruses. New records are added to the database on a daily basis by the anti-virus developers to keep the database up-to-date. This database is crucial for virus scanning as the viruses whose signatures are not there in this database will escape detection.

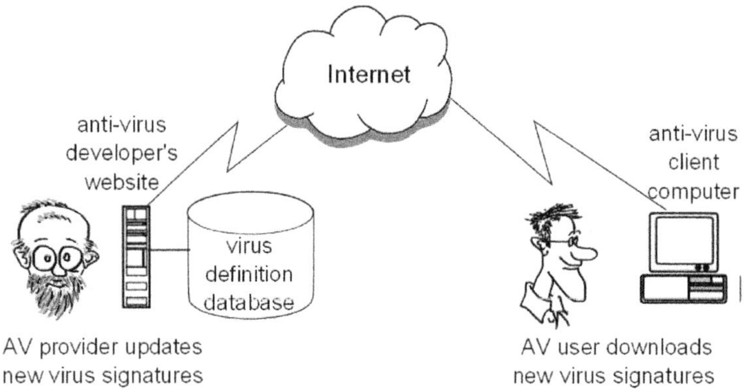

As new viruses are created almost on everyday, the size of virus definition files become very large and takes excessive amount of time to download. This situation becomes worse especially in slow and unreliable Internet connections. Some of the disadvantages are as below.

- Anti-Virus researchers have to extract signatures from new viruses and update the database. This requires lot of technical work.
- The users have to download the update on a regular basis. The network administrators have to implement the updates in the whole network.
- Updating the signature database is not a onetime phenomenon. It has to be updated on a regular basis both by the anti-virus developer and by the anti-virus users.

- The virus definition database has to be separately prepared and made available for different operating systems and different versions of the anti-virus software.

- With the increase in virus signatures the size of the database increases which increases network overhead and becomes difficult to download.

Contradiction

Contradiction	*We want to update the virus database in order to detect the latest viruses, but we don't want to update virus database on a regular basis as the job is boring and time consuming.*

Analysis of contradiction parameters

Improving Parameter: Volume of Transmission (download size)

Worsening Parameter: Loss of time, Ease of maintenance

Alternative Interpretation

One option is to reduce the number of signatures in order to reduce the size of the signature database, but that will affect the quality of scanning.

Contradiction	*The virus definition database should contain the signatures of thousands of viruses. But the size of the virus definition database should be very small.* *Physical contradiction- the size of the database should be large enough to contain the definitions of all viruses and small enough for faster download.*

Analysis of Contradiction Parameters

Improving Parameter: Volume of Transmission (download size)

Worsening Parameter: Reliability (of scanning)

Ideal Final result:

IFR Ideally the process of virus scanning should require no virus signatures or virus definition file.

IFR The virus signatures are generated automatically in the client machine so that there is no need to download them.

IFR If the user has to download a virus definition file then its size should be very small.

IFR The same virus definition file should work for all different versions and operating systems. Alternatively the same file should be automatically converted to work with different versions.

IFR The virus definition files are automatically distributed by the anti-virus venders and/or automatically collected/downloaded/updated by the anti-virus users.

Possible solutions

- Most modern anti-virus programs implement self-updating features to connect the user's computer to the anti-virus developer's site and download the updated virus definitions from the developer's website (TRIZ Principle-25: Self Service).
- To maintain compatibility with different platforms and different versions- the virus data may be updated in one database which is then converted to other formats (TRIZ Principle-36: Conversion).
- Implementing web-based scanning using the updated files directly from the anti-virus company's website (TRIZ Principle-17: Another Dimension). **Limitation**: This method is also internet dependent.
- The anti-virus developer should keep periodical updates in separate independent files so that the user (or client computer) downloads only the additional files and merges with the existing files (TRIZ Principle-1: Segmentation, Principle-5: Merging).
- Downloading only the newly added signatures (i.e., incremental) instead of downloading the whole signature database. For example, the client computer will compare the existing data files on the computer with the updated data files on the developer's site and download only those signatures which are added or updated (TRIZ Principle-21: Skipping).

INVENTION-61: Automatic updating of antivirus applications using push technology

Patent 6269456 (invented by Hodges et al, assignee Network Associates, Inc., July 2001) provides a method of updating the anti-virus updates automatically using push technology.

According to the invention, the updated signature files and other updated anti-virus information are loaded onto a central anti-virus server, while the push agent software is installed on the client computer. When the client computer is connected to the Internet, the push agent software operates in the background to receive updated anti-virus files from the central anti-virus server across the Internet (TRIZ Principle-25: Self Service). This method reduces the burden of the users as well as network administrators.

INVENTION-62: Selectively updating only the modified virus definitions

Patent 6622150 (invented by Kouznetsov et al., Assignee- Networks Associates Technology, September 2003) discloses a method of storing, distributing and accessing computer virus definition data using a structured database.

According to the invention, each virus contains a virus definition record indexed on a unique ID. When the client connects the server to download the updated virus definitions, only the updated virus definition records are sent to the client (TRIZ Principle-2: Taking Out). The local database engine modifies the local virus database by adding, removing or replacing existing virus definition records (TRIZ Principle-5: Merging).

INVENTION-63: Reducing malware signature set size through server-side processing

Patent 8239944 (invented by Nachenberg et al, assignee- Symantec Corporation, Aug 2012) suggests a method of reducing size of malware signature sets through server-side processing.

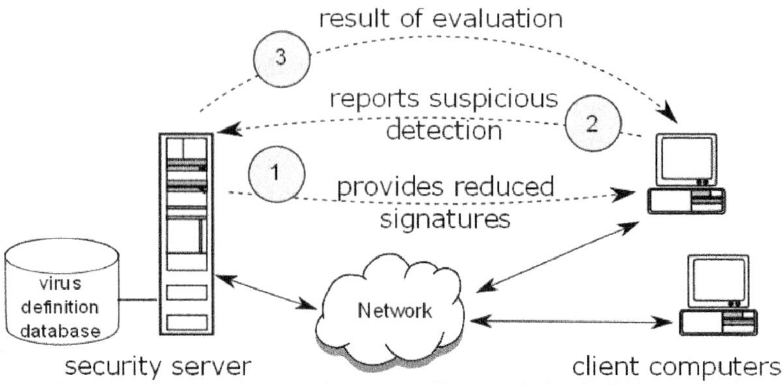

According to the invention, the anti-virus program will operate with a reduced set of malware signature which may generate a higher rate of false positives or suspicious. The anti-virus client will report all these suspicious entities to the security server. Based on the data reported by the client, the server will evaluate whether the signature detection is a false positive or a legitimate detection and informs to the client. If the evaluation indicates that the detection is a false positive, then the client releases the entity. On the other hand if the evaluation indicates that the detection was genuine, then further actions are taken.

Chapter 20.

Detecting and Preventing Boot Sector Viruses

20.1 What is Boot Sector Virus

The boot record is the first piece of code that is loaded into the memory when the computer is booted from a floppy or hard disk. All floppy diskettes and hard disks contain this small program known as boot record or Master Boot Record (MBR). The MBR is quite necessary for the booting operation. The boot sector is typically 512 bytes long and typically the first sector of the boot partition on the disk that contains the boot record.

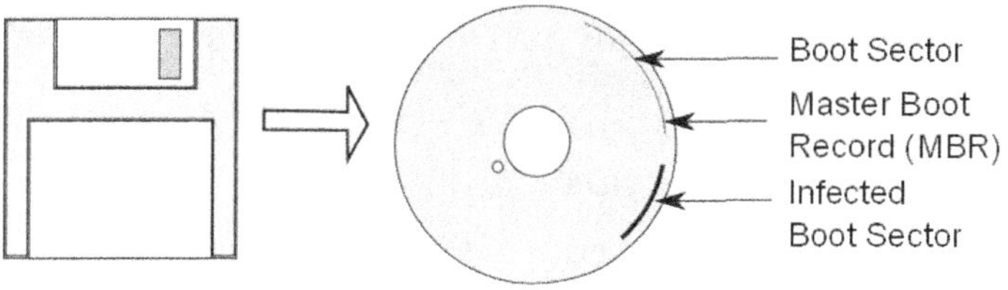

Boot Sector Virus Infection

The Boot Sector viruses or Master Boot Record (MBR) viruses are called so because they infect the boot records. They insert themselves into the boot sector of the disk by replacing the MBR with their own malicious code. When the computer is booted the virus code is loaded instead of the original boot record.

20.1.1 Characteristics of boot viruses

- Boot viruses infect the boot sectors. They replace the original boot sector with the virus code.

- Most boot viruses are 512 bytes long, that is the length of the boot sector itself.
- Boot sector viruses are generally carried by floppies and other transferable media.
- Boot viruses remain resident in the memory and infect every media used with the computer.
- As the boot sector is loaded before the operating system is loaded, the virus is loaded at the time of every booting and fools any virus protection system that is loaded afterwards.

20.1.2 How does it spread

The boot sector viruses generally transfer through infected floppy disks. When a diskette, infected with a boot sector virus, is placed into a computer system and the system is allowed to boot, the "virus transfer code" executes and transfers the virus to the hard disk by overwriting the disk's original boot sector with its own code.

The worst part of the thing is that the computer need not have to actually boot from the floppy in order to be infected. The computer can be infected from a non-bootable floppy if the floppy is infected with boot a boot sector virus. For example, a user may receive an infected diskette from an innocent source. If he puts the floppy in the drive and turns on the computer then the computer will look for the boot sector in "A:" drive and load the boot sector virus.

20.1.3 Why is it dangerous

Boot sector viruses are often more dangerous than file viruses. Since the master boot record (MBR) executes every time the computer is started, the boot sector virus always gets loaded on to the computer memory as soon as the computer boots. Then it hooks the Interrupt 13h vector which controls the hard disk, floppy and other disk R/W access. This hook executes a piece of code during all Int 13h routines and causes the boot record of any device accessed to be infected with the virus code. This way the hard disk remains permanently infected with that boot sector virus and even if there is a virus detection facility installed on the hard disk, it fails to detect the presence of the virus and its activities and remains powerless to prevent the infection.

Some boot sector viruses replace the original MBR and do the function of MBR through their own code. Some boot sector viruses damage the boot sector thereby making the disk inaccessible. The user gets a message like "non system disk or disk error".

20.1.4 Why is it difficult to detect Boot Sector Viruses

Since the master boot record executes every time the computer is started, the boot sector virus is loaded from the beginning and remains resident in the memory till the computer is shut down. As the virus is loaded before the OS is loaded it can easily fool the anti-virus programs loaded afterwards. It remains permanently in a computer until the system is totally damaged and fails to boot.

20.2 Methods of solving Boot Sector Virus problem

- ⇨ Verifying the authenticity of the boot sector before loading (TRIZ Principle-9: Prior Counteraction). Ideally the boot sector itself should check its authenticity (TRIZ Principle-25: Self Service).
- ⇨ Loading the anti-virus program before loading the boot sector (TRIZ Principle-13: Reversing).
- ⇨ Keeping the boot record in a secured place of the hard disk so that the virus cannot access it (TRIZ Principle-2: Taking out).
- ⇨ Booting from a separate boot ROM or similar "read only" medium that cannot be written by the virus. **Drawback**- using a separate boot ROM will add to the cost/ complexity to the system.
- ⇨ Avoid floppy read during boot up unless required (Note: this is no longer an issue now. But this was a concern when floppies were in use during nineties.)

20.3 Verifying authenticity of the boot sector before loading

The boot sector virus becomes powerful because it gets loaded along with the boot sector before the operating system is loaded. This advantage of the boot sector virus allows it to enjoy a safe haven. As all other virus detection mechanisms are loaded after the operating system is loaded they become powerless to detect or prevent the boot sector infection.

Ideal Final Result

IFR The computer should be able to boot without a boot record or the boot record should be virus resistant.

IFR The boot sector should check itself for genuineness before loading. Any infection should be automatically disinfected.

Possible Solution:

One of the most effective solutions is to compare the boot sector code with the original/ genuine boot sector code before loading into the memory. If there is a difference between the two then the boot program is deemed as infected.

But the question arises where to find the original or genuine boot sector code that is not infected? (i) one option is to store a copy of boot sector in a protected area of the hard disk, (ii) another option is to store a copy of the boot sector in a ROM chip, (iii) another option is to compare the boot sector code with another copy in an external storage device, (iv) another option is to compare with a copy provided by the anti-virus program.

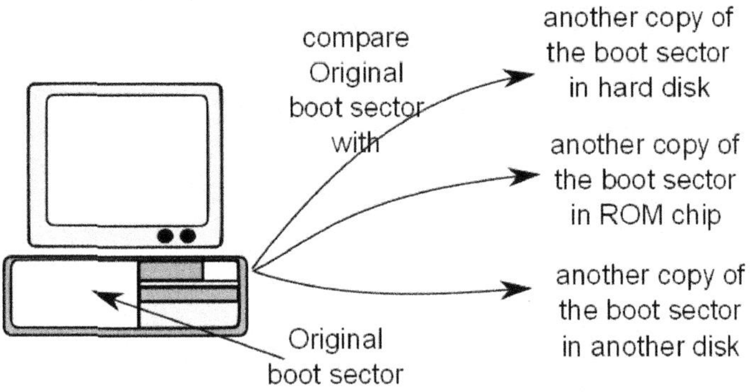

Verifying genuineness of boot Sector

INVENTION-64: Using a trusted BIOS for virus detection and removal

It may be better to check the validity of MBR without depending solely on the computer's OS or BIOS, because there are chances of OS or BIOS getting infected by stealth viruses.

Patent 6802028 (invented by Ruff et al., assignee PowerQuest Corporation, Oct 2004) uses a separate BIOS called "trusted BIOS" which is kept inaccessible to viruses. This BIOS is designed specifically for virus detection and removal. While booting, the method compares the standard BIOS and the trusted BIOS. If any inconsistencies detected, the method relies on the trusted BIOS and removes the infected BIOS and reconstructs boot sectors and MBRs. This method allows a computer to boot safely without depending on a possibly infected OS or possibly infected BIOS.

INVENTION-65: tracking the boot history to take preemptive corrective actions

Although computers typically boot from hard disks, there may be situations has to boot from an alternative source like floppy disk, memo disk or CD ROM etc. and get infected.

Patent 7590834 (invented by Challener, et al., assignee- Lenovo Singapore Pte. Ltd, Sep 2009) advises to track the boot history to know whether the computer was booted from an alternative source and if so a preemptive corrective action is undertaken (TRIZ Principle-9: Prior Counteraction).

The invention understands that there is a higher risk involved in booting from sources other than the hard disk. So it tracks the history of booting to determine whether the computer was booted from the primary boot source or not. If the computer was not booted from the primary boot source, preemptive corrective actions like a virus scan and other anti-virus actions are automatically initiated.

20.4 Loading Anti-Virus before loading the operating system

As the boot sector virus loads itself into the memory before anything else is loaded it remains powerful than anything else that is loaded afterwards. An anti-virus is an OS dependent program and can be loaded only after the OS is loaded. But this method has very limited functionality, as the boot sector virus would have already loaded into the memory by that time.

Ideal Final result:

IFR Ideally the anti-virus should be loaded before the boot sector virus is loaded so that it can check the genuineness of the boot sector.

Possible Solution:

- Store the anti-virus in a ROM chip and load it before the boot sector virus is loaded, i.e., before the Operating System is loaded.
- Keep a copy of the boot sector in a secured place and replace the code when the original boot sector is infected.

INVENTION-66: Storing anti-virus in a hidden partition to prevent boot sector viruses

Patent 5559960 (invented by Jonathan Lettvin, Sept 1996) suggests to create a hidden partition in the hard disk to store the anti-virus program and a small operating system called BTOS (Bootstrap Time Operating System). The BTOS is loaded at the startup to load an anti-virus program before the ultimate operating system is executed.

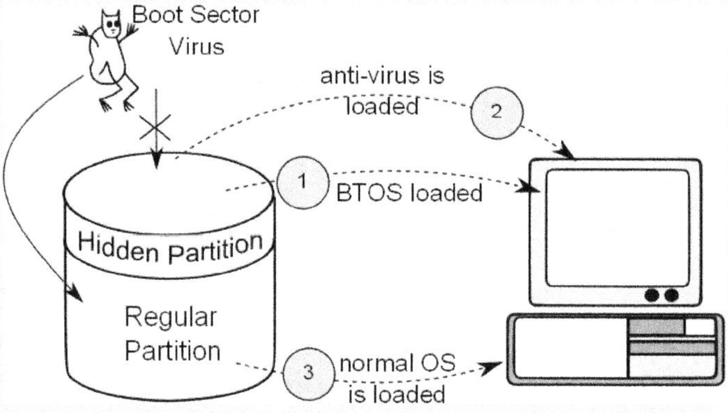

The objective of the invention is to provide a startup disk that can execute anti-virus program before the bootstrap-time viruses are executed (TRIZ Principle-13: Reversing, Principle-9: Prior Counteraction).

INVENTION-67: Storing anti-virus in a flash ROM to prevent boot sector viruses

Patent 5802277 (invented by Cowlard, Sep 1998) suggests to store the virus signatures and virus detection code in a Flash ROM. The virus detection code is executed after POST (Power On Self Test) and before passing control to a bootable media, whether a hard disk or floppy. Thus a new step of virus detection is introduced in between the steps of POST and loading the boot sector (TRIZ Principle-24: Intermediary, Principle-9: Prior Counteraction).

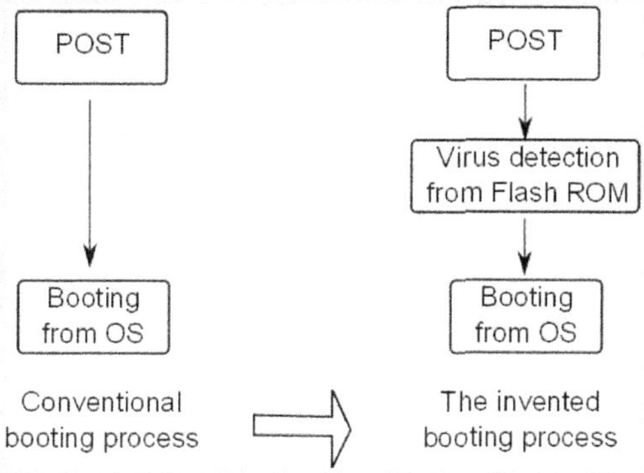

If we look at TRIZ Inventive Standard 1.2.1, it says if there is a harmful interaction between two elements (or substances), the problem may be solved by introducing a third element (or substance) between them. In this case the Flash ROM is a third element (or substance) that solves the problem.

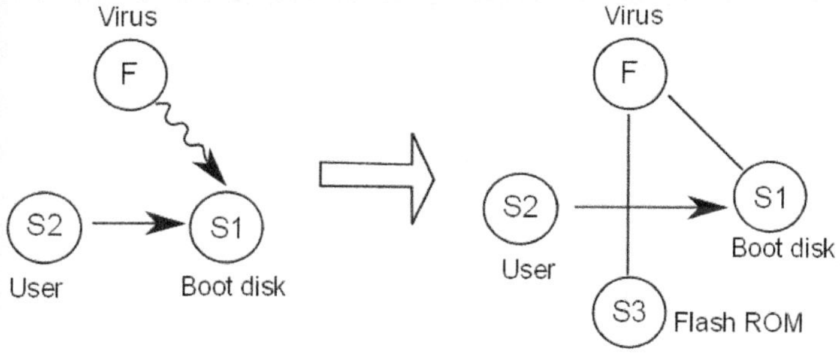

Introducing flash ROM for virus detection
Inventive Stadard 1.2.1

The virus signatures and virus detection program in the Flash ROM checks for the presence of any boot sector virus in the boot disk and passes the control to the boot code only if it does not find any boot sector virus.

INVENTION-68: Virus scanner operating at the pre boot phase

Patent 7549055 (invented by Zimmer, et al., Assignee- Intel Corporation, Jun 2009) suggests to load a trusted pre-boot scanner during pre-boot phase that operates primarily in the pre-boot phase of computer operation.

The code of the trusted pre-boot scanner may be written according to TCG (Trusted Computing Group) specification as a Trusted BIOS Base (TBB). The trusted virus scanner may scan a selected number of files (such as files loaded in RAM and Master Boot Record) or all files (such as files accessible during pre-boot phase) as necessary.

20.5 Booting from an uninfectable media

A computer typically boots from the hard disk and occasionally from external disks like floppies, flash disks and CD ROMs. However all these types of media are subject to virus infection. Systems may boot from a CD ROM or ROM chip or similar to avoid boot sector viruses.

Ideal Final result:

IFR Ideally the boot sector should be stored in an uninfectable media. In other words the computer should boot from a media that is not infectable.

Possible Solution:

- As a ROM cannot be written to it cannot be infected by viruses. This technique was used by McAfee's ROMSHIELD. ROMSHIELD is an IC chip that was designed to fit into the boot ROM socket found on most Ethernet LAN adapters. The ROMSHIELD chip intercepts the boot process and scans the boot sector and partition sector for boot sector viruses. After booting is over it also scans every diskette inserted into the computer for presence of boot sector viruses before the diskette is accessed.

- EFI (Extensible Firmware Interface) is another industry standard which intended to replace the DOS (Disk Operating System). EFI is a non-volatile RAM which is supposed to be executed before any other operating systems are loaded. Patent 6907524 (invented by Huntington, et al., assignee Phoenix Technologies Ltd., June 2005) suggests to copy

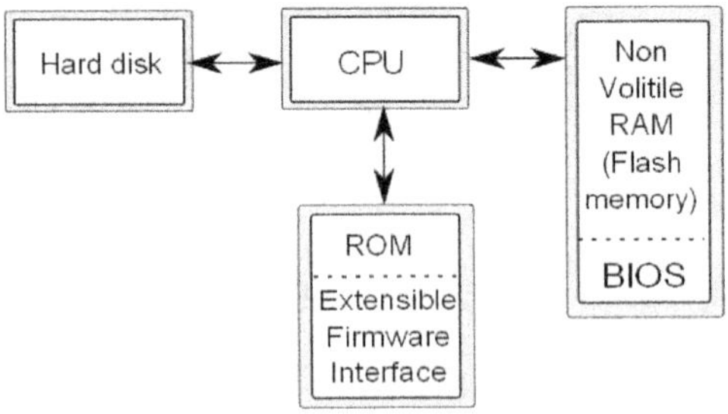

Patent 6907524

the boot sector of the hard disk to the non-volatile memory of EFI based operating system. When the computer is booted the boot sector is read from the non-volatile EFI memory bypassing the boot sector of the hard disk thereby avoiding any potential boot sector viruses.

INVENTION-69: Hardware based anti-virus system

Patent 7657941 (invented by Zaitsev, assignee- Kaspersky Lab., Feb 2010) suggests to use a hardware based anti-virus module in combination with AV application for better security. The hardware AV module has its own CPU and memory and is located between the PC and hard disk. The AV databases are updated in a two-phase approach to ensure security.

INVENTION-70: Using trusted operating environment for malware detection

Often rootkits intercept scanner activities and return "file missing" error. As the rootkit returns a wrong file to the scanner, the scanner fails to detect any virus infection as it fails to access the desired file.

Patent 8104088 (invented by Khilnani et al, assignee- Microsoft Corporation, Jan 2012) suggests using a trusted operating environment, which consists of a trusted operating system and a trusted anti-virus tool embodied in a removable data storage medium, such as a CD or USB drive. The computer is first booted from this removable data storage medium using the trusted operating system. Then the trusted anti-virus tool scans the computer and checks for the virus signature updates in the computer. After this virus scanning the computer is rebooted.

20.6 Avoiding floppy seek while booting

It is important to note that if a boot sector infected floppy is there in the drive when the system is booting then the system reads the infected boot record from the floppy and gets infected. **Thus just by an attempt of booting from the infected floppy can infect the system, even if it does not actually boot from the floppy and even if the floppy is not bootable.** Thus in most cases the infection takes place because the user had forgotten to remove the floppy disk from the drive.

Ideal Final result:

There should be no need to boot from floppy drive and the system should not seek floppy drive while booting (Note: this IFR is already achieved as the modern computers are no more booting from floppies).

The system should be able to know whether a disk is infected and avoid booting from an infected disk.

Possible Solution:

- Disable "floppy seek during boot up" option in the CMOS setup or bring the option down to the bottom of the list of bootable devices (TRIZ Principle-9: Prior Counteraction). **Drawback**: it will be difficult again to boot from the floppy by changing all the options in CMOS.

- The system should boot without reading data from the boot sector, as in case of non-disk-based Operating Systems (TRIZ Principle-28: Mechanics Substitution).

- The user should check the floppy drive for presence of any disk every time she boots the computer system. **Limitations**: the user may not be present or may be unmindful at the time of booting.

INVENTION-71: Alerting user to remove floppy to prevent boot-sector virus

In many cases the infection takes place because the user forgets to remove the unwanted floppy disk from the floppy drive. Patent 6550007 (invented by Baxter, et al., assignee Dell USA, April 2003) prevents boot sector infection by doing a simple job of displaying an alert message to the user before trying to boot from a floppy.

According to the invention the computer, while booting, first checks if there is a floppy in the drive. If it finds a floppy then it alerts the user that the computer system is about to boot from the floppy disk before actually doing so. If the user responds in the affirmative, then the computer boots from the floppy disk and the operation proceeds as usual. If the user responds in the negative (or does not respond within a predetermined time), then the floppy disk boot is skipped and the computer system attempts to boot from the next device listed in its boot table.

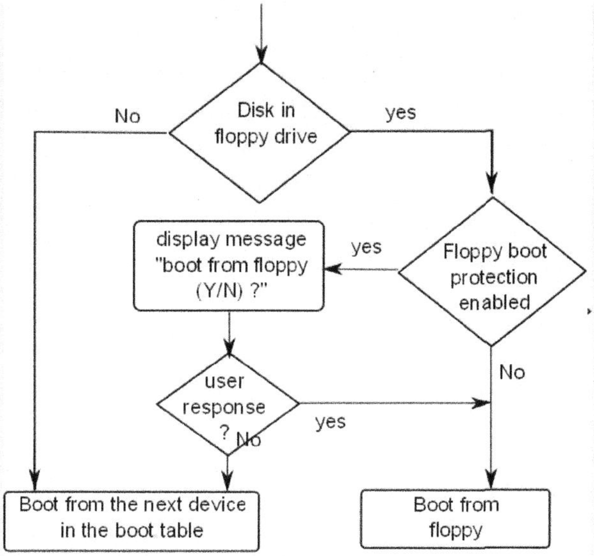

Floppy boot protection system

The invention is based on the assumption that most infections occur because of the failing of human memory to remove the floppy disk from the drive after its use is over. The invention solves this problem just by asking the user whether she wants to boot from the floppy (TRIZ Principle-23: Feedback) and skipping to read the floppy unless responded positively.

20.7 The downtrend of boot sector viruses

As we saw in Chapter-6 on Ideality, every system is moving towards an ideal stage. In the context of boot-sector viruses, an ideal stage is an environment without having the fear of any boot sector virus. The system has almost reached its ideal stage as we are seeing the downtrend of boot sector viruses.

As we saw in chapter-9 the continuously increasing capacity of storage devices has made the floppies obsolete. The increasing size of the executables and applications required to be distributed in CDs that are immune to virus infection.

The trend of increasing capacity of removable storage devices:

Floppies 1.2 MB → CDs 700 MB → DVDs 4.7 GB → HD DVD → Blu-ray

As the boot sector viruses were predominantly spreading through floppies, the obsolescence of floppies put an end to their spreading.

Self-repairing operating systems

Most operating systems today protect their boot sectors using various methods which make the boot sector viruses difficult to survive. For example the System File Checker (SFC) mechanism in recent versions of Microsoft Windows (XP and later) checks the consistency of system files during boot up and replaces them if found altered (TRIZ Principle-25: Self Service).

Chapter 21.

Detecting and Preventing File Viruses and Macro Viruses

21.1 Introduction to File Viruses

File viruses are the most common form of viruses. There are many file types that are designed to run automated actions during ordinary usage of the file. These files can be called as dangerous types[#] because they are potential to contain viruses or spyware that might damage your computer. They are potential to execute the virus code just by clicking at them. For example the files like program files (*.exe), batch files (*.cmd and *.bat), and script files (*.vbs and *.js), MS DOS programs (*.com and *.pif), screen saver file (*.scr) etc. are very much susceptible to virus infections.

Some viruses use files with two extensions in order to make dangerous files look like safe files. For example, Document.txt.exe or Photos.jpg.exe. Although these files are actually .exe files they may often confuse the user to be a text or picture file. As it is rare for a legitimate file to have two extensions, it is better to be careful before opening such files. However, file types like .txt or .jpg are safer to download than programs or macros.

[#] "Recognizing dangerous file types", http://windows.microsoft.com/en-in/windows-vista/recognizing-dangerous-file-types

Similarities between File Viruses and Macro Viruses

We are combining file viruses and macro viruses in the same chapter as they have many characteristics in common. Both of them belong to the typical virus category which are different from other malware like worms or Trojans. Both of them have the very typical characteristic of a virus to insert their code into other files in the process of infection. Both of them take shelter in their host files and are dependent on their host files for survival and execution.

Differences between File Viruses and Macro Viruses

However, they have critical difference in terms of how they are written, how they execute and what type of files they infect. The file viruses are written in assembly (low-level) languages while macro viruses are written in scripting (high level) languages. The file viruses infect and stay inside the executable files while the macro viruses infect and stay inside document files such as Microsoft Access files (*.mdb) or Microsoft Word files (*.doc) or Microsoft Excel files (*.xls) that allow embedded script operations. Thus the code of the file viruses are executed directly by the operating system while the code of the scripting based macro viruses are executed by the macro interpreter of the MS Office or similar environment. We will discuss more on the macro viruses later in this chapter.

21.2 Patterns of infection of file viruses

Generally a virus infects a computer program by inserting its viral code into the program. There are various patterns of infection. Some viruses insert themselves at the beginning of the file while some viruses insert their code at the end of the file. Some of the important patterns are as follows.

- Appending and prepending infection- the appending virus appends its code to the end of the host program and the prepending virus prepends its code at the beginning of the host program. The virus removes the initial few bytes of the program to insert a jump instruction to the virus code.

- Companion infection- creates a companion to an .exe file by creating a .com file with the same name. When the user types the program name (without extension) the OS gives priority to the .com file and loads the virus file.

- Overwriting- some viruses overwrite the original files with the copy of virus files. This is the worst type of infection. As the original files are overwritten they cannot be disinfected or recovered.

- Cavity filing or space filling – the virus attempts to install itself in an empty space available inside the program.

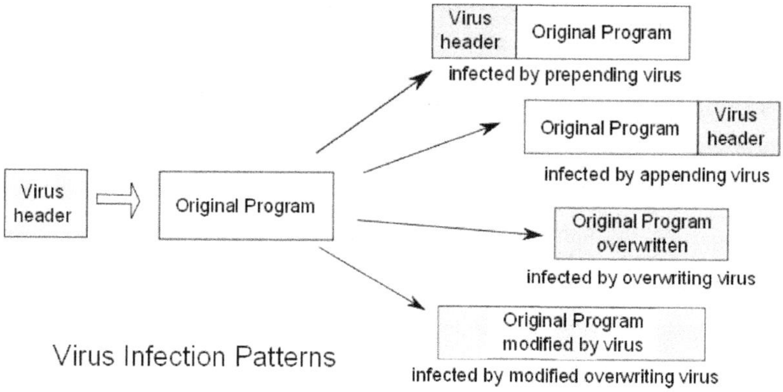

Virus Infection Patterns

How do the infected files execute

Although some viruses (like overwriting viruses) make damage to the files they infect, most viruses allow the host file to execute in its normal way. The virus adds its code to the end of the original program and adds a jump instruction at the beginning of the program code so that the virus code is executed before the original program. At the end of the virus code there will be another jump to the beginning of the original program so that the original program runs after the execution of the virus code.

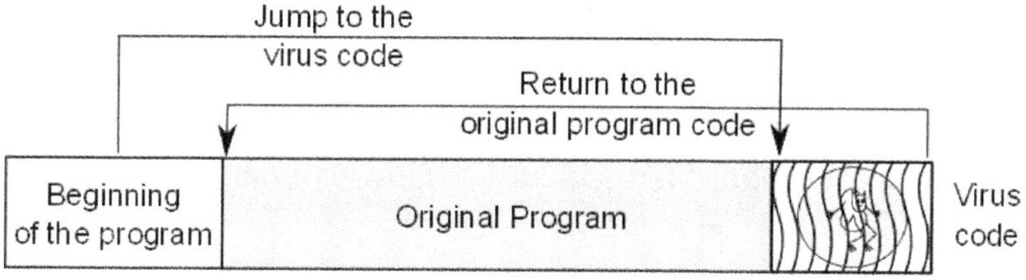

Typical Execution of an Infected Program

This way the virus code runs every time the infected program runs and does its intended actions. But the user does not get any indication about the execution of the virus code as the host program runs in its desired way.

21.3 Methods of repairing infected files

There are several actions that an anti-virus program may initiate when a virus is found. The first attempt of any anti-virus product is to repair the infected file. If a repairing is not possible then the anti-virus prefers to take other possible measure.

In case of simple infections the original program code remains in one single block. The anti-virus program follows a process that is exactly the reverse of virus infection in order to repair the infected file. For example, in the previous example of the appending virus, the anti-virus has to first remove the virus code and repair the first few bytes of the host program to remove the jump instruction. In other words, the process of disinfection is nothing but a reverse application of the process of infection (TRIZ Principle-13: Reversing).

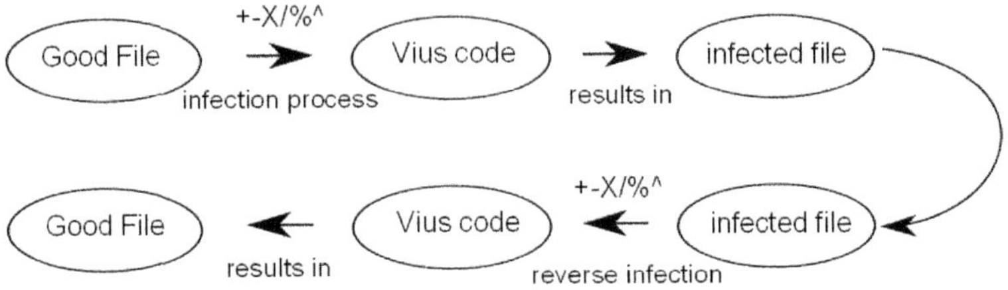

Repairing an infected file using reverse infection

- If the infected file is partially damaged by the virus then the anti-virus may apply various heuristic methods to recover the original code.

- Many anti-virus products keep a backup of critical OS files in protected locations. If any of these files gets infected or corrupted or damaged, the anti-virus replaces the infected files with their corresponding uninfected copies.

- If the anti-virus cannot repair a file because of an unknown pattern of infection, then it puts the file into quarantine, with a hope of repairing it in future.

- If the infected file is totally damaged and there is no hope of recovering it, then the anti-virus has to delete the file.

Limitations of Virus Cleaning

- The cleaner must know the exact characteristics of the virus and the pattern of its infection. It cannot remove an unknown virus.

- The virus should be the same as the virus known to the cleaner. If a virus is wrongly detected to be a different virus, then the cleaner will do wrong operations and result in building a junk file.

- Some viruses have different family members with different features; for example, the Jerusalem/PLO family now contains more than 100 mutants. The cleaner must determine the exact virus type to clean it successfully.

- Many polymorphic viruses have variable lengths and they maintain the original instructions encrypted. The conventional cleaners are unable to clean the MtE (Mutation Engine) infected programs.

21.4 Restoring virus Infected Systems

Sometimes the computers are not able to boot because of virus infection. But scanning or cleaning is possible only after the computer boots. So the most important thing is to restore a damaged computer before initiating a virus scanning.

- Patent 6347375 (invented by Reinert et al., assignee Ontrack Data International, Feb 2002) suggests to boot the local computer from a bootable virus utility operating program and establish communications with a remote computer. Then the local computer downloads a remote data recovery program from the remote computer to the memory of the local computer and executes the data recovery program in the memory of the local computer. Then the local computer downloads a virus scanning and repair utility from the remote computer to the memory of the local computer and executes the virus scanning and repair utility at the local computer. This method uses a remote scanning and repairing mechanism contrary to the conventional method of local scanning and repairing (TRIZ Principle-17: Another Dimension).

- If the computer is already infected, then it cannot download the necessary anti-virus programs or virus definition files from the Internet. Patent 7353428 (invented by Cheston, et al., Assignee- Lenovo Singapore Pte. Ltd, Apr. 2008) discloses a method of downloading anti-virus needs from a pre-authorized trusted anti-virus server. According to the invention the client computer is disconnected from the network and reconnected only with the trusted anti-virus server by applying a filter in the network interface card (NIC) driver by the primary operating system (OS) or the secondary OS or a service processor (SP) or by a virtual machine manager (VMM) depending on which is available at the client computer (TRIZ Principle-2: Taking out). After a trusted connection is established the anti-virus fix is automatically installed without requiring any end-user action. After the anti-virus fix is installed and the client computer is rebooted, the client computer is allowed to reconnect the full network.

INVENTION-72: Safe restoring of un-backed up data from a failing system

There is a need to recover the files from the most recent backup while ensuring that the restored files don't contain viruses. Patent 7222143 (invented by Childs, et al., assignee- Lenovo Pte Ltd., May 2007) proposes to use a locked partition with an alternate operating system for this purpose. The locked partition is accessible only by the alternate operating system and not accessible by the primary operating system.

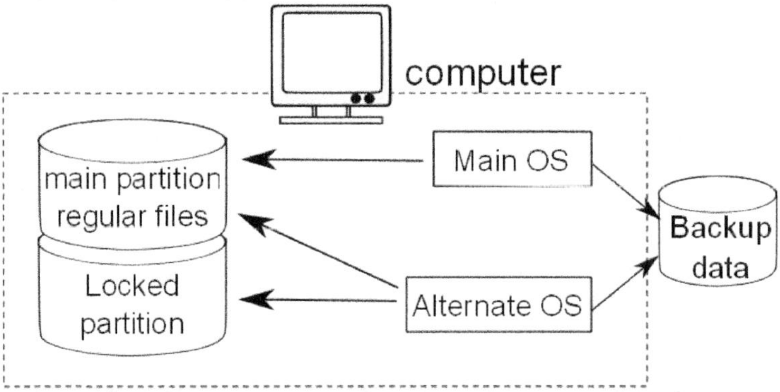

While restoring the failing system, the alternate operating system determines which files have been modified since the most recent backup and runs a virus scan on those modified files and uncorrupts the corrupted files. Thus the alternate operating system recovers all the modified files from the main partition to the locked partition, either uninfected or disinfected by the virus scanner. After the data restored from the last backup, the files which have been modified since last backup are replaced with the files recovered in the locked partition. Thus the system recovers files since the most recent backup while ensuring at least part of the restored files don't contain any viruses.

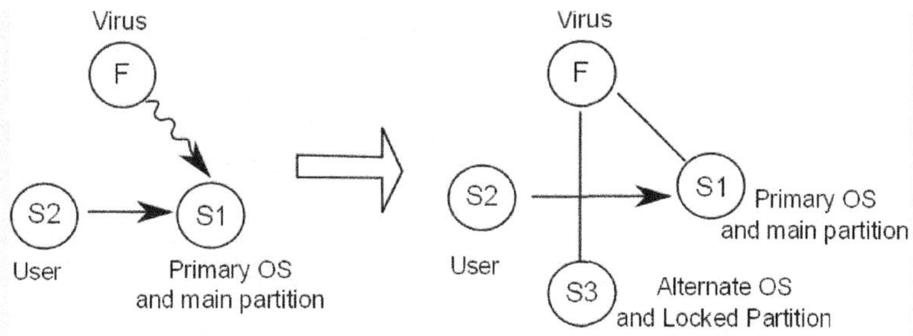

Introducing an alternate OS
and a Locked Partition (Patent 7222143)
Inventive Stadard 1.2.1

This is an example of TRIZ Inventive Standard 1.2.1, which says if there is a harmful interaction between two elements (or substances) or the element (or substance) and the action (or Field) the problem can be solved by introducing a third element (or substance) between them. In this case virus has a harmful effect on the main operating system and the main partition of the disk. To invention provides a solution by introducing a third element (or substance), i.e., an alternate OS and a locked partition.

21.5 Methods of Dealing with File Viruses

- Some anti-viruses move the infected files and store in a separate directory for quarantine. But this method is not safe as the user may run the infected files in the quarantine folder and infect the computer. Hence a further method is to rename the files with a different extension (TRIZ Principle-35: Change Parameter) and often to encrypt the file in order to prevent the file being used (TRIZ Principle-36: State Change and Conversion).

- The memory resident viruses are dangerous. Even if the files are healed by the anti-virus they are infected again by the resident virus. The resident virus does not go easily. It is necessary to remove the virus from memory and shut down the computer. Patent 6240530 provides a method of exterminating memory resident viruses by following four automatic steps, viz., (i) virus detection and identification, (ii) memory cleaning, (iii) restarting the system from and external OS and (iv) exterminating the virus.

INVENTION-73: Protecting executable programs through backup and restore

One of the methods to avoid infection is by making the executable file "read only". But sometimes it's necessary to make changes in executable files during normal course of action. In those cases the anti-virus raises an alarm signal, which may be misleading.

Contradiction	*Generally an anti-virus generates an alarm signal when the vital codes of a program are modified by a virus and prevents the operation. But if the anti-virus alarms all such modifications then that would generate a lot of false positives. On the other hand, if the anti-virus waits to see whether the vital codes are modified or not, then the anti-virus cannot prevent the infection.*

Patent 6073239 (invented by Eyal Dotan, assignee In-defense Inc., June 2000) solves this problem by backing up the program and vital data immediately before any modification is attempted (TRIZ Principle-15: Dynamize, Principle-26: Copying).

When a virus or other writing operation attempts to write a program, the method intercepts the operation and backs up the program in a different location. Then the method determines whether the writing operation is attempting to modify the **significant** data, such as, entry point, which could be a virus like operation. In case the attempt is to modify the **significant** data an alarm is generated and writing is denied. If the data is already modified, then the program is restored to its initial state and all modifications made to the program are undone.

INVENTION-74: Scrambling infected files to prevent spreading infection

Patent 6401210 (invented by Templeton, assignee Intel Corporation, June 2002) suggests to scramble the virus infected files and safely store them in a special directory like virus bin. The scrambled infected file rules out the possibility of being used. The invention uses an unscrambler logic to unscramble the virus infected file to reproduce the virus infected file in future if necessary.

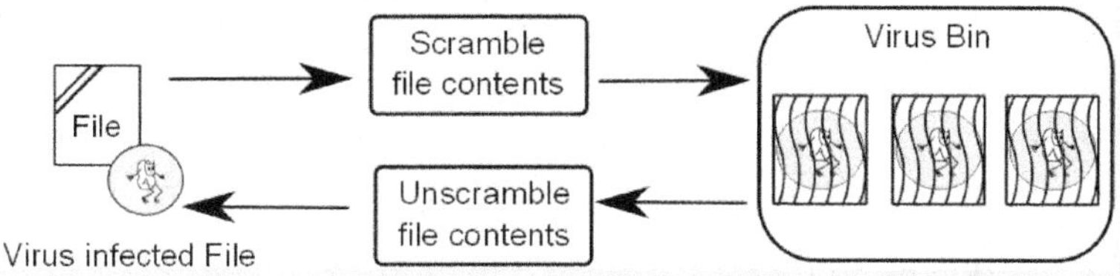

The invention uses scrambling techniques to make the infected files unusable (TRIZ Principle-36: State Change or Conversion) and isolate them to a virus bin (TRIZ Principle-2: Taking out).

21.6 Preventing Infection by restricting access to Files and Disks

As the virus has to change a file in order to infect it, one of the solutions to avoid infection is to make the file or the disk write protected. However this method has serious limitations, as the executable files often need to be modified for genuine reasons. Similarly write protecting disks or drives or partitions create many problems in normal computer operations.

Patent 7340775 (invented by Tarbotton, et al., Assignee- McAfee, Inc.. Mar. 2008) discloses a method of protecting computers by precluding writes to critical files. The method monitors the requests to write to files on the computer and prevents writing to critical files, critical file locations, trusted applications, operating system files etc. thereby preventing possibility of virus infection.

INVENTION-75: Preventing executable file from running unless the file has been certified

Patent 7376977 (invented by Jindal et. al., Assignee- Lucent Technologies Inc., May. 2008) teaches to avoid virus infection by executing only "certified" files (TRIZ Principle-35: Change Parameter).

According to the invention the applications are authenticated and authorized by valid users who are authorized to certify. This way the viruses and malware are never certified to run. When the computer receives an instruction to run an executable file, the computer first checks if the executable file is certified to run or not. If the executable file is not certified, then the computer system prevents the executable file from running.

If the executable file is certified then the computer further checks if the executable file has been modified since the time it was certified. If the file has been modified, then the computer prevents the file from running. (TRIZ Principle-9: Prior Counteraction).

INVENTION-76: Preventing executable files from running unless the files are aged than a specific period

Patent 7483993 (invented by - Nachenberg, Assignee- Symantec Corporation, Jan. 2009) suggests to block a computer program or code to run unless it has been residing on the computer longer than a specified time limit.

According to the invention, the system administrator (or user) feeds a time limit as an access control rule for the computers in the network. When a computer code is to be executed, the time stamp (when the code was first introduced to the computer) is compared with the current time to determine how long the code has been there on the computer. If the code has been there on the computer longer than the time limit, then the computer code is permitted to execute. This method blocks execution of viruses and macros during virus outbreaks.

Patent 8195953 (by Yue et. al., Jun 2012) suggests to integrate the security function within the target software itself that includes the abilities and normal behavior of the program. When the program is invoked the security function compares the normal behavior (in the ability section) with the actual behavior. This method protects the software both from traditional virus attacks and from modern worms, Trojans and other threats.

21.7 Introduction to Macro Viruses

A "macro" is a series of instructions, such as, menu selections, keystrokes and/or commands that are recorded by a macro recorder or programmed manually by a programmer. Macros are generally triggered by physically pressing a key or by internally calling the macro name. But macros can also be arranged to execute automatically without any user input. Some macros are embedded within application data files to remain hidden.

The macro viruses reside in macros and use "macro instructions" to perform unintended and sometimes damaging actions. As the macros reside in documents the macro viruses are document-based. They generally reside in word processing documents, spreadsheets and presentation files. The macro virus attacks a document by inserting a copy of itself into the file.

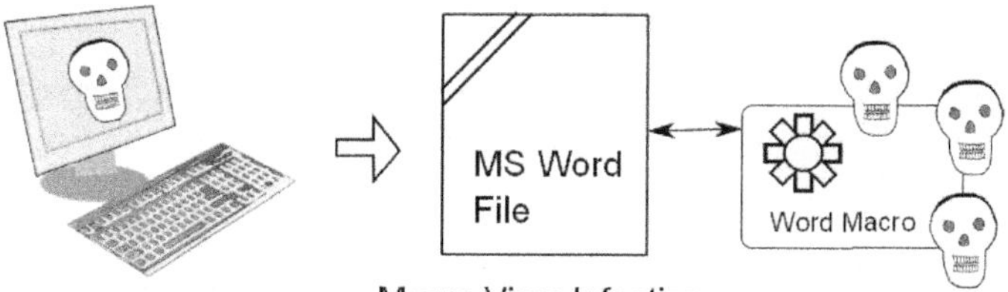

Macro Virus Infection

Macro viruses can be stored in files with any extension and can spread via file transfer or even by e-mail. As the documents are now being widely shared through networks and over the Internet, the document-based viruses have become more prevalent. The macro viruses reside in data files without knowledge of the user and may execute upon some user actions or even without manual triggering by the user.

History of macro virus

Macro viruses were created in late nineties much later compared to file viruses and boot sector viruses. In march 1999, a macro virus, known as the "Melissa virus" rapidly spread to millions of computers worldwide, causing hundreds of millions of dollars in lost productivity and snarling computer networks with large volumes of email traffic. There were many other infamous viruses like "Word Prank Macro" virus or "Concept" virus. All these macro viruses are document-based viruses and they infect documents created by MS Office and similar environments. The macro viruses are becoming more prevalent, because the documents are now widely shared through networks and over the Internet, even more than the sharing of diskettes in the past.

How do they work

While most file viruses and boot sector viruses are written in assembly language, the macro viruses are written in macro languages. The macro viruses reside inside the body of MS Office documents. The macro language is interpreted by the host program (like MS Word) that provides the macro environment. For example Word macros are interpreted by MS Word. Macros may be classified as Word Macros, Excel Macros etc.

Macro viruses generally copy themselves to new document files using macro copy commands. Often it attacks the global template called

NORMAL.DOT so that the subsequently edited documents get infected with virus macros.

Characteristics of macro viruses

- A macro virus resides in documents like word processing or spreadsheet. It can be stored in files with any extension.
- Macro viruses don't (and cannot) reside in executable files.
- Macro viruses are written in macro languages like VBA. Macro viruses cannot be written in assembly language or low-level languages, as those languages are not understood by the macro interpreter.
- Macro viruses generally infect the global setting files such as word templates (*.dot files) so that the subsequently edited documents are contaminated with the infective macros.
- The macro virus can infect a document, which the user has edited and saved using the application, and thinks to be genuine. The infection takes place without the user's knowledge.
- Macro viruses may act when specific keys or actions are triggered.
- While viruses written in assembly languages fail to execute even with slightest corruption, many macro viruses still work (although erratically) even after getting corrupted.
- The macro viruses can be called platform independent, as any application that supports macros is a potential platform for macro viruses. For example, a macro virus in an MS Word file not only works on Windows but also works on Macintosh. **Limitation**: but all macro commands will not work in all platforms. For example, if a macro makes a Win32 API function call, the same will not work in a Mac system. Besides many macro viruses don't work when transferred from one language of MS Word to another language of MS Word as the commands like "FileOpen" in English will not be understood by the other languages.
- Macro viruses spread at a high speed through emails and sharing of documents through Internet.
- Some macro viruses have mass mailing capability like worms. For example, Melissa was a macro virus that spread fast by its capability of mass mailing.

21.8 Problems in detecting macro viruses

The macro viruses are easy to create but difficult to detect. Even for a virus scanner it is difficult to decide which macro is a virus and which macro is not, as a user macro may also create files, send emails and do all such activities that a macro virus can do.

The difficulties of detecting macro viruses are mainly as follows:

- As the macro programming languages are easy to learn, a large number of new macro viruses with high variation are created on every day.
- Integrity checking of the document files does not work for macro viruses, as the susceptible documents are usually edited by users. Hence, keeping hash values or snapshots for each of these modifications is not possible.
- Signature scanning can detect macro viruses. But this method is not very effective as there are plenty of new macro viruses created on every day whose signatures are yet to be updated in the signature database.
- There are some polymorphic macro viruses which change their codes in every infection. Signature scanning or hash comparison is not effective to detect those viruses. Code emulation, although effective, is time consuming.
- A heuristic scanning is most effective to detect macro viruses of all types. But prior art heuristics are good at detecting new viruses that are variants of known viruses, but not so good at detecting new viruses that are not variants of known viruses.
- All macros are not viruses. It is difficult to differentiate good macros and bad macros. A macro virus may act like an ordinary macro such as accessing files, sending emails etc. It's not easy to determine whether a macro is suspicious or not.
- It is often extremely difficult to remove the malicious macro without removing the user macros. But the objective of an anti-virus is to retain the user macros and remove the virus macros.
- Sometimes corrupted macro viruses generate new variants of macro viruses which executes although not in the desired way. These variants are difficult to detect, as the checksum of the

original macro virus does not match with the corrupted macro virus.

- Sometimes while converting MS Word documents from one version to another the macro virus is also converted to the target version thereby creating new variants of viruses.
- Sometimes macro viruses infect documents that are already infected by macro viruses. This process creates new form of macro viruses in a natural process.
- The MS Office virus protection settings are stored in the Windows registry. Hence it becomes easy for a virus dropper to change the settings and activate the virus.
- There are two different techniques of infection. One is the virus will add the virus macro to a document. Another is the virus will modify the existing user macro(s) in the document. The second form of infection is difficult to detect and remove.

Ideal Final Result:

IFR The macro programming languages should not allow creating macro viruses.

IFR The MS Office and similar environments should not support execution of macro viruses.

IFR The MS Office and similar documents should have built in defense for Macro viruses.

IFR The uninfected macros should have some special characteristic to differentiate them from the infected macros.

21.9 Improvements in detecting Macro Viruses

Although signature scanning can detect macro viruses, it is not very effective as there are numerous new viruses with unknown signatures. Even if a comprehensive signature scanner were available, it would quickly become obsolete because of the ongoing generation and production of new / unknown macro viruses.

INVENTION-77: Detection and Removal of Viruses in Macros

Deleting the macro infected document or deleting the infected macro is not a good solution. Ideally the anti-virus should remove viruses from macros without deleting macros or host documents. Patent 5951698 (invented by Chen, et al.) proposed a method which operates by scanning through a document looking for suspect macro operations.

The invention includes a macro locating and decoding module, a macro-virus scanning module, a macro treating module, a file-correcting module and a virus information module. The macro locating and decoding module determines whether a targeted file includes a macro. If a macro is found, it is decoded and stored in the data buffer (TRIZ Principle-2: Taking out).

Then the scanning module accesses the decoded macro and scans it to determine whether it includes any suspect instructions. Then the macro-treating module removes the suspect instructions to produce a cleaned or sanitized macro.

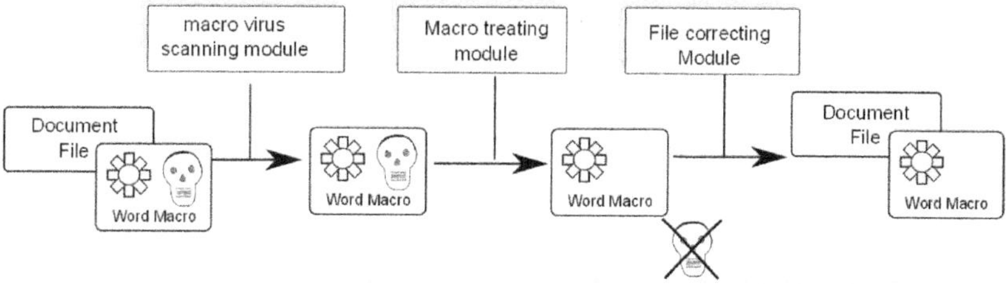

Finally the file-correcting module accesses the targeted file with infected macro and replaces the infected macro with the treated macro produced by the macro-treating module (TRIZ Principle-5: Merging).

MS Word includes a conversion tool to convert documents of one version to another for compatibility. But while converting documents the macro viruses inside the documents are also converted. This way the same macro virus gives birth to new variants by upward conversion and downward conversion creating many different signatures. How to detect all these variants with a single signature? The problem is solved by the following technique.

First, all different macro formats are converted to one single canonical form. The virus detection is done on the canonical form using a single definition (TRIZ Principle-36: Conversion, Principle-33: Homogeneity). This method eliminates the need for maintaining and comparing different signatures for different formats of the same macro virus.

- The early versions of MS Word did not have any scope to detect macro events. Later Microsoft released a patch called "scanprot.dot" to trap certain open file events and examine whether the file is opened for possible virus infection. Patent 5956481 (invented by Walsh, et al., assignee Microsoft Corporation, Sep 1999) suggested to implement the patch program as an internal component of MS Word application. **Limitation**: the degree of protection has to be much more than that is currently provided in MS Office environment.

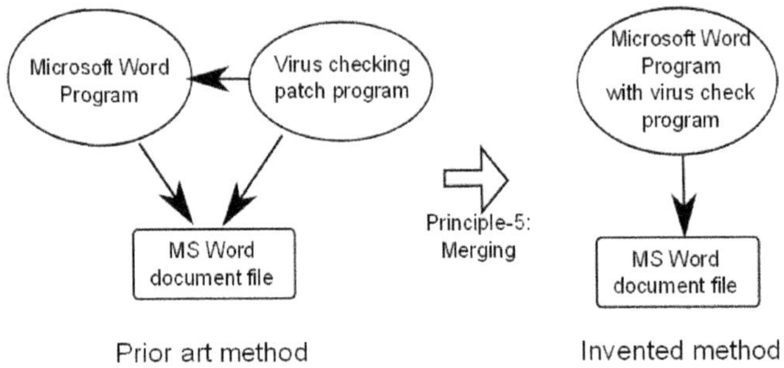

- MS Word 2000 and later versions included options make macro security to high in order to allow only digitally signed macros and thereby silently disable virus macros. **Limitations**: this method helped only commercial macros but did not help user macros as the common users were not expected to get digital certificates by paying money.

- Most known macro viruses use the methods of the CodeModule object to proliferate (InsertLines, AddFromFile) and CodeModule object is accessible through the VBProject object which can be turned on and off. So turning it off can avoid a large number of viruses. **Limitations**: these value setting is stored in an obvious location in the registry which can be changed by any virus. "Even before the final version of Office XP was released, there were already 2 viruses, Listi.A and Pcut.A that are perfectly capable of working effectively in Office XP."[#]

[#] Macro Virus Protection in the Microsoft Office Line, Part Two, http://www.symantec.com/connect/articles/macro-virus-protection-microsoft-office-line-part-two

INVENTION-78: Macro virus detection method

It is not easy to determine whether a macro is suspicious or not. Patent 6577920 (invented by Hypponen, assignee Data Fellows Oyj, June 2003) suggests checking the macros against three databases, viz., (i) the database containing signatures of known viruses, (ii) database containing signatures of certified commercial macros and (iii) database containing certified user created (local) macros.

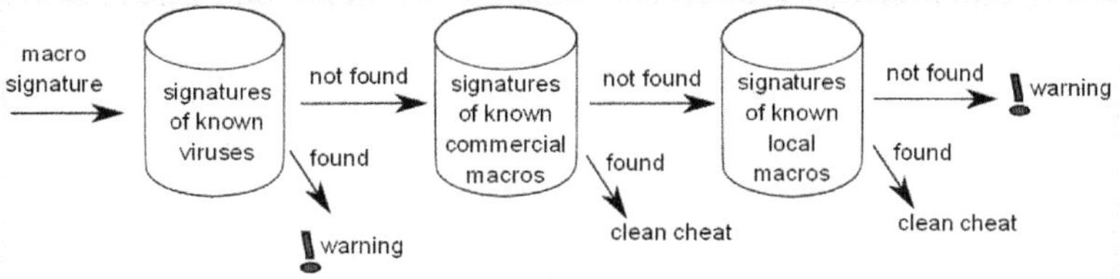

Macro virus detection method, Patent 6577920

As it is not possible to detect all new macro viruses accurately, the method suspects all macros, which are not known to be either commercial macros or certified local macros, to be macro viruses (TRIZ Principle-16: Partial or Excessive Action). If the signature of the macro is found in first database or not found in the second or third database then the user is given an alert.

INVENTION-79: Static analysis to detect macro viruses

The conventional static heuristics method can detect new viruses that are variants of known viruses, but not so good at detecting new viruses that are not variants of known viruses. Patent 6697950 (invented by Ko, assignee Networks Associates Technology, Feb 2004) teaches a method of static analysis for detecting macro viruses in a document without using emulation techniques.

First, a token analyzer converts macro operations into tokens. Then those tokens are fed into a parser that parses the tokens into intermediate form (TRIZ Principle-1: Segmentation, Principle-28: Mechanics Substitution).

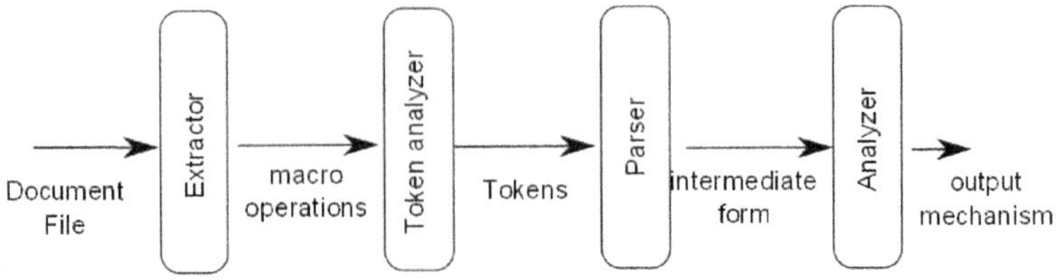

Macro virus detection method

Next the analyzer retrieves profile information about suspect macro operations from profile database and then performs flow analysis on the macro operations. This flow analysis determines the values for variables within the macro operations. Then the analyzer compares the macro operations against a profile containing information about suspect macro operations.

INVENTION-80: Using static heuristics to detect a class of macro virus

Some macro viruses use obfuscation techniques like encryption to hide from signature scanning. Patent 7069589 (invented by Schmall, et al, assignee- Computer Associates Think, Inc. Jun 2006) teaches a static heuristic to detect complex macro viruses.

According to the invention the heuristic analyzer analyzes a subject file and finds it suspicious if a scan string is found more than predefined number of times. For example, a VBA_Rnd (Visual Basic randomize) function must be used at least 8 times within the examined macro in order to trigger the heuristic rules.

INVENTION-81: Applying heuristics to detect macro viruses

Patent 7089591 (invented by Chi, assignee Symantec Corporation, Aug 2006) teaches to detect the macro viruses by scanning their generic behaviors, i.e., moving the code to the global environment (to be used by the application for all documents) and then copying the code to a local environment (to be used for a specific document).

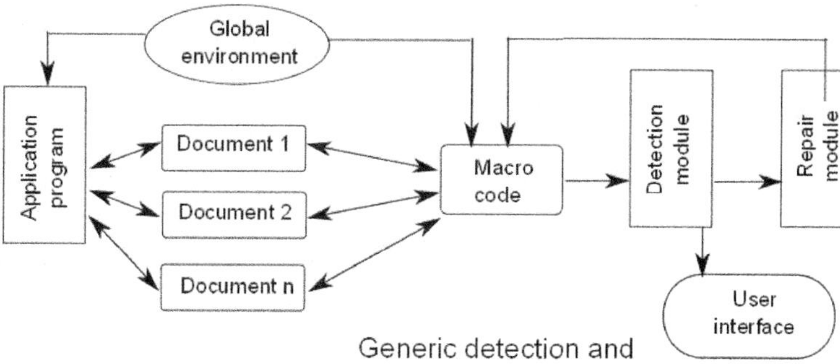

Generic detection and elimination of Macro Viruses

According to the invention, a detection module analyses the code to determine whether the macro contains instructions ***to be moved to a global environment and to be copied to a local document***. When these two conditions are satisfied the detection module declares that a macro virus is present within the code.

Patent 7093135 presents a method to automatically detect macro viruses written in VBA compliant programs. First a validation component scans various codes for virus infections and allocate validation keys to uninfected codes. A master database of keys are kept on a central server. The workstation machine scans the documents for macros and checks whether the macro has a validation keys.

Chapter 22.

Detecting and Preventing Email Viruses

22.1 What is an Email Virus

An email virus is a virus that generally infects the emails or spreads through the emails. Generally the virus attaches itself to an email and travels on the Internet through the email. Some email viruses send emails using the addresses from the address book of the victims' computer.

The creator of an email virus keeps in mind that the email travels from one computer to other though the Internet. He tries to exploit this capability of the email to fortify the virus. He exploits the strengths and weaknesses of the email messaging system and utilizes the email technology to spread the virus quickly to distant geographical locations.

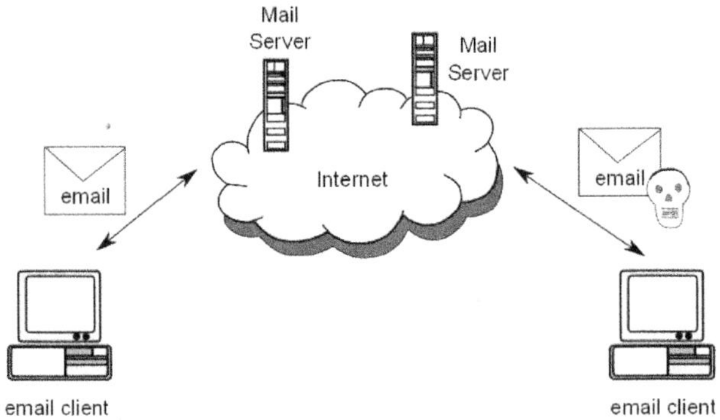

Virus spreading through emails

For example, the users may have email accounts through their employers or through an Internet application service provider (like Yahoo and Hotmail) or through an Internet service provider that provides Internet access. The email servers contain mailboxes for the users and each mailbox contains various email messages including attached documents.

As an email can contain any type of file as an attachment, the email virus generally tries to attach itself to the regular genuine emails. Besides, it may also send email messages to other computers including destructive viral codes. The infamous "ILOVEYOU" virus was sending copies of its virus code to every email address stored in the victim's computer.

Characteristics of Email viruses

Email virus is not a basic category of malware like viruses or worms. Any malware whether virus or worm or Trojan that spreads through emails can be called as email virus.

- The email viruses spread themselves by using email and Internet technology.
- The infected mails typically contain destructive viral codes as attachments.
- As an email can contain any type of file as attachment it can contain different types of viruses.
- Some email viruses send virus emails from the victim's computer to the addresses stored in the victim's address book.
- The email viruses can travel through any communication network, such as LAN, WAN or Internet.
- As emails can be sent to any part of the world, the email viruses can spread very fast across geographical locations.

22.2 How do they work

An email virus tries to exploit the loopholes of email protocols. For example, the existing email standard (RFC 2821) allows anyone to send an email with any origin indicated at the "From" field. This feature is exploited by spammers and email viruses.

Many email viruses are nothing but mass mailing worms. The Melissa Virus (1999) was the first mass mailing worm in a global perspective. Later SirCam and Klez also demonstrated more sophistication. Most mass mailing worms use their own SMTP engine to send emails directly, some of them also use a local SMTP relay if they find one.

Strategies followed by Email viruses

⇨ The email viruses generally send emails to the email addresses available in the victim's address book. These emails escape through firewalls and spam detectors as they originate from trusted senders.

- ⇨ As the mail is sent from the computer of a known person, the recipient believes that the mail has actually come from the known person and opens it.
- ⇨ The email virus attaches the viral code to the email and executes when the user opens the attachment.
- ⇨ It uses social engineering tactics to convince the user to click on the attachment or on a link in the email which leads to the execution of a malware.

Note: An email virus does not infect an email program, such as, outlook.exe. This type of job is done by file viruses.

22.3 Problems in detecting email viruses

The conventional methods of virus detection are not efficient for detecting email viruses. The problem becomes worse as because the emails travel from machine to machine on the Internet involving not only the senders and receivers but also other machines like servers and gateways. Besides, the method of storing emails is different in different clients and different servers which makes the job extremely difficult for a scanner. Let's look at different types of problems faced in detecting email viruses.

The main problems concerning email viruses are as follows:

- The email viruses originate from genuine sources. Hence it is difficult to differentiate the genuine emails and virus emails.
- The email attachment may look like a useful executable file or a zip file to perform some task and may not appear to contain a virus. But when the user opens the email attachment the computer becomes infected with the virus.
- Scanners cannot access emails stored by email clients as they use proprietary encryption for storing emails. The real time scanner (or on-access scanner) has to wait for the moment when the user tries to open an email or attachment.
- The scanners cannot access the emails or attachments in an email server like ccMail, MS Exchange, Davinci etc. because they encrypt the content of email and attachments for privacy reasons.

- The traditional anti-virus software is designed to detect file viruses, boot sector viruses, macros viruses etc. But they are not suitable for scanning emails. An email can be complicated in structure containing many different files as attachments. Some methods like Integrity checking don't work for checking emails.

Social Engineering threats

Some email viruses try to convince the recipient to perform some action by giving deceptive messages. For example, the message in the email may convince the recipient to click on a link to read some important message, or unzip the attached file containing your bank statement etc., which in turn infects the computer.

Sometimes the mail shows "you have message from facebook" or "twitter" or "linkedin" or other commonly used social networking sites confusing the user to be a genuine email and urging to click. The following is an example which appears to be a message from linkedin but in reality a spam mail. The links are not redirected to linkedin site but to very different site. Clicking on the links can result in virus infection.

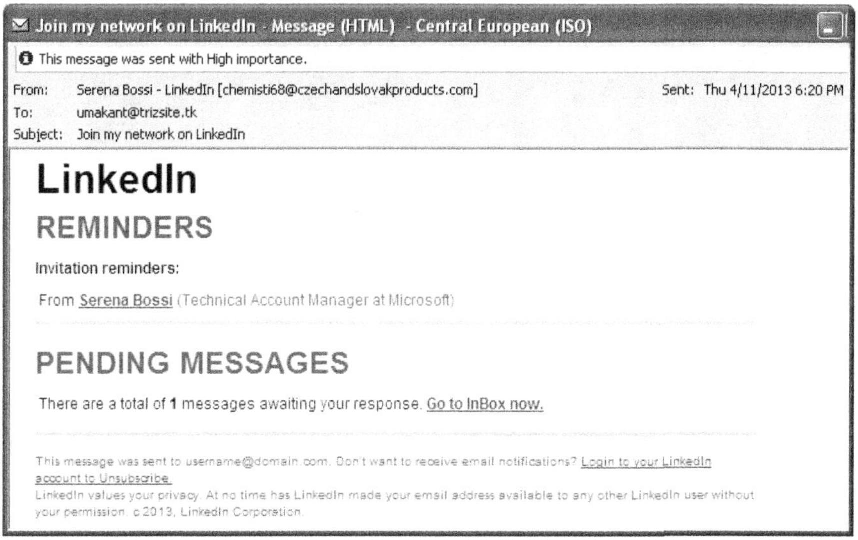

Sometimes the virus writers (or viruses) pack their executables in password protected zip files and provide the password and unzipping guidelines through the email. As the emails look convincing to the user, the user follows the given process to unzip the file and executes the virus.

Prevention mechanism

In order to prevent infections from websites the web browsers are designed not to allow websites to initiate a download without explicit consent of the user. So the user has to click on a link or a button to trigger the download.

But as we saw in the example the links or buttons or popups can confuse and misguide a user to click on a dangerous link. There are other situations where a popup says "Would you like to optimize your internet access?" the user might choose "yes" and land up in downloading the spyware. In some cases no matter whether the user clicks "yes" or "no" the spyware is downloaded.

22.4 How to prevent email viruses

Let's take a commonsense approach of how the email viruses can be tackled. The email origins from the source machine, goes through firewall (optionally), then through email server, routers and gateways till it finally reaches the receiver. Under the scenario there are various points of scanning and controlling the email viruses.

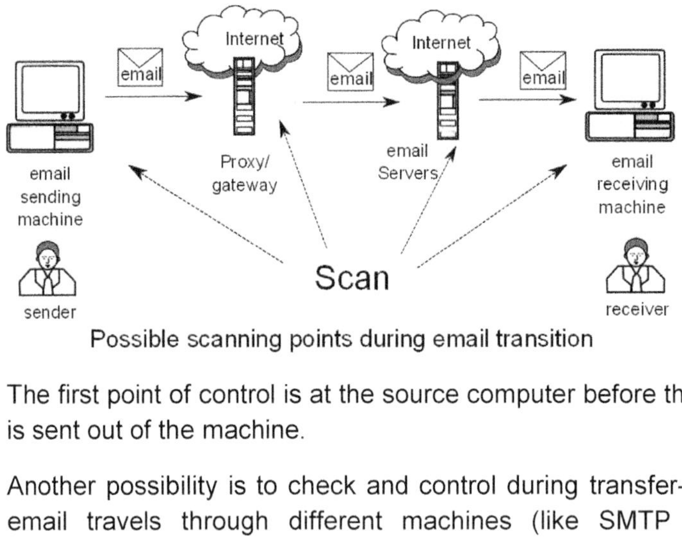

Possible scanning points during email transition

- The first point of control is at the source computer before the email is sent out of the machine.
- Another possibility is to check and control during transfer- as the email travels through different machines (like SMTP server, gateways, mail forwarders, POP3 servers etc.) there is possibility of scanning the mail in any of these machines.
- If the virus mail escapes all these points of scanning and reaches the destination then it has to be finally detected and treated at the destination machine.

22.5 Preventing email viruses at source

Although ultimately the receiver has to scan the email in order not to get infected, the mails should better be scanned in the source machine before they can go out of the source machine or network.

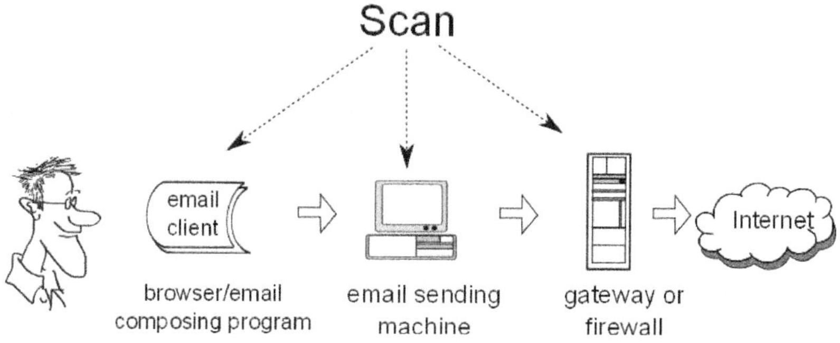

Email scanning points at sender's side

Ideal Final result:

IFR The source machine should not allow any email infection.

IFR If there is any email infection, it should be detected at the source machine and cleaned before they are sent out.

Possible Solutions

- The email viruses spread without suspicion because they often originate from genuine sources. There should be a method to protect the address book and make it inaccessible to viruses.

- The email virus often sends mails automatically without the knowledge of the sender. There should be a mechanism to control or prevent sending mails automatically.

INVENTION-82: Detecting email viruses by matching recipient address with randomly selected addresses

Patent 6763462 (invented by David Marsh, assignee Micron Technology, July 2004) discloses a method of detecting viruses in email applications by matching the recipient addresses by randomly selected addresses.

The invention generates random numbers and associates with specific email addresses in the address book. Each time the email application transmits an email message; the virus checker is invoked to inspect the recipient address of the outgoing message. If the email address corresponding to the random numbers matches with one or more of the recipient address, then the virus routine alerts the user of a potential virus activity.

22.6 Scanning emails at the Mail Server or Gateway

Anybody will admit that it is not wise to allow the virus mails to travel from the sender's computer all throughout the way to be scanned at the recipient's computer. If the virus could not be controlled in the sender's machine then it should at least be scanned on the mail servers and gateways before the infected mail can reach the recipient's computer to infect (TRIZ Principle-10: Prior Action). However, there are difficulties involved in scanning emails on the route during transfer.

- ⇨ Scanning emails on different types of clients and servers involve different types of methods.
- ⇨ The scanner has to have a mechanism of decrypting the mailboxes in the mail server in order to scan the emails.
- ⇨ There may be multiple servers and intermediate machines. Scanning the same emails again and again on different machines would result in wastage of time and resources.

Possible solution

- ⚒ Specialized scanners may be installed on gateways to scan incoming/ outgoing mails. One may configure either to scan all emails or to scan emails only with attachments. One may also define to block emails having attachments like, .com, .exe, .vbs, .scr etc. one may use other heuristics as to block emails having specific subject lines.
- ⚒ Patent 6785732 (invented by Bates et al., assignee IBM, Aug 2004) suggests an email checking method in the web server. When an email is detected with a virus, the message is either repaired or discarded and both the sender and the recipient are informed via email that the message contained a virus.

Further Problem

Scanning email servers does not work for proprietary email servers like ccMail, MS Exchange, Lotus Notes etc. which store emails in encrypted formats for privacy reasons. The anti-virus programs cannot break the proprietary encryption in order to access the attached files.

Contradiction	*The mail servers use proprietary encryption mechanism to maintain the privacy of the emails. If they reveal the decryption algorithm to anti-virus makers they cannot maintain the required privacy of the mails. On the other hand the anti-virus cannot scan the encrypted mail files without getting the decryption algorithm.*

Analysis

Improving Parameter: Confidentiality

Worsening Parameter: Security

Ideal Final result:

IFR The virus scanner should be able to detect viruses even in the encrypted mailboxes.

Problem Analysis

If we do an S-Field analysis here we find that there are two elements (or substances), viz., the mail server (S1) and the scanning engine (S2). We want the scanning engine (S2) to access the mail server (S1) for scanning the mails. But the scanner cannot access the encrypted mails in the servers (insufficient relation).

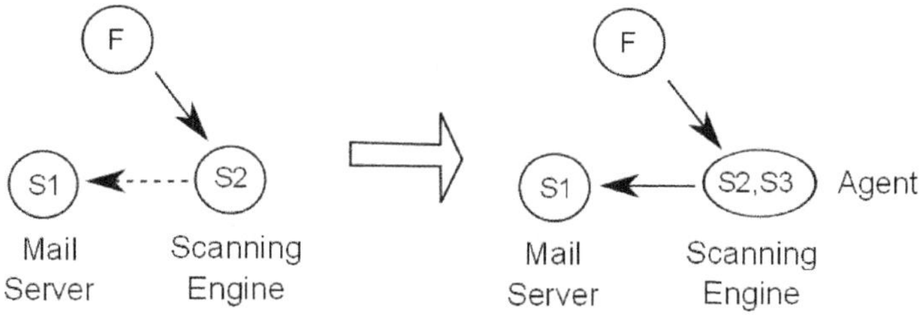

Using an Agent to access Emails
Standard 1.1.2

If we refer to the Inventive Standards, this situation can be solved by transiting to an Internal Complex SFM (Standard 1.1.2) or transiting to an external Complex SFM (Standard 1.1.3).

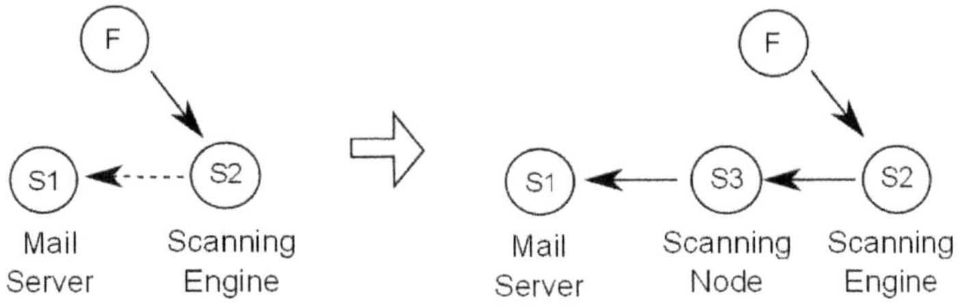

Using a client node access Emails for scanning
Standard 1.1.3

There are two patents below which solve this problem using these two methods. Patent 5832208 uses an Agent which can access the attachments of the mail server (Standard 1.1.2). Patent 5889943 uses a separate virus scanning node which downloads the emails from the postal node (Standard 1.1.3).

INVENTION-83: Using an agent for scanning emails in mail servers

Patent 5832208 (invented by Chen et al, assignee Cheyenne Software International, Nov 1998) proposes to place a software agent on the server computer to scan emails on the server computer. The software agent provides an interface between the anti-virus module and the message system (TRIZ Principle-24: Intermediary).

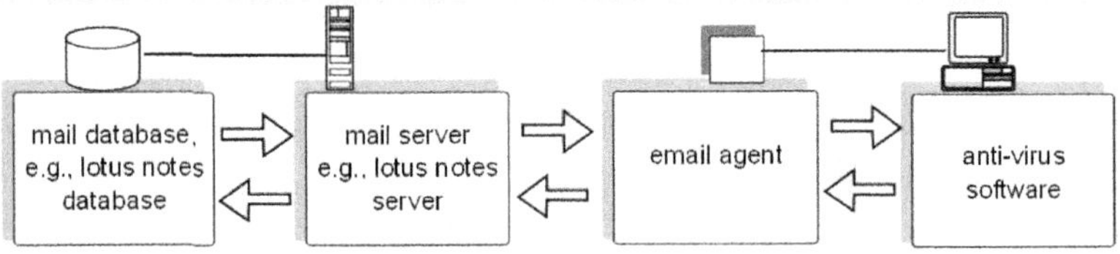

Using an agent for scanning email server

According to this method when an email message is forwarded to a mailbox, the agent is immediately invoked. If an attachment is present in an email message the agent first detaches and forwards the attachments to the anti-virus application (TRIZ Principle-2: Taking out). Then the anti-virus does a complete scan of all the email messages including the attachments. If a virus is found then it is cleaned and reattached with the original email message (TRIZ Principle-5: Merging).

INVENTION-84: Using a postal node to scan emails in the email server

Patent 5889943 (invented by Ji et al., assignee Trend Micro Incorporated, March 1999) proposes a method slightly different from the above. It proposes use a client node to poll the emails from a postal node for scanning.

According to the invention, the first node is a client node and the second node is an email postal node (like pop server). The second node (postal node) contains email messages. The first node (client node) polls the unscanned mails from the postal node and scans for viruses.

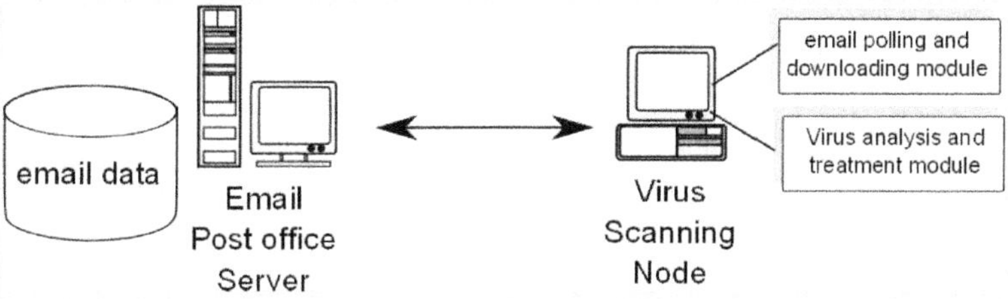

The messages are polled, scanned and treated automatically without any user triggering (TRIZ Principle-25: Self service).

Let's see another invention based on the same strategy of scanning the emails on a separate machine. However, the method of implementation is slightly different. In the above invention a client node was downloading the emails from a post office server to scan the mails, whereas in the following invention, the post office server is forwarding the infected emails to a quarantine server (or virus processing server).

INVENTION-85: Scanning emails by a remote email scanning server

Patent 6701440 (invented by Kim et al, assignee Networks Associates Technology, March 2004 and Patent 7299361, Nov 2007) discloses a method of remote virus scanning which is useful for web-based email service providers (like Yahoo and Hotmail) who store emails in centrally controlled servers.

The system includes a remote e-mail receiving server which receives the incoming e-mail message. Then a virus-detection program scans the e-mail message for virus. If no infection is detected then the mail is sent to the email sending (SMTP) server. On the other hand, if any infection is detected the mail is sent to a remote email virus processing server.

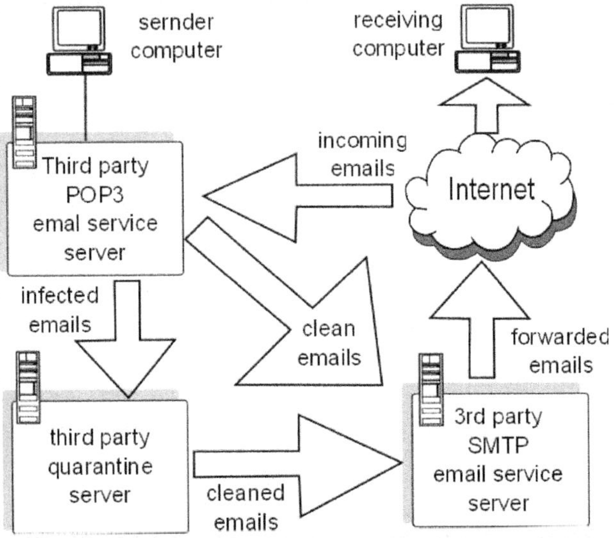

The remote e-mail virus-processing server attempts to clean the infected e-mail message and sends the cleaned email to the email-sending (SMTP) server which forwards the mail to the destination e-mail address.

🛠 Patent 7484244 (invented by - Nagoya, et al, Assignee- Duaxes Corporation (JP), Jan. 2009) discloses a similar method of detecting macro viruses in email attachments but with no OS dependency. The invention suggests to deploy an inspection computer that is connected to the mail server. When the emails are transferred from the mail server, the inspection server opens the attachments in order to execute the macros. Then it detects whether the macro is trying to access to certain I/O port by using a I/O check board and issues a warning when such an attempt is detected.

INVENTION-86: Up-to-date scanning of emails at a network gateway

Patent 7516489 (invented by - Lahti, Assignee-F-Secure Oyj, Apr. 2009) discloses a method of scanning for latest virus signatures at a network gateway. According to the invention the anti-virus application is installed at the email gateway of the network. When the anti-virus provider detects a new virus, it sends a notification to the anti-virus application (TRIZ Principle-23: Feedback). The notification may be pushed to the anti-virus application using HTTP or SNMP protocol or using mechanisms like Backweb.

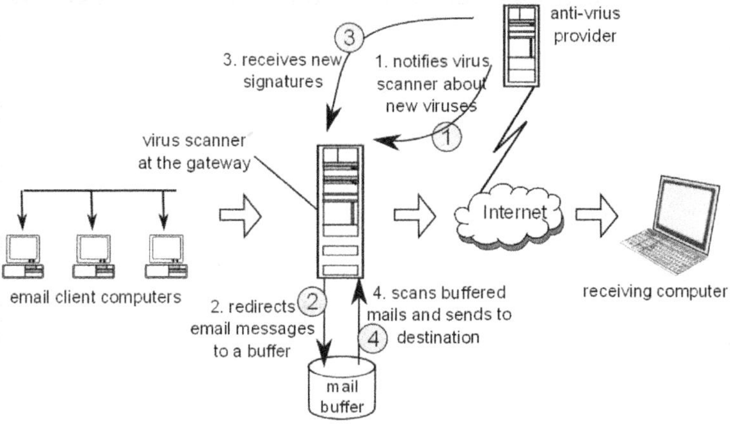

When the anti-virus application (on the gateway) receives the notification, it redirects the emails and/or attachments to a buffer for safe storage. After that it gets the signatures of the new viruses and scans the previously buffered emails. This method allows the scanner to use the latest discovered virus signature thus minimizing possibility of infection.

In the previous paragraphs we discussed how the emails are scanned on the email servers before they are delivered to the destination computer. Although the methods work fine, there are some drawbacks.

Further Problem:

- One of the major drawbacks of scanning emails on the transit is that there is a possibility of scanning the same mail again and again on different servers and finally on the recipient's machine which is a mere wastage of time and resources. There is a need to avoid repetitive scanning.

Possible Solution

One solution to the above problem is to attach a "Checked to be virus free..." certificate to the email after it is scanned. This helps the subsequent machines to skip the message from scanning again. The scanner on the recipient's machine may also rely on this "virus free.." certificate and open the mails without scanning again. **Limitations**: a virus may alter the status of an email to be "virus free.." and escape scanning.

INVENTION-87: Certifying emails to be free from viruses after scanning

Patent 7107618 (invented by Gordon et al, assignee McAfee, Sep 2006 and Patent 7533272 by same inventors, May 2009) discloses a method of certifying "virus free" status of emails to avoid repetitive scanning of emails.

The method scans an email before it is sent from the computer and attaches a certificate identifying that the email is free from viruses. The certificate is also sent along with the email to the recipient computer (TRIZ Principle-5: Merging). This certificate assures the recipient that the data received has been checked for viruses and is safe to open.

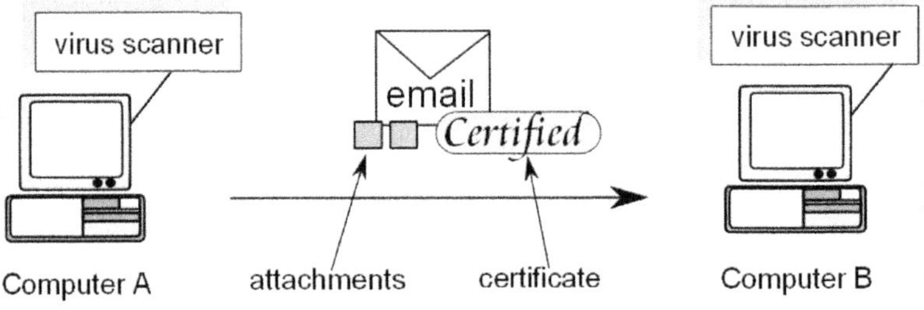

Avoiding repetitive scanning by using "Virus free" certificates

The certificate may sate that "the email has been scanned for viruses ..." and "certified ..." etc. The certificate may also contain a logo of the virus scanning company that indicates that the email has been scanned for viruses. Moreover, a digital signature may be attached to the email stating that the email has not been tampered while in transit from the sending computer to the receiving computer.

22.7 Detecting email virus at the recipient's machine

If the email virus cannot be controlled at the sender's machine and not in the mail servers then it will finally arrive at the destination computer. If the destination computer has an anti-virus it will be scanned there in the destination computer. However, there may be some difficult situations.

⇨ The recipient may not have an anti-virus installed on his computer.

⇨ The anti-virus database at the recipient computer might have not been updated.

⇨ The virus email may attach zip files and use social engineering tactics to convince user to unzip files.

⇨ The conventional anti-virus can scan only individual files. Hence detection is possible only when the receiver tries to open the infected files after downloading them.

Ideal Final result:

IFR The virus emails should have been scanned and cured before they could reach and infect their destination computers.

IFR The recipient should be able to open the emails without fear of virus infection even if he does not have an anti virus or his anti-virus has gone out of date.

Possible solution

⚒ In order to prevent email viruses Microsoft implemented a virus-protection feature in MS Outlook. This feature does not allow outlook to open (or run) any file with regular executable extension. **Limitation**: Although it does not run the executable files directly it allows to save the executable files. Besides the viruses / virus writers pack their executables in zip files which escape various protection features.

⚒ When the anti-virus suspects an infection in the email but fails to disinfect the file it may decide to delete the attachment in order to prevent a possible infection. **Limitation**: In such cases the recipient gets the email but not the attachment. **Contradiction:**

We want to view the infected file, but we don't want to take the risk of infecting the computer.

INVENTION-88: Displaying infected files and emails in a safe format

Patent 7263561 (invented by Green et al., Assignee- McAfee, Inc. Aug. 2007) teaches a method of viewing an infected file without taking the risk of infecting the computer.

The invention converts the virus infected file from its original format to a new format which is virus safe. The method may convert the file to an HTML file without scripts or to an ASCII text file or any other file having only text and not any scripts. The intended recipient can view the contents of the infected file without infecting his computer (TRIZ Principle-2: Taking out, Principle-36: State Change and Conversion).

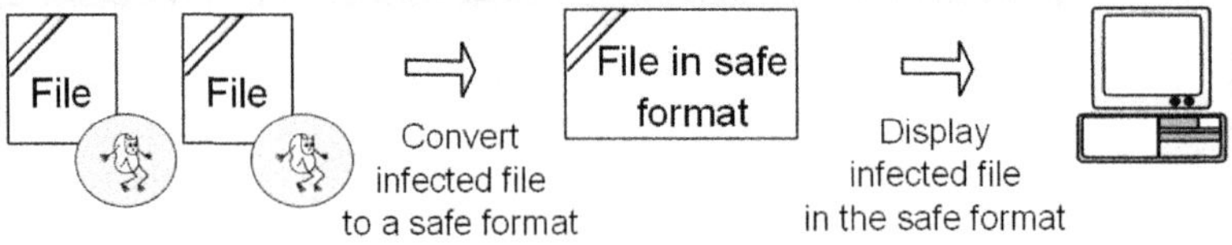

Converting infected file to safe format
before displaying to user

This is an example of Inventive Standard 1.2.2. The infected email has a harmful effect on the client machine. But the relationship has to be maintained. In this case, standard 1.2.2 suggests to introduce a third elements (or substances) which is a modification of first or second element (or substance).

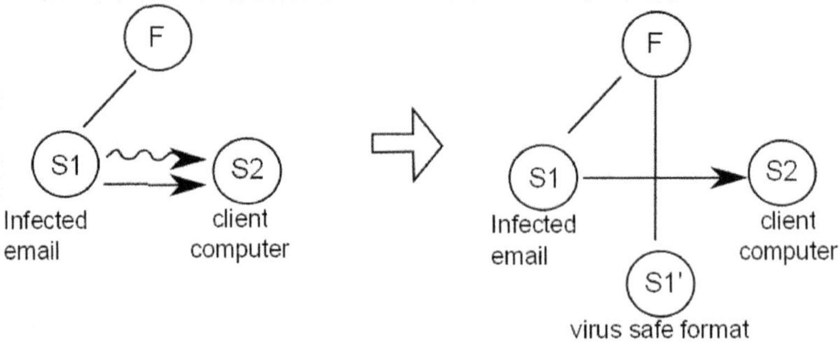

Converting email to safe format, Standard 1.2.2

This method is useful in situations where the remedies for a virus is not available. The intended recipient can view the contents of an infected file without infecting his computer.

INVENTION-89: Implementing a sacrificial server to convert email-attachments to non-executable format

All conventional methods provide a solution only after detecting a virus as a virus. But sometimes a virus may skip detection or identifying a virus to be a virus can be too late. Patent 7913078 (invented by Stewart et al., assignee- NIL, Mar 2011) suggests using a sacrificial server to scan emails and convert email attachments to a non-executable format in order to avoid possibility of infection. (Note: The objective of this invention is very similar to that of the previous invention and uses the same Inventive Standard 1.2.2.)

According to the invention a sacrificial server (either physical or virtual) may be implemented in the network. All the executable programs and other suspicious parts of incoming email messages are forwarded to the sacrificial server. The sacrificial-server converts them to non-executable format (such as PDF) and sends to the recipient. The sacrificial server is then checked for virus activity. After the execution is completed, the sacrificial server is rebooted (TRIZ Principle-34: Discard and Recover).

INVENTION-90: Using a Hypervisor area for testing email viruses

Hypervisor is a technology that allows multiple Operating Systems to run on the same client. Patent 7996901 (invented by O'Sullivan, et al., assignee- Lenovo (Singapore) Pte. Ltd., Aug, 2011) discloses detecting email viruses using hypervisor technology.

According to the invention, the computer will have a type-1 hypervisor capable of running multiple operating systems. (Type-1 hypervisors provide better performance as they directly run on the hardware unlike type-2 hypervisors which run on an operating system.) The hypervisor may open a second operating system from the beginning or open up the second operating system on demand.

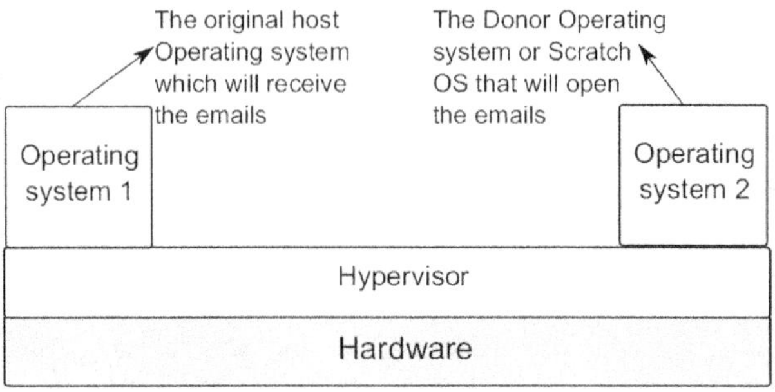

The hypervisor system, Patent 7996901

This second operating system (or donor operating system or "scratch OS") will work as a scratch pad. The emails sent to the recipient will be opened under this second operating system which will determine whether the email contains a virus. Once the email activities are complete the "scratch OS" can be discarded (TRIZ Principle-27: Cheap and disposable). Thus the user operating system will have no damage.

22.8 Verifying the authenticity of the sender

- The email viruses generally send emails to the addresses collected from the victim's address book. As the sender's address remains valid and genuine it becomes difficult to differentiate between the genuine mail and virus mail.

- The existing e-mail standard can verify the validity of an email address, but cannot verify whether a particular message has been actually sent from a particular address. This drawback helps the spammers to misuse email addresses for wrong purposes.

Possible Solutions

- One solution to this problem is implementing PKI and using certificates of external trust centers. **Drawback**: this will involve distribution and maintenance of large number of security keys which is complex and expensive.

INVENTION-91: Authenticating emails without scanning and without opening

Patent 7523496 (invented by Bickford, et al., Assignee- International Business Machines, Apr. 2009) discloses a method of authenticating emails (to ensure that they have originated from the genuine source and hence free from viruses) without opening the emails.

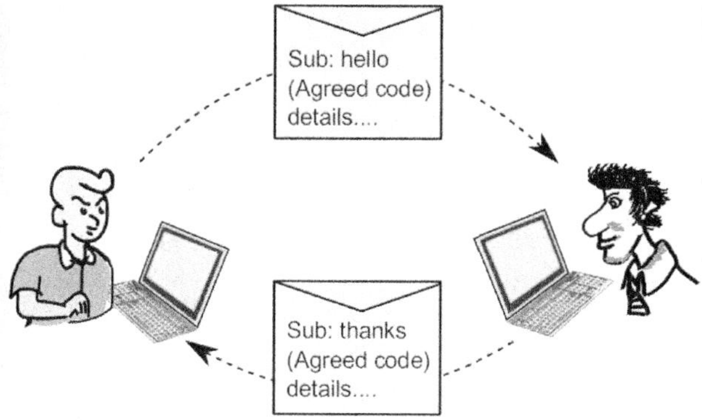

Using privately agreed authentication code

According to the invention, the sender and the recipient of the emails agree beforehand on an authentication key, such as a simple natural-language phrase, which identifies the originator to the recipient. The authentication key is included in an open field (such as the subject line) of the email so that the recipient can examine it without opening the email.

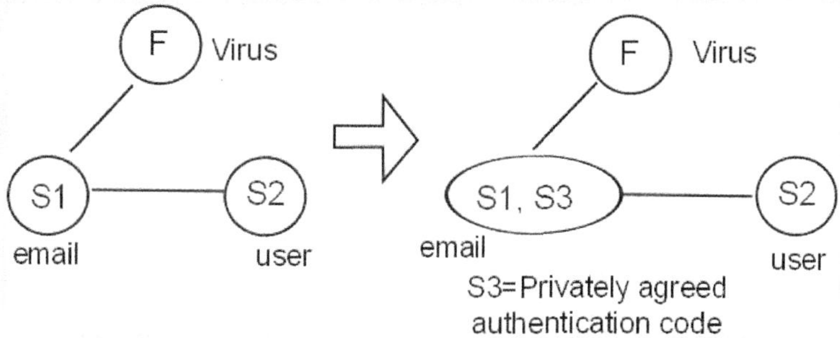

This is a good example of Standard 4.2.2. An email (S1) in its original form is difficult to diagnose whether it has originated from the right source. This is solved by adding a privately agreed auth code (S3) into the email (S1) thereby creating an internal complex S-Field. When the recipient receives the email it first checks whether the expected authentication key is present. If the authentication key is not present or is different from the previously agreed authentication key, then the recipient may suspect and reject the email.

Patent 7752440 (invented by Faynberg, et al, assignee- Alcatel-Lucent USA Inc, Jul 2010) teaches to prevent email spam and virus distribution by authenticating the origin of email message. The invention defines a set of mechanisms to reasonably ensure that the email message has come from a genuine location and sent by the person indicated in the "From:" Field. In order to verify authenticity, the method sends a query directly to the alleged originating server (or does this function through a AAA server). The method not only authenticates the sending address but also the sender server. If the response to the query is negative, then the message is discarded. This method avoids the need for implementing complex methods of PKI and security certificates for authenticating the sender.

- Patent 7854007 (invented by Sprosts, et al, assignee- Ironport Systems, Inc., Dec, 2010) provides a series of heuristic tests to examine the sender reputation information. The heuristics include the name and type of file attachment to a message, the size of the file attachment, the amount of similar file sizes attached to received messages, the amount of similar file names attached to received messages and the names of attachments of known viruses. Besides some heuristics are checked on the message sender, subject or body etc. Each of these heuristic has threat scores. The messaging gateways contain various content filtering logic. They count the threat parameters against a period of time. That means too many messages showing higher threat parameters indicates a virus outbreak. When the virus threat score value is greater than a specified threshold the message gateways store the message in a quarantine queue instead of immediately delivering message to the recipient. As the message gateways suspend delivery of messages the method provides sufficient time for updating the anti-virus and prevent outbreaks at early stages.

22.9 Detecting and Managing Outbreak of Email Viruses

One of the worst problems of email viruses is that they can grow and transmit very fast. Hence these types of viruses are capable of causing virus outbreaks or epidemics that can easily spread to a large geographical location just within hours. The problem becomes worse because;

- The viruses typically use addresses from local address book which are considered as trusted addresses and not detained by the spam filters or by the gateway.
- The traditional methods of scanning individual emails don't tackle outbreaks efficiently.
- During outbreaks a huge number of virus mails transit from computer to computer consuming excessive bandwidth and choking the network traffic.

Ideal Final result:

IFR The email system should be intelligent to carry only the genuine messages and drop the virus codes.

IFR The email address book of a computer should not be accessible to a virus.

Possible Solution:

- The virus outbreaks may be controlled by scanning emails at various stages, such as, (i) during composition and uploading at the sender's computer, (ii) during transfer through SMTP servers, mail forwarding servers, mail distributing servers, POP3 servers, and (iii) during receiving and opening emails and attachments at the client computer.
- Patent 6898715 (detailed later) proposes to automatically execute various counter measures like blocking E-mail attachments, hiding E-mail address books etc. upon detection of virus outbreaks. The method automatically shuts down the email server in case of extreme situations.
- Patent 6886099 and 7093293 (detailed earlier) provide a method of detecting virus outbreaks by monitoring some measurement parameters. The measurement parameters are like "how many email messages are sent having identical message title", "how many emails are sent with identical file attachment", "how many emails are sent having attachments of a given type", "how many emails are sent having attachments of executable files" etc. If the measurement parameters cross a predetermined threshold level

within a given measurement period then the system indicates the outbreak of a computer virus.

- Patent 7690038 (invented by Simon Ko, assignee- Trend Micro Incorporated Mar 2010) provides an automatic tracking of vulnerability and clean up system. The invented anti-virus system logs the in-transit e-mails in a computer network. When the anti-virus engine gets an updated pattern file it checks the log whether the network has been exposed to a computer virus that is identified in the updated pattern file. In such a case it initiates one or more of the following antivirus actions.

  a) send a vulnerability assessment report to the network administrator; b) send an e-mail notification to the network administrator about the virus; c) send an e-mail notification to a user of a client computer that has received an e-mail carrying the virus; d) automatically disinfect a client computer that has received an e-mail carrying the virus etc.

Chapter 23.

Protecting Networks from Worms and Network Viruses

23.1 Introduction to Worms and Network Viruses

Worms are stand-alone computer programs that copy themselves from one machine to another using the resources of the computer system and network infrastructure. They exploit the vulnerabilities of the networks and operating systems and find their way to transmit from one computer to another. Some worms called "host computer worms" run entirely on the host computer and use the network connections only to copy themselves to other computers. Some other worms called "network worms" consist of multiple parts running on different machines using the network connections for communicating between themselves. As the worms primarily exploit network connections to replicate themselves, they are also known as Network Viruses.

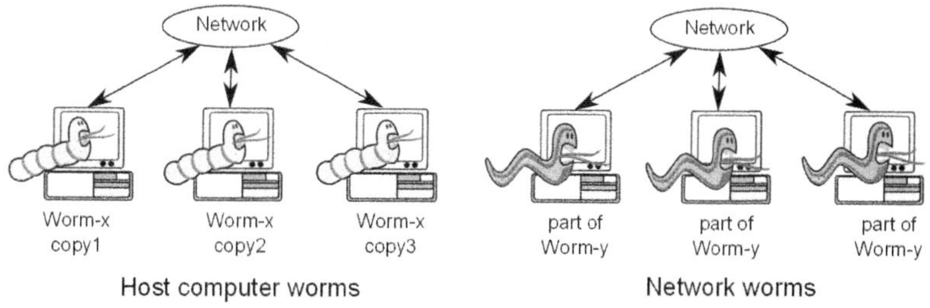

The worms have the potential to cause incalculable damages. The cost of some of the worm outbreaks in past were very high. The economic damage and lost productivity done by the Goner, Code Red II, Blaster, SoBig, Netsky and Sasser worms were significant. History says Code Red worm outbreak in 2001 affected millions of Windows NT and Windows

2000 computers causing damages causing billions of dollars. In Aug 2003, the Sobig virus/worm infected millions of MS Windows computers connected through Internet. In January 2004, Mydoom worm infected millions of computers. Luckily most of the current day worms are relatively benign.

During early days the worms were considered to be more of a nuisance than a threat. But today, with the popularity of Internet, worms have become more complicated and capable of performing a wide range of malicious activities, including data stealing, lunching of Denial-of-Service (DoS) or even delivering other viruses and Trojans. There are different types of worms. An email worm spreads copies of itself using email messages, IRC-worm spreads copies of itself through IRC (Internet Relay Chat) channels and SMS worms spreads through SMS (Short Messaging System).

23.1.1 Characteristics of Worms

Worms are self-contained viruses. They are independent programs capable of executing by themselves. Unlike viruses they don't depend upon a host program to execute.

- ⇨ Unlike typical viruses, the worms don't attach themselves to other files or depend upon other files to execute. They are capable of executing without being triggered by any user.
- ⇨ Worms are capable of communicating to other machines through network connections.
- ⇨ Worms make use of network connections and network technology to copy themselves to other machines and even to other networks.
- ⇨ Many worms are transferred through emails. Some worms are capable of generating emails, which are called mass mailer worms.
- ⇨ As the worms exploit specific features and vulnerabilities of network protocols they are protocol dependent. That means the worms written for one protocol (e.g., DECNET) will not work for another protocol (e.g., TCP/IP).
- ⇨ As a network may connect large number of computers, the worms/network viruses are susceptible to outbreaks that may infect a large number of computers within a very short time.

- Many worms don't have any payload. Some of them have payload of a DoS attack against specific websites. But most of them cause network congestion because of overloaded traffic on the network.
- Since most worms are created in an indoor network environment, they are not adequately tested or audited on large-scale networks.

23.1.2 Similarities between Worms and Viruses

Worms come under the broad category of viruses because many features are common between worms and viruses.

- Worms also replicate themselves like viruses. Without replication the worm cannot grow or survive.
- Both viruses and worms are malware and infect innocent computers. All virus scanners do scan the worms too.
- Like viruses the payload of worms may not immediately manifest. Some viruses or worms wait patiently as benign programs until their events are triggered to become active.

23.1.3 Differences between Worms and Viruses

The following are the differences between worms and the typical viruses.

- Viruses infect other programs by attaching themselves to the target programs. On the contrary the worms are independent programs and don't attach their code to other programs.
- Viruses have to modify their host files at the very first instance of their infection. On the contrary worms can spread without changing or damaging any file.
- Viruses and worms follow different methods to transmit. As viruses are dependent on their host programs they can move from system to system when somebody carries the infected file through a transferable media or copies the infected files from one computer to another or downloads an infected file from Internet. But worms have the capability to transmit independently from one computer to another through network connections.
- The viruses can execute only when their host programs execute. On the contrary worms can execute independently on various triggers like system boot, internet connection etc.

- Viruses generally infect the files on the same computer where they reside. They move to another system only when somebody copies the infected file. But worms don't depend on human beings to transfer to other systems. They can look for potential victims through the network connection and spread by themselves. In that sense, the worms can spread faster than viruses.

23.1.4 Worm Infection Strategy

- Through emails– most worms transmit their code by sending emails. They collect email addresses from victim's address book or collect from different victims or collect from search engines like google. Some worms do email address harvesting through ICQ, newsgroups and similar sources.

- Attacking vulnerable IP addresses- many worms scan the IP addresses in the network and find if any of them has any vulnerability to attack. For example, it may check whether the potential victim has a blank password or weak password to get access over the system. It may make a dictionary attack to check for a weak password or capture passwords on the fly.

- Some worms assume that the system of a particular type (such as a particular version of Windows) will have a specific vulnerability and then launch the attack.

- The author of the worm may use social engineering techniques to pursue the recipient to execute the code or directly execute the code by using other triggers.

- Some worms attack backdoor compromised systems. If the backdoor has blank password or weak password it can occupy the system through the backdoor.

- Network protocols are generally based on open standards for enabling flexibility. But feature is a weakness of the protocols that is exploited by the worms for communication and replication.

23.1.5 The four stages of Worms' lifecycle

Florian Buchholz et al. explain four stages of a Worm's lifecycle ("Digging for Worms, Fishing for Answers"). After analyzing the behavior of several worms they find a four-stage lifecycle of the worms, viz., target selection, exploit, infect and propagate. In the first stage the worm looks for a possible victim computer. Next it exploits the vulnerability of the victim computer. Then it infects the victim by changing file systems, deleting files and doing all kinds of circus it intends to do. Finally, it comes to a stage where it is capable of propagating to other machines.

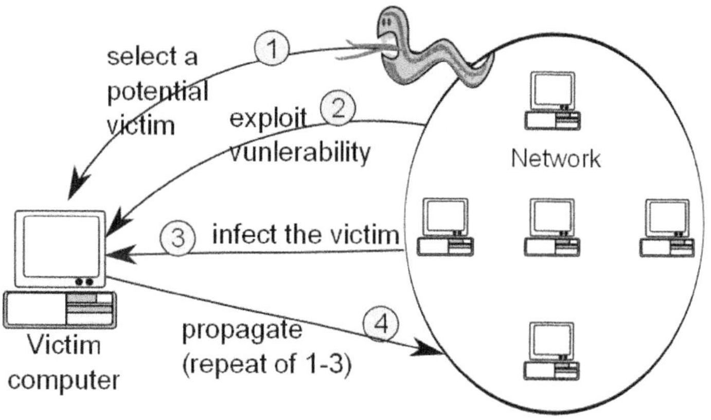

Four stages of worm infection

The fourth stage is actually the repetition of first three stages but from the newly infected machine. While the first three stages were inbound connections to the new machine, the fourth stage involves outbound connections from the new machine to other machines.

23.1.6 Why is it important to tackle the Network Viruses

A virus or worm in a network environment is a serious concern and needs to be tackled in a more systematic way. That is because;

- A network virus has special capabilities to copy itself to other computer and spread fast to other computers in a network environment by exploiting the features and capabilities of the networking technology.
- As the worms/ network viruses propagate through network they can increase network activities and thereby degrade the network performance and even choke or paralyze the network traffic.
- It is difficult to disinfect all the computers in a network. If any single system is left uncleaned, it will reinfect the whole network.
- Network viruses are a threat globally to the Internet. Epidemics can spread fast in networks, whether LAN, WAN or Internet.

Worms can transfer confidential data. Many worms start a server on a particular port and create a backdoor for the hackers.

23.1.7 The contradiction of avoiding network viruses

One solution to avoid network viruses is to disconnect your computer from all networks (TRIZ Principle-2: Taking out). But there are often strong reasons and requirements for accessing the network and Internet. A person may have to work in a LAN in the office environment for exchanging files with co-workers. A current day computer user has to connect Internet to access emails and other information.

Contradiction	*We want to connect our computer to LAN and Internet in order to share data, files and emails. But we don't want to connect our computer to LAN or Internet, as that might cause a virus infection.*

Analysis

Improving Parameter: Connectivity

Worsening Parameter: Security

When we convert this contradiction to a physical contradiction, the same parameter "Connectivity" becomes both "improving" and "worsening" parameter, as it causes both benefits and harms.

23.1.8 Ideal situation

IFR Ideally we should have seamless connection to the network for data transfer but we should have no fear of viral infection

23.2 How to prevent viruses/ worms from entering the network

Prevention is better than cure. If the virus can be prevented from entering the network then there is no need to scan each computer or each file of a computer or each packet transferred between computers. Let's see what preventions can be taken to keep the viruses out of a network.

- Maintaining workstation security– that includes installing anti-virus on individual workstations, installing operating system patches, removal of unwanted services, removal of unwanted file sharing and access rights etc. These precautions allow Internet connection but disallow virus infection (TRIZ Principle-9: Prior Counteraction).

- **Limitations**- (i) installing and upgrading anti-virus on each computer requires a lot of maintenance activities. (ii) Installing virus-detection software on each individual computer consumes a lot of system resources on each computer which could have been utilized for other purposes. (iii) The traditional scanning method is file based which cannot deal with the network traffic directly. The scanner has to wait until the infected file is fully downloaded to the user's system. (iv) When the files are moved from one computer to another, the already scanned files are also scanned again in the destination computer, which wastes time and system resources.

- It is also necessary to install anti-virus programs on the servers and gateways and fix up all vulnerabilities of servers through updates and patches so that the worms will not be able to copy themselves to the server.

- Placing a proxy server or firewall or other intrusion detection devices at the Internet connections which can detect and prevent unwanted connections. If the worms cannot get into the network then they cannot cause infection.

- After a virus is detected and cleaned in a network, the details of that virus may be added to the firewall of the network in order to prevent the virus reentering the network.

- Application security – which involves developing application code with security in mind thereby leaving no security flaws for the intruders. The application should have validation routines to handle all types of bad/ invalid data fed by the user.

- Educating the users- not only the system administrators, the end users should also understand the risks and vulnerabilities of the system, so that they can be careful about email attachments, weak passwords and using detachable storage.

- Network policy- the system admin should implement a proper network policy. The malware policies should be included in IT policies and IT policies should be properly implemented.

- Another method to prevent worm propagation is by "address blacklisting". The worm propagating IP addresses may be blacklisted so that none of their packets are accepted by any host.

- A viral outbreak is more than just viral infections of individual files. When there is a viral outbreak a large number of systems may get infected. The anti-virus should be alert on virus-outbreaks to prevent other computers in the network from being infected (TRIZ Principle-9: Prior Counteraction). It is necessary to quarantine the infected machine as soon as possible otherwise the infection can spread throughout the network.

23.3 Methods of detecting Worms and Network Viruses

When the preventive measures fail to block a virus from entering the network there should be detection systems for detecting it as soon as possible. The detection may be done at individual machines or through a central scanning server or on the fly while the data is being transferred from one computer to another. The conventional scanning methods are host based and don't work efficiently for scanning viruses in a network. Some special techniques of scanning network viruses are as follows.

Network virus detection methods are divided into two main categories, viz., network traffic analysis and network packet analysis.

Network traffic analysis or traffic pattern analysis or flow based analysis- is done by monitoring the unusual traffic pattern in the network. As an infected computer typically transmits malicious packets to random IP address destinations, the method detects the sender of such random packets as infected. This is also known as "anomaly based detection".

Network packet analysis- is done by analyzing each single IP (or other) packet to detect if they contain any malicious code or code pattern. This method is useful during data transfer from one computer to another such as downloading data from a server. If an infection is detected during data transfer/ download, then the anti-virus program should cure the virus infection or delete the partially transferred/ downloaded file.

- In many cases, both the methods are used. For example, once an anomaly is detected in the traffic pattern, the focus is given to packet analysis in order to know the exact nature of infection.

- **Limitation:** (i) the network traffic pattern analysis requires complex calculations; (ii) one approach is to compare the traffic with a baseline. But this method is slow and cannot draw any conclusion based on regular fluctuations; (iii) some stealth worms may send very less number of packets which cannot be determined by network traffic analysis; (iv) these methods are prone to high rate of false positives; (v) analysis of network packets going through high-speed routers requires additional equipments coupled with the routers. This increases the cost and complexity of network management.

- Another method of statistical technique is "Sequential Hypothesis Testing" which is based on whether each connection request succeeded or not.

- The detection method should isolate the infected machine in a network automatically (TRIZ Principle-2: Taking out, Principle-25: Self Service) so that the infected machine cannot spread infection to other computers (Patent 7571483).

- Another method of worm detection is by implementing various simple heuristics in routers and gateways to monitor different characteristics of worms. This method identifies various worm-like behaviors. For example, if there are identical or repeated packets or malicious packets then an infection is suspected. The routers may be instructed to drop (i.e., reject) packets fulfilling specific conditions like having specific port numbers.

- **Limitations**- it is difficult to differentiate between the identity and behavior of good and bad code. Any mistake in a judgment may lead to false positives or false negatives. For example, "talking to a large number of hosts" is a worm like behavior. But some servers legitimately talk to a large number of hosts. It is difficult to suspect an infection just because a server (or client) is talking to a large number of hosts.

23.4 Implementing Virus Scanning though a Gateway or Firewall

The conventional anti-virus programs are installed on individual computers in a network which requires too much installation and maintenance activities. Another method is to install an anti-virus directly into the firewall.

In a firewall-based virus scanning, all the data transfer between the LAN and Internet is scanned at the gateway or firewall.

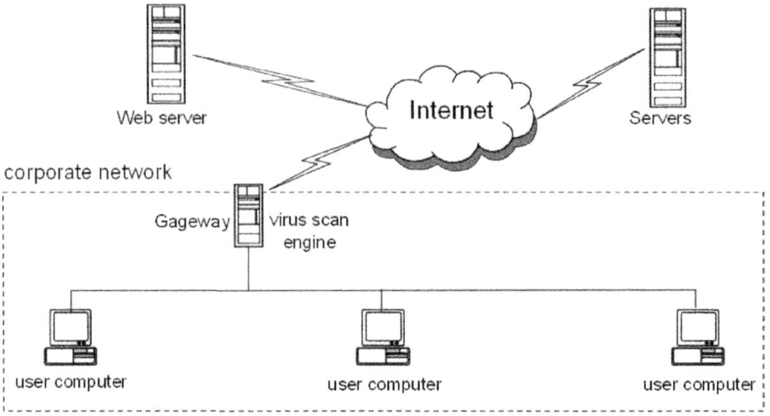

Gateway based Virus scanning method

Limitations of firewall based virus scanning

However, a firewall based virus-filtering feature is also not very effective because;

- A substantial amount of processing at the firewall degrades the network performance,
- Specialized computers for firewalls and gateways may require additional expenditure,
- The firewall has access to less operational data which leads to a less precise scanning compared to a client based virus scanning,
- Still requires an anti-virus at the individual machine to prevent infection from internal sources.

The Contradiction of firewall based scanning

Thus we saw that both the methods viz., implementing anti-virus at individual computers and installing anti-virus at the firewall, have specific advantages and disadvantages. On one hand a single point protection makes the scanning slow, whereas on the other hand installing the scanner on individual computers increases administrative overhead. This situation leads to the following contradictions.

Contradiction	*Implementing anti-virus on every computer protects individual computers from both external (Internet) and internal (within the LAN) attacks, but increases administrative overhead. We want to protect the computer but we don't want the administrative load.*
	Implementing anti-virus directly into the firewall reduces the administrative load but fails to provide protection from viruses spreading within the LAN. We want to reduce admin load but don't want virus infections from internal sources.

Analysis of Contradiction Parameters

Contradiction#1

Improving Parameter: Reliability

Worsening Parameter: Ease of Maintenance and Administration

Contradiction#2

Improving Parameter: Ease of Maintenance and Administration

Worsening Parameter: Reliability

Possible Solution

INVENTION-92: Distributed virus scanning by the client machines and central proxy server

Patent 6728886 (invented by Ji et al., assignee Trend Micro Incorporated, April 2004) discloses a technique of distributing virus scanning load between central scanning servers and local host computers without the need for managing anti-virus programs at each host computer.

According to this new scenario, the central virus scan servers will be implemented at central proxy servers in the LAN. If the browser of the host computer supports the technology of creating local scan engine then it will access the central proxy server to automatically download and create a local scan engine and/or local proxy server that will run on the host computer (TRIZ Principle-3: Local Quality). Once a local proxy server is created, the host will directly access the Internet bypassing the central proxy server. If on the other hand the browser of the host computer does not support the technology of creating local scan engine, then the data is transferred through the central proxy server and scan engine.

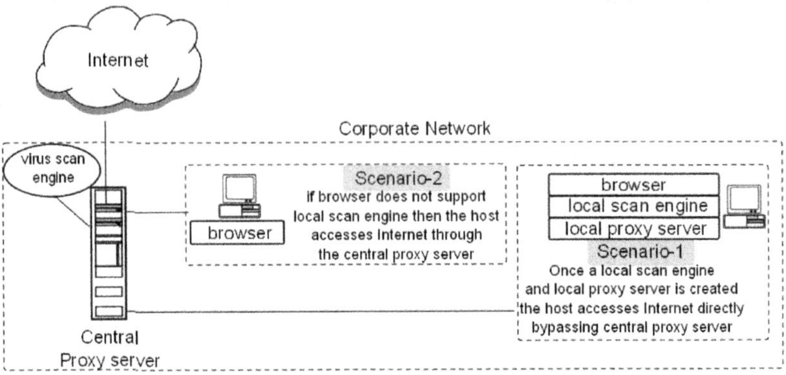

Distributed virus scanning arrangements, Patent 6728886

This method has the advantage of centrally managed virus scanning solutions while does not have the disadvantage of periodical updating and maintenance at each host computer. Besides, as many of the host computers will have ability for local scanning the load on the central server will be greatly reduced.

⚒ Patent 7512982 (invented by Takahashi, Assignee-Kabushiki Kaisha Toshiba (JP), Mar. 2009) teaches the possibility of detecting computer viruses in a computer network by looking at the presence of irregular data (Inventive Standard-4.2.1). According to the invention a detection computer is placed in between the local network and internet where a collection unit collects irregular data representing a possibility of computer virus, a decision unit decides whether the irregular data represents a computer virus and a notification unit notifies the computer network about the virus detection.

23.5 Virus Scanning through a Central Scanning Server

Another method of virus scanning in network is by implementing a central scanning server(/s). The clients or agents on individual computers intercept and transfer the suspect data to the central server for virus scanning and receive the results of scanning.

Advantages

- The anti-virus program and virus signature database is installed only on the central server and not on individual machines.

- Requires less maintenance as the scanning engine runs on one or a few central servers.

Disadvantages

- The clients have to transfer a large volume of data over the network, which slows down the network traffic and virus scanning operation.

- This situation becomes worse in a WAN or Internet scenario where the connections between hosts and servers are typically slow and costly.

Contradiction

Contradiction	*Implementing anti-virus through central scanning servers reduces administrative load on individual computers but requires a large volume of data to be transferred between the client and the server. We want the clients to send files to the central scanning server, but we don't want the network traffic to be overloaded because of file transfer.*

Analysis

Improving Parameter: Ease of maintenance and admin

Worsening Parameter: Volume of Transmission

Ideal Final result:

IFR The central server should scan the files but the client computers need not send the files to the central server.

IFR The clients should send files to the scanning server for scanning but without affecting the network traffic.

Possible Solution

- The volume of data transmission can be greatly reduced by transferring only the vulnerable parts of the file instead of transferring the whole file for scanning (vide invention below).

INVENTION-93: Improving scanning speed by transferring only vulnerable parts of the file to the scanning server

Patent 7020895 (invented by Albrecht, assignee F-Secure Oyj, Mar 2006) discloses a method reducing volume of data transfer between the agent and a server during virus scanning.

The inventor realizes that although a large volume of data is transferred by an agent to the scanning server, the scanning application actually looks at a relatively small portion of this data. Hence, according to the present invention it is not required to transfer the entire electronic file from the agent to the server, rather only those parts of the file which are of direct interest to the scanning application. For example, the scanning application may require the transfer of only a header portion of an electronic file. This method not only speeds up scanning operation but also improves network performance (TRIZ Principle-21: Skipping).

- There should be a way to scan the files at the central server without sending files to the central server. But how can the centralized server scan a file without getting the content of the file? The following invention may be interesting.

INVENTION-94: Improving scanning speed by transferring only file identification and checksum to the scanning server

Patent 7152164 (invented by Loukas, assignee- NIL, Dec 2006) discloses a method of scanning files in a central server without sending files to the central server.

According to the invention, the client computer sends only the identifications of files and some critical parameters like checksum which are tiny in size and require substantially less time and bandwidth. The file identifications may include the properties of the web content such as, source URL, source computer URL, content type, size, creation date, version number etc. along with check-sum of the web content and a data sample picked according to given rules (TRIZ Principle-30: Thin and Flexible). The tiny files again can be sent in compressed form to further reduce their size (Principle-37: Expansion).

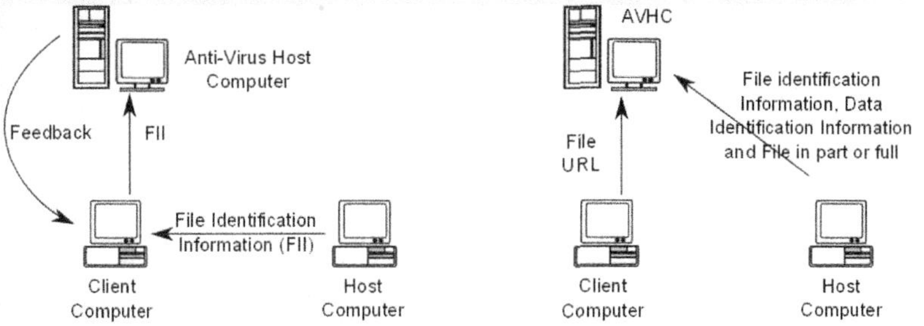

Scenario-1:
The client computer gets FII from host computer and sends to AVHC

Scenario-2:
The client computer sends URL to AVHC and AVHC gets FII from host computer

The anti-virus host computer (AVHC) compares the sent identifications with a database of identifications of other known virus infected files and other known virus infected web content. If the file is found to be infected then security measures are taken. If the anti-virus host computer does not have any information about the given file, it may directly fetch the file from the host computer by using the URL and file identification information and scan the content. This method avoids sending file to the AV server for scanning and eliminates need for installing AV on the client.

INVENTION-95: Managing non-protected computers in a network through a managing computer

Although there will be many computers in a network running up-to-date virus scanners there may be some computers which have not updated their anti-virus. In a network, the protection is as strong as the weakest link in the network. If some computers in a network are not protected, then the whole network becomes vulnerable to virus attacks. Patent 7269851 (invented by Ackroyd, assignee- McAfee Inc., Sep 2007) discloses a method of protecting non-protected computers in a network through a managing computer.

A managing computer receives a plurality of log data messages identifying detection of malware by various computers having up-to-date anti-virus connected to the network. The managing computer detects the patterns of malware detection across the network and triggers associated pre-determined anti-malware actions. The actions may include forcing specific computer to update their anti-virus data, or forcing specific computers to change their security settings or isolating specific computers from network etc.

A network can easily get infected if the newly added machines are infected. One method is to quarantine all newly introduced devices in a remediation Virtual LAN. **Drawback**- during the period of virus scanning and quarantine the new device will not have access to the network.

INVENTION-96: Network virus control through a virus control server

Patent 8245294 (invented by Zahra et al, assignee- Avaya, Inc., Aug 2012) teaches to create restricted access VLANs for each newly added device in order to prevent infection in the network.

According to the invention all newly added devices must be connected in such a way that all network traffic to and from the selected computer must pass through the virus control server. This method will prevent any possible infection from the newly added device (TRIZ Principle-24: Intermediary).

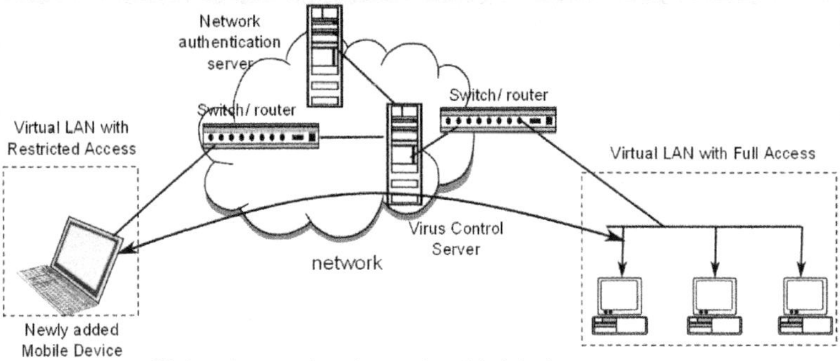

All data from and to the newly added device must pass through the Virus Control Server

The virus control server can further assign a security policy to the selected device for regulating network traffic between the selected device and the devices outside the subnet. When the device is quarantined (or the device is verified to be virus free) the virus control server releases the selected device from its quarantine sub-net so that at least some network traffic to and from the selected device bypasses the virus control server.

This way the virus control server connects and disconnects selected devices to the network depending on the vulnerability by identification of a virus (TRIZ Principle-15: Dynamize).

23.6 Improving on-the-way scanning and packet scanning

The conventional virus scanners don't have capabilities of scanning files while being downloaded. Hence the infected files continue to get downloaded to the user's computer without the user's knowledge and remain undetected on the user's system for a long time or passed on to other systems before detected by a scanner. It would be useful to screen all the data before they are downloaded or at the time of downloading (TRIZ Principle-10: Prior Action).

Methods of Packet Scanning

There are two types scanning network packets, one is "store scan forward scanning" and another is "stream scanning".

Store-scan-forward scanning

This method is generally used by file-based scanners. The scanner waits till all the data is received for a file. Once all the data for the whole file is received the scanner scans the whole file for viruses and then forwards the file to its destination. **Advantages:** Great flexibility, easily extendable, more reliable scanning, low failure rate. **Drawbacks:** Delay in file transfer, slow performance as the scanner has to wait for the whole file. The delay can be too much if the file size is large, because the scanner will have to wait till the last packet of the file has arrived.

Stream scanning

This is also called "real time scanning" or cut-through scanning. The method receives, scans and forwards the data packets, which are not files but parts of files. The scanned data units or packets are immediately forwarded to their destinations after scanning. Stream scanning can be implemented either in hardware or in software. **Advantages:** Causes no delay in file transfer- all activities, receiving, scanning and forwarding of data, take place concurrently. **Drawbacks:** Stream scanning is less efficient for virus detection. It has access only to future packets, but no access to previous packets. So it will have no access to the whole file and therefore cannot get the advantage of file scanning.

INVENTION-97: Screening computer data while going through telephone network

Patent 5987610 (invented by Franczek, et al., assignee Ameritech Corporation, Nov 1999, patent 6397335 May 2002) proposes to virus screen the data on the telephone network so that the end users can download computer data without any fear of getting virus.

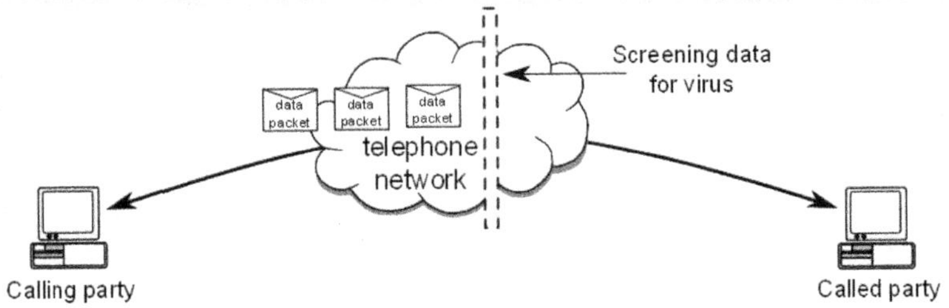

Virus scanning of data through telephone network

According to the invention, the telephone network, instead of simply passing the raw data, will screen the data for virus. If no virus is detected in the screening then the data is communicated to the second party. On the other hand, if a virus is detected then the telephone network performs necessary corrective actions. As the data is already screened for viruses prior to its delivery, it need not be screened for those viruses again at the user's computer (TRIZ Principle-10: Prior Action).

Data may be scanned while being downloaded from a server. If an infection is detected during download, then the anti-virus program should cure the virus or delete the partially downloaded file. This will prevent unnecessary downloading of infected files from the server which would later be deleted when detected to be infected.

INVENTION-98: Virus scanning while downloading data to a network client

Patent 6088803 (invented by Tso, et al., assignee Intel Corporation, July 2000) suggests to implement a virus checker in the network device. When the client requests for downloading a data the network device invokes the virus checker and scans the requested file as input (TRIZ Principle-15: Dynamize, Principle-9: Prior Counteraction).

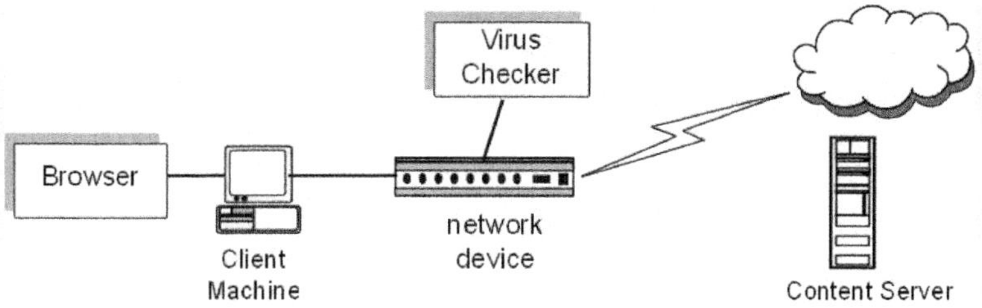

Implementing virus checker in network device

If the requested file does not contain a virus then the network device transmits the file to the client device, alternatively, if the file is detected to be infected then the network device interrupts transmission of data and transmits an appropriate message to the client device and/or the message server.

However, there is a problem in this method. While scanning the data packets at the time of downloading, the scanning may take slightly more time than downloading. But if the last part of an infected file is downloaded, then it may cause infection. Hence it is necessary to withhold the last part of the file to ensure that a virus-infected file does not reach the client device in its entirety.

Contradiction	*It is necessary to withhold the last part of the file in order to ensure that a virus-infected file does not reach the client in its entirety. But if the scanning operation takes too much time, then the operation may result in a time-out error. We need adequate time gap to finish virus scanning, but we don't want a time-out error.*

The invention solves this problem by feeding time gaps artificially between each individual segments. This method spreads a potentially large final delay over individual segments. In other words the delay required for scanning is spread over individual segments downloaded (TRIZ Principle-31: Hole, Principle-8: Counterweight, Principle-1: Segmentation).

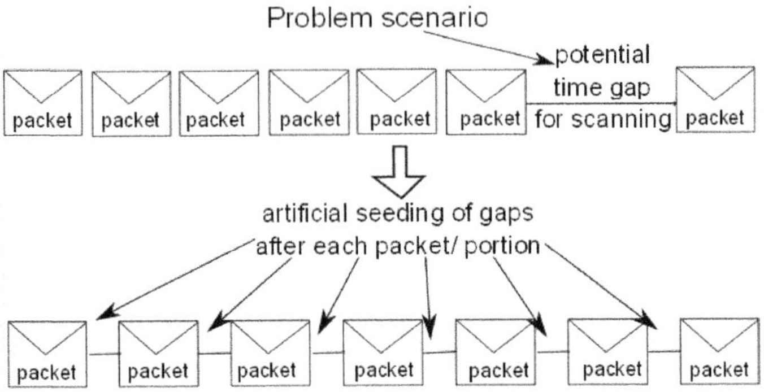

Solution by Patent 6088803

As the potential long gap is spread between individual packets, the gaps become smaller and avoid any timeout error.

Patent 7203960 (invented by Painter, assignee- Trend Micro, Inc, Apr 2007) proposes an anti-virus method which guarantees a maximum delay for scanning the streaming data. The method first scans a portion of streaming data and compares the scanning time against the maximum scan time. If the estimated scan time does not exceed the maximum scan time, then the incoming data stream is scanned for computer virus otherwise the data stream is transmitted without virus scan. The advantage of this method is that the scanning never exceeds beyond a maximum delay.

INVENTION-99: Passive scanning of network packets

Active scanning of network packets often slows down the delivery of packets. Patent 7461403 (invented by - Libenzi, et al., Assignee- McAfee, Inc., Dec. 2008) discloses a method passive screening which detects computer viruses and malware but without causing any interruption in the data packet stream.

According to the invention, all the incoming network packets are copied from the packet stream to an incoming message queue (TRIZ Principle-26: Copying). The network packets are reassembled and scanned by a network protocol specific scanner to identify computer viruses, malware and other bad content. As the incoming packets are processed passively (offline), there is no adverse effect on the network throughput.

- Patent 7716741 (invented by Forman, et al, assignee- IBM May 2010) provides a real time scanning by adding a virus scanning capability to a data transfer device. The invention stores a real-time virus checker on a controller. The virus checker scans data as it is being written to a file. If a virus is detected, the suspected file is flagged. Anti-virus software is then invoked to perform a scan of the entire suspected file. In this manner, demands on CPU resources to perform scans will be greatly reduced as only those files marked as possibly containing a virus need to be scanned, rather than scanning all the files on the entire data transfer device.

- Patent 8127356 (by Thiele, et al.) teaches to determine whether a packet is good or malicious by a series of programs. A first program checks whether the packet is a known exploit. A second program checks whether the packet is a harmless broadcast traffic. A third program checks whether the packet is a network administration traffic or other type of traffic that is harmless. If the packet does not belong to any of the above category then it is suspected as a new exploit candidate.

23.7 Advanced methods of detecting viruses in network

The conventional anti-virus programs use a "file scanning" approach which does not work properly in a network environment. Hence network scanners use various specialized methods to detect, locate and eliminate the source of the virus in a network.

- There are some malicious sites which can pass on malicious content when the user is just browsing the site. The malicious content may do harm to the computer or collect personal information about the user from the computer. One approach to solve this problem is to access the site by a virtual machine and analyze the content by using an analyzer tool. If accessing the links changes the state of the virtual machine then the site is declared to be harmful. **Limitations**: this method is difficult and time consuming. Besides websites are continuously changing.

- A network can get infected by newly added infected machines. One solution is to keep the new machines in a remediation VLAN till they are satisfactorily quarantined (described earlier).

INVENTION-100: Virus epidemic control by analyzing data flow and file modifications in a network

Patent 7062553 (invented by Liang, assignee Trend Micro, June 2006) teaches to analyze the traffic flow and file modifications to detect virus epidemics in a network environment. If any node is detected with an unpredicted traffic flow within a predetermined time interval, the method suspects the activity to be caused by a virus and initiates anti-virus tasks into the abnormal segment.

Similarly when two different files are detected to be modified identically within a predefined short period of time the method notifies the network server about the presence of a suspected malicious program in the network. On getting such notification the server transfers an anti-virus task to the suspicious area for taking prevention and damage control actions.

Patent 7089589 (invented by Chefalas et al., assignee Lenovo (Singapore) Pte. Ltd., Aug 2006) teaches to use a bait server to identify the offending clients in a network. The bait server's address is not published and no system should try to access it in normal situations. Hence, any attempt to access the bait server is considered suspicious.

INVENTION-101: Detecting virus infection by detecting randomness in destination addresses

Patent 7140041 (invented by Jeffries et al, assignee International Business Machines Corporation, Nov 2006) teaches to detect viruses by detecting the randomness in destination addresses.

The invention is based on certain assumptions on the characteristics of the malicious programs. For example, a malicious program typically has the characteristics like, a constant or nearly constant IP packet size, a constant or random IP source address and transfer will involve an unacknowledged datagram etc. The invented system analyzes the IP packets received by the gateway. If the destination addresses are detected to be too much random then the method suspects the presence of a worm or virus.

INVENTION-102: Identifying infected computers in a network by using smart switches

When a virus is detected in a network all measures are taken to clean the virus from the detected computers. But it is almost impossible to ensure that the virus has been eradicated for every computer in a large network. Patent 7418732 (invented by Campbell, et al., Assignee- Microsoft Corporation, Aug. 2008) teaches to identify the source of infection in a computer network by using "smart" switches and routers.

According to the invention the "smart" switches scan the network traffic packets for virus signatures. Due to the one-to-one connection of the switch to the physical computers, the source of a detected virus can be clearly identified.

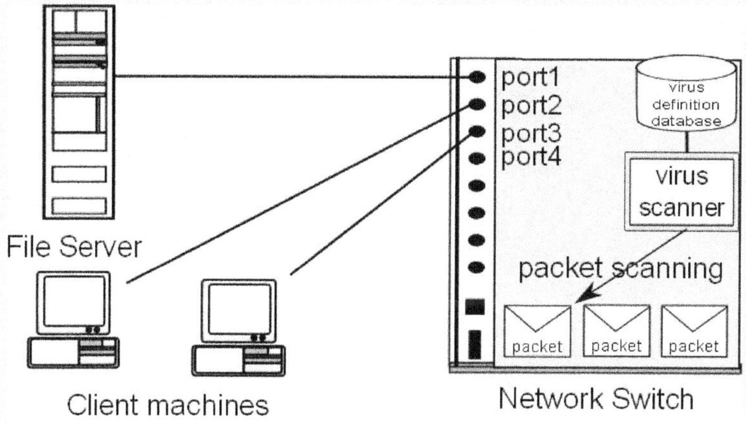

Scanning of data packets by Smart Switch

This type of scanning can be done either in an online or in an offline mode. In an online mode the packets are scanned for virus signatures before being forwarded to their destination ports. In an offline mode, a copy of the packets is saved into a packet queue for scanning.

Patent 7779474 (invented by Garbow, et al, assignee- Trend Micro Incorporated, Aug 2010) teaches to detect virus in a network by analyzing the changes in registry entries and/or file attributes. According to the invention the watch controller program in the client sends every change in the registry entry to a monitor in the network. If the number of changes in any client exceeds a threshold then the monitor suspects a virus infection in that client.

INVENTION-103: Using a pre-scanner card for inspecting network traffic

The network scanning may be either store-scan-forward scanning or stream scanning. Stream scanning gives a faster throughput but it can detect fewer viruses because it can do only forward scanning. Patent 7992206 (invented by Painter, et al., assignee- Trend Micro Incorporated, Aug, 2011) disclosed a two tier scanning by a front-end pre-scanner card and a back-end complex scanner.

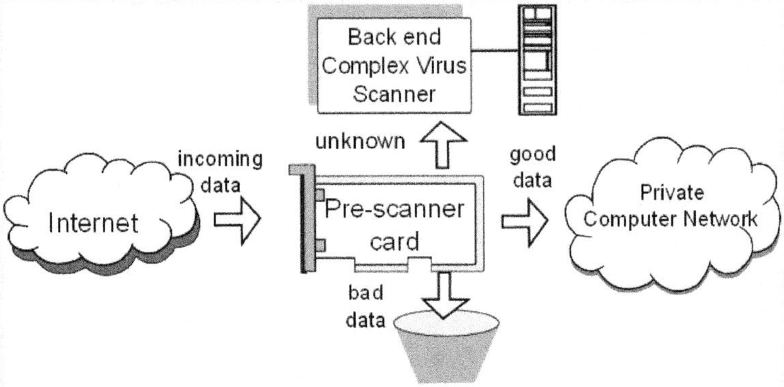

Scanning traffic using pre-scanner card

The invented add-on pre-scanner card is pluggable and removable into a local bus of a computer in a network. This pre-scanner card receives the network packets and scans them to determine whether they contain any virus. This works as a pre scan exercise to decide which of the payloads need further scanning and which of the packets don't need (TRIZ Principle-10: Prior Action). If the pre-scanner card fails to determine whether the packet is infected or not then the packets are passed to the computer for a detailed scanning by a file-based scan engine.

- Patent 8019689 suggests to use a reputation server to maintain reputation scores of individual hosts. These reputation scores indicate whether a host is trustworthy or not. The security module at the client obtains the reputation score of the target site from the reputation server and avoids the site the score is indicated as malicious.

- There are some stealth worms which send very minimal packets (such as a few packets per week) which are difficult to be diagnosed by using traffic anomaly methods. There are other stealth worms which adjust the transmission rate of their packets according to the actual network traffic thus maintaining a very low signal-to-noise ratio (SNR). Patent 8181249 (described earlier) teaches to detect stealth worms by sending bait packets from one or more bait addresses in order to conduct a "sting" operation. While the normal hosts will not react to the bait packets the compromised hosts will try to explore the bait address by sending probe packets (TRIZ Inventive Standards 4.2.3).

INVENTION-104: Detecting contaminated system through traffic pattern anomalies

Flow-based analysis is implemented into network routers for monitoring unusual traffic patterns. Deep-packet analysis is based on tracking back each single malicious IP packets. The prior art flow-based analysis is based on the worm behaviors. Patent 8020207 (invented by Chow et al., assignee- Alcatel Lucent, Sep 2011) discloses a new method of detecting the anomalies in the traffic pattern.

According to the invention the packets associated with different protocols are counted for each port distinctly for each direction. Such packets include ARP requests, TCP/SYN requests and acknowledgements, TCP/RST packets, DNS/NETBEUI name lookups, out-going ICMP packets, UDP packets etc. the method examines the header data of each protocol data unit (PDU) and identifies a type of attack based on the count values and the rules. When a packet causes an individual count or combination of counts to exceed a threshold, appropriate action is taken.

INVENTION-105: getting malware pattern by comparing the inventory of a client machine with the merged inventory

Patent 8091127 (invented by Bradicich et al, assignee- International Business Machines Corporation, Jan 2012) provides a new heuristic method of malware detection by comparing the file attributes of a client computer with an inventory of file attributes.

The invention first collects a baseline inventory of file signatures from each client computer system and creates a merged inventory in the central server. The file attributes may include file size, file date, file path and file path etc.

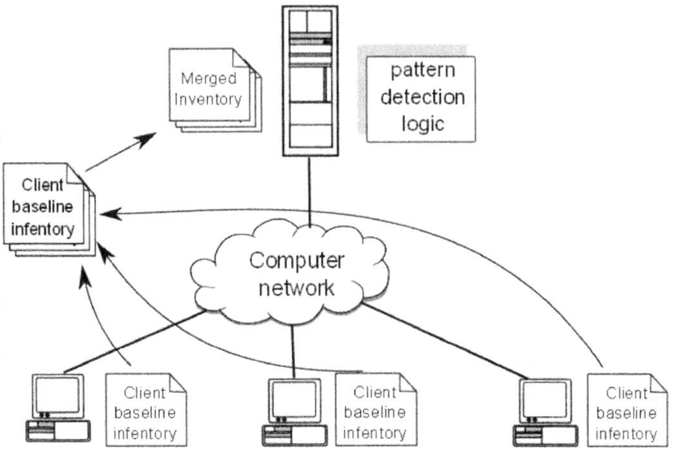

Heuristic Malware Detection by
Comparing Client Inventory with Merged Inventory

Then changes in each updated client inventory is compared to the merged inventory and in response to the comparison; a deviant pattern of file attribute changes can be detected in the current inventory survey. Thereafter, the deviant pattern can be classified as either benign event or a malware attack. Once a deviant pattern has been classified as malware attack, malware removal logic is invoked in the offending client computing system.

🛠 Patent 8151073 (invented by Chouery., assignee- FAC Systems Inc., Apr, 2012) suggests an innovative method of detecting viruses by analyzing hard disk LED activities. According to the invention, the system storage has an external alarm configured to monitor the drive activity of the LED of the storage device. The monitor compares the actual load time for the file to the expected load time. If a virus spends an unexpected amount of time attempting to access a storage medium the alarm is triggered. (TRIZ Inventive Standard 4.2.1. measuring another parameter that is linked to the action (or Field) that is required to be measured.)

23.8 Protecting File servers and Internet Servers

The viruses not only infect stand-alone machines, they also infect servers. Even if all individual workstations are protected, that will not ensure that the servers are also protected automatically. It is also necessary to install anti-virus on file servers, email servers, web servers and other servers too.

Although most of the scanning tactics are same for a client machine and a server, it is more important to control the overhead of the anti-virus on a server. As a server may have hundreds of users and large number of files, the overhead of a virus scanner can be significantly high.

23.8.1 Improvements on Scanning a File Server

A file server stores a large number of files and accessed by a large number of concurrent users. When a file in the file server is infected with a computer virus, many users are adversely affected. The conventional virus scanners are designed for workstations and not optimized for file servers. There is a need to optimize the performance of virus scanners to operate on file servers.

INVENTION-106: Optimizing virus scanning for a network file server

Patent 7155461 (invented by Miyata, et al., assignee- Hitachi Ltd. (Japan), Dec 2006) suggests a method for optimizing server scanning. According to the invention, the file server and scan server work cooperatively. When a file is scanned and found not infected with a virus then the file server system updates the last scan time and the last updater (the user who last scanned the file) in the file configuration information. If the last scan time is earlier than the last update time of the virus pattern then the file server asks the scan server to scan the file for virus. But scan is omitted for a file if the last scan time is after the last update time of the virus pattern. (TRIZ Principle-21: Skipping). As the file server opens the file without virus scanning, the method accelerates file access.

INVENTION-107: Scanning multiple versions of a file in a shared file system environment

A quick scan generally scans the home directory of each user and various shared directories accessed by different users. But the per-user versions of the shared files in a virtualized file system environment are generally not scanned in a quick scan session.

Patent 8065730 (invented by Sobel et al, assignee- Symantec Corporation, Nov 2011) suggests to scan the virtualized files in a quick scan in order to ensure proper security. A file retrieval module first determines if a file is virtualized and the malware detection module then determines whether the virtualized version of the file contains any malware.

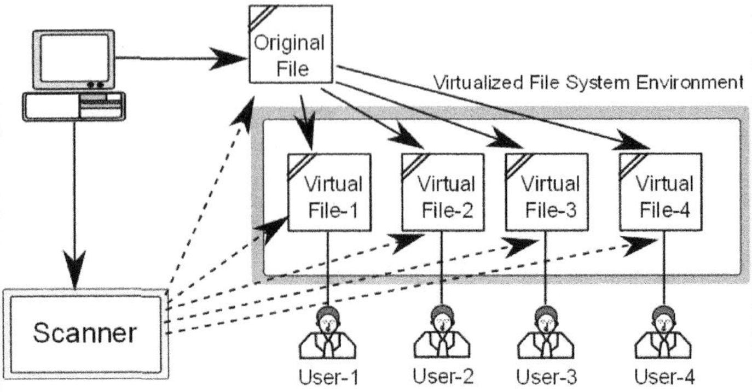

The scanner scans the original file and all virtualized copies
US Patent 8065730

This method ensures better security as it not only scans the original file but also scans temporary or virtualized copies of the file created for different users.

INVENTION-108: Method of scanning files in a Network Attached Storage (NAS) server

When a NAS (network attached storage) server receives file operation requests from client computers, the scan server, connected to the NAS server, execute a virus scan on the requested files. This method has the following problem.

If the file is too large then scanning may take long time causing a time-out error. If the time-out is avoided by skipping part of the file from scanning then that may skip a virus which may infect the NAS server (Contradiction).

Patent 8166548 (invented by Saika, assignee- Hitachi, Ltd., Apr 2012) provides a method of scanning large files without causing any timeout. According to the invention, when the first computer writes data to NAS it sends a request to the scan server to scan the written data. The scan server partially executes a virus scan on the written data. Thereafter the first computer writes the rest of the data to the NAS and the scan server is configured to execute the remainder of the virus scan. This method increases the response speed and thereby prevents a possible timeout caused by executing a virus scanning.

23.8.2 Preventing infections in web-servers and Internet

Servers

When a web server is infected with virus, all the clients connecting to that web server are exposed to infection. For example, all the client machines downloading infected content from that server are liable to get infected. Server infections need to be tackled immediately otherwise they can spread viruses very fast to many clients and cause viral outbreaks.

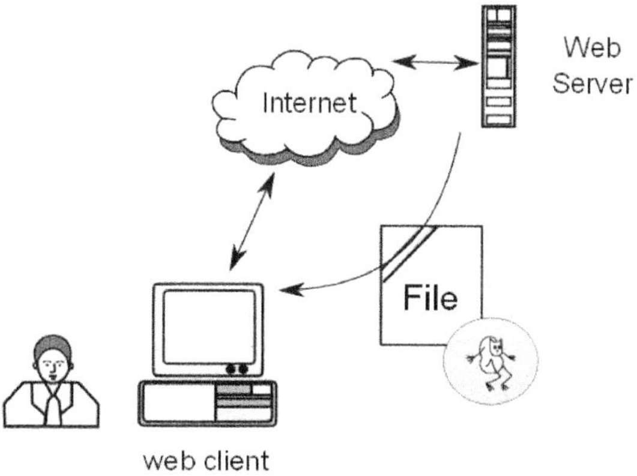

Infected files downloaded from web servers

Any Internet based server whether a mail server or database server or ftp server or web server or LDAP server or other type of server, is highly exposed to malware attacks. This is because all of them use static IP addresses and their location, identification, function etc. are all exposed to the public. The attackers get enough time to apply different methods and take repeated attempts to break through the security system.

Problems involved in scanning web servers

- The prior art anti-virus programs run on a single computer system. The anti-virus installed on a client system cannot check or determine whether the content of the server is virus free or not. The anti-virus has to be installed on the server machine too.
- The conventional anti-viruses scan the computer at file level; they don't scan the streaming data that are downloaded from Internet, such as, streaming shockwave files to display video on the client's machine.
- The file based virus scanners cannot deal with the network traffic directly. Hence, they have to wait for the file to be fully downloaded and saved in the disk in order to initiate a virus scan.

But this situation has two drawbacks, (1) the infected file is downloaded unnecessarily thus increasing the network traffic, (2) the infected file may cause damage to the computer if not detected and deleted immediately after the download.

- Every site manage is not necessarily good. Some site managers may knowingly leave infected files on the web server.
- Scanning server computers may involve huge amount of system resources.

Ideal solutions

IFR Ideally the content of web-servers should be free from viruses so that the clients downloading content from the web servers would not be infected.

IFR Ideally the client should be able to know which file of the web server is infected and avoid downloading that file.

Preventing infections from and to Internet Servers

As the Internet based servers are connected to numerous clients it is highly desirable to install a virus checker on individual servers in order to reduce possible infections to the servers and the clients connected.

- ✓ One solution is to implement a virus scanner on the gateway which is the entry / exit point to the external network. **Limitations**- the gateway-based scanners don't provide adequate protection.
- ✓ A certificate server may certify the content of the web servers. This will help users to know which content in the server is reliable and which content is not. **Limitations**- Implementing certificates and encryption involves lot of additional configurations and expenses.
- ✓ Enabling distributed virus scanning may improve the efficiency of scanning in a distributed network.
- ✓ The search engines may scan the contents of different websites and display the reliability of the contents in the search results (Patent 6721721 below).

INVENTION-109: Integrating virus-checking functionality into search engines

Many users search the web through search engines like "google" and click on the search results to access the desired web page. As the web page is searched by a reliable search engine, the user generally feels confident about the content. But practically the content can be infected by malicious codes, as the content is not provided by the search engine but by different individual servers.

Patent 6721721 (invented by Bates et al., assignee International Business Machines Corporation, April 2004) proposes a method of integrating virus-checking functionality into a database search environment.

According to the invention the search results of the search engine would display virus-status information against the records in the result set. For example, the virus free contents may be marked as "√" and infected contents may be marked as "X" and contents not scanned may be marked as "?". This way the user is informed about the reliability of the web pages while she is viewing the search results.

Patent 6789201 (invented by Barton et al., assignee Networks Associates Technology, Aug 2004) presents a toolbar plug-in for the browser which is capable of providing virus-related services, such as, virus-related information, virus-related news, searching for viruses in virus database, virus related statistics and other such services. Although the concept of yahoo toolbar was there in the prior art, there was no concept of a virus toolbar.

INVENTION-110: Implementing anti-virus in a web server to check emails and site content

Patent 6785732 (invented by Bates et al., assignee International Business Machines Corporation, Aug 2004 and Patent 7177937 Feb 2007) presents a method of implementing anti-virus in a web server that checks emails, downloadable files and website content for possible viruses.

According to the invention, when a client requests to download emails, attachments and other downloads, the content is scanned at the server. If the downloaded file contains a virus the file is deleted and an error message is sent to the web client informing that the file was deleted because of virus. Similarly, when a requested link or URL is known to contain a virus, a message is sent to the web client stating that the URL contains a virus. When the client requests for a new link or URL the web page is processed before being sent to the user.

Besides, the client may request the web server to perform virus checking on a particular drive on the web client. Upon receiving such request the web server may download a client virus checker to the web client that scans the client drive for viruses and informs the client about the results.

We discussed about certifying data and emails as virus free (Patent 7107618 and Patent 7533272) in last chapter. The same method can also be used to certify the content of websites. The content available for download on a host site is scanned and a certificate is displayed identifying the content to be virus free.

INVENTION-111: Implementing bottom-up analysis to detect malicious content of a website

Some sites can pass on malicious content to the user computer while the user is just browsing the site. These malicious contents can do harm to the client computer or steal valuable data from the client computer. Patent 8161130 (invented by Stokes et al, assignee-Microsoft Corporation, Apr 2012) suggests a bottom up approach to detect the malicious content of a website.

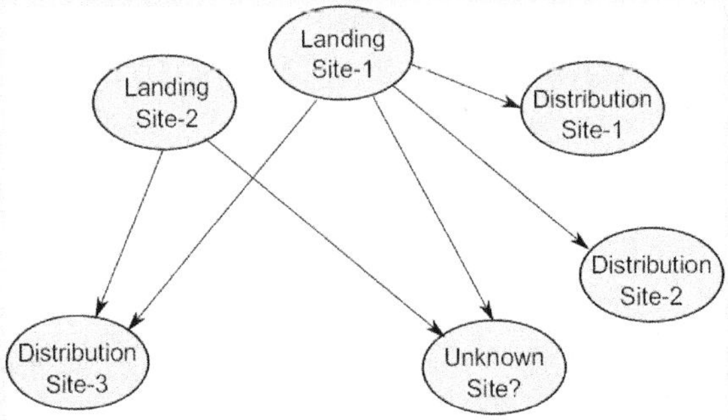

Bottom up approach to identify malicious sites

The invented method analyses the content of a site to determine whether the site hosts malicious content or benign content. Then the analysis module identifies the landing sites linked to the distribution sites. These linked sites are identified as suspect sites for further analysis. This approach is called as "bottom up" approach because it is initiated by the detection of potentially problematic distribution sites. The approach can also perform linking analysis to identify a suspect network site based on a number of alternating paths between that network site and a set of distribution sites that are known to host malicious content. The approach can also train a classifier module to predict whether an unknown landing site is a malicious landing site or a benign landing site.

- Some security venders maintain a whitelist of known trustworthy websites to allow access. Similarly some venders use blacklists of known untrustworthy websites to prevent access. This method reduces infection from untrustworthy servers. **Limitations**: The trustworthiness of servers maintained in whitelists and blacklists gets outdated soon as the new sites emerge on every day. **Solution**: Some security software vendors, instead of following blacklists, use various heuristics to identify untrustworthy sites.

- Patent 8019689 (invented by Nachenberg) suggests to use a reputation server which calculates the reputation score of different websites. The security module on the client computer obtains the reputation score from the reputation server and decides whether to connect to the server or not.

23.9 Protecting computers from Viruses in a Peer to Peer Network

In a peer-to-peer (P2P) networking environment the participant computers directly communicate with each other without the help of an intermediate server. There are also P2P clients who transfer data/ files directly through Internet. This method of transferring files facilitates transfer of viruses along with the files. It is necessary to protect computers in a P2P network.

INVENTION-112: Protecting computers in a P2P network by deploying a protect server

Patent 8056133 (invented by Yao, et al., assignee- Trend Micro Incorporated, Nov, 2011) discloses protecting computers in a P2P network by implementing P2P protect servers and P2P protect client applications.

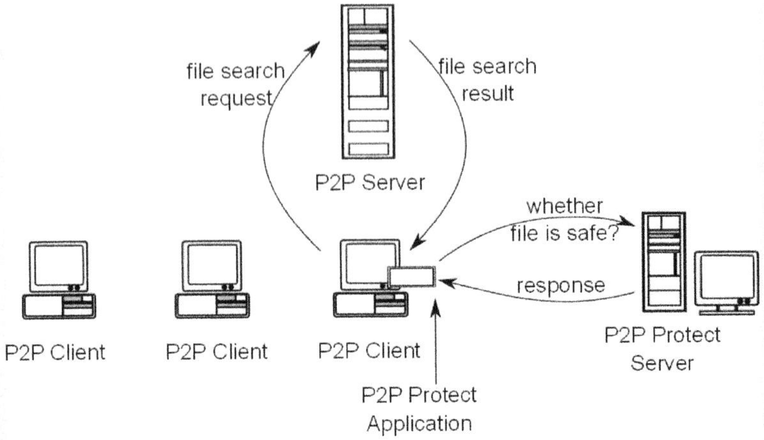

Protecting clients in a P2P network using P2P Protect Server

According to the invention, a P2P protect server (which is different from P2P server) will include a crawler to locate P2P client computers and obtain files available for P2P data transfer. Then the P2P protect server will employ a scan engine to scan those files for computer viruses and store the results of the scanning in a database. P2P protect applications will run on the client machines which will request P2P protect servers for information about virus infection on specific files. This way the P2P client computer can know the infection status of a file and take a decision whether to download the file or not.

INVENTION-113: Method of automatic inoculation in a Peer-to-Peer network

Generally an infected system is unaware that it has infected files until it receives an updated virus signature that detects the undetected virus. Patent 8091134 (invented by Benton, et al., assignee- Lenovo (Singapore) Pte. Ltd., Jan, 2012) discloses a method of automatic virus detection and inoculations by peer computers in a peer to peer network.

According to the invention the computers may be connected peer to peer in a network environment. When the infected computer system sends an infected file to the detecting computer system. The detecting computer system detects the virus in the infected file, retrieves virus information corresponding to the virus (such as the name of the infected file, the identifier, or name, of the virus, the virus definitions used to identify the virus, and any instructions needed to eradicate the virus), and automatically sends the virus information back to the infected computer system over the network (TRIZ Principle-23: Feedback).

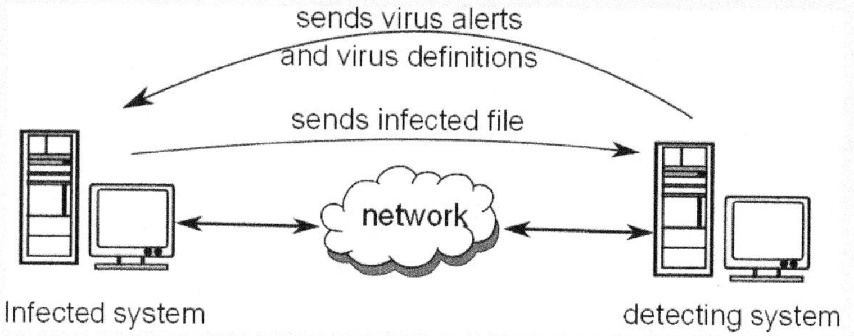

The invention has the benefit that even if the infected computer does not have updated anti-virus it can update its anti-virus definitions from the peer computers automatically upon detection of such a virus.

23.10 Preventing virus outbreaks

A virus outbreak is extremely dangerous as it infects a large number of computers in a network or in multiple networks. This requires disinfecting each and every machine in the network. After each machine has been checked and disinfected. If any infected machine is left out then it would infect the network again.

Generally anti-virus programs search for viruses and disinfect computer files that have been infected. But they are not quite efficient to handle virus outbreaks. As an outbreak is considered to be more than just infection of individual files, mere detection of individual viruses are not enough. It is necessary to take appropriate measures to detect and prevent virus outbreaks in the network.

There are proposals for a nation-wide internet worm control system. If the geographical location of a worm can be detected at an initial state, then various steps may be taken to prevent the worm from spreading to other geographical locations.

INVENTION-114: Countermeasures for dealing with virus outbreak

Patent 6898715 (invented by Smithson, et al., assignee Networks Associates Technology, May 2005) suggests a robust method of dealing with virus outbreaks. According to the invention, when a virus outbreak is detected, a predefined sequence of counter-measures is automatically (or manually) followed to invoke anti-virus counter measures.

Examples of predefined actions to be followed upon detection of a virus outbreak:

... downloading latest virus definitions
... performing a complete virus scan
... blocking email attachments
...
... shutting down email server.

The counter-measures can include reducing virus notification, increasing scanning options, blocking E-mail attachments, hiding E-mail address books and the like. This method automatically provides an appropriate response to the virus outbreak even if there are no IT support personnel present in the environment (TRIZ Principle-25: Self Service, Principle-9: Prior Counteraction).

INVENTION-115: Method of hindering the propagation of worm-like viruses in a network

Patent 7278019 (invented by Norman, Assignee- Hewlett-Packard Development Company, L.P. Oct. 2007) discloses a method hindering the propagation of worm-like viruses in a network.

The invention puts a detection computer (or reactor computer) in a network. The detection computer monitors activities of other computers and detects the presence of an infected computer that attempts to contact an unused network address. When an infected computer is detected, the detection computer sends the remediating means to the identified computer system to hinder the operation of the computer virus.

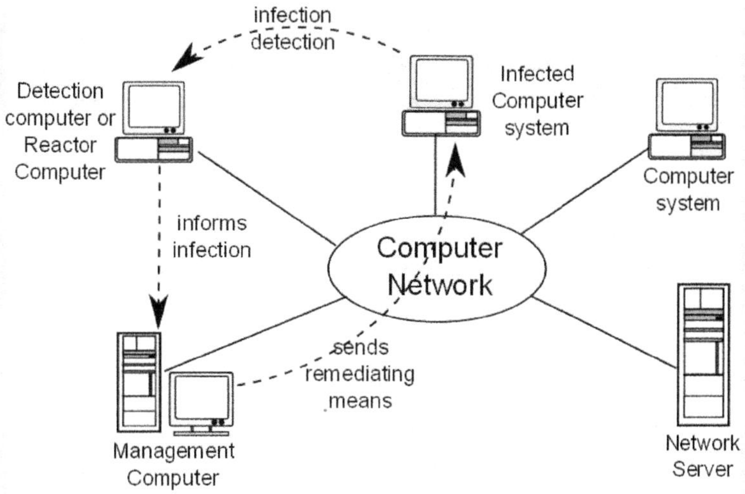

Alternatively, the network may further comprise of a management computer, which upon receiving command signals from detection computer, sends the remediating means to the identified computer. The remediation operations may include a virus killer or a virus remediating program or virus mitigating programs to hinder the operation of the computer virus.

- US Patent 7293177 (Inventor- Lahti, et al., Assignee- F-Secure OYJ, Nov 2007) provides a simple solution of "locking" the infected files. The method first scans the files using an anti-virus application. If the file is not infected, then it is closed. On the other hand if the file is infected then the file is left as open and non-sharing, so that other applications running on the computer cannot operate on the infected file (TRIZ Principle-35: Parameter Change).

- Some viruses which pose only a minor threat to one system may pose a substantial threat to another system. Therefore it is necessary to assess the risk of a virus properly. Patent 7409720 (invented by Cambridge, et al., Assignee McAfee, Inc., Aug. 2008) discloses a method of assessing the risk level depending on the past infections caused by the virus. If a new virus is similar to the viruses that have previously caused significant infections within the system, then the method warns the system or organization about the possible higher risk level associated with that new virus.

- Another solution to solve network virus proliferation is through Network Admission Control (NAC), marketed by Cisco Systems Inc. **Limitations**: NAC agents can defend against only those threats which are pre-defined in their signature files.

- Patent 7571483 (invented by Bascle, et al, assignee- Lockheed Martin Corporation, Aug 2009) suggests a method of detecting the network device that is the source of virus activity. Once the infected device is detected the device is automatically disabled and thereby isolated from the network. If any user is associated with the detected device then the user is also disabled and prevented from accessing the network (TRIZ Principle-2: Taking out). Isolating the infected device and/or the associated users prevents further infection and reduces vulnerability of a network.

INVENTION-116: Detecting virus related epidemics based on connection strength coefficient

The conventional methods like signature scanning etc. cannot predict virus epidemics spreading through emails. There is a need to detect epidemics during infancy and control its propagation. Patent 7743419 (invented by Mashevsky et al., assignee- Kaspersky Lab, ZAO, Jun 2010) discloses a method of automatically detecting epidemics based on known activity level of malware programs in the world.

According to the invention, the source of an epidemic is calculated and analyzed based on statistical data in real time. The statistics is collected for a time frame and for a geographical area. The prediction is made based on a calculated value of "connection strength" coefficient. The connection strength reflects a volume of information exchange (i.e., number and quality of connection channels) between different geographical locations like countries. The main goal is to detect an epidemic in its infancy and monitor its spread across different countries in real time. If the epidemic is caused by a network worm then notifications can be issued to all the users informing them about the protection against the worm.

INVENTION-117: Controlling virus outbreaks by suspending email delivery

Patent 7748038 (invented by Olivier, et al, assignee- IronPort Systems, Jun 2010) provides a method of detecting and managing computer outbreaks by analyzing messages having virus like characteristics. The virus outbreak information is determined by one or more second messages that have the same or similar characteristics associated with the viruses as the first message. When a series of virus like messages are detected, a virus outbreak is declared. In such a case the messaging gateway can suspend delivery of messages. This method provides sufficient time to update an anti-virus program that can control the virus.

23.11 Enhancing Network Security Measures

We discussed about various methods of implementing anti-virus software in a LAN. One is to install the anti-virus directly into the firewall, another is to install on individual computers, another is by a central scanning server etc. Each one has its advantages and disadvantages. However it is necessary to ensure complete network security.

INVENTION-118: Using a probe to ensure network security

Patent 6205551 (invented by Grosse, assignee Lucent Technologies, March 2001) discloses a method of determining the clients that are not configured in accordance with the desired network security features of the computer network.

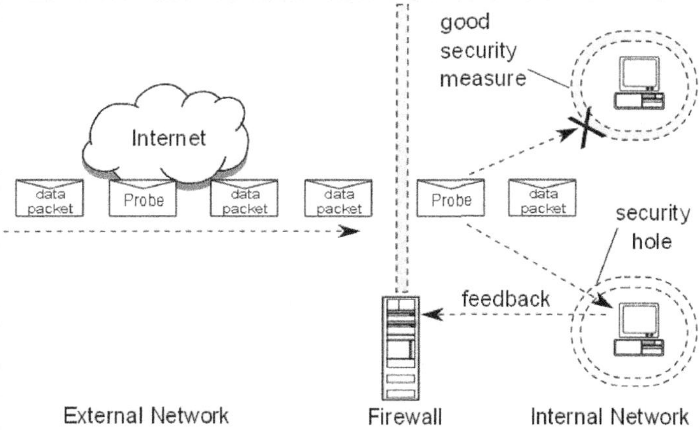

Inserting probes to detect security holes

The method inserts a probe (typically configured as a virus in the form of a Trojan horse) within the incoming files in the computer network. If the client is properly configured then the probe (Trojan horse) will not execute. However if the client is misconfigured (i.e., not in compliance with the network security measures) then the probe (Trojan horse) will execute a security alert indicating that the client is vulnerable to a security breach.

This method reduces the workload of a network administrator. The network administrator need not go from computer to computer to identify which machine is not in compliance with the standard security measures. The probe executes an alarm in the firewall indicating the clients that are vulnerable. This helps the network administrator taking appropriate action to correct those clients which are misconfigured (or not in compliance with the desired security measure of the private network).

INVENTION-119: Integrating anti-virus policy into the firewall

Patent 7010807 (invented by Yanovsky, assignee SonicWALL, March 2006) discloses a method of protecting computers in a local area network by implementing a anti-virus policy programmed into the firewall (TRIZ Principle-7: Nested Doll).

According to the invention, the LAN's anti-virus policy (such as, which version of which anti-virus is permitted etc.) is programmed into the firewall or other Internet access module (IAM). This policy is applied to all the client computers in the LAN. Any client computer not meeting the anti-virus policy is not permitted to access the Internet.

INVENTION-120: Preventing virus attacks by restricting unsafe clients to access wireless LAN

Generally a network's access point allows a wireless client computer to access the network regardless of whether the wireless client computer has adequate anti-virus protection. Patent 7424745 (invented by Cheston, et al., Assignee- Lenovo (Singapore) Pte. Ltd., Sep. 2008) discloses a method of preventing virus attacks by restricting clients to access a wireless LAN unless the client has installed specified anti-virus programs.

According to the invention, the access point of a wireless network maintains a list of pre-requisite anti-viral programs that must run on the wireless clients. When a wireless client sends a request to access the network, the access point verifies whether the wireless client has all the necessary anti-virus programs installed. If the client computer has all the requisite anti-virus programs then the access point allows it to access the network otherwise sends an anti-virus request to a pre-authorized anti-virus program server to install necessary software and fixes on the wireless client. After the anti-virus fix is installed on the client computer, the access point removes the restriction and allows the client computer to access the wireless network. (TRIZ Principle-2: Taking out, Principle-25: Self Service, Principle-9: Prior Counteraction).

INVENTION-121: Rejecting client requests at proxy unless the client's anti-virus is updated

Patent 7383579 (invented by Catanzano, Assignee- AT&T Delaware Intellectual Property, Inc., Jun. 2008) discloses a method of determining a computer's anti-virus protection status.

According to the invention, when a client sends a request to the server, the version of the client's anti-virus software is included in the request (either as a code, or a text string or a date string or some other code).

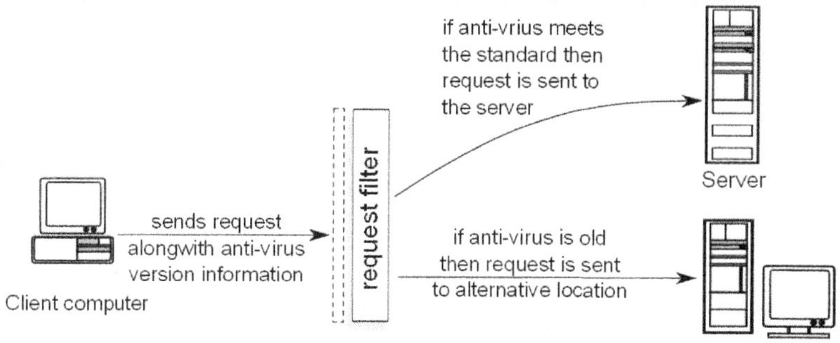

Redirecting client requests
if anti-vrius version does not meet the standard

A request filter (which is implemented either in the computer or in the router or in the proxy server or firewall) examines the version of the anti-virus protection software present on the user's computer. If the version of the anti-virus software is sufficient then it allows access. If the version of the anti-virus software on client machine is not sufficient, then it redirects the request to an alternate destination. This method provides anti-virus compliance of individual users without the need for a system administrator.

🛠 A similar solution is also prescribed in Patent 7591001 (invented by David Shay, assignee- Liquidware Labs, Inc., Sep 2009) that advises to ensure the security status of another computer before establishing a network connection to it. The method requests and receives the second computer's security status before establishing a network connection to it. This exchange of information should take place as one of the first few packets exchanged during the network connection. The security status may include the anti-virus status and updates, firewall status, installation of operating system patches etc. This enables a computer to determine whether the other computer's security status is compliant with its security policy before establishing the network connection, thus reducing the risk of infection by a virus, worm, or the like.

INVENTION-122: Segregation of traffic for security purposes

It is necessary to provide an effective detection and enforcement policy for network viruses, worms, spyware, bots and other malware. Patent 7698548 (invented by Shelest et al., assignee- Microsoft Corporation. Apr 2010) suggests to segregate network traffic into two or more separate categories defined by security values for ease of monitoring and enforcing policies.

For example the communication traffic may be segregated by the characterization that whether the traffic is associated with user interaction or not. (Another method of segregation may be according to identifiers of the data packets.) The traffic security policy may include a detection policy or an enforcement policy or both. The detection policy may include determining whether the segregated communications traffic flow involves malware. The enforcement policy may include a malware policy.

INVENTION-123: Limiting outgoing connection attempts to slow down spreading of computer viruses.

Worms can spread themselves from one computer to other by sending copies of themselves through emails and other means. Patent 7784096 (invented by Kaniyar et al., assignee- Microsoft Corporation, Aug 2010) suggests limiting the number of outgoing TCP connection attempts to arbitrary IP addresses in order to slow down spreading of viruses. This is useful to any computer at any given time regardless of whether an anti-virus software is installed on the system or not.

Chapter 24.

Detecting Encrypted, Polymorphic and Metamorphic Viruses

24.1 Rise of Virus Creation Techniques

As the anti-virus programs adopted various advanced scanning techniques, the conventional viruses found no place of survival. The virus creators focused on how to provide protection to their viruses, make their creation survive under adverse situations and escape from different scanning techniques. They implemented various anti-anti-virus techniques to make their viruses more resistant to anti-virus programs.

Some of the most important virus obfuscation techniques implemented are Encryption, Polymorphism and Metamorphism. But creating such hi-tech viruses are extremely difficult. To simplify virus creation process, some virus writers developed virus construction kits and made them readily available on the Internet. Some of the virus construction kits are NGVCK (Next Generation Virus Construction Kit), VCL32 (Virus Creation Lab), VBS Worm Generator etc.

24.2 The Encrypted Viruses

Encryption is an obfuscation technique that hides the actual code of a virus. The encrypted virus includes an encrypted viral body and a decryption routine (or "decryption loop"). When a file infected with an encrypted virus executes, the decryption routine first takes over the control and decrypts the encrypted viral body. Then the decryption routine transfers control to the decrypted viral body which does its intended mischief. While infecting other files, it also copies the decryption routine along with the encrypted viral body to the target file.

Feature analysis

- The encrypted virus must contain a decryption routine to decrypt the virus body before execution.
- As the viral body is encrypted that cannot be easily changed to create new variants of the virus.
- The virus creator having the source code or virus-creating engine can create many viruses with minor alterations. No similarity between the family members will be visible because of encryption.

Strengths

- As the viral body is encrypted, it is not commonly visible to simple scanning. Decrypting the viral body is neither easy nor safe.
- Although some methods try to decrypt the encrypted code of the viruses it can take substantially long time.

Weaknesses

- Although the viral body is encrypted and thus remains hidden from view, the decryption routine is common in each infection of the virus. The anti-virus software can detect these viruses by searching the signature of this unchanging decryption routine.

24.3 Methods of detecting Encrypted Viruses

As we saw above the encrypted viruses can be detected by scanning the signatures of their unchanging decryptor. Although this is an easy method of detecting simple encrypted viruses it does not give any idea about infection pattern to cure the infected file. Hence it is often necessary to decrypt the viral body in order to know the infection process.

Possible solution

- One solution to solve this problem is emulation. The emulator allows the virus to execute freely within the virtual computer. When the virus executes within the virtual computer its decryption routine decrypts its viral body and makes visible to the anti-virus software.
- However, there are new types of viruses (e.g. Win32/Magistr.B.Worm) which do not store the encryption key in the virus body, rather calculates the key using the machine name.

Solution- But the anti-virus can still know the encryption code as it is constant for that machine. But what if the virus is encrypted in one machine and transferred to another machine?

INVENTION-124: Detecting encrypted viruses using probabilistic encryption key guessing

When an encryption key is derived from a previous machine and the file is transferred to a different machine, the case looks impossible to solve because the anti-virus is presented with unknown data encrypted by an unknown key. For example, the file is infected in the server and transferred to the clients. The same problem also happens when a user changes his machine name. In such cases the anti-virus has no way to know the original computer name or retrieve the decryption key. Patent 7260725 (invented by Carmona, et al., Assignee- Computer Associates Think, Inc., Aug 2007) discloses a method of discovering the encryption key using a method called probabilistic encryption key guessing.

The invented method analyzes the encrypted data to determine the most frequently occurring encrypted byte in the encrypted data. Then it calculates an encryption key based on the most frequently occurring encrypted byte and a corresponding expected original byte of the original data (Inventive Standard- 4.2.4. measure something that is already there in the environment). For example, a 32 bit executable code for Intel processors contains a lot of 0's and 255's. So whatever data is most frequently occurring in the encrypted data is probably the encrypted form of the original value zero.

This method helps the anti-virus to reverse calculate the key from the encrypted data. After getting the encryption key the encrypted data is decrypted to restore the original data (TRIZ Principle-13: Reversing).

24.4 Polymorphic Viruses and Encrypted Polymrphic Viruses

A polymorphic virus uses a polymorphic engine to change its code every time it runs without changing the original algorithm. Thus the viral body of the polymorphic virus is different in each infection although they do the same functionality.

As the polymorphic viruses don't have any specific type of signature, the conventional pattern matching method of signature scanning fails to detect such viruses. Emulation is the best method to reveal the polymorphic obfuscation. Most polymorphic viruses use an encryption routine to help the virus hide from detection. These are called as encrypted polymorphic viruses.

Encrypted polymorphic viruses

As the decryption routines of encrypted viruses are detectable by the signature scanning, the virus writers implemented mutation engines to create different decryptors in each different infection. Encrypted polymorphic viruses, as the name suggests, bear the characteristics of both encrypted viruses and polymorphic viruses (A good example of TRIZ Principle-5: Merging). The code within the virus includes an encryption routine to help the virus hide from detection and a decryption routine to decrypt it before its execution.

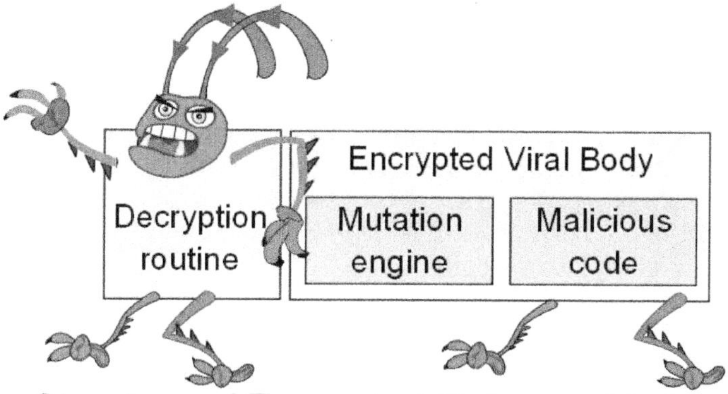

Structure of Encrypted Polymorphic Virus

Such type of polymorphic viruses are often difficult to detect. They not only have different signatures in each infection but also generate different decryption routines in each infection. As there is nothing constant in the polymorphic encrypted viruses, they have no signatures and therefore not detectable by signature scanning.

During execution of encrypted polymorphic virus the control first goes to the decryptor. The decryptor decrypts the viral body and passes the control to the decrypted viral body. The viral body then creates a new decryptor and encrypts itself to create a new virus which looks totally different from its predecessor.

Feature analysis

- The viral body of a polymorphic encrypted virus is encrypted and hence not visible to outside.
- The virus comprises a decryption routine and an encrypted viral body. The encrypted viral body includes a static viral body and a "mutation engine".
- Polymorphic viruses use mutation techniques to change their decryptors in every infection. As the decryptor is changed and the viral body is encrypted with different encryption keys an encrypted polymorphic virus has no part that remains constant on each infection.
- In most polymorphic viruses, the virus does not mutate. Rather the mutation engine generates a virus decryption routine and uses this routine to encrypt the static virus body and the mutation engine.
- The polymorphic virus uses a decryptor at the top of an execution flow. The virus first decrypts the encrypted viral code and hands over the control to the main viral code.
- The encrypted polymorphic viruses must decrypt their viral body before they can execute.
- They are detected by code emulation when they decrypt their viral body in a virtual computer.
- As no part of two polymorphic viruses are common, they don't have specific signatures. They are not detectable by conventional signature scanning or pattern matching.
- Although behavior monitoring can detect viral behavior it can detect so only after its execution by which time it would have caused the infection.

Problem of detecting Polymorphic Viruses

As the polymorphic viruses don't have any static strings, they cannot be detected by conventional signature scanning. But there is a way of detecting them. As they have to decrypt their body before execution it is possible to scan their body when they execute. But allowing the virus to execute is a risky situation and can easily infect the computer. This situation creates a contradiction.

Contradiction	*The anti-virus can read the decrypted viral body during runtime when the decryptor decrypts the viral body. But if we run the infected program then we may well damage our computer system. We want to run the infected program to see its decrypted viral body, but we don't want to run the program as that will infect and damage the computer system.*

Analysis

Improving Parameter: Reliability of scanning

Worsening Parameter: Security (Risk of getting infected)

Ideal Final Result

IFR Ideally we should be able to see the decrypted code of the virus body without running the virus-infected file.

IFR Alternatively we should be able to run the infected file without causing any damage to the computer.

Solution

The first IFR is unfortunately not possible with the current technology. The second IFR is possible through code emulation. The encrypted polymorphic virus can only be detected in a sandbox or emulator. When the virus decrypts its body in the virtual memory the anti-virus has to capture the viral code from the memory of the virtual machine and scan for viral signatures.

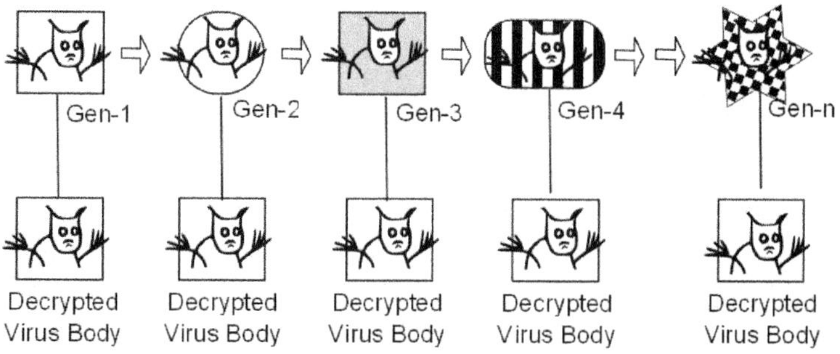

The decrypted Virus Body is the Same for Different Generations of Polymorphic Viruses

Although the encrypted viral body varies in each infection, when unencrypted, they provide the same constant viral body in memory. Hence the anti-virus can detect the virus infection by scanning the decrypted viral code in the virtual memory of the code emulator.

24.5 Metamorphic viruses

As the polymorphic viruses could be detected at the time when decrypted, the virus creators tried to further complicate the process of concealment. They tried to change everything of a virus in each infection which gave rise to metamorphic viruses.

A metamorphic virus may or may not have an encryptor. The complete body of a metamorphic virus is changed in every infection even without using any encryption that makes it completely undetectable by any kind of signature scanning. Emulation does not help detection as it does not leave any identifiable code block in the memory that can be detected by a signature scanning.

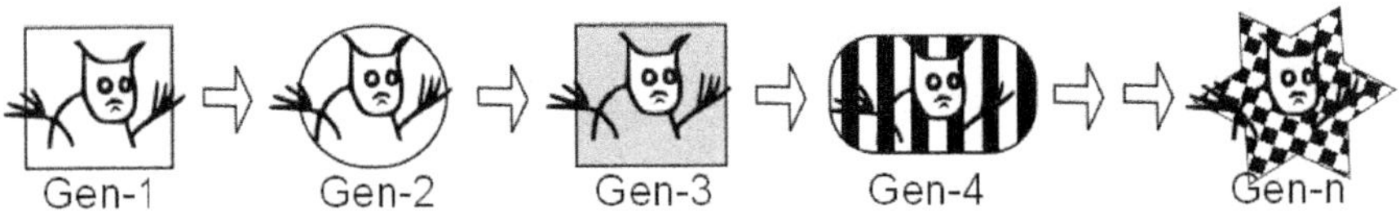

Changing Structure of Metamorphic Viruses

While polymorphic viruses show their viral body which is found to be identical at the time of execution, metamorphic viruses don't give such a chance. They are always different, whether before execution or at the time of execution.

Feature analysis

- The metamorphic viruses go one step beyond the encrypted polymorphic viruses as it changes its everything from infection to infection including its core viral body. Metamorphism is also called as body-polymorphism.
- The metamorphic viruses cannot be detected by signature scanning as they don't have any fixed string as signature. They don't have anything in common anywhere in any generation.

24.5.1 How does the metamorphism work

As the intention of the metamorphic virus is to change its body every time it infects, it has the capability of reprogramming itself. First it translates its own code to a temporary format, then edit that temporary format following certain rules (like instruction reordering, code permutation, register renaming, code shrinking, code expansion, garbage insertion etc.) and then writes itself back to the normal code again. Even the metamorphic engine is also changed. All these are done by the virus itself.

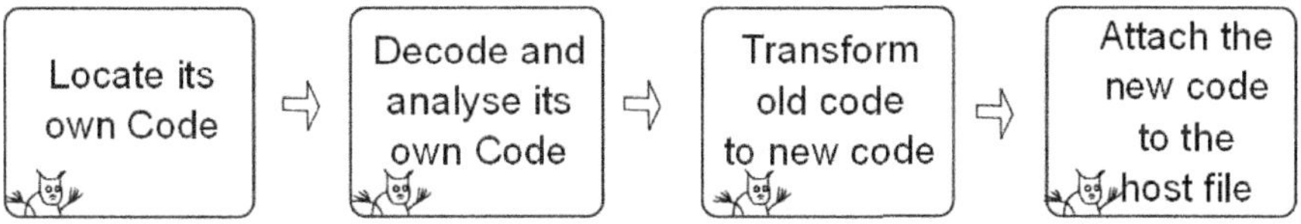

Steps of Transforming Metamorphic Viruses

24.5.2 The ideal Final Result for the Virus Creators

So far we have discussed many IFRs for anti-virus users and anti-virus developers. Let's now see what is the IFR before the anti-virus creators.

IFR The metamorphic viruses should be of highly metamorphic, i.e., widely different from each other.

IFR The code of the virus programs should look very similar to ordinary benign programs so that they cannot be differentiated through any method of detection.

Contradiction before Virus Creators

However, achieving this goal is also not so easy for the virus developers. They face the following contradiction.

Contradiction	*Each instance of the virus code should be substantially different from each other so that they cannot be detected as linked to each other. But at the same time they should have something common to produce the core functionality of the virus such as subject identification, mutation and infection.*

Techniques used by metamorphic viruses

The metamorphic viruses use different techniques to change their virus bodies and solve the above contradiction. Depending on the implemented techniques a metamorphic virus can be very complex and hard to detect.

- ⇨ One technique of metamorphism is transposition or rearrangement of instruction order. Such reordering of instructions is possible if there is no dependency existing between them.
- ⇨ Another such technique is to change the register usage. Although the virus uses the same code it uses different registers in its new generation.
- ⇨ Reordering of subroutines- another technique is to use permutation to reorder the virus' subroutines. This is a stronger technique and can create a large number of variations.

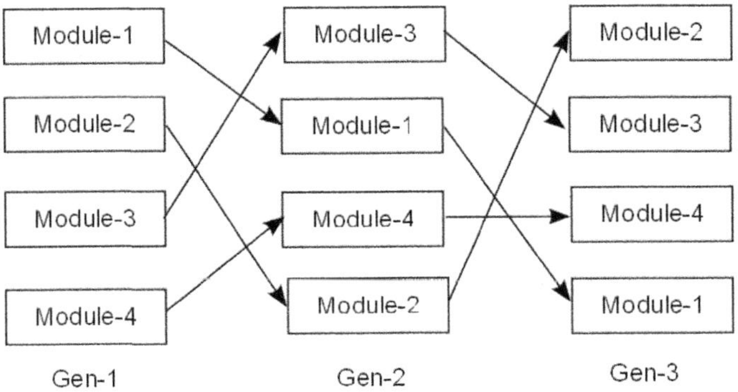

Module reordering by Metamorphic Viruses

- ⇨ Another technique is to insert garbage instructions between core instructions. Garbage instructions are either created or copied from different locations. The garbage instructions skipped by jump instructions and are not executed by the virus. Hence they have no impact on the virus functionality.
- ⇨ Another method is code-polymorphism which replaces one set of instructions with another set of instructions that does the same function. For example,

```
XOR   BP,BP          ;db 31h, 0edh
```

Can be replaced with the code below,

```
SUB   BP,BP          ;db 29h, 0edh
```

Which does the same thing. If there are too many such code substitutions that becomes a nightmare for any anti-virus.

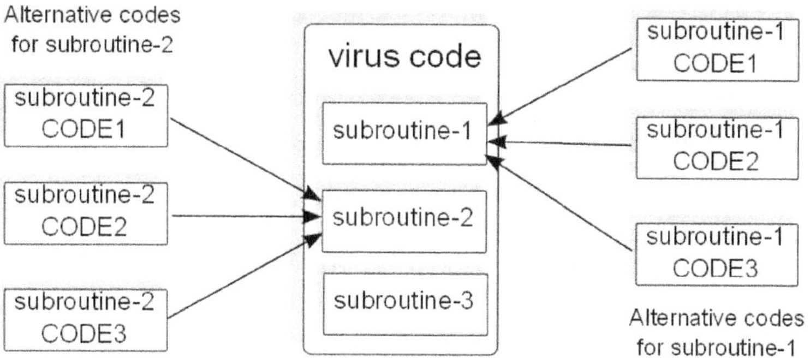

Code substitution by Metamorphic Viruses

➩ Creating metamorphic viruses requires very high programming skills. But there are virus generation kits like NGVCK (Next Generation Virus Generation Kit) which can create highly metamorphic viruses.

24.6 Methods of detecting Polymorphic and Metamorphic Viruses

Metamorphism is a strong concept to generate undetectable viruses. But there are still some techniques to detect metamorphic viruses.

✓ Although the metamorphic viruses change their code on every infection, they still have to maintain some similarity to produce the same functionality. The anti-virus researchers try to detect those similarities.

✓ As most of the metamorphic viruses are created by virus creation toolkits, they will have some codes in common, which the anti-virus researchers have to detect.

✓ NGVCK (Next Generation Virus Generation Kit) generated viruses are highly metamorphic and almost non-detectable. But these viruses are too different from other viruses and normal programs. HMM and other techniques can detect these viruses by detecting the difference of their structure.

- ✓ Most Metamorphic viruses can be detected by analyzing the code. Their codes have some similarity between themselves and have some difference from normal programs.
- ✓ Using machine learning techniques with HMM, data mining, neural networks etc. When these modules are trained more they become more capable of detecting metamorphic viruses.

Possible solutions

- ⚒ Some metamorphic viruses are detected through code emulation in a virtual machine. If the virtual machine well mimics the system functionalities, the virus cannot differentiate between the real machine and virtual machine and executes its code in the virtual environment. The anti-virus applies various techniques such as heuristic scanning, behavior checking etc. to detect the suspicious code during code emulation.
- ⚒ CDPE (cue-directed program emulation) is also a successful method which assumes that at least one section of the polymorphic virus code is static and consistent from generation to generation. The emulation proceeds until the file is fully decrypted. The frequently found codes in decryption loops are called "boosters" and rarely found codes in the decryption loops are called "stoppers". If a number of stoppers are detected before detecting a booster then the file is decided as uninfected. On the other hand if a number of boosters are detected before detecting a stopper then the scanning proceeds an infection is decided.
- ⚒ Patent 5826013 (by Nachenberg) discloses a polymorphic virus detection module which comprises a CPU emulator for emulating the target program and a virus signature scanning module for scanning the decrypted virus code. The method uses the instructions and interrupt usage profiles of the mutation engines of the known polymorphic viruses rather than depending upon the heuristic stopper and booster code sequences. (TRIZ Principle-35: Change Parameters).

INVENTION-125: Detecting polymorphic viruses based on redundancy of viral code

The polymorphic and metamorphic viruses often contain a significant amount of redundant or ridiculous code. Patent 7266844 (invented by Teblyashkin, et al., Assignee- McAfee, Inc. Sep. 2007) discloses a heuristic detection of polymorphic viruses based on redundancy of its viral code.

The invention analyzes the computer program to detect if the level of such redundant or ridiculous code exceeds a threshold level. If the number of such instructions exceeds the threshold level, then the computer program is treated as containing a computer virus (Inventive Standards 4.2.4- Measure something that is already there in the environment). This technique is useful in identifying new and polymorphic viruses.

Patent 7356736 (invented by Natvig, Assignee- Norman Asa, Apr. 2008) discloses a simulated computer system for detecting encrypted, polymorphic, metamorphic and other computer viruses. The invented system logs all accesses and nature of accesses to system resources in a totally simulated and controlled environment. The viruses feel that they are running in a normal computer environment and infect the virtual files in the virtual hard disk. The anti-virus program detects the viruses by analyzing the access logs to the simulated resources.

Patent 7409717 (invented by Peter Szor, Assignee- Symantec Corporation, Aug. 2008) discloses a method of detecting metamorphic computer viruses through register signatures. While executing in an emulated environment, the viruses produces specific register values when given a set of inputs. The register values are then examined whether they match with any of the register signatures stored in the virus database module to verify presence of a virus.

INVENTION-126: Detecting polymorphic viruses by data driven lexical analysis

Patent 7636945 (invented by Chandnani, et al., assignee- Computer Associates Think, Dec 2009) discloses a method of detecting script language viruses. The apparatus includes a script language processor, a detection data processor and a detection engine. The script language processor prepares language description data corresponding to at least one script language. The detection data processor prepares detection data for viral code corresponding to the script language virus. The detection engine lexically analyzes a data stream using the language description data and the detection data to detect the viral code.

The language description data may correspond to language definition rules and language check rules. The data stream may be converted to a stream of tokens, wherein the lexical analysis is performed on the token stream. The script language virus detection apparatus may be a computer program stored on a computer readable medium and/or transmitted via a computer network or other transmission medium. (cannot understand!!)

INVENTION-127: Detecting metamorphic viruses by analyzing register values

Patent 7937764 (invented by Peter Szor, assignee- Symantec Corporation, May, 2011) teaches detecting metamorphic viruses by analyzing register values.

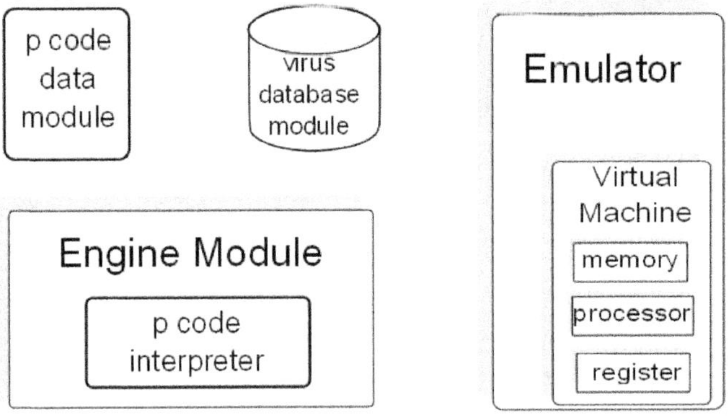

Virus Detection System

The method detects a computer virus in a file by executing the file in a virtual machine. The method records the values of the register values in the virtual computer. Then the virus detection system analyses the recorded values of the virtual registers during emulation of the file indicates an order that is indicative of a computer virus.

ITERATION	REG 0	REG 1	• • •	REG N	OPCODE
0000	0000	0000		0000	4AFF
0001	ACFD	0000		0000	8BDS
0002	046F	0000		0000	58
0003	B406	DB88		042A	BF0C0000
0004	FF23	619E		042A	8B1A
0005	74A0	53C0		042A	5A
0006	0000	1199		FF84	89B4BA181100
0007	04FE	1199		FF84	B640
0008	1475	1199		FF84	894E04

FIG. 6

A virus detection system (VDS) holds a database of the register signatures. The VDS examines a file that might contain a computer virus and identifies potential entry points in the file. While emulating each potential entry point, the VDS builds a register table that tracks the values of virtual registers. Then the VDS analyzes the register table to see whether the file contains a virus.

Chapter 25.

Patented Anti-Virus Solutions in Chronological Order

Problem:

The boot sector virus overwrites the disk's original boot sector with its own code so that the virus is loaded into the memory before anything else. Since the boot sector is the first item of data accessed during the boot up of a computer system, a virus in that location is difficult to eliminate.

Patented Solution:

The problem can be solved by loading the anti-virus before the boot sector virus is loaded. But how can an anti-virus be loaded before loading the operating system? Patent 5559960 (invented by Jonathan Lettvin, Sept 1996) suggests to have another small operating system called BTOS (Bootstrap Time Operating System) which will run at the startup to load an anti-virus before the computer executes an ultimate operating system. (TRIZ Principle-13: Reversing, Principle-9: Prior Counteraction).

Problem:

But the question arises as where to store the bootstrap anti-virus that will be loaded by BTOS before loading of the ultimate operating system. Because wherever you store the anti-virus, it is subject to viral infection. How to keep the bootstrap anti-virus safe and hidden from virus infection?

Patented Solution:

Patent 5559960 and Patent 5826012 (invented by Jonathan Lettvin) proposes to create a "hidden partition" (TRIZ Principle-32: Color Change) by utilizing the spare sectors and tracks in the disk that is not reflected in the size and geometry information stored in the BIOS parameter block of the disk (TRIZ Principle-22: Turn harms to benefits). As the OS cannot access this partition, there is no reason or scope for a virus to assume or access this hidden storage space.

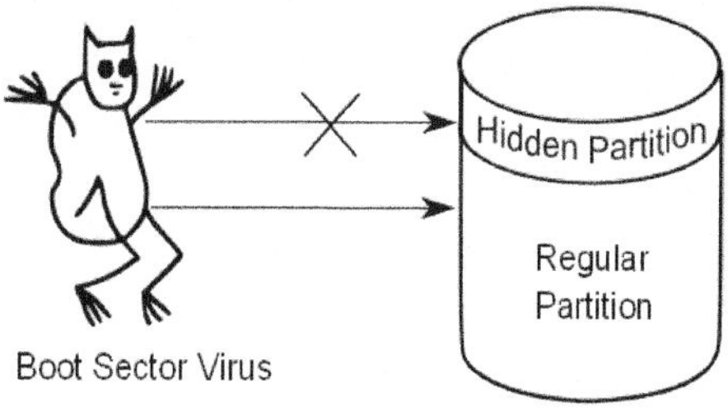

Problem

Sometimes the virus writers reverse engineer the protection mechanism included in the anti-virus program in order to enable their viruses to escape the available detection mechanism.

Patented Solution

Patent 5684875 (invented by Hans Ellenberger, Nov 1997) suggests a polymorphic protection method which installs only a few selected algorithms each time the anti-virus is installed (TRIZ Principle-3: Local Quality). Hence even if a virus writer reverse engineers the detection method he can view only limited number of algorithms which are installed on that machine. Even if the new viruses include the counter measures for those algorithms they cannot escape for long as they will be detected by another installation having a different set of algorithms.

Problem:

The conventional anti-virus mechanism detects virus only after the virus enters into a system and often after performing its intended activity. There is a need for a method that can search, detect and eliminate viruses before they enter into a computer system.

Patented Solution:

Patent 5842002 (invented by Schnurer et al, Nov 1998) teaches to introduce a foreign operating system (different from the operating system intended to be protected) into the data stream before the data arrives at the computer system. This foreign OS creates a virtual world that simulates the host computer system (TRIZ Principle-7: Nesting, Principle-26: Copying) and encourages the virus to perform its intended activity.

When the virus starts its disruptive behavior within the simulated host computer system it is caught and removed.

Problem:

Some prior art anti-virus programs do not allow any modification to executable files in order to avoid virus infection. But this method may lead to false positives, as writing to an executable file can be a legal operation. **Contradiction**- if the anti-virus will wait to verify whether the writing operation is modifying the "significant data" in order to determine the virus operation, then that would allow the virus to modify the program.

Patented Solution:

Patent 6073239 (invented by Eyal Dotan, assignee In-defense Inc., June 2000) solves this problem by backing up the program immediately before any modification is made. When a virus or other writing operation attempts to write any data to the program, the method intercepts the operation and backs up the program in a different location. Then the method determines whether the writing operation is attempting to modify the **significant** data (such as, the "entry point"), which could be a virus like operation. If the writing operation is attempting to modify the **significant** data then an alarm is generated and writing is denied. If the data is already modified, the method restores the program to its initial state and undoes all the modifications that the virus might have made to the program. (TRIZ Principle-26: Copying, Principle-34: Discard and Recover).

Problem:

The conventional virus scanning utilities, installed on the end-user systems, cannot detect infections during download. While downloading files from Internet, the infected files are still downloaded to the end-user's storage device and remain undetected on the user's system for a long time or passed on to other systems before detected by the scanner.

Patented Solution:

There is a need to prevent infected files from being downloaded to the end-user's machine. Patent 6088803 (by Tso, July 2000) teaches to install a virus checking software on the network device for checking virus while downloading data to a network client (TRIZ Principle-24: Intermediary). hen a client requests for a data object, the network device invokes the virus checker and scans the requested file as input. If the requested file does not contain a virus then the network device transmits the file to the client computer, alternatively, the network device interrupts transmission of data and transmits an appropriate message to the client computer and to the message server.

Problem:

Some prior art anti-virus systems make the boot partition "read only" in order to protect the system from virus attack. But Microsoft Windows requires many files in "windows" directory (inside boot partition), which are supposed to be written to. Besides the network software and virtual memory manager may require write access to either "windows" directory or root directory or both. Hence making the boot partition "read only" can cause the system to halt.

Contradiction- we want to make the boot partition "read only" in order to protect it from virus attack. But we don't want to make the boot partition "read only" as the operating system and other critical programs require write access to the boot partition.

Patented Solution:

Patent 6092161 (invented by White et. Al, assignee Arendee Limited, July 2000) provides a new method of protecting the boot partition by creating a Write Many Recoverable (WMR) partition. The invented method allows the boot partition to be written without limit during a session. However, at the start of a new session, all the changes to the partition are undone and the partition is restored to its original state. In other words, if a partition is virus-free to start with, it will remain virus-free at the start of each new session (TRIZ Principle-34: Discard and Recover).

Problem:

A large number of computer viruses are memory resident in nature. These viruses monitor commands of a BIOS or DOS from within the memory. The traditional virus scanners can only detect a virus in the system area but cannot exterminate a virus that is resident in the memory. Therefore, even if a file is healed from virus, it is infected again by the memory resident virus. A manual extermination process is difficult and error prone. There is a need for a simple and risk-free method to exterminate the memory resident viruses.

Patented Solution:

Patent 6240530 (invented by Togawa, May 2001) provides an optimum virus extermination method in four steps without imposing much burden in operation. The first step involves virus detection and identification. The second step involves memory clearing. The third step involves restarting the system by fetching an operating system from outside. The last step includes extermination of the virus. All these steps are implemented automatically thereby avoiding the possibility of errors that would have occurred during a manual extermination process (TRIZ Principle-25: Self service).

Problem:

The prior art scanners use single virus signatures to scan individual viruses. This method provides low reliability and detects false positives. There is a need to use unique combination of signatures and patterns for high reliability in scanning.

Patented Solution:

In contrast to the traditional scanning approach of one virus- one signature, Patent 6338141 (invented by Wells, Jan 2002) suggests to use a combination of many signatures and flags to scan any virus (TRIZ Principle-40: Composite). By using multiple signatures for each virus the invention allows to verify infections with a high degree of certainty and avoid false identifications.

Problem:

Sometimes a computer may fail to boot because of virus infections. It may not be able to access Anti-Virus software from the hard disk or update virus signature files from the Internet. Even if a computer is able to boot, it may not have access to latest virus scanning software. There is a need to provide up-to-date virus scanning utilities to the users even if the computer is not able to boot because of viral damages.

Patented Solution:

Patent 6347375 (invented by Reinert et al., Feb 2002) provides a method of up-to-date virus scanning of a local computer by a remote computer even in situations where the normal operating system of the local computer is not operable. The invention provides a bootable virus utility operating program to boot the local computer and establish communications between the local computer and a remote computer. Then the local computer downloads a remote data recovery program from the remote computer to the memory of the local computer and executes the data recovery program in the memory of the local computer. Then the local computer downloads a virus scanning and repair utility from the remote computer to the memory of the local computer and executes the virus scanning and repair utility at the local computer. The invention provides a remote scanning and repairing mechanism contrary to the conventional method of local scanning and repairing (TRIZ Principle-17: Another Dimension).

Problem:

Often users forget to remove floppy disks from a floppy drive. In such cases if the floppy is infected with boot sector virus then the computer gets infected when attempts to boot from the floppy. One solution is to remove floppy seek option in the CMOS setup. But it will be difficult again to boot from the floppy by changing all the options in CMOS.

Patented Solution:

Patent 6550007 (invented by Baxter, et al., April 2003) solves this problem simply by displaying an alert to the user. When the computer finds a floppy in the drive it alerts the user that the computer system is about to boot from the floppy disk before actually doing so. (TRIZ Principle-23: Feedback). This method enables the user to remove the floppy disk from the drive if he does not intend the computer system to boot from the disk (TRIZ Principle-9: Prior Counteraction).

Problem:

A virus uses several techniques to spread itself and operate secretly. Can't the anti-virus use all those techniques to catch and remove viruses?

Patented Solution:

Patent 6813712 (invented by Luke, Nov 2004) discloses a beneficial counter virus agent for detecting viral infection of a computer system. This counter virus is released deliberately with a pre-determined population level. The counter virus attaches itself to other files for replication. But it maintains its own population level by self-destructing or infecting other files depending on the population level. In this way the population of the counter virus is maintained unless the counter virus infects another (unauthorized) virus, in which case the replication mechanism of the unauthorized virus overcomes the population control mechanism of the counter virus. This resulting increment in the population reveals the existence of the unknown virus (TRIZ Inventive Standard 4.2.2). The advantage of this method is that it can detect new and unknown viruses.

Problem:

The conventional anti-virus programs are meant for searching and disinfecting individual computer files. But they are not efficient to handle virus outbreaks. A virus outbreak is more than just individual viruses and unless controlled can wreck havoc in large number of computers.

Patented Solution:

Patent 6898715 (invented by Smithson, et al., May 2005) discloses a predefined sequence of steps that is automatically (or manually) followed to invoke counter measures against virus outbreaks. The counter-measures include reducing virus notification, increasing scanning options, blocking e-mail attachments, hiding e-mail address books and the like. This method automatically provides an appropriate response during virus outbreak even if the IT-support personnel are not present (TRIZ Principle-25: Self Service, Principle-9: Prior Counteraction).

Problem:

An on-access scanner scans a file when an access is attempted to the file. The scanner has to intercept file access events for scanning the file. But there are some drawbacks in this method. For example, intercepting a file during access may cause file access errors. Besides, if the scanning takes longer time, the user may believe that there has been a software/hardware malfunction.

Patented Solution:

Patent 6931540 (invented by Edwards et al., Aug 2005) provides an improvement in the on-access method. The virus detection actions are selected based on the type of the files being accessed and the process accessing them. For example, executable files and macro files etc. are more likely to propagate virus than data files or image files and hence requires more security measures to be executed. Similarly, some processes, like findfast.exe in windows, open a large amount of files which may not need to be scanned securely because there is no risk of a virus propagation. This method allows for more efficient use of system resources while maintaining an appropriate level of security measures.

Problem:

Often virus writers try to attack anti-virus systems in various ways. For example, a virus may produce highly compressed versions of very large files knowing that the anti-virus has to decompress the file in order to scan the viruses within it. As the decompressed file is sufficiently large, the anti-virus may take extremely long time to scan or may consume excessive amount of physical memory available requiring extensive use of virtual memory thereby impacting the performance of the system.

Contradiction- if a protracted scanning is not terminated then the anti-virus system may impact the performance of the system. But timing out a protracted scanning may inappropriately terminate a usual scanning operation in a slow or overloaded computer thereby compromising vulnerabilities.

Patented Solution:

Patent 6968461 (invented by Lucas, et al., Nov 2005) advises to time out a protracted scanning but provides an additional level of sophistication by comparing the size of the computer file being scanned with the actual time taken for scanning. The scanning method first calculates a measurement value based on the amount of data processing performed during scanning operation and then triggers a break only if the said measurement value exceeds a threshold value. That means if the size of a file is large, then it is not early terminated as it may legitimately require a large amount of data to be processed during scanning operation (TRIZ Principle-15: Dynamize, Principle-16: Partial or excessive action).

Problem:

There are some network environments where the virus-scanning engine runs on a central server and the agents on individual machines transfer data to the central server for scanning. But this method requires transfer of a large volume of data over the network and thereby slows down the network traffic and virus scanning operation particularly if the agent and the server exist at different locations.

Patented Solution:

Patent 7020895 (invented by Albrecht, Mar 2006) figured out that although a large volume of data is being transferred by an agent to the scanning server, the scanning application actually looks at a relatively small portion of this data. Hence, it is not required to transfer the entire electronic file from the agent to the server, rather only those parts of the file which are of direct interest to the scanning application (TRIZ Principle-21: Skipping). For example, the clients may transfer only the header portion of an electronic file thereby greatly reducing the volume of data transferred to scanning server thereby speeding up the scanning operation and improving network performance.

Problem

It is advantageous to scan files through central scanning servers, as there is no need to install and maintain anti-virus engines on individual computers. But the disadvantage is that the clients have to transfer large volume of data to the scanning server over the network, which slows down the network and scanning operation.

Contradiction- we want to scan files by a central scanning server (because that reduces maintenance activities) but we don't want to send files from individual clients to the central scanning server (because that affects network performance).

Patented Solution

Patent 7152164 (invented by Loukas, Dec 2006) discloses a method of scanning files in a central server without the need of sending files to the central server. According to the invention, the client computer need to send only the identifications of files, which are tiny in size and require substantially less time and bandwidth. The file identifications include the properties of the web content such as, source URL, source computer URL, content type, size, creation date, version number etc. along with check-sum (TRIZ Principle-30: Thin and Flexible).

The anti-virus scanning server compares those identifications with a database of identifications of other known virus infected files or web contents and takes security measures if found a matching in the database.

Problem

If a computer-storage is corrupted due to the malfunction of any hardware or virus infection, then the files can be restored from the previously stored backup. But in such cases the files that have been modified since the last backup cannot be recovered. Besides if the backed up data contains a virus, then the system may still remain contaminated and the files may again be corrupted.

Patented Solution

Patent 7222143 (invented by Childs, et al., May 2007) discloses a method of safe restoring a previously un-backed up data during a system restore by using a locked partition with an alternate operating system. The locked partition should be accessible only by the alternate operating system and not by the primary operating system (TRIZ Inventive Standards 1.2.1- Introduce a third element (or substance) to remove the harmful interactions between two elements (or substances).

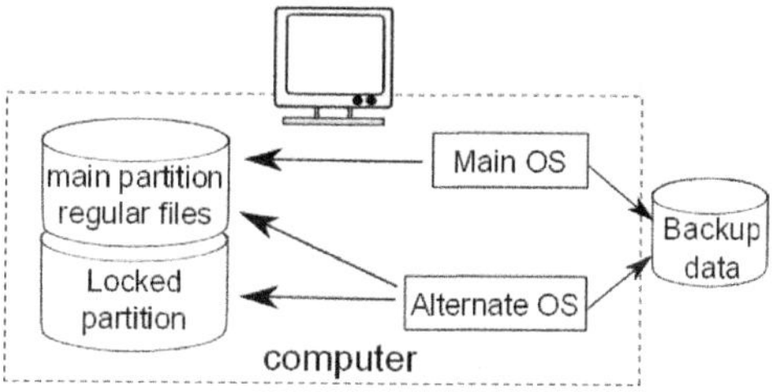

While restoring the failing system, the alternate operating system determines which files have been modified since the most recent backup and runs a virus scan on those modified files and uncorrupts the corrupted files. Thus the alternate operating system recovers all the modified files whether uninfected or disinfected by the virus scanner. After the data restored from the last backup, the files which have been modified since last backup are replaced with the files recovered in the locked partition. Thus the system recovers files since the most recent backup while ensuring at least part of the restored files don't contain any viruses.

Problem

Analyzing viruses and extracting virus signatures is a difficult and time taking job. As there are a large number of new viruses, a manual extraction of virus signatures increases the time gap between virus creation and release of detection mechanism.

Patented Solution

Patent 7234167 (invented by Teblyashkin, et al., Jun 2007) discloses a fingerprint generation logic that extracts virus signatures automatically by comparing the infected copy of the files with the non-infected copy of the same files. The method also generates the virus removal data automatically (TRIZ Principle-25: Self Service). Thus the invention helps rapid generation of fingerprint data and virus removal data.

Problem

There are many trial software distributed via internet which carry computer viruses. These viruses may alter or cause damage to the operating system. Some prior art techniques like Connectix Corporation's Virtual PC and VMware use virtual disks to discard unwanted changes. But there is a need to implement that technique in a regular PC in order to test trial software, trial data and trial mail data.

Patented Solution

Patent 7240239 (invented by Kuniyasu Suzaki, Jul 2007) suggests using a virtual computer that can reset the state after trying out the trial software. According to the invention, there is no need to create an installer for the evaluation version. The application developer copies and distributes the trial software along with a snapshot of an active OS. This way the trial user can try out the emulated version without taking any risk of non-recoverable damage from computer viruses (TRIZ Principle-26: Copy, Principle-27: Cheap and disposable).

Problem

Some viruses like Win32/Magistr.B.Worm do not store the encryption key in the virus body. They calculate the key using the machine name. But the anti-virus can still know the encryption code, as it is constant for that machine. But the problem becomes worse when a user changes his machine name or the infected file is copied or moved to a different machine. The case looks impossible to solve because the anti-virus is presented with unknown data encrypted by an unknown key.

Patented Solution

Patent 7260725 (invented by Carmona, et al., Aug 2007) discloses a method of curing encrypted computer viruses using a method called probabilistic encryption key guessing. The method first analyzes the encrypted data to determine the most frequently occurring encrypted byte in the encrypted data. Then it calculates an encryption key based on the most frequently occurring encrypted byte and a corresponding expected original byte of the original data. For example, a 32 bit executable code for Intel processors contains a lot of 0's and 255's. So whatever data is most frequently occurring in the encrypted data is guessed to be the encrypted form of the original value zero (Inventive Standard- 4.2.4. measure something that is already there in the environment).

Problem

The polymorphic viruses follow different techniques to continuously change their code to have different code sequences in successive infections. The conventional anti-virus programs fail to detect such viruses, as they don't follow any specific code pattern.

Patented Solution

Patent 7266844 (invented by Teblyashkin et al., Sep. 2007) discloses a heuristic detection of polymorphic viruses based on the redundancy of viral code. The invention recognizes that the polymorphic viruses often contain a significant amount of redundant or ridiculous code. It first analyzes the computer program to detect if the level of such redundant or ridiculous code exceeds a threshold level. If the number/occurrences of such instructions exceed a threshold level, then the computer program is treated as containing a computer virus (Inventive Standards 4.2.4- Detect by measuring something that is already there in the environment).

Problem

Anti-virus venders have to update virus definition data periodically. While a delay in distributing virus definitions can cause tremendous damage and lost productivity, a quick untested release of virus definitions can raise false positives and cause serious confusions.

Contradiction- we want the software venders to perform more comprehensive internal testing in order not to allow false positives, on the other hand we want to release the updates fast.

Patented Solution

Patent 7290282 (invented by Renert, et al., Oct. 2007) proposes to release the virus detection modules to the clients including a constraints module. The constraints module is a special module which allows specific clients to test the new heuristics and provide test reports to the software server. (TRIZ Principle-23: Feedback).

Problem

Most new viruses are just modifications of old viruses. But the anti-virus provider has to identify the pattern of each modified virus and create an update for the anti-virus users. There should be an easy solution for the rewritten, modified or recognized malware which are dealt previously.

Patented Solution

Patent 7376970 (invented by Marinescu, May 2008) discloses a method of proactively protecting rewritten and reorganized malware. According to the invention a virtual operating system is emulated for execution of the programs to determine if the programs are malware created. During simulation, a behavior signature is generated based on the API calls issued by potential malware. This behavior signature is analyzed to determine whether the simulated executable is a malware.

Problem

There are many identical files on each individual machines on a network which are scanned on respective machines. Thus the same files are repeatedly scanned in subsequent executions of the anti-virus software. Besides the same files are repeatedly backed up even if not changed since last backup.

Patented Solution

Patent 7398399 (invented by Palliyil, et al., Jul. 2008) provides a method of avoiding repetitive scanning of duplicate files in a network. First it identifies identical resources on different computers in a network by comparing the hash values for each resource. Once the identical resources are identified, the information is used for different purposes. For example, the identical resources may not be virus scanned or backed up again. This method reduces overall processing overhead of virus scanning and backup operations.

Problem

While simple computer viruses work by copying exact duplicates of themselves, encrypted viruses include an encrypted viral body and a decryption routine, polymorphic viruses generate a new decryption routine each time it infects a file and Metamorphic viruses vary the instruction in the viral body with each infection. These types of viruses cannot be detected by conventional methods like signature scanning.

Patented Solution

Patent 7409717 (invented by Peter Szor, Aug. 2008) discloses a method of detecting metamorphic computer viruses by using register signatures. The invention finds that the viruses when executed produce specific register values when given a set of inputs. This is generally true even for code-altering metamorphic viruses. Thus the emulating module of the invention executes the computer program instructions in a virtual machine and uses the register signatures to detect metamorphic and other types of viruses. If a register signature matches then the selected file is probably contains a virus. (TRIZ Inventive Standard 4.2.1.)

Problem

It is often hard to identify the physical computer that houses the virus especially in a large network. For instance, the culprit may be an old, long-forgotten, server sitting somewhere in a closet or under a laboratory bench, with a non-descriptive device name that does not tell where the machine is. How to find exactly which computer in the network is housing a virus?

Patented Solution

Patent 7418732 (invented by Campbell et al., Aug. 2008) discloses a method of using network switches and routers for identifying the source of attacks in a computer network. The invention uses "smart" network switches to scan network traffic packets passing through the switches for virus signatures. As the switches are physically connected one to one with each computer, a virus detection at the switch can clearly identify the source of a virus.

Problem

Generally a network's access point allows a wireless client computer to access the network regardless of whether the wireless client computer has adequately installed and run the required anti-virus programs. This practice causes a viral threat to the network from unsafe clients.

Patented Solution

Patent 7424745 (invented by Cheston et al., Sep. 2008) discloses how to prevent potential virus attacks on the network by restricting unsafe clients. According to the invention, when a wireless client sends a request to access the network, the access point verifies whether the wireless client has all the necessary anti-virus programs installed. If the client has all the requisite anti-virus programs only then it is allowed to access the network otherwise a request is sent to a pre-authorized anti-virus program server to install necessary software and fixes on the wireless client (TRIZ Principle-2: Taking out, Principle-25: Self Service, Principle-9: Prior Counteraction).

Problem

Recently various types of spyware have emerged including adware, dialer software and other equivalents which cause various problems for the computer users. But scanning spyware by a standalone spyware scanner is a duplicate effort that causes a performance impact on the computer.

Patented Solution

Patent 7441273 (invented by Edwards, et al., Oct. 2008) suggests to integrate spyware detection capabilities with the virus scanner. According to the invention the same virus scanner will have options and capabilities to scan spyware. If the user opts for scanning the spyware then the registry is scanned for detecting spyware. When the virus signatures are updated from the internet, the spyware signatures will also be updated together at the same time (TRIZ Principle-5: Merging). This option saves system resources and scanning time.

Problem

There is a need for a real time system for tracking of viruses worldwide to search and identify the parties that might have been involved in the origination or distribution of viruses.

Patented Solution

Patent 7496960 (invented by Chen, et al, Feb. 2009) discloses a method of real-time tracking of viruses from various computers by a central tracking server.

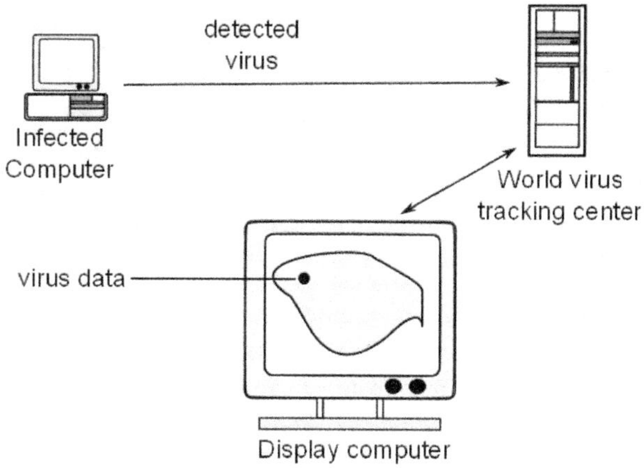

The invention proposes to deploy a central tracking server to receive data pertaining to the anti-virus scanning results from each computer on the network. This server provides a small program or applet that resides in the temporary memory of the client computer. The client computer invokes a scan and sends the details of viruses to a World Virus Tracking Center (WVTC) after the scanning is over. The WVTC displays the geographical maps that show the viruses encountered in each country. This system can proactively help preventing the spread of such viruses.

Problem

The conventional scanning methods are not enough to detect the advanced stealthy viruses. There is a need for more heuristics to detect such viruses easily and effectively.

Patented Solution

Patent 7519997 (invented by Alexander Shipp, Apr. 2009) discloses a method of detecting virus infection by comparing the frequency distribution analysis of the program code with that of the expected distribution of a program created with the same compiler. The invention first determines which compiler was used to create that program code. After determining the compiler, the method reverse engineers the program (TRIZ Principle-13: Reversing) and performs a frequency distribution analysis of instructions found in the code to see whether it corresponds with an expected distribution for a program created with that computer. The method is based on the assumption that the programs created by a compiler follow a certain frequency distribution and if a program does not follow the expected pattern, may be suspected as infected.

Problem

The conventional anti-viruses scan the email viruses when the emails are opened by the recipients. But there are cases where the recipient may not have an anti-virus. There is a need for authenticating an email without opening the mail and without scanning through an anti-virus.

Patented Solution

Patent 7523496 (invented by Bickford, et al., Apr. 2009) discloses a method of authenticating emails (to ensure they have originated from the genuine source and hence free from viruses) without opening the emails.

According to the invention, the sender and the recipient of the email agree beforehand on a certain authentication key, which identifies the originator to the recipient. This authentication key is included in an open field (such as the subject line) of the email so that it can be examined by the recipient without opening the email. When the recipient receives the email it first checks whether the expected authentication key is present. If the authentication key present as expected then the email is verified to have originated from the trusted source. On the other hand if the authentication key is not present or is different from the previously agreed key, then the mail may be rejected as suspicious.

Problem

Some Trojan horse applications intercept keystrokes and email the recorded data to the hacker. Although many prior art anti-virus programs scan each application at load time they are not effective against main-in-the-middle attacks such as Trojan horses.

Patented Solution

Patent 7526654 (invented by Charbonneau, Apr. 2009) suggests to detect the attack of Trojan horses by comparing the hash value of the system memory with a previously computed trusted hash value. The Invention first stores a trusted hash value that is representative of a trusted state of the computer. Then the computer calculates the hash value of the current data stored in the memory and compares the new hash value with the trusted hash value. If the hash values are found to be different then the application is considered un-trusted and locked out.

Problem

Email coming from trusted sources may contain viruses. The content downloaded from Internet may contain viruses. There is a need for a system of certifying a data to be virus free so that the user can open them safely without scanning for virus.

Patented Solution

Patent 7533272 (invented by Gordon, et al., May. 2009) suggests to certify the data after scanning so that the data will not be rescanned when transferred from one computer to another. The certificate may contain a company logo or any type of logo that specifies that the email has been scanned for viruses. For example, an email may be certified at the source computer. When this certified email is received at the second computer the recipient may open it without scanning for viruses. The same certification method can be used to certify other content such as the content of a web site or the content of CD-ROMs etc.

Problem

Generally a virus scanning software starts working after the operating system is loaded. This method does not scan the viruses that are loaded during the pre-boot phase. There is a need for an improved scanning system which should provide protection even during pre boot phase.

Patented Solution

Patent 7549055 (invented by Zimmer, et al., Jun 2009) discloses a virus scanner that operates primarily in the pre-boot phase of computer operation. According to the invention, a trusted pre-boot scanner is loaded during pre-boot phase. The trusted virus scanner may scan a selected number of files (such as files loaded in RAM and Master Boot Record) or all files (such as files accessible during pre-boot phase) as necessary.

Problem

The conventional anti-virus scans a computer on a file-to-file basis. So if there are situations when the scanner is disabled for some time or the computer is started with a safe boot without the antivirus enabled then there is a possibility of some files being infected. In such cases the anti-virus has to go through a complete scan of all the files involving gigabytes of storage. There is a need for a simple precise scan in such situations.

Patented Solution

Patent 7581250 (invented by Sitze, Aug 2009) finds a solution by scanning only the changed sectors of the hard disk instead of scanning all the data in the hard disk.

The invention initially scans all the sectors of a disk. Afterwards it checks whether there has been any write operation to any sector of the hard disk. If there is any write operation then the specific sector is scanned otherwise the sector is avoided (TRIZ Principle-21: Skipping). This method works faster in case of above situations as it scans only the changed sectors of the hard disk. (**Note**- Patent 7401361 (by Freeman, Jul. 2008) also advised scanning of only the changed sectors instead of scanning the whole disk.)

Problem

If the client computer is already infected with worms, it may not be able to boot or may not be able to download the required anti-virus updates.

Patented Solution

Patent 7587765 (by Challener, et al., Sep 2009) advises to turn off the computer and reboot using Wake on LAN (WOL) and establish a secured connection to a pre-authorized trusted anti-virus server in order to download the anti-virus updates. According to the invention when there is an update available with the anti-virus server, it notifies the client computer about the availability of an update. In that case the client computer disengages from the network and reestablishes a link only with the trusted anti-virus server (TRIZ Principle-2: Taking out). After the anti-virus fix is downloaded and installed, the client computer is re-booted, and then allowed to reconnect to the full network.

Problem

As the numbers of viruses are increasing and the methods of scanning are becoming complicated, an on-demand scanning is taking ever increasing time to scan a computer. There is a need to reduce the time required for scanning.

Patented Solution

Patent 7644352 (invented by Grupe, Jan 2010) advises to copy the files of the computer to be scanned to a second computer and scan the files in the second computer (TRIZ Principle-26: Copying). The second computer scans the data and creates a log file identifying data having characteristics of a virus or banned file. The log file is then transferred to the source computer. The source computer then scans just the data identified by the log file. This method avoids the need for a complete scan in the source computer thereby saving time of scanning. (TRIZ Inventive Standard 4.1.2.)

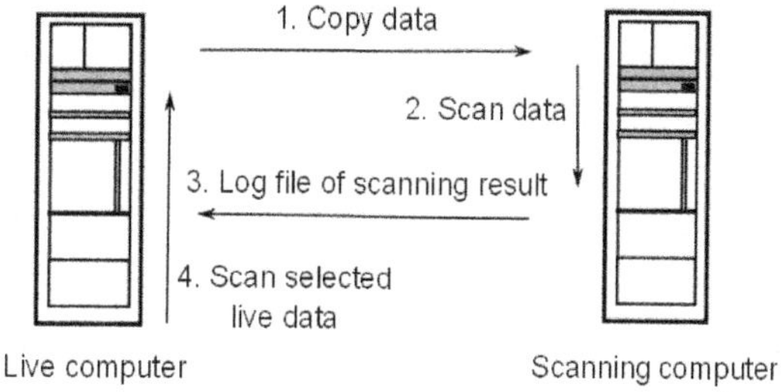

Dividing Scanning Load to a Second Computer
Patent 7644352

Problem

Some viruses like rootkits change the operating system files so that they do malicious functions, such as, key logging, opening backdoors etc. along with their original functions. One method is to identify the presence of a backdoor by scanning. But if a malware opens a port only at designated times, then the scanner may not detect such a port. Another method is to compare the system files with their non-infected copies. But if the malware has taken control of the system it may provide a clean version of the file for comparing hash.

Patented Solution

Patent 7627898 (invented by Beck et al., Dec 2009) detects a possible infection by comparing the properties reported by the suspect operating system and the properties reported by a clean operating system. If there is a difference between the files then the system is deemed to be infected. Alternatively the detection system may compare the reported properties generated by using a high-level scan (using APIs) and a low-level scan (using disk sectors) of the same suspect operating system. This can identify an infection if there is a difference between the two results.

Problem

The anti-viruses are often attacked by highly specialized viruses. There is a need to protect the anti-viruses from malware attacks.

Patented Solution

Patent 7640583 (invented by Marinescu et al., Dec 2009) suggests to hide the anti-malware program by using all the techniques that are generally used by a malware to hide its files. The method includes changing of the identification or file name of the item, changing of the signature of the item and/or changing of the size of the item. (TRIZ Principle-35: Parameter change). Alternatively, the anti-malware file may be randomly renamed performing polymorphism on the anti-malware file to alter the size and signature of the anti-malware file (TRIZ Principle-36: State change). These obfuscation techniques make it difficult for the malware to locate the anti-malware files in order to accomplish the desired task.

Problem

A conventional AV application has to be installed on top of the OS. This method slows down the computer operation as the AV application uses the same system resources as the OS. There is a need for an AV system that can remove all types of malware components including rootkits, but without utilizing computer system resources.

Patented Solution

Patent 7657941 (invented by Zaitsev, Feb 2010) suggests to use a hardware-based anti-virus module for curing infected computer systems. This AV system has its own CPU and memory and can be used in combination with AV application. It is configured to connect to a utility of a computer system that runs with system privilege. The hardware based anti-virus system is located between a PC and a disk device. The hardware-based AV system can be implemented as a separate device or it can be integrated into a disk controller.

Problem

Detecting signatures are very useful in both static (without executing the suspected program) and dynamic (executing the suspected program) methods. But metamorphic viruses change their instructions (and thereby signatures) without changing their functionality.

Patented solution

Patent 7739737 (invented by Christodorescu et al., Jun 2010) suggests to compare the "function signatures" that describes the function of the malicious code instead of comparing "codes strings" (TRIZ Principle-28:

Mechanics Substitution). This functional analysis is done by converting varying expressions into a standardized form prior to application of signature analysis.

Problem

The existing e-mail standard can verify the validity of an email address, i.e., to verify that the email exists. But there is no method to verify whether a particular message has been actually sent from a particular address. This drawback of the email system allows spam and virus emails.

Patented Solution

Patent 7752440 (invented by Faynberg, et al, Jul 2010) teaches to prevent email spam and virus distribution by authenticating the origin of email message. In order to verify authenticity, the methods sends a query directly to the alleged originating server (or does this function through a AAA server). The method not only authenticates the sending address but also the sender server (TRIZ Principle-23: Feedback). If the response to the query is negative, then the message is discarded.

Problem

Many viruses transmit themselves through encrypted archive files in order to avoid detection. The anti-virus program has to wait and scan when the user extracts the file from archive. Breaking the password for decryption exposes confidential information of legitimate archives.

Patented Solution

Patent 7797746 (invented by Fossen, et al, Sep, 2010) teaches how to scan without decrypting and without decompressing the contents of the archive file. The method compares the descriptive information of each of the contained files with the information on known malicious or undesirable computer files in order to determine if any of the contained files are malicious or undesired computer files. Thus the undesired computer files are detected in encrypted, compressed, password-protected and even in damaged archives without decompressing the archives.

Problem

The conventional anti-virus software scans only the base OS and not the virtual machines (such as Vmware) or the applications running on the virtual machine. The guest OS writes all its data in a single file and an anti-virus application on the base OS has no way to recognize the file and data on the guest OS. On the other hand individually scanning the file system of each virtual machine needs installing the anti-virus on each virtual machine and results in a lot of additional work.

Patented Solution

Patent 7802302 (invented by Nagarkar, et al, Sep, 2010) discloses a scanning manager that scans the file systems of all the associated virtual machines running on a base computer. In order to scan a virtual machine, the scanning manager identifies the file on the base machine that represents the virtual machine, freezes the virtual machine, and creates a snapshot thereof. The scanning manager restarts the frozen machine, and starts the snapshot. The files of the snapshot are mapped at a virtual machine level, and the resulting file mapping information is used to scan the files of the virtual machine at a base machine level. The mapping information is current as of the instant the snapshot was taken. The scanning manager can scan one or multiple or all virtual machine(s) running on the base computer, in conjunction with a full or partial scan of the base computer, or independently.

Problem

In a multi network environment, when a network is infected with viruses, it becomes difficult to distribute anti-virus updates to the client computers.

Patented Solution

Patent 7849508 (invented by Jung, et al, Dec, 2010, Patent 7917956, March 2011, Patent 7,934,260, April 2011, Patent 8146161, March 2012, Patent 8151353, April 2012) suggests a bypass connection for a multi-network virus immunization system. When the network is infected with viruses, the bypass connection is used for distribution of anti-virus agent (TRIZ Principle-17: Another dimension).

Problem

Sometimes a system may crash out of virus infection and may even fail to update its virus database. In such a case every time the user tries to reboot the computer the malware does more mischief like deleting more files or sending confidential data to criminal party.

Patented Solution

Patent 7930531 (invented by Chow et al., Apr, 2011) advises to use a USB flash disk with multiple partitions with different operating systems for recovering such an infected computer. When the host computer is infected the user will reboot the computer from the flash disk using a new OS image. The virus removal programs in the alternate OS can help recover from a virus in the primary OS (TRIZ Principle-17: Another Dimension).

Problem

The metamorphic viruses change their signature on every infection to avoid detection. Metamorphic viruses are not necessarily encrypted but their codes are different in each generation. As they have no static signatures they cannot be found by signature scanning.

Patented Solution

Patent 7937764 (invented by Peter Szor, May, 2011) teaches detecting metamorphic viruses by analyzing register values. The method executes the infected file in a virtual machine and tracks the register values of the virtual computer. The infection is detected by analyzing the register values.

Problem

Some anti-virus programs allow users to specify the type and name of files or folders to scan. But as the numbers and types of files increase, it becomes difficult for the user to remember all the names of files and folders to properly instruct the anti-virus program with regard to which files/ file types/ folders should be scanned.

Patented Solution

Patent 7953984 (invented by Chung et al., May 2011) suggests to include a search engine with malware detection engine to help malware detection (TRIZ Principle-5: Merging). The search engine is configured to receive data and commands from the malware detection application and return data pertaining to search results to the malware detection application. The scan engine of the malware detection application then scans the selected scan targets.

Problem

The network scanning may be either store-scan-forward scanning or stream scanning. Both of them have their own advantages and disadvantages. Store and forward scanning is slow, while stream scanning is less reliable.

Patented Solution

Patent 7992206 (invented by Painter, et al., Aug, 2011) disclosed an add-on pre-scanner card for scanning network traffic. The pre-scanner card receives the network packets and does a pre scan exercise to decide which of the packets need further scanning and which of the packets don't need (TRIZ Principle-10: Prior Action). If the packets are doubtful they are passed to a file-based scan engine for detailed scanning.

Problem

Each security software company has a collection of its own in-house developed virus signatures. It is necessary to prevent theft of these signatures by other venders. In a cloud-scanning technology, the software venders can "hide behind the cloud" and usurp their competitors' scanning technologies. There is no way to detect blatant stealing of a security vendor's products or signatures and hard work.

Patented Solution

Patent 8015284 (invented by Isenberg et al., Sep 2011) suggests using a bait file to detect theft of virus signatures by third party venders. The bait file is actually a non-malware file. But the signatures corresponding to the bait file are included in the signature database of the security vender which is made publicly available.

When a third party vender steals the signatures, the bait file signatures are also included in that. Later when the corresponding bait files are given to the third party vender for scanning the (actually uninfected) bait files are detected to be infected. This situation proves stealing of signatures.

Problem

The conventional virus scanner has to apply various detection methods and scan through thousands of virus signatures in order to detect a malware. However, there are still chances of false positives where a goodware is wrongly diagnosed and a malware. How to avoid such false positives?

Patented Solution

Patent 8028338 (Invented by Schneider et. al., Sep 2011) discloses a set of goodware characteristics which can be used to determine whether a file belongs to goodware. When a file is detected as malware the file is then scanned through the goodware characteristics in order to confirm the detection result. This method reduces the chance of false positive detections.

Problem

Different anti-virus software use different methods for detection of malware and other threats. Since they are all developed by different venders and follow different data communication and data storage formats, these applications are generally incompatible to each other. Because of their incompatibilities they cannot share virus detection information with each other. There is a need for an improved system for sharing of malware-related information.

Patented Solution

Patent 8056136 (invented by Zaitsev, Sep 2011) discloses the possibility of a centralized knowledge database of malware related information which can be shared by different anti-malware software venders. The centralized security system will accumulate information from different types of security threats and provides controlled access to the accumulated information to various security application modules through XML interfaces for receiving and parsing information.

This method takes advantage of different analytical methods of different anti-virus software. If one analytical method identifies the object to be malicious and another identifies the object to be non-malicious, then the interpreter module identifies correlations between one or more information parameters of the suspicious object and information parameters of other known malicious and non-malicious objects stored in the central knowledge database.

Problem

With the multitude of new viruses and proliferation of new viruses the execution of anti-virus software takes enormous time and puts significantly negative impact on the performance of the computer. Sometimes the impact becomes even more substantial than the impact posed by many potential viruses. There is a need for detecting and removing such undesired content without affecting the performance of the computer.

Patented Solution

Patent 8079084 (invented by Huang, et al., Dec, 2011) suggests improving virus detection speed by using a hardware co-processor (called virus coprocessor). The co-processor can be used for pattern recognition, string comparison; seek instruction and other such operations. The memory of the virus co-processor is capable of communicating with the memory of the main processor so that the results of virus scanning are available to the main processor (TRIZ Principle-8: Counterweight).

Problem

Generally the virus signatures are pulled from the anti-virus server either on user's request or at a scheduled time. In whatever case an infected system is unaware that it has infected files until it receives the next update which detects the undetected virus.

Patented Solution

Patent 8091134 (invented by Benton, et al., Jan 2012) discloses an automatic method of virus detection and inoculation in a peer to peer network. According to the invention when a computer sends an infected file to a peer computer the peer computer detects the virus in the infected file and automatically sends the required virus information back to the infected computer system over the network (TRIZ Principle-23: Feedback). Thus when the infected computer does not have updated anti-virus it can update the required virus definitions from the peer computer automatically.

Problem

It is necessary to keep the important files and virus definitions hidden and protected from viruses. One prior art technique is to keep the operating system files in a HPA (host protected area) of the hard disk. But there are possibilities of the HPA being attacked or changed and it is then difficult to find the backup files that have been tampered.

Patented Solution

Patent 8132257 (invented by Li, et al., Mar, 2012) suggests an anti-virus method based on a security chip. The security chip stores the key files such as BIOS code file, MBR code file, the hash values of operating system files and other important files. When the computer is powered on, the control program verifies the integrity of the system control program with the hash value stored in the memory of the security chip. If all the files are found alright then the computer is started otherwise the damaged/ infected files are retrieved from the backup. The security chip protects key files with more reliability (TRIZ Inventive Standard 1.2.1).

Problem

Sometimes a user may install more than one anti-virus programs with or without knowledge in order to protect the computer against malware. But installing two anti-viruses often causes deadlocks. Sometimes one anti-virus program's scanning may cause another anti-virus program to scan and the later scanning may cause the original anti-virus to scan again. This may lead to infinite loops of scanning. It is desirable to prevent deadlocks even when running more than one anti-virus programs.

Patented Solution

Patent 8171552 (invented by Chang, May 2012) discloses a method of executing more than one anti-virus programs simultaneously by using in a layered environment without causing deadlocks or execution failures. A layered driver or filter driver is a specific type of driver that sits above another driver and intercepts requests directed at the lower driver's objects (e.g., a function driver or a filter driver). The anti-virus program is installed in driver model, where the highest level driver passes on user-mode requests to the lowest level driver. As the driver stack remains common to both the anti-virus programs, a first filter driver associated with the first anti-virus program scans the target file and transmits a request to the second anti-virus program without causing any problem (TRIZ Principle-7: Nested Doll).

Problem

Although the integrity verification techniques has ability to detect polymorphic and metamorphic viruses, they can at best raise an alert on a particular file which later has to be carefully emulated and analyzed in the virus diagnosis phase within a virtual machine. The conventional methods of integrity verification do not indicate where the changes have taken place. This creates a new area of problem called "virus localization".

Patented Solution

Patent 8191146 (invented by Di Crescenzo et al., May 2012) suggests a cryptographic hashing for localizing viruses in a host file. This method returns a fixed-size, such as 128 or 160 bit hash for the file. The hash values are computed out of the file in such a way that any mismatch in the hash value can indicate the location of mismatch or virus infection.

Problem

It is difficult to define the heuristics to detect an unknown malware. Hence, most heuristics lead to false positives and false negatives. Practically a program itself (or its programmer) best knows its normal behavior and this knowledge should be utilized to detect the abnormalities.

Patented solution

Patent 8195953 (by Yue et. al., Jun 2012) suggests to integrate the security functions within the target software itself. For example, the program may contain an ability section containing the capability and behavior of the program. If the actual behavior of the program differs from its ability specifications then the program is suspected as infected. (TRIZ Inventive Standard 4.2.2. Internal complex SFM by inserting security functions within the file). This method protects the software from any kind of attacks whether in static state or during execution.

Problem

As the signature scanning has several drawbacks, the heuristic detection is used to overcome those drawbacks. Although the heuristically detected malicious code is remediated, other instance of the malicious code may remain on the computer system. It is necessary to detect the other instances of the malicious code in easy method.

Patented Solution

Patent 8225405 (invented by Peterson, et al., Jul 2012) teaches how to use file based signature scanning for viruses previously detected through heuristic methods. According to the invention, the host computer maintains a blacklist of virus signatures. When a virus is detected heuristically a virus signature for the malicious code is created locally on the host computer system and updated in the blacklist. Later the host computer is scanned using these locally created signatures. This makes the subsequent detection of the virus easy by scanning the file for the blacklisted signature, without going for an execution of the malicious code in an emulated environment (TRIZ Principle-10: Prior Action).

Problem

It is necessary to store critical system files in a secured location in order to protect them from virus infection. One method is to create a write-protected area in the hard disk. But this may not be adequately secured as write protection can be disabled by anybody having admin privileges. Another method is to use an additional hardware to keep files secured. But using additional hardware involves additional cost.

Patented Solution

Patent 8239959 (invented by Gellerich, Aug, 2012) discloses a method of write-protecting memory to prevent manipulation of files by hackers or virus infections. According to the invention a portion of the computer memory is converted to write protected which is exclusively operable from outside the computer's operating system. As the write protected area is made inaccessible from within the operating system it becomes fully protected from any kind of attack or infection.

Problem

A network must protect itself from infected machines. One method is to quarantine all newly introduced devices in a remediation Virtual LAN. But this has a drawback as the newly added device will not have access to the network until the device is fully virus scanned.

Patented Solution

Patent 8245294 (invented by Zahra et al, Aug 2012) suggests using a virus control server to quarantine infected computers. When a new machine is added to the network the virus control server assigns an IP address to the device through DHCP. During this period all traffic to and from the newly added computer must pass through the virus control server. After the quarantine is over the device is released to communicate bypassing the virus control server (TRIZ Principle-15: Dynamize).

Annex-1

The 40 Principles for Software/ IT

Principle-1: Segmentation

1.1 Divide a system or object into separate independent parts or sections

1.2 Make a system modular so that it becomes easy to put together and take apart

1.3 Increase the degree of fragmentation or segmentation

Principle-2: Taking out

2.1 Take out the undesired part or harmful function of an object

2.2 Take out the cause or carrier of an undesired property or function

Principle-3: Local Quality

3.1 Change the structure of an object or system or environment from uniform to non-uniform

3.2 If an object or system has multiple functions, change specific parts of the object to achieve efficiency in the corresponding function.

3.3 If an object or system has multiple functions, change specific parts of the object or system to make suitable for specific local conditions.

Principle-4: Asymmetry

4.1 If an object or system is symmetrical make it asymmetrical or introduce lines of asymmetries.

4.2 If an object is already asymmetrical, increase the degree of asymmetry

4.3 Change the shape of an object or system to suite external asymmetries

Principle-5: Merging

5.1. Merge in space- Physically join or merge identical or related objects or operations to work together in space.

5.2 Merge in time- Join or merge objects, operations or functions so that they act contiguously or parallel in time.

5.3. Merge both in space and time- Join or merge objects or functions to act together in both space and time.

Principle-6: Universality

6.1 Make a new object or system that performs multiple functions, thereby eliminating the need for multiple existing systems.

Principle-7: Nested Doll

7.1 Put one object or system inside another

7.2. Allow one object or system to pass through an appropriate hole in another

7.3. Increase the number of nesting, or Use a stacking or cascading arrangement

Principle-8: Counterweight

8.1 Where the weight of an object or system causes problems, combine it with something that provides lift

8.2 Where the weight of an object or system causes problems, make it interact with the environment to get lift

Principle-9: Prior Counteraction

9.1 Where the action causes stresses or harmful effects, introduce anti-actions and beforehand stresses to control the harmful effects.

Principle-10: Prior Action

10.1. Perform a useful action (either fully or partly) before it is needed

10.2 Pre-arrange objects so that they can come into action at the most convenient time and place

Principle-11: Cushioning

11.1 Introduce emergency backups to compensate for the potentially low reliability of an object

Principle-12: Equipotentiality

12.1 If an object or system needs to be lowered or raised, redesign the object's environment to bring balance and compensate that need

Principle-13: Reversing

13.1 Use an opposite or inverse action to solve the problem

13.2 Make movable objects fixed, and fixed objects movable

13.3 Turn the object, system or process 'upside down'

Principle-14: Curvature

14.1 Turn linear parts to curved parts, flat surfaces to spherical surfaces.

14.2 Use rollers, balls, spirals and domes

14.3 Change linear motion to rotary motion

Principle-15: Dynamize

15.1 If an object or system is rigid or inflexible make it movable or flexible.

15.2 Split an object or system into parts those are capable of moving relative to each other.

15.3 Make an object or system to be adaptive (by changing its functionality) to achieve optimal performance under different operational conditions.

Principle-16: Partial or Excessive action

16.1 If it is not possible to do the precise action or achieve the precise result, try to achieve 'slightly less' or 'slightly more' of the action or result.

16.2 If an action is crucial and a partial action can lead to problems, better do more or excessive

16.3 If an action is difficult or expensive, and can be easily done in future, better do it less or partial.

Principle-17: Another Dimension

17.1 If an object moves in a straight line or plane, consider moving outside the line or plane.

17.2 Use "another side" of a given object or system

17.3 Use 'another orientation' or 'layout' of a given object or system

17.4 Use another Method

Principle-18: Vibratation

18.1 Cause an object to oscillate or vibrate

18.2 Increase or change the frequency of vibration

18.3 Make use of an object or system's resonant frequency

Principle-19: Periodic Action

19.1 Replace continuous actions with periodic or pulsating actions

19.2 If an action is already periodic, change the frequency to suite external conditions

19.3 Use gaps between actions to perform other useful actions

Principle-20: Continuity of Useful Action

20.1 Make all parts of an object or system work continuously with full efficiency

20.2 Utilize or eliminate all idle or non-productive space, time and actions

Principle-21: Skipping (Hurry)

21.1 Conduct an action at very high speed to eliminate harmful side effects.

21.2 Skip unwanted steps to gain speed

Principle-22: Turn Harms to Benefits

22.1 Use harmful objects or actions to deliver positive effect

Principle-23: Feedback

23.1 Introduce feedback to improve a process or action

23.2 If feedback is already used, make it adaptable to variations in operating conditions

Principle-24: Intermediary

24.1 Introduce an intermediary between two objects, systems or actions

24.2 Introduce a temporary intermediary that disappears (or can be easily removed) after it has completed its function

Principle-25: Self Service

25.1 Enable an object or system to serve itself by performing installation, configuration, repair, maintenance and all other operations

25.2 Make use of waste materials or unused resources

Principle-26: Copying

26.1 Use simple and inexpensive copies in place of unavailable, expensive, complicated, dangerous or possibly vulnerable objects and systems

26.2 Replace an object, or action with an optical copy, infrared or ultraviolet copies.

26.3 Use virtual copies or simulations of an object or system or function.

Principle-27: Cheap and Disposable

27.1 Replace an expensive object or system with a multitude of inexpensive, short-living objects

Principle-28: Mechanics Substitution

28.1 Replace a mechanical means with a sensory (optical, acoustic, taste, touch or smell) or other (magnetic, electromagnetic, thermal etc.) means.

28.2 Change the internal mechanism, structure, format or code

Principle-29: Pneumatics and Hydraulics

29.1 Use gases and liquids instead of solid parts or components

Principle-30: Thin and Flexible

30.1 Incorporate flexible shells and thin films instead of solid structures.

30.2 Use flexible and thin films to isolate an object or system from its environment.

Principle-31: Hole

31.1 Make an object porous or add porous elements to an object

31.2 If an object is already porous, add something useful into the pores

Principle-32: Color Change

32.1 Change the color of an object, its part or its external environment, which can change the visibility of the object

32.2 Change the transparency of an object or its surroundings

Principle-33: Homogeneity (Compatibility)

33.1 Build interacting objects out of the same material (or materials having matching properties)

Principle-34: Discard and Recover

34.1 Discard the elements of an object or system which have fulfilled their functions

34.2 Restore the exhausted or consumable parts of an object or system during operation

Principle-35: Parameter Change

35.1 Change parameters of an Object or System

Principle-36: State Change and Conversion

36.1 Change the state of a file, program, data or device in order to get an useful effect

36.2 Convert an incompatible or unusable data, file, format or technology to a compatible and usable data, file, format or technology.

36.3 Migrate from old incompatible data, format or technology to compatible data, format or technology.

Principle-37: Expansion

37.1 Use expansion (or compression) of an object or component to achieve useful effect

Principle-38: Enrich/ Improve Quality

38.1 Replace an object or system with an updated or advanced object or system

38.2 Add special features or functions to improve an object or system

Principle-39: Calm (Inert Atmosphere)

39.1 Replace a normal environment with an inert one

39.2 Add neutral parts, or inert elements to an object or system

Principle-40: Composite

40.1 Use composite (or multiple) materials instead of uniform (or singular) ones.

Annex-2

List of Patents Cited

Sl	Patent Titles	Inventors	Patent details
1.	Method for recovery of a computer program infected by a computer virus	Mann, et al.	Patent 5408642, Assignee- Symantec Corporation, April 1995
2.	Automatic immune system for computers and computer networks	Arnold et al.	Patent 5440723, Assignee- IBM, Aug 1995.
3.	Methods and apparatus for evaluating and extracting signatures of computer viruses and other undesirable software entities	Kephart	Patent 5452442, Assignee- IBM, Sept 1995
4.	Software anti-virus facility	Jonathan Lettvin	US Patent 5559960, Sept 1996.
5.	Generic disinfection of programs infected with a computer virus	Kephart et al.	US Patent 5613002, Assignee- IBM, March 1997.
6.	Adaptive statistical regression and classification of data strings, with application to the generic detection of computer viruses	Kephart et al.	US Patent 5675711, Assignee- IBM, Oct 1997.
7.	Method and apparatus for detecting a computer virus on a computer	Ellenberger	US Patent 5684875, Nov 1997.
8.	Polymorphic virus detection module	Nachenberg	US Patent 5696822, assignee- Symantec Corporation, Dec 1997.
9.	Processor emulator module having a variable pre-fetch queue size for program execution	Nachenberg et al.	US Patent 5765030, Assignee- NIL, Jun 1998

Sl	Patent Titles	Inventors	Patent details
10.	Virus protection in computer systems	Cowlard	US Patent 5802277, Sept 1998.
11.	Boot-time anti-virus and maintenance facility	Jonathan Lettvin	US Patent 5826012, Oct 1998.
12.	Polymorphic virus detection module	by Nachenberg	US Patent 5826013, Assignee-Symantec Corporation, Oct 1998
13.	Anti-virus agent for use with databases and mail servers	Chen et al.	US Patent 5832208, Assignee-Software International, Nov 1998.
14.	Computer virus trap	Schnurer et al.	US Patent 5842002, Assignee-Quantum Leap Innovations, Nov 1998.
15.	System for creating virus diagnosing mechanism, method of creating the same, virus diagnosing apparatus and method therefor	Yamamoto	US Patent 5881151, Assignee-Fujitsu Limited, March 1999.
16.	Apparatus and method for electronic mail virus detection and elimination	Ji et al.,	US Patent 5889943, Assignee-Trend Micro Incorporated, March 1999.
17.	Method and apparatus for detecting a presence of a computer virus	Kephart, et al.,	US Patent 5907834,Assignee-IBM, May 1999.
18.	System, Apparatus and Method for the Detection and Removal of Viruses in Macros	Chen, et al.,	US Patent 5951698, Assignee-, March 1997.
19.	Method and apparatus for protecting data files on a computer from virus infection	Walsh, et al.,	US Patent 5956481, Assignee-Microsoft Corporation, Sep 1999
20.	Method to analyze a program for presence of computer viruses by examining the opcode for faults before emulating instruction in emulator	Nachenberg et al.	US Patent 5964889, Assignee-Symantec Corporation, Oct 1999.
21.	Computer virus screening methods and systems	Franczek, et al.	US Patent 5987610, Assignee-Ameritech Corporation, Nov 1999

Sl	Patent Titles	Inventors	Patent details
22.	Method for protecting executable software programs against infection by software viruses	Eyal Dotan	US Patent 6073239, Assignee-In-defense Inc., June 2000.
23.	System for virus-checking network data during download to a client device	Tso, et al.	US Patent 6088803, Assignee-Intel Corporation, July 2000.
24.	Method and apparatus for controlling access to and corruption of information in a computer	White et al	US Patent 6092161, Assignee-Arendee Limited, July 2000.
25.	Antivirus accelerator for computer networks	Waldin et. al.	US Patent 6094731, Assignee-Symantec Corporation, July 2000.
26.	Computer security using virus probing	Grosse	US Patent 6205551, Assignee-Lucent Technologies, March 2001
27.	Method of treating whitespace during virus detection	Kuo et al.,	US Patent 6230288, Assignee-Network Associates, May 2001
28.	Virus extermination method, information processing apparatus and computer-readable recording medium with virus extermination program recorded thereon	Togawa	US Patent 6240530, Assignee-Fujitsu Limited, May 2001.
29.	Method and system for providing automated updating and upgrading of antivirus applications using a computer network	Hodges et al.,	US Patent 6269456, Assignee-Network Associates, Inc., July 2001.
30.	Method and apparatus for computer virus detection, analysis, and removal in real time	Wells	US Patent 6338141, Assignee-CyberSoft, Jan 2002.
31.	Apparatus and method for remote virus diagnosis and repair	Reinert et al.,	US Patent 6347375, Assignee-Ontrack Data International, Feb 2002
32.	Dynamic heuristic method for detecting computer viruses using decryption exploration and evaluation phases	Nachenberg	US Patent 6357008, Assignee-Symantec Corporation, March 2002

Sl	Patent Titles	Inventors	Patent details
33.	Computer virus screening methods and systems	Franczek et al.	US Patent 6397335, Assignee-Ameritech Corporation, May 2002
34.	Method of managing computer virus infected files	Templeton	US Patent 6401210, Assignee-Intel Corporation, June 2002
35.	Computer systems	White et. Al,	US Patent 6526488, Assignee-Arendee Limited, Feb 2003
36.	BIOS-level floppy boot-sector virus prevention	Baxter, et al.,	US Patent 6550007, Assignee-Dell USA, April 2003
37.	Computer virus screening	Hypponen	US Patent 6577920, Assignee-Data Fellows Oyj, June 2003
38.	Method and apparatus for restoring data damaged by a computer virus on a magnetic information recording disk in a hard disk drive	Nam	US Patent 6584583, Assignee-Samsung Electronics, June 2003
39.	System and method for efficiently managing computer virus definitions using a structured virus database	Kouznetsov et al.,	US Patent 6622150, Assignee-Networks Associates Technology, September 2003
40.	Method and apparatus for detecting a macro computer virus using static analysis	Ko,	US Patent 6697950, Assignee-Networks Associates Technology, Feb 2004
41.	Method and system for protecting a computer using a remote e-mail scanning device	Kim et al	US Patent 6701440, Assignee-Networks Associates Technology, March 2004
42.	System and method for executing computer virus definitions containing general purpose programming language extensions	Pak et al.,	US Patent 6718469, Assignee-Networks Associates Technology, April 2004
43.	Virus checking and reporting for computer database search results	Bates et al.,	US Patent 6721721, Assignee-International Business Machines Corporation, April 2004
44.	Distributed virus scanning arrangements and methods therefore	Ji et al.,	US Patent 6728886, Assignee-Trend Micro Incorporated, April 2004
45.	E-mail virus detection utility	David Marsh	US Patent 6763462, Assignee-Micron Technology, July 2004

Sl	Patent Titles	Inventors	Patent details
46.	Fast virus scanning	Glover	US Patent 6763466, Assignee-Networks Associates Technology, July 2004
47.	Web server apparatus and method for virus checking	Bates et al.,	US Patent 6785732, Assignee-International Business Machines Corporation, Aug 2004
48.	Anti-virus toolbar system and method for use with a network browser	Inventor-Barton et al.,	US Patent 6789201, Assignee-Networks Associates Technology, Aug 2004
49.	Computer virus detection and removal	Ruff et al.,	US Patent 6802028, Assignee-PowerQuest Corporation, Oct 2004
50.	Viral replication detection using a counter virus	Luke	US Patent 6813712, Assignee-International Business Machines Corporation, Nov 2004
51.	Method and system for detecting viruses on handheld computers	Cox, et al.,	US Patent 6842861, Assignee-Networks Associates Technology, Jan 2005
52.	Computer virus detection	Smithson, et al.,	US Patent 6886099, Assignee-Networks Associates Technology, Apr 2005
53.	Test driver ordering	Vignoles, et al.,	US Patent 6898712, Assignee-Networks Associates Technology, May 2005
54.	Response to a computer virus outbreak	Smithson, et al.,	US Patent 6898715, Assignee-Networks Associates Technology, May 2005
55.	Extensible firmware interface virus scan	Huntington, et al.,	US Patent 6907524, Assignee-Phoenix Technologies Ltd., June 2005
56.	Method and apparatus for minimizing file scanning by anti-virus programs	Drew	US Patent 6928555, Assignee-Networks Associates Technology, Aug 2005. (continued later in patent 7441274, Oct 2008)
57.	System, method and computer program product for selecting virus detection actions based on a process by which files are being accessed	Edwards et al.,	US Patent 6931540, Assignee-Networks Associates Technology, Aug 2005

Sl	Patent Titles	Inventors	Patent details
58.	Apparatus and method for protecting a computer system against computer viruses and unauthorized access	Pritchard, et al.	US Patent 6931552, Aug 2005
59.	Test driver selection	Vignoles et al.,	US Patent 6938161, Assignee-Networks Associates Technology, Aug 2005
60.	"Method and apparatus for increasing virus detection speed using a database	Chess	US Patent 6952776, Assignee-International Business Machines Corporation, Oct 2005
61.	Distributed system and method for conducting a comprehensive search for malicious code in software	Muttik et al.,	US Patent 6963978, Assignee-McAfee, Nov 2005
62.	Providing break points in a malware scanning operation	- Lucas, et al.	US Patent 6968461, Assignee-Networks Associates Technology, Nov 2005
63.	Histogram-based virus detection	Nachenberg	US Patent 6971019, Assignee-Symantec Corporation, Nov 2005
64.	System and method for dynamically detecting computer viruses through associative behavioral analysis of runtime state	Kouznetsov,	US Patent 6973577, Assignee-McAfee, Dec 2005
65.	Tree pattern system and method for multiple virus signature recognition	Hursey, et al.,	US Patent 6980992, Assignee-McAfee, Dec 2005
66.	System and method for network virus protection	Yanovsky	US Patent 7010807, Assignee-SonicWALL, March 2006
67.	Remote computer virus scanning	Albrecht,	US Patent 7020895, Assignee-F-Secure Oyj, Mar 2006
68.	System, method and computer program product for eliminating disk read time during virus scanning	Hursey,	US Patent 7036147, Assignee-McAfee, April 2006

Sl	Patent Titles	Inventors	Patent details
69.	Detecting malicious alteration of stored computer files	Wolff, et al.,	US Patent 7043634, Assignee- McAfee, May 2006
70.	Virus epidemic damage control system and method for network environment	Liang,	US Patent 7062553, Assignee- Trend Micro, June 2006
71.	Detection of a class of viral code	Schmall, et al.,	US Patent 7069589, Assignee- Computer Associates Think, Inc., Jun 2006
72.	Method and apparatus for the detection, notification, and elimination of certain computer viruses on a network using a promiscuous system as bait	Chefalas et al.,	US Patent 7089589, Assignee- Lenovo (Singapore) Pte. Ltd., Aug 2006
73.	Generic detection and elimination of marco viruses	Chi	US Patent 7089591, Assignee- Symantec Corporation, Aug 2006
74.	Software virus detection methods and apparatus	Radatti , et al.	US Patent 7093135, assignee CyberSoft, Inc., Aug 2006
75.	Computer virus detection	Inventor- Smithson et al,	US Patent 7093293, Assignee- McAfee, Aug 2006
76.	Computer virus Virus checking and reporting for computer database search results	Bates et al.,	US Patent 7096215, Assignee- International Business Machines Corporation, Aug 2006
77.	System and method for certifying that data received over a computer network has been checked for viruses	Gordon et al,	US Patent 7107618, Assignee- McAfee, Sep 2006
78.	Identifying malware containing computer files using embedded text	Moore, et al.,	US Patent 7114185, Assignee- McAfee Inc.., Sep 2006
79.	Detecting dissemination of malicious programs	Jeffries et al,	US Patent 7140041, Assignee- International Business Machines Corporation, Nov 2006
80.	Network anti-virus System	Loukas	US Patent 7152164, Assignee-Nil, Dec 2006
81.	Network anti-virus System	Loukas,	US Patent 7152164, Assignee-Nil, Dec 2006

Sl	Patent Titles	Inventors	Patent details
82.	Information processing system	Miyata, et al.,	US Patent 7155461, Assignee- Hitachi Ltd. (Japan), Dec 2006
83.	Web server apparatus and method for virus checking	Bates, et al.	US Patent 7177937, Assignee- IBM, Feb 2007
84.	Self-destructing document and e-mail messaging system	Udell, et al.,	US Patent 7191219, Assignee- Clarios Corporation, March 2007
85.	Anti-virus method and system guaranteeing a maximum delay for streaming data	Painter	US Patent 7203960, Assignee- Trend Micro, Inc, Apr 2007
86.	Safely restoring previously un-backed up data during system restore of a failing system	Childs, et al.,	US Patent 7222143, Assignee- Lenovo (Singapore) Pte Ltd., May 2007
87.	Event reporting between a reporting computer and a receiving computer	Wolff, et al.,	US Patent 7228565, Assignee- McAfee, Inc. Jun 2007
88.	System and method for computer virus detection utilizing heuristic analysis	Jordan.,	US Patent 7231667, Assignee- Computer Associates Think, Inc.. Jun 2007
89.	Automatic builder of detection and cleaning routines for computer viruses	Teblyashkin et al.,	US Patent 7234167, Assignee- McAfee, Inc., Jun 2007
90.	Input and output control means for computer system storage and a software execution method using same	Kuniyasu Suzaki	US Patent 7240239, Assignee- National Institute of Advanced Industrial Science and Technology (JP), Jul 2007
91.	On-access malware scanning	Muttik, et al.,	US Patent 7243373, Assignee- McAfee, Inc., Jul 2007
92.	Process-based selection of virus detection actions system, method and computer program product	Melchione	US Patent 7251830, Assignee- McAfee, Inc., Jul 2007
93.	Pre-approval of computer files during a malware detection	Barton, et al.,	US Patent 7257842, Assignee- McAfee Inc.., Aug 2007
94.	Virus detection system	Carmona , et al.,	US Patent 7260725, Assignee- Computer Associates Think, Inc., Aug 2007

Sl	Patent Titles	Inventors	Patent details
95.	Systems and methods for making electronic files that have been converted to a safe format available for viewing by an intended recipient	Green, et al.,	US Patent 7263561, Assignee- McAfee, Inc., Aug 2007
96.	Heuristic detection of polymorphic computer viruses based on redundancy in viral code	Teblyashkin et al.,	US Patent 7266844, Assignee- McAfee, Inc., Sep 2007
97.	Managing malware protection upon a computer network	Ackroyd.,	US Patent 7269851, Assignee- McAfee Inc.., Sep 2007
98.	Method of hindering the propagation of a computer virus	Norman	US Patent 7278019, Assignee- Hewlett-Packard Development Company, L.P., Oct 2007.
99.	Software audit system	Tarbotton et al.,	US Patent 7281267, Assignee- McAfee, Inc., Oct 2007
100.	Fuzzy scanning system and method	Peter Szor,	US Patent 7284273, Assignee- Symantec Corporation, Oct 2007
101.	Reducing false positive computer virus detections	Renert, et al.,	US Patent 7290282, Assignee- Symantec Corporation, Oct 2007
102.	Preventing virus infection in a computer system	Lahti, et al.,	US Patent 7293177, Assignee- F-Secure OYJ, Nov 2007
103.	Remote e-mail scanning system and method	Kim, et al.,	US Patent 7299361, Assignee- McAfee, Inc., Nov 2007
104.	Mechanisms for banning computer programs from u	Tarbotton, et al.,	US Patent 7302584, "se", Assignee- McAfee, Inc., Nov 2007
105.	System and method for tracking computer viruses	Parish, et al.,	US Patent 7310818, Assignee- McAfee, Inc., Dec 2007
106.	System, method and computer program product for precluding writes to critical files	Tarbotton, et al.,	US Patent 7340775, Assignee- McAfee, Inc., Mar 2008
107.	Polled automatic virus fix	Cheston, et al.,	US Patent 7353428, Assignee- Lenovo Singapore Pte. Ltd., Apr 2008
108.	Simulated computer system for monitoring of software performance	Natvig	US Patent 7356736, Assignee- Norman Asa., Apr 2008, continued in 8069372, Nov 2011

Sl	Patent Titles	Inventors	Patent details
109.	System and method for proactive computer virus protection	Marinescu	US Patent 7376970, Assignee- Microsoft Corporation, May 2008 (This patent is continued in patent 7877802, Jan 2011.)
110.	Defense against virus attacks	Jindal et.al.,	US Patent 7376977, Assignee- Lucent Technologies Inc.., May 2008
111.	Systems and methods for determining anti-virus protection status	Catanzano,	US Patent 7383579, Assignee- AT&T Delaware Intellectual Property, Inc., Jun 2008
112.	Restoration of data corrupted by viruses using pre-infected copy of data	Bucher,	US Patent 7392542, Assignee- Seagate Technology LLC, Jun 2008
113.	Method and system for anti-malware scanning with variable scan settings	Pavlyushchik	US Patent 7392544, Assignee- Kaspersky Lab, ZAO, June 2008, (the patent was continued in patent 7725941 granted later in May 2010)
114.	Apparatus, methods and computer programs for controlling performance of operations within a data processing system or network	Palliyil, et al.,	US Patent 7398399, Assignee- International Business Machines Corporation, Jul 2008
115.	System and method for reducing virus scan time	Freeman, et al.,	US Patent 7401361, Assignee- Lenovo (Singapore) Pte. Ltd., Jul 2008
116.	Metamorphic computer virus detection	Peter Szor,	US Patent 7409717, Assignee- Symantec Corporation, Aug 2008
117.	Virus prediction system and method	Cambridge, et al.,	US Patent 7409720, Assignee- McAfee, Inc., Aug 2008
118.	Heuristic detection of malicious computer code by page tracking	Peter Szor,	US Patent 7418729, Assignee- Symantec Corporation, Aug 2008
119.	Network switches for detection and prevention of virus attacks	Campbell, et al.,	US Patent 7418732, Assignee- Microsoft Corporation, Aug 2008
120.	Anti-virus fix for intermittently connected client computers	Cheston, et al.,	US Patent 7424745, Assignee- Lenovo (Singapore) Pte. Ltd., Sep 2008

Sl	Patent Titles	Inventors	Patent details
121.	Virus scanner system and method with integrated spyware detection capabilities	Edwards, et al.,	US Patent 7441273, Assignee- McAfee, Inc., Oct 2008
122.	System and method for providing passive screening of transient messages in a distributed computing environment	Libenzi, et al.,	US Patent 7461403, Assignee- McAfee, Inc., Dec 2008
123.	Heuristic detection of computer viruses	Nachenberg	US Patent 7478431, Assignee- Symantec Corporation, Jan 2009
124.	Temporal access control for computer virus prevention	Nachenberg et al.,	US Patent 7483993, Assignee- Symantec Corporation, Jan 2009
125.	Apparatus, method, and system for virus detection	Nagoya, et al.,	US Patent 7484244, Assignee- Duaxes Corporation(JP), Jan 2009
126.	Virtualized protective communications system	Bantz, et al.,	US Patent 7493654, Assignee- International Business Machines Corporation, Feb 2009
127.	Tracking and reporting of computer virus information	Chen, et al.,	US Patent 7496960, Assignee- Trend Micro, Inc. (JP), Feb 2009
128.	Anti-computer viral agent suitable for innoculation of computing devices	Liang,	US Patent 7512808, Assignee- Trend Micro, Inc. (JP), Mar 2009
129.	Computer virus generation detection apparatus and method	Takahashi,	US Patent 7512982, Assignee- Kabushiki Kaisha Toshiba (JP), Mar 2009
130.	Anti-virus protection at a network gateway	Lahti,	US Patent 7516489, Assignee- F-Secure Oyj, Apr 2009
131.	Method of and system for heuristically detecting viruses in executable code	Alexander Shipp,	US Patent 7519997, Assignee- Messagelabs Limited, Apr 2009
132.	Authenticating without opening electronic mail	Bickford, et al.,	US Patent 7523496, Assignee- International Business Machines, Apr 2009
133.	Method and system for detecting a secure state of a computer system	Charbonneau,	US Patent 7526654, Assignee- Nil, Apr 2009

Sl	Patent Titles	Inventors	Patent details
134.	System and method for certifying that data received over a computer network has been checked for viruses	Gordon, et al,	US Patent 7533272, Assignee- McAfee, Inc., May 2009
135.	Pre-boot firmware based virus scanner	Zimmer, et al,	US Patent 7549055, Assignee- Intel Corporation, Jun 2009
136.	System and method for reducing the vulnerability of a computer network to virus threats	Bascle, et al.,	US Patent 7571483, Assignee- Lockheed Martin Corporation, Aug 2009
137.	System, computer program product and method of selecting sectors of a hard disk on which to perform a virus scan	Sitze,	US Patent 7581250, Assignee- Lenovo (Singapore) PTE Ltd, Aug 2009
138.	Storage conversion for anti-virus speed-up	Challener, et al.,	US Patent 7581252, Assignee- Lenovo (Singapore) PTE Ltd, Aug 2009
139.	Secure storage tracking for anti-virus speed-up	Challener, et al.,	US Patent 7581253, Assignee- Lenovo (Singapore) PTE Ltd, Aug 2009
140.	Virus scanner system and method with integrated spyware detection capabilities	Inventor- Edwards, et al.,	US Patent 7581254, Assignee- McAfee, Inc., Aug 2009
141.	Automatic virus fix	Challener, et al.,	US Patent 7587765, Assignee- International Business Machines Corporation, Sep 2009
142.	Method and apparatus for tracking boot history	Challener, et al.,	US Patent 7590834, Assignee- Lenovo Singapore Pte. Ltd, Sep 2009
143.	System, apparatuses, methods and computer-readable media for determining the security status of a computer before establishing a network connection	David Shay,	US Patent 7591001, Assignee- Liquidware Labs, Inc., Sep 2009
144.	Portable antivirus device with solid state memory	Andrew Lee,	US Patent 7591018, Assignee- Trend Micro Incorporated., Sep 2009
145.	Method and system for detecting infection of an operating system	Beck et al.,	US Patent 7627898, Assignee- Microsoft Corporation, Dec 2009

Sl	Patent Titles	Inventors	Patent details
146.	Detection of polymorphic script language viruses by data driven lexical analysis	Chandnani, et al.,	US Patent 7636945, Assignee- Computer Associates Think., Dec 2009
147.	Systems and methods for converting infected electronic files to a safe format	Green, et al.,	US Patent 7640361, Assignee- McAfee, Inc., Dec 2009
148.	Method and system for protecting anti-malware programs	Marinescu et al.,	US Patent 7640583, Assignee- Microsoft Corporation, Dec 2009
149.	Content scanning of copied data	Grupe,	US Patent 7644352, Assignee- McAfee, Inc., Jan 2010
150.	Hardware-based anti-virus system	Zaitsev,	US Patent 7657941, Assignee- Kaspersky Lab., Feb 2010
151.	Method of, and system for, heuristically detecting viruses in executable code	Alexander Shipp	US Patent 7664754, Assignee- Symantec Corporation, Feb 2010
152.	Network security system with automatic vulnerability tracking and clean-up mechanisms	Simon Ko,	US Patent 7690038, Assignee- Trend Micro Incorporated, Mar 2010
153.	Communications traffic segregation for security purposes	Shelest et al.,	US Patent 7698548, Assignee- Microsoft Corporation, Apr 2010
154.	Systems and methods for determining anti-virus protection status	Catanzano,	US Patent 7707636, Assignee- AT&T Intellectual Property, Apr. 2010
155.	Apparatus, methods and articles of manufacture for computer virus testing	Radatti, et al,	US Patent 7716736, Assignee- Cybersoft, Inc., May. 2010
156.	Method and system for offloading real-time virus scanning during data transfer to storage peripherals	Forman, et al,	US Patent 7716741, Assignee- IBM, May. 2010
157.	Emulation system, method and computer program product for malware detection by back-stepping in program code	Muttik et al.	US Patent 7739100, Assignee- McAfee, Inc., Jun 2010
158.	Method and apparatus to detect malicious software	Christodorescu et al.,	US Patent 7739737, Assignee- Wisconsin Alumni Research Foundation., Jun 2010

Sl	Patent Titles	Inventors	Patent details
159.	Method and system for detection and prediction of computer virus-related epidemics	Mashevsky et al.	US Patent 7743419, Assignee-Kaspersky Lab, ZAO., Jun 2010
160.	Method and apparatus for managing computer virus outbreaks	Olivier, et al,	US Patent 7748038, Assignee-IronPort Systems, Jun 2010
161.	Method and apparatus for reducing e-mail spam and virus distribution in a communications network by authenticating the origin of e-mail messages	Faynberg, et al,	US Patent 7752440, Assignee-Alcatel-Lucent USA Inc, Jul 2010
162.	Rapid virus scan using file signature created during file write	Challener et al.,	US Patent 7752667, Assignee-Lenovo (Singapore) Pte Ltd., Jul 2010
163.	Reducing false positive computer virus detections	Renert, et al,	US Patent 7757292, Assignee-Symantec Corporation, Jul 2010
164.	Method and system for delayed write scanning for detecting computer malwares	Edwards, et al,	US Patent 7757361, Assignee-McAfee, Inc., Jul 2010
165.	Computer virus screening methods and systems	Franczek, et al,	US Patent 7774840, Assignee-NIL, Aug 2010
166.	Virus detection in a network	Garbow, et al,	US Patent 7779474, Assignee-Trend Micro Incorporated, Aug 2010
167.	Outgoing connection attempt limiting to slow down spreading of viruses	Kaniyar et al.,	US Patent 7784096, Assignee-Microsoft Corporation, Aug 2010
168.	Computer virus check method in a storage system	Nakatsuka, et al,	US Patent 7788488, Assignee-Hitachi, Ltd, Aug 2010
169.	Detection of undesired computer files in archives	Fossen, et al,	US Patent 7797746, Assignee-Fortinet, Inc., Sep 2010
170.	Method and apparatus for detecting and removing kernel rootkits	Liu, et al,	US Patent 7802300, Assignee-Trend Micro Incorporated., Sep 2010
171.	Single scan for a base machine and all associated virtual machines	Nagarkar, et al,	US Patent 7802302, Assignee-Symantec Corporation., Sep 2010

Sl	Patent Titles	Inventors	Patent details
172.	Computer virus and malware cleaner	Nason, et al,	US Patent 7836500, Assignee-eAcceleration Corporation., Nov 2010
173.	Detecting compromised computers by correlating reputation data with web access logs	Neystadt, et al.	US Patent 7882542, Assignee-Microsoft, Feb 2011
174.	Virus immunization using entity-sponsored bypass network	Inventor-Jung, et al,	US Patent 7849508, Assignee-The Invention Science Fund I, LLC, Dec 2010
-	Multi-network virus immunization	Jung et al.,	Patent 7917956, Assignee-The Invention Science Fund I, LLC, March 2011
-	Virus immunization using entity-sponsored bypass network	Jung et al.,	Patent 7,934,260, Assignee-The Invention Science Fund I, LLC, April 2011
-	Multi-network virus immunization with separate physical path	Jung et al	Patent 8146161, Assignee-The Invention Science Fund I, LLC, March 2012
-	Multi-network virus immunization with trust aspects	Jung et al	Patent 8151353., -do-, Apr 2012
175.	Identifying threats in electronic messages	Sprosts, et al,	US Patent 7854007, Assignee-Ironport Systems, Inc., Dec 2010
176.	Web server apparatus and method for virus checking	Bates, et al,	US Patent 7895340, Assignee-Trend Micro Incorporated, Feb 2011
177.	Image forming apparatus and control method thereof	Ouchi,	US Patent 7895658, Assignee-Kabushiki Kaisha Toshiba, Feb 2011
178.	Temporal access control for computer virus prevention	Nachenberg et al.,	US Patent 7904573, Assignee-Symantec Corporation, March 2011
179.	Computer network virus protection system and method	Stewart et al.,	US Patent 7913078, Assignee-NIL, Mar 2011
180.	Multi-partition USB device that re-boots a PC to an alternate operating system for virus recovery	Chow et al.,	US Patent 7930531, Assignee-Super Talent Electronics, Inc.., Apr, 2011

Sl	Patent Titles	Inventors	Patent details
181.	On-demand cleanup system	Saguiguit et al.,	US Patent 7934261, Assignee- Trend Micro, Inc., Apr, 2011
182.	Metamorphic computer virus detection	Peter Szor,	US Patent 7937764, Assignee- Symantec Corporation, May, 2011
183.	Enhanced malware detection utilizing transparently integrated searching	Chung et al.	US Patent 7953984, Assignee- Trend Micro Incorporated, May 2011
184.	Computer resource optimization during malware detection using antivirus cache	Batenin	US Patent 7962959, Assignee- Kaspersky Lab ZAO, Jun 2011
185.	Method, system and program product for maximizing virus check coverage while minimizing redundancy in virus checking	Ramer,	US Patent 7979904, Assignee- International Business Machines Corporation, Jul 2011
186.	Pre-scanner for inspecting network traffic for computer viruses	Painter, et al.,	US Patent 7992206, Assignee- Trend Micro Incorporated, Aug, 2011
187.	Hypervisor area for email virus testing	O'Sullivan, et al.,	US Patent 7996901, Assignee- Lenovo (Singapore) Pte. Ltd., Aug, 2011
188.	System and method for certifying that data received over a computer network has been checked for viruses	Gordon et al,	US Patent 7996902, Assignee- McAfee, Aug 2011
189.	Pre-boot firmware based virus scanner	Zimmer, et al,	US Patent 8010799, Assignee- Intel Corporation, Aug 2011
190.	Discerning use of signatures by third party vendors	Isenberg et al.,	US Patent 8015284, Assignee- Symantec Corporation, Sep 2011
191.	Deriving reputation scores for web sites that accept personally identifiable information	Nachenberg	US Patent 8019689, Assignee- Symantec Corporation, Sep 2011
192.	Containment mechanism for potentially contaminated end systems	Chow et al.	US Patent 8020207, Assignee- ALCATEL LUCENT, Sep 2011
193.	Modeling goodware characteristics to reduce false positive malware signatures	Schneider, et. al.	Patent 8028338, assignee Symantec corporation, Sep 2011

Sl	Patent Titles	Inventors	Patent details
194.	Protecting computers from viruses in peer-to-peer data transfers	Yao, et al,	US Patent 8056133, Assignee- Trend Micro Incorporated, Nov 2011.
195.	System and method for detection of malware and management of malware-related information	Zaitsev,	US Patent 8056136, Assignee- Kaspersky Lab Zao, Sep 2011
196.	Anti-malware scanning in a virtualized file system environment	Sobel et al,	US Patent 8065730, Assignee- Symantec Corporation, Nov 2011
197.	Detection of undesired computer files in archives	Fossen et al.,	US Patent 8074280, Assignee- Fortinet, Inc., Dec, 2011 (Also patent 8,151,355,, April 2012. Patent 8,166,550, Apr 2012)
198.	Virus co-processor instructions and methods for using such	Huang, et al.,	US Patent 8079084, Assignee- Fortinet, Inc., Dec, 2011
199.	Heuristic malware detection	Bradicich et al,	US Patent 8091127, Assignee- International Business Machines Corporation, Jan 2012
200.	System and method for autonomic peer-to-peer virus inoculation	Benton, et al.,	US Patent 8091134, Assignee- Lenovo (Singapore) Pte. Ltd., Jan, 2012
201.	Behavioral detection based on uninstaller modification or removal	Chen et al,	US Patent 8099784, Assignee- Symantec Corporation, Jan 2012
202.	Trusted operating environment for malware detection	Khilnani et al,	US Patent 8104088, Assignee- Microsoft Corporation, Jan 2012, later Continued in patent 8230511, July 2012.
203.	System, method and program product for detecting unknown computer attacks	Thiele, et al.	Patent 8127356, assignee- IBM, Feb 2012
204.	Anti-virus method based on security chip	Li, et al.,	US Patent 8132257, Assignee- Lenovo (Beijing) Limited, Mar, 2012
205.	Security system for computers	Chouery,	US Patent 8151073, Assignee- FAC Systems Inc., Apr, 2012
206.	Bottom-up analysis of network sites	Stokes et al,	US Patent 8161130, Assignee- Microsoft Corporation, Apr 2012

Sl	Patent Titles	Inventors	Patent details
207.	Computer system and method for scanning computer virus	Saika,	US Patent 8166548, Assignee-Hitachi, Ltd., Apr 2012
208.	Simultaneous execution of multiple anti-virus programs	Chang	US Patent 8171552, Assignee-Trend Micro, Inc., May 2012
209.	Malware detection system and method	Chow et al.,	US Patent 8181249, Assignee-Alcatel Lucent, May 2012
210.	Virus localization using cryptographic hashing	Di Crescenzo et al.,	US Patent 8191146, Assignee-TTI Inventions C LLC., May, 2012
211.	Computer program with built-in malware protection	Yue et. al.,	Patent 8195953, assignee Trend Micro, Inc., Jun 2012
212.	Heuristic detection malicious code blacklist updating and protection system and method	Peterson, et al.,	US Patent 8225405, Assignee-Symantec Corporation, Jul, 2012
213.	Reducing malware signature set size through server-side processing	Nachenberg et al.	US Patent 8239944, Assignee-Nachenberg, Aug 2012
214.	Network based virus control	Zahra et al.,	US Patent 8245294, Assignee-Avaya, Inc., Aug 2012
215.	Method and data processing system to prevent manipulation of computer systems	Gellerich,	US Patent 8239959, Assignee-International Business Machines Corporation, Aug, 2012
216.	Rapid heuristic method and system for recognition of similarity between malware variants	Malanov et al.,	US Patent 8250655, Assignee-Kaspersky Lab, ZAO, Aug, 2012
217.	Selecting malware signatures to reduce false-positive detections	Griffin, et al.,	Patent 8239948, assignee-Symantec Corporation, Aug 2012
218.	On Demand Virus Scan	Amundsen	US Patent application 20080141375, June 2008,
219.	Virus resistant computer with data interface for filtering data	Lawrence Kates	US patent application 20090183253, July 2009
220.	Method for upgrading anti-virus software and terminal and system thereof	Wanchun Zhang,	Patent application 20100132042, May 2010

Bibliography

1. Altshuller G., "Creativity as an Exact Science: The Theory of the Solutions of Inventive Problems", Gordon & Breach Publishers, 1988.
2. Altshuller G., And Suddenly the Inventor Appeared. Translated by Lev Shulyak, Technical Information Center, USA. 1996.
3. Altshuller G., Forty Principles, Translated by Lev Shulyak. Technical Innovation Center, Worcester, MA. 1998
4. Yuri Salamatov, "TRIZ: The right solution at the right time", Translated by Maria Stragaia and Sergei Yakovlev, 1999
5. Savransky, S. D, "The Engineering of Creativity", CRC Press, 2000
6. Umakant Mishra, "Improving Graphical User Interface using TRIZ", pothi.com, 2009
7. Umakant Mishra, "TRIZ Principles for Invormation Technology", https://www.createspace.com/3981801, Revised and Enlarged Edition, 2010
8. Vladimir Petrov, "Logic of ARIZ", TRIZJournal, Nov 2005, http://www.triz-journal.com/archives/2005/11/09.pdf
9. Vladimir Petrov (edited), "System of Standard Inventive Solutions"
10. Darrell Mann, "Hands on Systematic Innovation", by CREAX press
11. S.D. Savransky "A few words about the Altshuller's contradiction matrix " TRIZ-Journal, August 1997
12. Articles on TRIZJournal, www.trizjournal.com
13. Articles on TRIZsite journal, www.trizsite.tk/trizsite/articles
14. Ideation International, "TRIZ- Roots, Structure and Theoritical Base", 2005, http://www.ideationtriz.com/new/materials/TbTRIZRootsStructureTheoreticalBase.pdf
15. Frans Veldman, "Heuristic Anti-Virus Technology", http://mirror.sweon.net/madchat/vxdevl/vdat/epheurs1.htm

16. Babak Bashari Rad, Maslin Masrom and Suhaimi Ibrahim, "Evolution of Computer Virus Concealment and Anti-Virus Techniques- A short Survey", International Journal of Computer Science Issues, Vol 8, Jan 2011

17. Peter Szor, Peter Ferrie, "Hunting for Metamorphic", Symantec Security Response., http://enterprisesecurity.symantec.com/PDF/metamorphic.pdf

18. Peter Szor, The Art of Computer Virus Research and Defense, http://computervirus.uw.hu/index.html (online html)

19. Peter Szor, articles on computer viruses, http://www.peterszor.com/virusresearcharticles.html

20. CARO Naming Scheme, http://www.caro.org/naming/scheme.html

21. CW Sandbox, "Behavior Based Malware Analysis", http://mwanalysis.org/

22. The CERIAS Intrusion Detection Research Group, "Digging for Worms, Fishing for Answers", http://www.acsac.org/2002/papers/68.pdf

23. John Aycock and Alana Maurusat, "Future threats", http://ssrn.com/abstract=1412008

24. European Institute for Computer Antivirus Research website, http://www.eicar.org

25. F-secure weblog archieves, http://www.f-secure.com/weblog/archives/

26. Knowledge base, Sophos Anti-virus, http://www.sophos.com/en-us/support/knowledgebase

27. Jieh-Sheng Lee, Jieh Hsiang, and Po-Hao Tsang, "A Generic Virus Detection Agent on the Internet", 1997, IEEE, 30th Annual Hawaii International Conference on System Sciences, vol. 4.

28. Performance test reports of various popular anti-virus programs at http://www.av-comparatives.org,

29. Security articles at SANS intitute website, http://www.sans.org/reading_room/whitepapers/malicious/

30. Symantec Security articles on Symantec website, www.symantec.com/connect/security/articles

31. Virus and threat descriptions at f-secure, http://www.f-secure.com/v-descs/, http://www.f-secure.com/en/web/labs_global/threats/descriptions

32. VLAD (Virus Labs and Distribution) website, www.wiw.org/~meta/vlad.php

33. Proceedings of Bulletin Conferences, Virus Bulletin Magazine, http://www.virusbtn.com/virusbulletin

34. Wing Wong, "Analysis and detection of Metamorphic computer viruses", May 2006,

35. Zuwei Tian, Xingming Sun, Hengfu Yang, "A Scheme of PE Virus Detection Using Fragile Software Watermarking Technique", International

36. Journal of Digital Content Technology and its Applications. Volume 5, Number 2, February 2011

37. Morten Christiansen, "Bypassing Malware Defences", 2010, SANS Infosec Reading Room. http://www.sans.org/reading_room/

38. Essam Al Daoud, Iqbal H. Jebril and Belal Zaqaibeh, "Computer Virus Strategies and Detection Methods"

39. Feng Xue, "Attacking Antivirus", Nevis Networks, http://www.blackhat.com/presentations/bh-europe-08/Feng-Xue/Whitepaper/bh-eu-08-xue-WP.pdf

40. M. Stamp, Information Security: Principles and Practice, Wiley Interscience, 2005

41. Wing Wong and Mark Stamp, "Haunting for Metamorphic Engines", 2006

42. Wojiech Podgorski, "Artificial Intelligence Methods in Virus Detection and Recognition- Introduction to heuristic scanning", http://podgorski.wordpress.com

43. Ankit Fadia, "Unofficial Guide to Ethical Hacking", MacMilllan, 2001

Glossary

- ARIZ- is the Russian acronym for "Algorithm of Inventive Problem Solving", a TRIZ tool for solving complex problems.
- Almost exact identification (or nearly exact identification)- when the identification is not exactly accurate but good enough to declare as identified.
- Armored viruses – viruses that are specifically written to make it difficult for an antivirus researcher to find out how they work and what they do.
- Checksum- a computed value based on the content of the file. The checksum changes when the content of the file changes.
- Companion viruses – viruses that spreads by creating a similar file (say, dothis.com) which runs instead of the targeted file (say, dothis.exe). When the user writes "dothis" and presses enter, the virus file (dothis.com) runs instead of the targeted files as the .com files have a higher preference of execution in the OS.
- Contradiction- a contradiction happens when two different parameters conflict with each other. For example, the display unit should be large for better visibility and at the same time should be small for portability.
- Contradiction Matrix- presentation of all contradiction parameters in the form of a tabular matrix, where the x-axis presents all improving parameters and the y-axis presents all worsening parameters. The cells of the table contain the Inventive Principles which can address the contradiction.
- Contradiction parameters- the parameters, such as, weight, volume, speed, temperature, security, vulnerability etc. which can improve or worsen a situation.

- DoS (Denial of Service) – the system slows down to a non-functional stage because of excessive resource depletion or excessive bandwidth consumption.
- Drive-by infections- the malware is downloaded without a user's knowledge when he is visiting a site or viewing a streaming media.
- Droppers- the non-viral malware that installs other malicious programs like viruses or worms.
- Exact Identification- when the viral body is exactly matched with its signatures uniquely identified for that specific virus.
- False negative – is an instance of wrongly labeling a malicious program as a benign program.
- False positive- is an instance of wrongly labeling a benign program as malicious program.
- False positive rate- the number of false positive instances divided by the total number of benign instances.
- Firewall – a protective barrier, which can be implemented on a single computer or on a network, for controlling traffic and blocking unwanted inbound connections from external network or Internet.
- Gateway- is a computer between the internal network (LAN) and external network (or Internet) may be implemented as a proxy or firewall to monitor and control the incoming/outgoing traffic.
- Heuristic scanning- the method of searching for virus like characteristics from various aspects.
- Host computer- any computer is called as a host in Internet convention. A host may be a workstation or server or may hold other responsibilities in a network.
- Host program- any genuine program which can be infected by virus. During viral infection the virus code is attached to the host program.
- Ideal Final Result (IFR)- the ultimate extent of looking at a solution.
- Ideality- is a situation when the system has all benefits of the current system without having any drawbacks or limitations.

- Inventive Principles- the 40 principles of TRIZ which can be applied to solve any kind of contraction in an inventive problem.
- Inventive Problem- a problem where the conventional solutions lead to further problems.
- Inventive standards- are structured rules for solving technical problems. TRIZ provides 72 inventive standards divided in five different classes.
- Keylogger – a small program or hardware device that records each keystroke typed on the keyboard of a computer.
- Malware- any type of malefic software including adware, spyware, worms, viruses, Trojans, backdoors, keyloggers etc.
- Metamorphic viruses- the viruses that change the code of their body in every occurrence of infection.
- Nearly Exact Identification – faster than Exact Identification Scanning. It does not accurately tell the name of the specific variant of the virus but good enough to identify an infection.
- NGrams – are consecutive binary sequences inside a program code. Generally the NGrams of benign software are different from the NGrams of malicious software.
- Off access scanning- scanning a file when it is not in use.
- On the fly scanning – scanning when an email or file is on the way before it is finally opened, similar to on-access scanning.
- On-access scanning- the method of scanning a file just before it is requested for opening.
- Parasitic virus – virus that spreads by attaching itself to files and runs first before running of the host file.
- Pay load – the portion of virus that contains the disastrous code that the virus ultimately intends to do.
- Physical Contradiction- a contradiction where the same parameter conflicts with itself.
- Polymorphic viruses- the viruses which change the code in their body in every replication.

- Problem Explorer- understanding and analyzing a problem by exploring the problem environment, the resources and constraints,
- Proxy Server- is a gateway between the internal and external network. A proxy provides protection by having two IP addresses, one visible to the internal network and another visible to outside.
- Resources- a TRIZ method to identify and utilize the resources like, time, energy, information, substances etc. that are already available to a system.
- S-Fields- a method of analyzing problems by drawing relationships between Elements (or Substance) and Actions (or Fields).
- Technical Contradiction- a contradiction where two different parameters conflict with each other, e.g., a menu should display all necessary menu items, but it should not hide other important information on the screen.
- Trends of evolution- a tool to predict the future evolutions of a product based on the past trends of similar other products.
- TRIZ- acronym for Russian word "Teoriya Resheniya Izobretatelskikh Zadach", which means "Theory of Inventive Problem Solving".
- True positive- is a malicious code that is correctly tagged as malicious and hence correctly classified.
- True negative – is a benign code that is correctly tagged as benign code, that means correctly classified.
- Virus database – the database containing information such as signatures, behaviors and removal methods of known viruses.
- Virus Signature – is a unique sequence of bytes that may be found in a virus program code but unlikely to be found elsewhere.

Index